The Political Theory
of Conservative Economists

The Political Theory
of Conservative
Economists

Conrad P. Waligorski

 University Press of Kansas

In memory of my parents,
Josephine and Barney Waligorski

Published by the University Press of Kansas (Lawrence, Kansas
66045), which was organized by the Kansas Board of Regents and is
operated and funded by Emporia State University, Fort Hays State
University, Kansas State University, Pittsburg State University,
the University of Kansas, and Wichita State University

Library of Congress Cataloging-in-Publication Data

Waligorski, Conrad.
    The political theory of conservative economists / Conrad P.
Waligorski.
        p.   cm.
    Includes bibliographical references (p.)
    ISBN 0–7006–0459–6 (alk. paper)
    1. Liberty. 2. Equality. 3. Democracy. 4. Free enterprise.
5. Chicago school of economics. 6. Social choice. I. Title.
JC585.W28 1990   89–28791
323.44–dc20   CIP

Printed in the United States of America
10 9 8 7 6 5 4 3 2 1

The paper used in this publication meets the minimum requirements of the
American National Standard for Permanence of Paper for Printed Library Materials
Z39.48–1984.

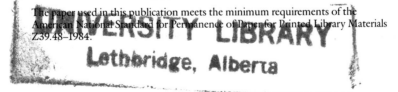

Contents

Preface

Ideas matter. They are the filter through which people see, organize, interpret, and attempt to change the world. Economic theories, concepts, views, and proposals dominate contemporary public debate over traditional political questions about the meaning and content of the good society and state. Economic issues have always been central to liberalism; indeed, some authors attempt to define liberalism almost exclusively in economic terms. This book examines several such authors. It explicates the political ideas, values, policy prescriptions, and interrelation of politics and economics among conservative economists, emphasizing James Buchanan, Milton Friedman, and Friedrich A. Hayek, with occasional reference to George Gilder, Ludwig von Mises, George J. Stigler, and others sharing similar views on the operation of the market and its relation to politics. These authors—four of whom have won the Nobel Prize in economics—provide intellectual justification for returning to a laissez-faire state, offering support and policy advice for conservative governments in the United States, Britain and elsewhere. The conservative economists present a coherent repudiation of the liberal-democratic welfare, regulatory and interventionist state. Their economic reasoning and policy preferences encourage them to redefine and narrow such political values as democracy, freedom, equality, and justice, reducing popular participation and both the moral and empirical bases for active government.

This book examines the *normative political* ideas of conservative economists; their definition, justification, and interpretation; and some of the policies that follow from them. It explores the interrelation of political science, economics, and philosophy to bring out the values and assumptions of a significant group of economists, each of whom aspires to influence public policy. Conservative economists have had an enormous impact, but there has been little analysis of their political assumptions, ideas, and proposals. They advocate versions of popular American values, especially in their politically oriented writing, but they attempt to monopolize how these values are defined and applied. Based on their economic model, these theorists claim that their interpretations of such fundamental political ideals as democracy or freedom are the only legitimate ones for modern liberal democracies. This claim is highly suspect. Words have multiple meanings, and sharing and using the same word, formal value, or principle means nothing until we sort out incompatible meanings and applications, obstacles to the implementation of principles, and opinions about policies that fulfill these principles. People often interpret familiar ideas in new and unique ways, so changing their meaning and application that they gain new substance and advance policies fundamentally different from those supported by another interpretation or set of assumptions. For example, we may all value freedom but strenuously disagree over its meaning. Agreeing that we advocate freedom, or any other value such as individualism, equality, or justice, is the beginning of discussion, not its end. There is no way of knowing what any value means until one knows the circumstances under which a person can and may practice it, acceptable manifestations of the value, obstacles to it, and so forth. Disagreements over these questions amount to qualitative differences in values and ideologies.

In the same way that one can analyze the political ideas of an Augustine, Martin Luther, John Calvin, or Reinhold Niebuhr without writing a book on theology, it is possible to write about economists' politics without writing an economics text. Conservative political economy can best be understood within the context of other interpretations of fundamental political values. Therefore I occasionally contrast past and present theorists and their arguments with the conservative economists and their arguments. In doing this, I am not commenting on the validity or invalidity, usefulness or lack of usefulness of their economic theories, even though I may have strong opinions about them. I am not concerned whether their economics preceded their political theory and philosophy or their political philosophy is the basis for their economics. But it is important that the conservatives' politics and philosophy support their economics and that there is nothing in their political theory which calls their economics into question. For this reason, I emphasize political writing and those shared assumptions and predispositions that are relevant to the conservative economists' political concepts and policy proposals, not each author's purely economic work. I am concerned more with understanding their rarely studied political theory, and what they are attempting to say to our contemporary world, than with criticizing it.

Conservative economic arguments provide a powerful belief system in the conflict for the soul of modern liberal-democratic government: what will it do, to whom will it resond, what will be its future constitutional structure, who will benefit from what kind of policy, what do citizens—if the word has meaning—owe one to another, what is the good liberal-democratic society. These are political and moral questions. Though they have an economic component, they extend far beyond the confines of economic theory. Economists may therefore find parts of this book confusing, dealing with familiar ideas in a different and threatening manner. Political scientists may find parts to be obvious. Perhaps this is inevitable when talking to both groups simultaneously. However, it is economists who will find most that is new or different. They may not recognize all of the assumptions discussed or may claim there is no such thing as natural law or theories of justice in economic theorizing. I agree, if one looks only at words, not their meaning. Conservative theories contain the functional equivalent of these and many other normative political ideas, and it is that which concerns me as a political theorist.

Several people have urged me to make a statement of my political beliefs. I became interested in the conservative economists when I was asked to review one of James Buchanan's books. I am a liberal, of the reform variety, meaning that I believe that there are many obstacles to realization of fundamental values; that under some circumstances government may be an obstacle to realization of basic values and under others it may be a necessary means to removal of obstacles; that there are few easy answers; that freedom, equality, individualism, democracy, participation, and tolerance are expansive concepts; and that, when circumstances change, modifications of policy are necessary to protect fundamental principles. Some readers may also detect echoes of Burke in some of my comments. They will not be wrong.

A number of people in political theory, economics, and philosophy have made important contributions to this book through their support and criticism. I thank them very much for their help and advice. Daniel M. Hausman, Douglas Rae, and Warren J. Samuels read this book in manuscript. It is a better book because of their diligence, suggestions, and proposals, and I owe them a special debt. I also thank the anonymous reviewers at the *Social Science Journal* who reviewed an early version of chapter 5 and the editors of that journal, who gave permission to use the material here. Several people have commented on parts of this book that were originally presented as conference papers, once again proving the seriousness with which panelists take their often difficult task. I especially thank Emily Gill, Gerald Houseman, Joel Kassiola, and Paul Kress. David Gay has been a friend and colleague, introducing me to information, theories, and ideas relevant to the authors discussed in this book, while always challenging my perspective. Steven Zega read part of this manuscript and made numerous perceptive comments. My good friend Thomas Hone has enriched my thinking and has been a constant encouragement. So has Booth Fowler. I thank the staff of the University Press of Kansas for their assistance. Finally, I thank my wife, Ann Waligorski. She understood how important this project has been to me. Errors in interpretation and facts are mine.

Part One

Introductory Arguments

Chapter One

Introduction

Conservative economics is also a normative theory of politics. Economists regularly engage in political theory, masking normative judgments with seemingly objective economic analysis. This book examines and explicates the political ideas and recommendations of important contemporary conservative economists who are revising fundamental political values to conform to their economic model. Chapter 1 discusses why these theorists are called conservative, who they are, why they may be examined as a group, and how economic theory can be analyzed as normative political theory. Later chapters examine the basis for and content of the conservative economists' political theory.

Conservative economics is a response to and has hastened the apparent collapse of the post–World War II neo-Keynesian orthodoxy on the interrelation of politics and economics. The political-social dislocations produced by economic traumas in the last twenty-five years gave conservative economists an opportunity to gain support for their long-standing rejection of Keynesian policies and interventionist government. As in other periods of perceived analytic and policy confusion, when existing explanations appear inadequate, people often turn to older political-social-economic models. Regardless of their actual value, these models provide a paradigmatic moment – an ideal point when virtue and policy seem to have coincided – from which dissatisfied theorists and politicians can appeal against the declining convention. The renewed emphasis in Anglo-American countries on restoring a pre-Keynesian microeconomic market model of political economy represents such a revival. Drawing upon an older public philosophy, conservative economists reject Keynesian economic and political justification of interventionist government.

The conservatives' political and economic theory has little room for intervention, regulation, welfare, or active citizens and government. Based upon their assumption of a natural economic order, conservative economists propose radically reduced public involvement in economics and rigid separation between politics and economics. Though economic issues dominate political debate, governments will no longer attempt to ensure that the market oper-

3

ates, provide extensive welfare, or reduce the uneven impact of market changes or problems. The conservative market comprehensively explains human behavior and institutions; organizes society; defines moral and political values such as democracy and obligation; sets public goals; judges politics; and seeks to replace participatory, interventionist, regulatory, and welfare politics with spontaneous, cooperative market behavior. By asserting that all human behavior is reducible to and understandable as self-interested market behavior, the conservative economists limit the need for and possibility of political, social, and moral analysis and concerns separate from the market, thus voiding consideration of the political and social effects of their economic ideal while making political prescriptions. Limited politics and political norms inevitably follow.

In surveying the normative political content of conservative economists' market politics, I am concerned with the political component, relevance and impact of their economic theories and policy proposals and do not analyze all economic theories of politics. Throughout, I assume that economics and politics are closely interrelated—a proposition the conservative economists accept—and that when economic theory makes political prescriptions, it may be analyzed as normative political theory—a statement the conservative economists reject. Political theory has a rich history—from Aristotle to Thomas Jefferson to John Rawls—of inquiring into the type of economy likely to support preferred polities. Conversely, Adam Smith, Thomas Robert Malthus, Herbert Spencer, and John Maynard Keynes each defined the type of polity necessary to his economy. John Stuart Mill and Karl Marx are claimed by both disciplines. There are virtually no "pure" political or "pure" economic theories. All share concerns over distribution and allocation of resources, the role of government, justice, equity, equality, stability, freedom, and the nature of popular control. Moreover, political legitimacy, class and regional conflict, social stability, and the rise and decline of nations often have an economic cause and component.

Even if political science and economics have been conceptually and academically separate for a century, the distance between political and economic analysis has traditionally been slight. John Locke, for example, influenced economic as well as political thought. Though ostensibly political, his *Second Treatise of Government* analyzed the development of property and money, while presenting a simplified labor theory of value. Indeed, political and economic concerns were inseparable: "[T]he chief end . . . [of civil society] is the preservation of Property,"[1] broadly understood. His assumption that individualism, property, freedom, and exchange are natural is one of the intellectual sources of conservative political economy.

Writers mixed political and economic analysis throughout the eighteenth and nineteenth centuries. Though Adam Smith was primarily an economic theorist, his economics deeply influenced subsequent liberal conceptualizations of politics. To Smith, trade and barter were natural. The attempt to better one's condition, and the propensity to exchange one thing for another, created markets and the division of labor. Free markets exist wherever people are allowed to pursue their own interests within a framework of minimal government. In the absence of government intervention, such a market would produce both order and prosperity. Although Smith was one of the first theorists to make a deliberate effort to separate politics from economics, that distinction, even in *Wealth of Nations*, is neither perfectly clear nor fully developed.

A glance at the daily newspaper illustrates that today the interrelation of politics and economics is crucial in both theory and public debate. Charles Lindblom summarizes this point: "In all the political systems of the world, much of politics is economics, and most of economics is also politics."[2] The major theorists presented in this book would agree with the sentiment but not its expression. For them, politics is understandable through economics, and their goal is substantial political and policy modifications to reduce public and governmental intervention in economic life. They do not quarrel with the statement that everywhere governments are urged to intervene to protect, promote, and regulate the economy; that people expect and demand laws and regulations to control and eliminate problems and dislocations flowing from depressions, the development of new industries, and the vicissitudes of working conditions; that there is no such thing as an unregulated economy; that business often insists upon the regulation and intervention that are a major source of the growth in government. Their argument is that such demands for government intervention in the economy are illegitimate; they must be removed from the political agenda and majorities and governments stripped of the power and means to accommodate them. The market must be freed. The assumptions and arguments which lay the foundation for these policy recommendations are elaborated in the following chapters.

Conservatism

Labels are important. They can be shorthand expressions for an entire philosophical or ideological approach. Even when used in the most simplistic manner, as in media references to the "conservative wing" of the Chinese Communist party or Iranian "revolutionary moderates," they classify similar approaches, simplify (or oversimplify) the world, and express popular political, social, and economic positions—though there is no necessary correlation between being "conservative" or "liberal" on political issues and being "conservative" or "liberal" on economic or social issues.

Economists such as James Buchanan, Milton Friedman, F. A. Hayek, George Stigler, William Hutt, and others are considered conservative because of their faith in markets and mistrust of government. Some of them, however, call themselves "liberals" and dislike the name "conservative." Hayek emphatically rejects the conservative label, calling himself a true liberal "in the original, nineteenth-century sense" as opposed to "accidental accretions" that have attached to liberalism. This true liberalism, "The Abandoned Road," emphasizes economic freedom and the operation of spontaneous forces and represents "the individualistic tradition that has created Western Civilization." It is opposed to both conservatism and "pseudo-liberalism which in the course of the last generation has arrogated its name."[3] William H. Hutt believes that "the word 'liberal' has been stolen by those who are hostile to what used to be known as 'liberalism.'"[4] Friedman also dislikes "[t]he change in the meaning of the term liberalism," which has been most marked in economics where expanded government services and regulation undermine freedom and corrupt the meaning of liberalism. The "rightful and proper label" for his highly influential *Capitalism and Freedom* is liberalism.[5] "I'm not a conservative. . . . .I'm a liberal in the traditional sense."[6]

Writers disagree over what to call such theorists. That critics of liberalism frequently call them liberals, and critics of conservatism call them conservatives, answers nothing. Disagreements remain at a more sophisticated level. In two recent books published by the University of Minnesota Press, the author of the volume entitled *Liberalism* called Buchanan, Friedman, Gilder, and Hayek classical liberals, whereas the author of the volume entitled *Conservatism* called Friedman and Hayek conservatives. Hayek is included in both *The Liberal Tradition in European Thought* and *The Conservative Tradition in European Thought*. The contemporary traditional conservative Russell Kirk, who is skeptical about the individualistic tradition, claims that writers such as von Mises and Hayek "are at once liberal and conservative." Echoing Burke's *Appeal from the Old to the New Whigs*, Hayek considers himself an "Old Whig," upholding traditional principles of liberty.[7] Such disagreement is common.

Each statement is partly correct because each focuses on a segment of reality, ignoring other elements, and elevates a partial insight into a complete picture. There are many forms of conservatism and liberalism within the liberal-democratic framework. Conservative economists share the values and assumptions of eighteenth- and nineteenth-century liberalism. Economists such as Buchanan, Friedman and Hayek—or politicians such as Herbert Hoover, Ronald Reagan, George Bush and Margaret Thatcher—*are* liberal, if one focuses on the principles and policies of nineteenth-century Anglo-American, individualistic liberalism. They start from an individualistic perspective, assuming self-interest is the primary motivation. Freedom, particularly economic freedom, is their principal value. Ownership and use of private property are the most important aspects of economic freedom. The conservatives accept equal opportunity, defined as careers open to talent. They agree with parliamentary democracy and a broad, though not necessarily universal, suffrage. They conceive of society as distinct from the state, spontaneous, superior, and cohering naturally. Government is the realm of coercion and should be limited to enforcing general laws that are equally applicable to everyone and to protecting the population from foreign aggression. Since no one can be trusted with coercive power, and since markets limit power, guarantee individual freedom, and reward people according to their contribution to the welfare of others, markets should be the primary means for organizing cooperative behavior.

Despite this catalog of classical liberal principles and policies, the economists discussed in this book will be called conservative because the label is appropriate within the context of contemporary politics. Indeed, they *are* conservative if we focus on their interpretation of traditional liberal principles; the policies they claim are necessary to implement those principles; and their refusal to let liberalism evolve–evidenced by their claim that reform liberalism, which began with such writers as T. H. Green in the nineteenth century and argues for development of new policies, including government intervention to protect enjoyment of basic liberal principles, is not real liberalism. Emphasis on the primacy of a self-regulating autonomous market that promotes freedom, equality, democracy, and justice and curbs human depravity; limited government defined as nonintervention in economic affairs; limitation of economic rights to narrow competitive and property rights; denial of the relevance of social justice; the claim that freedom and equality are solely negative concepts (i.e., no interference); and individualism conceived as being left alone to compete rather than having real choice in lifestyles–all are conservative positions given contemporary perception of political-economic reality.[8]

There is, however, another lesser noticed and more important link to conservatism in these authors. Conservatism is not simply a bunch of policies or defense of the status quo but frequently embodies principles shared by many varieties of conservatives. Economists such as Buchanan, Friedman, and Hayek hold several assumptions in common with traditional conservatives such as John Adams, Edmund Burke, and Benjamin Disraeli and contemporaries such as Russell Kirk. These assumptions and principles extend beyond the policy of the day, forming a core of principles that Anglo-American conservatives share regardless of specific policy differences. Historically, these assumptions and principles have formed the philosophical heart of traditional or classical conservatism in its conflict with classical liberalsim. These principles and assumptions include skepticism and doubts about human reason and ability, emphasis on the complexity of society, belief that there is an objective order existing separate from human will or volition, opposition to equality, and mistrust of popular rule. These assumptions are major themes in the rest of the book.

From its beginnings traditional conservatism has been skeptical about mankind. Human nature cannot be trusted. *Reason and ability are severely limited*, whether by sin or by insufficient intelligence, and people cannot easily or radically change the existing system. Contemporary conservative economists assert fundamental human ignorance and inherent limits, using those precepts to defend market relations and to attack government involvement in economics. Emphasis on the *complexity* of the spontaneous system or market reinforces the importance of limited human ability. Society is complex, fragile, and held together with the glue of order and hierarchy; its growth should not be interfered with. Because of the inherently dynamic nature of market society, conservative economists claim that collectively people are not intelligent enough to intervene successfully in intricate market relations; that—in a combined political, moral, and economic argument—intervention worsens problems, undermines freedom and efficiency, and is unfair; that no matter how uncomfortable we feel, we must accept the existing system and cannot reform it according to our wishes or morality; and that acceptance of market results as the best possible outcome is a necessary limitation on the human temptation to interfere in natural relations.

Most conservatives assume that an *order* exists separate from human will, that it prevails in human relations, and that it is to be discovered, not created or imposed by conscious human behavior. This order is not maintained because people know how it functions, but because they are brought up in a certain way to accept and fit into it. Order accompanies or creates higher standards, separate from human volition and guiding behavior independently of narrow self-interest and concern for the immediate present. Wherever they find this order—in natural law or tradition for classical conservatives, or the spontaneous market for market conservatives—this superior standard provides guidance for correct behavior.

If there is natural order in human relations, *equality* can upset that order. Conservatives of all varieties mistrust equality, claiming it violates the fundamental human drives associated with order. Traditional and market conservatives dislike equalization efforts and usually consider inequality as natural and desirable to the functioning of the good society, though market conservatives allow more room for the talented to rise within market society. Both types of conservatives agree that wealth and birth are natural distinctions, ones with which government should not interfere lest it upset the guiding order of society. Thus property and inheritance must be preserved as natural and essential to the functioning of the system. Because popular political power frequently fosters equality, each group of conservatives *mistrusts popular rule*. Though modern conservatives no longer reject democracy, they would limit its application. Flawed human nature and the needs of the market combine to place limits on democracy, to prevent it from destroying the good society.

This does not mean that traditional and market, or individualist, conservatism are identical. They are separate varieties of conservatism, appealing to distinct justifications and often opposed on policy issues. They disagree over paternalism, the nature of community, intergenerational links, and the individual's control over property. But both share a bleak picture of human nature which sets rigid limits to human possibility. Their common belief that deliberate intervention is likely to go wrong, that human reason and ability are severely constrained, and that people must collectively accept their fate within the existing order are in marked contrast to liberal optimism that conscious, deliberate change for the better is possible.

The popular meanings of liberalism and conservatism have changed over time. For this reason I occasionally contrast market or individualist conservatives with reform liberals such as John Maynard Keynes, John Kenneth Galbraith, and Lester Thurow.[9] Market conservatives have deep roots in early nineteenth-century liberalism, especially that developed by Malthus and David Ricardo, but in their policies and proposals, they are among the most influential conservatives of this century. Writing in societies where some form of liberal values is officially accepted and justifies public policy, these authors claim the tradition of liberalism but drastically narrow its meaning and application. They allow no room for growth – no adaptations of policy to promote historical liberal values in altered circumstances and no role for government to protect the public from a changed market. They dream no great dreams of liberating men and women in all aspects of their lives, as did John Stuart Mill, who in mid-century began to modify the policies of laissez-faire to promote the principles of liberalism.[10] To the authors examined in this book, modifying policy cannot protect a principle such as freedom but instead destroys it. Policy becomes overriding principle – leave the market alone – and alternative policies and principles, even from within historical liberalism, must be subordinated to this fundamental policy-principle-guide.[11] This emphasis on an autonomous market and market relations as the paradigmatic model for all behavior makes these authors conservative in the latter part of the twentieth century.

Theorists Discussed

Three economists are emphasized throughout this book: James Buchanan, Milton Friedman, and Friedrich Hayek. Others who share and supplement their views are occasionally discussed, but these three symbolize, and in large part developed, the normative and empirical justification for the modern conservative political-economic alternative to interventionist government. Differences in individual economic theories are insignificant in the context of the focus of this book: conservative economists' shared image of political reality. These three authors present a complete, coherent political theory. They are variations on a theme, with striking similarities in their philosophical assumptions, dislikes, vision of an ideal economy, and political and social preferences and beliefs.[12]

James Buchanan was born in 1919 and received his Ph.D. in economics from the University of Chicago in 1948. He developed the widely accepted and increasingly influential "public choice" school of economic analysis, which studies the constitutional and contractual basis of political and economic decision making. His work attempts to apply economic principles to political decision making, claiming that the same analytic assumptions and models—particularly individual utility maximization—that seemingly explain economic behavior also explain political behavior. Buchanan received a Nobel Prize in economics in 1986. In his Nobel Prize lecture, he credited the Swedish economist Knut Wicksell (1851–1926) with influencing such aspects of his work as methodological individualism and the idea that politics is a complex exchange mechanism. His arguments provided some of the philosophical underpinnings of the Gramm-Rudman-Hollings deficit reduction law and proposals for a balanced-budget amendment to the United States Constitution. His public choice analysis is widely accepted as giving insight into the workings and failure of modern liberal-democratic regimes and furnishes support for reforming them. Buchanan has spent most of his career teaching economics in universities.

Milton Friedman has been the most active politically. Born in 1912, he received his Ph.D. in economics from Columbia University in 1946. Most of his teaching career was at the University of Chicago, where, as with Buchanan and Stigler, he was influenced by Frank Knight. Though Friedman distinguishes between his scientific and popular work, he is concerned primarily with how his economic proposals may affect public policy and has been the most active economist since Keynes in attempting to "construct theoretical models . . . [that] lead to policy recommendations . . . [and] generate public opinion in support of them".[13] Consciously aiming at a wide audience, Friedman has influenced and shaped policy in the United States, Britain, Israel,[14] Latin America, and Iran. His economic theory, politics, and policy proposals are closely related, in that he has created an entire political-economic model for modern society, rooted in his picture of a free market. He has attempted to influence public policy through a column in *Newsweek*; a television program, "Free to Choose"; numerous pamphlets; and several popular books. His influential

Capitalism and Freedom (1962), claiming a causal link between freedom and capitalism on one side and oppression and government on the other, had sold more than 430,000 copies by 1980, when it was still selling at the rate of more than 25,000 copies a year. The first run of *Free to Choose*, promoted by a $50,000 advertising budget, printed 100,000 copies.[15] Friedman received a Nobel Prize in economics in 1976. His deepest professional impact is through monetarism. Critics often refer to the "Chicago Boys"[16] as disciples of Friedman. He acted as a writer and adviser to Barry Goldwater's presidential bid in 1964, helping develop Goldwater's tax plan, despite its fiscal rather than monetarist orientation. In 1968, less active than in 1964, he advised Richard Nixon. Friedman offered advice to the government of Chile in 1975 and on occasion to other governments. Ronald Reagan, Margaret Thatcher, and Menachem Begin incorporated some of his proposals.[17] In the United States, he actively supported tax limitation proposals, such as Proposition 13 in California. Whether it is balanced-budget proposals, opposition to increases in taxes and the minimum wage, or pejorative distinctions between taxpayers and tax receivers, these policies exemplify philosophical assumptions and policy proposals of conservative economists.

Friedrich Hayek is widely read, and his critique of social justice is accepted by the preceding authors. Born in 1899 in Vienna, where he studied with Ludwig von Mises, Hayek has had an active intellectual career in economics and philosophy. He was at the University of Chicago from 1950 to 1962. An opponent of Keynesian political economy since the 1930s, he has been of fundamental importance in uniting, inspiring, and creating modern conservatism. He also had an impact on David Stockman's economic theories.[18] *The Road to Serfdom*, his first political book, was condensed in the *Reader's Digest*.[19] In 1947 he founded the Mont Pelerin Society which organizes and unites conservative economists and has provided a forum for analysis and development of neoclassical political economy throughout the postwar ascendance of Keynesian public policy. Hayek's professional economics emphasizes monetary theory and the economic system as a coordinating mechanism, and he received the Nobel Prize in economics in 1974, along with Gunnar Myrdal. His policy proposals were widely accepted in postwar West Germany.[20]

Several authors will be discussed occasionally: William Hutt, a South African economist; George Stigler, Nobel Prize winner in economics, 1982; George Gilder; Thomas Sowell, on whose dissertation committee Stigler and Friedman served;[21] Robert D. Tollison; Gordon Tullock; and Richard E. Wagner. Except for Gilder, each is a professional economist.

All possible authors are not included, for several reasons. First, this book emphasizes currently active economists who are engaged in writing about politics in order to change contemporary political economy and does not discuss those, such as Kenneth Arrow, who share similar assumptions but are not politically active. Second, I focus on current writers[22] and occasionally employ historical examples or contrasts with other theorists and antecedents for interpretative juxtaposition,[23] so that theorists are viewed in an intellectual context rather than in terms of the always problematic and never satisfactory question of influence. Thus economists such as Frank Knight, Ludwig von Mises, Vilfredo Pareto, Joseph Schumpeter, and Knut Wicksell receive only passing notice. Finally, this book emphasizes the political theory of conservative economists, not–with the sole exception of George Gilder–the economics of conservatives; thus Robert Nozick, an important philosopher who shares many assumptions and arguments with the conservative economists, is not systematically included. Throughout, this book focuses on the attempt of contemporary conservative economists to redefine basic political values, the role of economics in politics, and the role of government in the economy.

Common Elements

Though the major conservative economists share a common world view, there are many methodological and theoretical differences among them. Monetarism (Friedman) is incompatible with supply-side economics (Gilder). Competition is less important for Gilder than for Buchanan, Friedman, or Hayek. Gilder is much less of a classical thinker than Friedman or Hayek. Buchanan places some of Hayek's beliefs that the market cannot be improved "into the Panglossian category" and is uneasy with some of Hayek's economics, but he believes Hayek's system is consistent with his own public choice approach. Buchanan has more room for individual rational choice, contract, and deliberate construction of rules and institutions than does Hayek, who has the dimmest view of human possibilities. Hayek, unlike Friedman, believes that capitalism (a term Hayek dislikes) works with imperfect knowledge. Economists can explain what happened but should not try to predict what *will* happen. Friedman wants governments to follow a fixed rule regulating the quantity of money, whereas Hayek believes this to be impossible and wishes to allow private enterprise to issue currency. Friedman believes a commodity-based currency would not work, whereas Hayek wants private issuers of money to experiment with one. Hayek is less oriented toward statistics and quantitative analysis than are Buchanan, Friedman, and Stigler, the latter two being quite gifted in the field. Buchanan has less faith than Friedman, Gilder, or Hayek in the market as a perfect instrument for distribution and production of order; to him, it is simply better than the alternatives. He therefore allows some intervention to promote equal opportunity. As does Stigler, he distinguishes between socialism and the welfare state, liking neither. Hayek and Friedman rarely make that distinction. Friedman writes most about current issues, Buchanan emphasizes constitutional structure rather than day-to-day political questions, and Hayek is more concerned with philosophical issues in political economy than are the others. Friedman is less concerned than Buchanan or Hayek with traditional questions of order and respect for established rules.[24]

These differences are a small part of the story. Fundamental political, policy, and philosophical agreement bind these authors together. Hayek, Friedman, and Buchanan have been officers in the Mont Pelerin Society, and Friedman, Stigler, Frank Knight, and Ludwig von Mises attended the first meeting in 1947. Buchanan, Friedman, and Stigler admit to having been influenced by Knight. Some of the less frequently noted economists, such as Gordon Tullock, have been coauthors with Buchanan. Buchanan refers to Knight and Friedman as "men with whom, broadly and generally, I agree on principles of political-philosophical order." Friedman acknowledges that he has been "influenced by a fresh approach to political science that has come mainly from economists," including Buchanan, Stigler, and Tullock. He has learned much of his "philosophy" from "Frank Knight . . . Friedrich A. Hayek, George J. Stigler."[25] Stigler believes his approach differs from Tullock and Buchanan "primarily in its strong empirical orientation."[26] Each accepts the basic concept of methodological individualism.

These authors may not form a single school, but they speak the same language; share similar values, ends, assumptions, themes, and vision of the good society; and employ the same deductive structure in their political arguments. Their common world view, shared dislikes (especially of Keynesianism), and similar recommendations unite them. Their arguments and approaches to economics and politics build on one another, interweaving themes to produce a coherent political economy and public philosophy. Their ideas may be discussed as a trend or movement, in the same way that one can analyze the common arguments and policies among Sophists, eighteenth-century liberals, or contemporary democratic socialists.

The major element in this shared world view is a picture of the market as the most important social regulatory mechanism. There is extraordinary consistency in the conservative economists' market-based political-social recommendations, conclusions, and criticisms. Each writer believes that the needs of the economy should limit and control politics, because it is inferior to market economics. Whether the focus is on Buchanan's constitutionalism, Hayek's rule of law, or Friedman's monetarism, the conclusion is that public discretion must be limited. Intervention into economics is always dangerous and counterproductive. Reduced and limited government is an axiomatic corollary. The good polity will follow general laws, applicable to all, curb popular participation and intervention into natural markets, and limit democracy to election procedures. Whatever the situation, the economic market produces order and fairness, while politics produces chaos and destroys freedom. The economic market controls and channels human passions into constructive, potentially harmonious ends; politics gives free rein to and multiplies the worst effects of human greed. Given human nature, government cannot create or pursue the common good, produces nothing of value, and always serves particular interests. This means that economic intervention inevitably and disastrously fails or at best robs some people for the undeserved benefit of others. Although the market may sometimes produce undesirable outcomes, its results are generally for the best, especially in the long run, whereas public intervention in the long run is unjust, oppressive, and destructive.

There are no important political or social issues, policies, concepts, or conclusions on which the major authors disagree. As a group they call for and justify a fundamental change in the guiding philosophy, policy goals, and methods of operation of modern, welfare-oriented, interventionist liberal-democratic systems. Given their common starting economic and philosophical perspective, each develops one or another part of their collective public philosophy. Pictures of freedom, justice, equality, and democracy are complementary. Each would be comfortable living in the ideal world of the others. Although my arguments do not always apply to each author, they fit as a group and as an alternative political model. Different combinations of theorists are discussed in each chapter, but the book discusses only issues upon which at least two major authors agree, notes who takes what position, and where they may occasionally disagree.

Economic Theory as Normative Political Theory

Theorists such as Adam Smith and Karl Marx have inspired fundamental changes in the economic and political orders of Europe and North America. Conservative economists seek to emulate that influence. They believe it is appropriate and necessary to make policy recommendations in order to create their ideal market society. Their ideas provide the philosophical basis for much of the current American, British, and Canadian social-economic policy. This is not to claim that they have directly shaped specific policies, but through their books, journals, membership in foundations and think-tanks, and occasionally direct advice to politicians, they have influenced opinion leaders, decision makers and sometimes the mass public. As individuals and as a group, they are attempting to provide a complete alternative to interventionist political economy.

Economic theories have normative and political implications when economists define and employ political ideas and values such as freedom or democracy; condemn most of the existing western political enterprise as inefficient, dangerous, and in need of major renovation to conform to supposedly nonpolitical standards; distinguish the private from the public; prescribe public goals and policy; shape public images of what is possible; and propose altering the structure and behavior of governments to achieve a superior system reflected in economic theory. Assumptions about human motivation, normal class relations, and what constitutes ethical behavior are politically relevant when they limit the extent and nature of legitimate policy debate, define political problems, and structure acceptable solutions to whatever is conceived as a problem. This applies across the political spectrum equally, to liberal, socialist, and Marxist economic theorists.[27] Even specification of the way in which politics and economics are to be studied—and in the west, liberalism rather than a rival such as Marxism defines the expected relation between politics and economics—is a political judgment. Moreover, when violence, revolution, and despair result from economic conditions, the nature of the economic theory attempting to deal with those conditions becomes of primary importance to politics[28]—particularly if an untestable theory claims superiority over political or social considerations.

Normative political theories share several common elements. These include assumptions about the *nature of order*, either in the universe (as with Plato and much natural-law theory), polity, society, economy, or all four. Normative theories contain explicit or implicit assumptions about *human nature or motivation*—beliefs about why people behave as they do. The picture of order, coupled with human nature or motivation, usually defines proper *distribution*, whether it is justice, offices, power, status, or wealth that is being assigned to people. Assumptions about order and human motivation also delimit what is *natural* and must be accepted from what is susceptible to successful intervention. Major theories attempt to *define and explain basic concepts* such as justice, freedom, authority, and the good life. These conceptions are usually tied to and limited by an author's notions of order and human nature and in turn limit the range of acceptable public behavior. Moreover, every significant normative theory contains a *justification*; that is, an appeal to standards higher than mere human volition—the Forms, history, the dialectic, the will of the people, utility, laws of nature, natural law, or, in the case of classical economics, a naturalistic ethic, the impersonal market—that attempts to "prove" the "correctness" and "truth" of that theory and its recommendations. Most important, normative theories create *guidelines for policy prescriptions*—who should rule and why, the nature of social welfare, how to achieve freedom, justice, equality, and so forth—that define legitimate goals and the proper means to attain them.

Conservative economics is both an economic theory and a normative theory of politics. First, it contains each of the components of normative theories.

It starts from essentially philosophical, indeed metaphysical, assumptions about the nature of reality, order, harmony, human nature, natural relations, distribution, and Newtonian-like causality. Second, it attempts to define basic political ideas: freedom, individualism, equality, democracy, justice, power, obligation, coercion, order, public morality, the nature of social cohesion, the ends and goals of society, welfare, and legitimate political problems. Third, conservative economists make comprehensive political and policy recommendations based on their starting assumptions. Many of these—less active government, abolishing the minimum wage, curbing labor unions, a reduced role for popular participation, elimination of widely held beliefs that governments should attempt to mitigate economic dislocations—require major political and social changes. Even the definition of a problem and acceptable solutions is, therefore, heavily value laden.

The inevitability of some value-laden analysis affirms the importance of appreciating starting assumptions. The history of science illustrates[29] that values and preconceptions order and shape observations and color attempts to explain the world. Human beings never approach a phenomenon with a blank slate. The more important something is to our world view or the more involved we are in outcomes, the more likely we will see what we expect. This is particularly so with human behavior, though it is present in even the most rigorous scientific endeavors. Whether based on religion, formal philosophy, or myth, our ideologies, values, starting assumptions, and expectations about normal behavior provide a framework for analyzing and interpreting the world.[30] Ideologies and values explain and interpret reality for people who hold them, conditioning what people see and how they explain another's behavior. They give clues to what is legitimate and illegitimate, a real alternative or an impossible fantasy, and what one must attend to and what can safely be ignored. They shape what is considered acceptable evidence. People rarely fight and kill over "facts." In many of the great controversies of normative political economy and politics, the facts narrowly understood are hardly in dispute. Rather, people fight over beliefs, values, and often incompatible interpretations of facts—whether a particular "fact" is significant and whether a specific situation does or does not fit a value criterion.

The controversy over abortion in the United States may be the quintessential example. There is no disagreement over the "facts" of an abortion. All sides agree on what an abortion *is*, how one occurs, what results from an abortion. The issue is not facts but interpretation of those facts. What is the moral and political significance of an abortion? Why and when is it a problem requiring a public solution? Is the fetus human or not? Who has rights? The fetus? The potential mother? Both? Others? If both have rights, whose right should be paramount, and is there a stage in the pregnancy when one set of rights overrides the other? What is the role of government in protecting the rights of whoever has rights? No amount of merely technical data can answer these questions. This applies to many political-economic controversies. For example, is the minimum wage legitimate, particularly when conservative and liberal economists agree that it can increase unemployment? Is that increase politically or socially significant, and if so, how? Does it make further intervention to address any new unemployment legitimate, or forbid any intervention? Is the status of women a problem or not? Unemployment? Poverty? Air pollution? Violence on television? Sexually explicit magazines? If yes, by what criteria are they so defined? Who should deal with these problems and what means may they employ? Answers cannot be determined by technical means, though these invariably affect one's view of the moral and political issues.

The role of preferences and values must be remembered when examining claims about politics that originate in any economic theory. Political theorists have been too reluctant to examine economic theories, especially those of conservative economists. The moral, philosophical,[31] and political assumptions in economic theories do not invalidate them. However, unspoken and often unacknowledged presuppositions color what an individual, a nation, or a generation considers normal, obvious, a concern, legitimate, or otherwise. The next chapter examines some of the most important assumptions that form the foundation of the conservative economists' critique of modern politics. These assumptions give clues to what is or is not a problem, which problems should be addressed by public intervention and which left alone, and where the burden of proof will be placed. They help explain, even if they do not determine, why these theorists think as they do and how they reach their political and social conclusions. The remainder of the book examines the political theory associated with these assumptions.

Chapter Two

Starting Assumptions:
The Philosophical-Economic
Foundations for a Political Argument

The free market wouldn't allow Scrooge to exploit poor Bob.
—Edwin Meese, December 15, 1983.

Assumptions shape perceptions of and responses to the world. This chapter reviews six politically crucial assumptions that form the foundation for conservative political theory and policy recommendations. It does not discuss all of the conservative economists' assumptions, only those that are relevant to their political theory and model. Some of these concepts are not economic as such but are the structuring beliefs and principles that lie beyond economics. The assumptions discussed in this chapter are: that the theory is (relatively) value free and objective; that human nature or motivation is individualistic; that self-interest is the primary human drive; that self-interest creates order; that the market embodies this order; and that the market is the model for politics. These preconceptions form an untestable "vision" of how the world does and should operate.[1] They structure and dominate the conservative economists' understanding of politics and political values.

These "working ideas about the nature of the whole of reality"[2] are a mixture of political, philosophical, and economic concepts based on normative and empirical claims. Authors switch between normative and empirical, description and prescription, without alerting us to the change. In most cases assumptions are definitional in nature and presented as universally applicable. They set limits to political possibility, forming the foundations of an alternative design for the democratic polity. The conservatives' beliefs encourage them to divide the world into either/or terms, promoting absolutist political-social thinking without shadings of ambiguity or the possibility of compromise between values or policies.

18

Objectivity Claims

Values shape behavior, how people view the world, what they consider important, where they place the burden of proof in controversies, how they decide what is a problem, and what is an acceptable solution to problems. The conservative economic theorists claim that their analysis is *objective*, and, for Friedman, *positive, scientific, and value-free*, providing an impartially correct standard by which to judge politics.

The claim of a superior standard entered political theory with Plato, but the modern assertion that economics can be positive and value-free dates at least to David Ricardo in his debate with Malthus and was developed in the late nineteenth and early twentieth centuries by such theorists as Vilfredo Pareto. Friedman takes a strong position. For Friedman, "[T]here are no value judgments in economics." He assumes that wide agreement on technical issues eliminates value conflict.[3] Economic theory is independent of and separate from normative and ethical judgment. "Science is science and ethics is ethics."[4] Economics is theoretically capable of producing knowledge equivalent to the natural sciences—"[p]ositive scientific knowledge that enables us to predict the consequences of a possible course of action."[5] This is a continuing theme, illustrated in his essay "The Methodology of Positive Economics."[6] Friedman's economics "is, or can be, an 'objective' science, in precisely the same sense as any of the physical sciences." It is independent of and the basis for normative judgments, not vice versa.[7] Results are the only test. Are its predictions generally accurate and confirmed by experience? Despite the virtual impossibility of testing his theories, determining what *is* a result of assumptions, or deciding in a nontautological manner what is an acceptable outcome, Friedman claims that it is irrelevant to look at his assumptions. Assumptions specify when a theory will be valid; they do not determine or affect its actual validity. Friedman undercuts potential criticism by occasionally claiming that he links economic hypotheses to actual behavior and policy recommendations with an "as if" statement. One can examine real-world behavior "as if" people conformed to hypotheses such as always trying to maximize returns: "It is only a short step . . . to the economic hypothesis that under a wide range of circumstances individual firms behave *as if* they were seeking rationally to maximize their expected returns . . . and had full knowledge of the data needed to succeed in this attempt." He believes that "[t]ruly important and significant hypotheses will be found to have 'assumptions' that are wildly inaccurate descriptive representations of reality."[8]

Friedman intends that this position be taken seriously. Discussion of values is an evasion. Disagreements are related to conflict over scientific economics, not preferences or assumptions. Differences on how to achieve an end do not result from value judgments. Moreover, he seems to confuse values with motives. He condemns "the widespread tendency to attribute policy differences to differences in value judgments. This tendency arises because it is often so much easier to question a man's motives than to meet his arguments or counter his evidence." Too often people assume that those who disagree are simply "'bad.'"[9] He believes that there is, or should be, a technical solution to every disagreement. Thomas Sowell echoes this, emptying value conflict from political economy, in his assertion that different factual interpretations, empirical assumptions, and images of causation, rather than values, separate rival perspectives.[10]

Friedman takes the most extreme position, but others accept elements of this view. Though critical of a positivist approach, Buchanan contends that "the only test for 'realism' of assumptions lies in the applicability of the conclusions." He sees his position as "neutral with respect to ideological or normative content." Though making a sharp distinction between science and morals, Buchanan acknowledges that "[l]ike [Knut] Wicksell my purpose was ultimately normative rather than antiseptically scientific." Despite admitting a normative component to his concerns, Buchanan often claims that his economic model of behavior is predictive and descriptive, having no prescriptive or ethical element. Although he admits that calling his exchange theory the key to a *better* political system is normative, this insight is lost when he makes policy recommendations. Even if he is not necessarily offering hypotheses for empirical refutation, he asserts that some of his propositions are potentially testable. Market thinking makes economics scientific, independent of value judgments. The idea of spontaneous order is itself a principle of science, based upon observation and "the exchange paradigm."[11] Ryan Amacher acknowledges that economic analysis "may embody implicit value judgments and ideological biases," but "one simply has to be careful to avoid these pitfalls."[12] He does not tell how.

Though Hayek does not claim that economics can be a science in the same way as does Friedman, he believes that his central concept of spontaneous order is correct, objectively true, and a valid statement of how the world actually operates. It is based upon observation of social evolution, but though it has "scientific status," it is not testable as such. Social and policy debate are "capable of a definite scientific treatment." Controversies between nonsocialists and socialists are not caused by value differences but "rest on purely intellectual issues capable of scientific resolution." Economics is the only science that comprehends all of humanity and therefore provides the basis for judging other institutions.[13]

Hayek employs science in a more traditional, less positivist sense than Friedman. Methods used in physical science are not applicable. The purpose of economics is to explain, not predict. As with Buchanan, Hayek is willing to acknowledge that his work contains normative elements, though both authors claim that their conclusions follow from the naturalistic market rather than normative values. Hayek's policy claims, however, are as strong as those of Friedman and Buchanan. More important, despite lack of agreement over the exact nature of science and economics, these authors agree that their economics is scientific and objective and that their policy recommendations are the only possible ones for modern democracies. Their images of order, human nature, and the concomitant market are not hypotheses to be debated but objectively valid statements about an existing, natural system of human relations. Conservative economics is not another ideology but provides lasting principles and a true picture of reality that are valid bases for correct policy advice.[14]

It would be easy to add more examples of this extraordinary claim, which, consciously or not, fulfills two policy objectives. First, it makes the system invulnerable to criticism. Second, it attacks the liberal assertion that there are no neutral policies—that every policy contains normative judgments that make necessary and legitimate choices about who will benefit from what types of public policy. For example, Lester Thurow claims that value judgment is inevitable. Definitive experiments are impossible, and "unobservable variables" are common. Efficiency statements are no different from equity statements. "Both depend upon an underlying set of discussable value judgments." "Prescription dominates description." It is not possible to rationally or empirically claim that people are rewarded according to contributions in a neutral market; therefore, we have no choice but to make deliberate distribution choices. Traditional economics has become an ideology, "a political philosophy, often becoming something approaching a religion."[15] The conservative economists vehemently reject this position. Political and economic stability require acceptance of their objectivity claim. Introducing deliberate choice *inevitably* undermines the efficient operation of the economic system and political values such as freedom and democracy which are based upon it.

The problems with this crude positivism are immense. An objectivity claim reflects acceptance of a particular guiding principle or method of reasoning. The conservative economists deny the structuring impact of context and perspective, claiming universal validity for their theory. There is no outside platform upon which one can stand to look into their model. As with Plato, the only sound test assumes the validity of the starting premises. This model of science presupposes an objective reality, separate from observation, and unvarying, discovered laws of nature. As with spontaneous order, these laws are not created by observers, are not imposed upon reality, and do not change with the observer but are implicit in what is observed. Because they reflect reality, moral injunctions and wishful thinking cannot affect them, nor can they be modified merely to accommodate temporary desires. The conservatives' premises may be hypothetical (though they rarely say so), but their political and policy conclusions are not.

The method of analysis is largely a priori, deductive reasoning. Despite the mathematical talent of several of these writers, there is a strong anti-empirical bias in their thinking. Propositions are often true by definition. Political proposals are not offered as hypotheses for analysis but as categorical statements, true because the economic premises from which they are deduced are true. Testing, falsification, and experiment are rarely possible or attempted. Experience cannot prove the validity or invalidity of assumptions[16] or conclusions. There are no explanations of results that are divorced from such normative values as freedom or efficiency.

All theories, especially those dealing with people and values, share the problem that preferences inevitably affect a theorist's work. This does not invalidate the search for understanding but cautions against easily accepting claims of complete neutrality or universal applicability. Except for Hayek's on occasion, the conservatives' objectivity claims ignore the controlling role of perception and the possibility that assumptions may lead to choosing a method of confirmation that confirms the assumptions. Causal linkages, especially between government intervention and economic problems or between capitalism and freedom, are asserted without controlled experimentation or clear causal connections. This is a simple picture of science, defined as observation and deduction, which misses the crucial role of deciding what is a fact, how facts are related, and how analytic methods are selected.[17]

Human Nature

All political, social, and economic theories contain and are based upon a theory of human nature[18] or motivation. Assumptions about human nature explain how people behave, provide clues as to how they should behave, set adamantine boundaries to politics, determine the legitimacy and illegitimacy of public action, and hint at desirable public policies. The extent and scope of freedom, the meaning of equality, the nature and content of democracy, the existence of public morality, the nature of obligation and social ties, and the limits and possibilities of public policy and collective action are all contained in a theory's picture of human nature. In seemingly empirical theories, images of human nature or motivation affect what is considered proper methodology, what can safely be ignored, what behaviors must be attended to, and what requires an explanation.

There are many conflicting theories of why people behave as they do.

Classical liberalism, capitalism, and liberal democracy are based upon a mildly hopeful premise, that improvement is possible. As Thomas Jefferson summarized, "Although I do not, with some enthusiasts, believe that the human condition will ever advance to such a state of perfection as that there shall no longer be pain or vice in the world, yet I believe it susceptible of much improvement, and most of all, in matters of government and religion, and that the diffusion of knowledge among the people is to be the instrument by which it is to be effected."[19] The traditional liberal emphasis on freedom, tolerance, and education would make no sense unless one assumed that people are, or are potentially, capable of understanding and pursuing their interests and effectively participating in governance. Optimistic assumptions may encourage the conclusion that people can understand and creatively improve their situation, individually or collectively. On the other hand, a pessimistic approach generally entails the belief that people are permanently limited by sin, ignorance, tradition, or fate and that there is little they can do to improve their lot. If people are essentially evil, weak, sinful, corrupt, or irrevocably ignorant, then it makes no sense to argue for freedom; people will only abuse it. Democracy becomes dangerous nonsense—the ignorant masses need strong leadership, or else they will destroy that little bit of order known to the few who have some insight into the nature of reality.

As an example, capitalist and socialist theories are divided by many things, especially by rival images of human motivation—what people may achieve and how they ought to behave. As a child of liberalism, capitalism assumes that people are fairly competent, naturally competitive, and are most dependable when their self-interest is involved. Government policy succeeds when it allows people the freedom to competitively pursue their interests but must otherwise be limited. Socialism, and especially Marxism, has assumed that people are naturally creative and cooperative. Competition is an aberration resulting from defective economic and social institutions that must be corrected to release human energies. In some varieties of this thinking, government may have extensive power to recreate the world in the image of the perfected person.

Assumptions about human nature are not always characterized by such dualism; there are many degrees of shading and complexity among arguments. The crucial point is that conceptions of human nature deeply affect interpretations of what is due to people, what is the nature of obligation, what people consider possible or legitimate, and what is desirable behavior. Whether one looks at the debate over equal rights for women, Burke's attack on the French Revolution, Lenin's claim that the unaided proletariat is capable of nothing more than trade unionism, Hitler's murderous effort to purge Germany of racially "inferior" stock, or the gentle debate between John Adams and Thomas Jefferson over who is a member of the natural aristocracy, assumptions about human nature and motivation animate each conflict. Will people save or spend a tax cut? Are racial groups equal? Are differences between women and men politically significant? Economically? Socially? Responses to these questions are not graven in stone. Though societies frequently have given incompatible answers, these rival answers have seemed obvious and right from within each society's dominant value system and picture of human nature. To understand a theory and its claims, one must understand its assumptions about human nature and motivation.

Conservative political economy is based on classical liberal theory. While sharing many values with such liberals as John Maynard Keynes or John Kenneth Galbraith, the conservative position has more limits and fewer qualifications. It is closer to Malthus than to Adam Smith, but Smith is the starting point for their analysis. For Smith, in *The Wealth of Nations* (1776), people are fundamentally alike—individuals competent enough to see and seek their own interests within a given setting. They necessarily pursue their own good, but not to the extent of Thomas Hobbes's war of each against all. Cooperation results from seeking one's own ends. Pursuit of economic self-interest—"[t]he natural effort of every individual to better his own condition"—is the motivating force behind the invisible hand, which tends to promote human harmony in market-like situations. Assuming a large number of small producers, sellers, and buyers, with no one dependent upon any other participant, self-interest, if pursued within the limits of legal and moral codes, tends to promote the welfare of others. One could improve one's position only by producing a better product, selling a product at a lower price, or both. Even though man is self-interested, man is also a social animal, and the extensive division of labor which arises out of self-interest illustrates that interdependence.[20]

The conservatives' assumptions about behavior and motivation seem to override their science claims. When discussing political or market behavior, the issue of objective, value-free science is mostly forgotten, and analysis starts from human nature. The economists' assumptions about human possibility and the role of the market in harmonizing human behavior shape all their arguments and conclusions. Given basic human drives, the market becomes the arena of cooperation and safe competition and is the key to reconciling egoistic individuals. The conservatives take human nature as fixed and largely independent of moral, cultural, and social influences. These factors may modify *how* people seek self-interest but not their inevitable attempt to do so. People cannot be trusted outside the market and need strong spurs to cooperation. Opportunities for satisfying greed are the most productive incentives to proper behavior. In a form of secular Calvinism,[21] life is seen as virtually penal in character. Men[22] are purposeful but isolated, having few ties. Interests and pains are incommensurable.

Conservative man is mired in profound ignorance, overwhelmed by passion for his own interests. Each author agrees that humans can never know enough, or sufficiently divorce self-interest from decisions, to plan for the entire economy. Rather than justifying protective government intervention, ignorance requires that collectively people leave things alone, accepting the results of evolutionary change in the economy. Though ignorant of the larger picture, individuals know the immediate circumstances they confront and are free to attempt to act within that situation if there is no outside, coercive interference. Individuals are thus independent and free to act, because the market reconciles and harmonizes their conflicting efforts. Groups must not be free to act because there are insufficient limitations upon their ability to act.[23]

The conservative economists are in complete agreement about what motivates people. In all environments, regardless of context, individuals compete to satisfy *self-interest*[24] in market-like situations. Individual self-interest is the key to conservative political economy, providing a powerful explanatory and predictive tool—the only interpretative device needed to understand economics, political behavior, and the inevitable failure of government intervention into economic relations. As the most important element in human nature and politics, pursuit of self-interest provides a "natural" limit to public action. Economics is identified with analysis of the pursuit of individual self-interest. Economic behavior is separated from total behavior. All motivation, perception, and behavior are individualistic. Each person is engaged in self-chosen, utility maximizing,[25] purposeful action, directed toward individual and individually chosen ends. In all circumstances, individuals pursue self-interest regardless of the structuring function of role playing, public opinion, context, or institutional goals which either mask self-interest or represent a temporary coincidence of individual self-interests. These theorists assume a close connection between individual interests and preferences "and social outcomes";[26] i.e., that it is correct to say that politics reflects the psychological and moral makeup of individuals. They look at collectivities—groups, corporations, political parties—and see only individuals. The political or social whole can be understood in terms of the part—individual pursuit of self-interest.

Self-interest is the most "dependable spur" to motivate people. Altruism, or "human kindness," always fails before self-interest. Self-interest is whatever people strive for, including money making and peer approval. "It is whatever it is that interests the participants, whatever they value, whatever goals they pursue."[27] Self-interest fuels competition in the market and in politics but simultaneously ensures cooperation. There is one choice: allow individuals to seek their own self-interest in markets which limit the destructive pursuit of self-interest or the vain hope of government beneficence.[28] Trust in government simply loosens restraints. The market performs better than government because it generates minimum standards of respect for law, property, and the rights of others which curtail destructive expressions of self-interest.[29] When people appear to behave in an altruistic manner, they are engaging in self-interested activity from which they derive psychic income. The only non-market limit on pure, individual self-interest is the recent assertion that a man's family is part of his definition of self-interest.[30]

Self-interest produces competitiveness, and to the conservatives, competition serves several functions. It controls and rewards behavior, makes consumers sovereign, ensures market adjustment, provides the alternative to government direction of the economy, removes temptations for public provision of services, and thus promotes cooperation, freedom, and equality. Given limited human knowledge and ubiquitous self-interest, neither intelligence nor goodwill can create the order and institutions needed by society. Undirected experimentation through competition provides the means by which individuals and societies advance, making it the only way to overcome human limitations. Although competition does not guarantee the best possible outcome, it ensures maximum use of available knowledge and skill.[31]

Self-interest and *individualism* are not identical, but in the conservative economists' formulation, individualism is reduced to allowing pursuit of self-interest in market-like situations. Self-interest is the key element in individualism as well as in all aspects of politics and public policy, including conservative critiques of democracy, freedom, and equality. The market theory of economics and politics is individualistic. Individuals are the major, perhaps the only relevant, focus of attention. To the extent that a social whole exists, it results from and reflects individual action and behavior. Common interest is Hobbesian, encompassed by the pursuit of self-interest and by the system that forces cooperation—here the market rather than government. Neither values nor relative standing induce behavior, except when envy leads to egalitarian demands.

Individuals and individual ends are the subject matter of economics (and should be for politics), as opposed to "'social engineering'" which means "the uses of individuals as means to nonindividual ends."[32] Common interest is fulfilled by pursuit of self-interest in the market, individuals invariably seeking self-interest regardless of context. This is the basis of Buchanan's "methodological individualism." Buchanan states that individuals are the ultimate decision makers. Economics and economic analysis of politics focus on individual actions and choices in all circumstances. This supposedly makes economics scientific, gives it superior status to other social sciences, and enables it to be predictive. People are presumed to act according to individually determined preferences. Individuals are the sources of their own valuations and always attempt to maximize autogenously derived conceptions of self-interest, usually envisioned as increases in wealth but always involving a desire for more. In the absence of individual interest there is no interest. Postulating supra-individual interests is unscientific and allows those who claim to speak for a greater interest to exercise their own self-interest–control over others.[33] Institutions are important[34] because they shape how individual interest is expressed and whether it has a beneficial (markets) or harmful (politics) impact.[35] The conservatives agree, however, that institutional purposes are always subordinated to individual ends, which "explains" the inevitable failure of all redistribution and intervention policies and "proves" that socialism is impossible. Though Buchanan is aware that institutional context affects individual definition of utility maximization, serious analysis of how individuals interact–one of the basic concerns of political science–is missing from each theorist.

The other authors agree that there are no collective goals and purposes, only individual ones, that everything people do is to promote their self-interest, and that this is the key to making political-economic recommendations. Self-interest is a universal motivation, intuitively obvious and the starting point for subsequent analysis. Despite his emphasis on "spontaneous order," tradition and evolution, Hayek considers himself a true individualist in the traditions of Locke, Hume, Smith, and Burke. Individualism is the alternative to socialism because people understand only their own immediate circumstances, and no one can comprehend an entire social-economic order. True individualism requires spheres of independent action–the economy–where people may attempt to achieve their ends. Like Buchanan, Hayek assumes that analysis starts with individual actions and purposes, which create institutions as the unintended consequence, not the purpose, of most interaction. Order follows from individuals pursuing self-interest and in turn provides the proper framework for that pursuit. Thus only individuals engage in purposeful action, not groups. Social goals are simply the "coincidence of individual ends." There is no way to adequately compare people. As previously mentioned, individual self-interest is not egosim and includes a man's family.[36] Friedman accepts essentially the same arguments. Though Gilder rejects much classical theory and adds a creative element to his heroes of capitalism that is missing from the others, his individualism is also contrasted with collectivism and is fulfilled by individual action in the market.[37]

The self-interest dictum does not advocate that people treat one another with selfishness, brutality, or lack of compassion. Nor is it a warrant for law breaking. Rather, it claims that people always put self-interest first, howsoever they define it. Whatever a person does, even if it seems foolish or suicidal to an outside observer, is done in that person's self-defined self-interest, not for moral or group ends.

Individualism is not necessarily a normative concept. Buchanan's initial formulation of methodological individualism, when stated in if/then terms, can serve as a fruitful, nonnormative starting point for analysis. It takes on normative implications when it becomes the basis for policy prescriptions—a point Buchanan admits but fails to carry into policy advice—and is operationalized as the only valid expression of individualism. In the conservative formulation, individualism means the right to compete in markets; it does not address many of the classical liberal concerns with allowing and encouraging autonomy and spontaneity outside the market.[38] Indeed, impersonal, natural forces, beyond conscious or collective control, determine general behavior and individual life chances.

Conservative economists claim that individuals bear the consequences and rewards of their actions—as in Malthus's classic argument, even in an overpopulated society, "[h]e who performs his duty faithfully will reap the full fruits of it"[39]—but that they have no power to constructively change the system. The individual may be the focus of analysis, but individualism, like freedom, equality, democracy, and justice, is procedural only. *Procedural individualism* is not concerned with success or outcomes, only with the existence of procedures that allow individuals to attempt to compete. It is not a substantive concept and has nothing to do with self-development, self-expression, successful achievement of goals, or the valuing of individual differences, all of which open the possibility of legitimate public intervention to help people achieve their goals. As such, it is a system-maintaining concept, because individual fate does not matter as long as the system that allows for interaction is maintained.[40] Individualism means behavior in the pursuit of self-interest that is never outside the rules of the market. It is satisfied by the assumption that people choose and act based on their own purposes and by allowing them to seek their interests in the free market. Individual valuation is acceptable only if expressed in conformity with the market. Otherwise, pursuit of individual self-interest is destructive and must be limited by constitutional restraints.

This individualism is neither the result of empirical analysis nor a proposition offered for testing, but is the irreducible starting point for analysis. The conservatives may be correct about self-interest and individualism, but they are excruciatingly vague about the content and meaning of self-interest. Self-interest is the conservatives' Ptolemaic earth: Everything circles around it and all counter evidence is made to fit within the system. The concept cannot be refuted or falsified.

If self-interest means measurable financial interest, then the self-interest axiom is clearly false,[41] since that ignores other things of value as well as role playing, conditioned responses, noninstrumental behavior, and accepting group norms. If it refers to esteem, reputation, or psychic income, then we enter realms of higher metaphysics, where every action is of necessity self-interested because that is how conservative economists have defined human nature.

Humans act only in self-interest; therefore whatever a person does, even if it costs a great deal of money, peace of mind, or status, is in his or her self-interest. In this context, only the individual is admitted as judge. By studiously avoiding specification of the meaning of self-interest, conservatives can employ the concept to defend any policy or outcome, such as inequality, which results from market relations, and to attack any welfare, tax, or redistribution policy. Such policies can serve no public interest but instead cloak the self-interest of tax eaters—welfare recipients, majorities, and bureaucrats.

The self-interest argument depicts a world that must either be this way or that, with no possible midpoint. Rousseau or market individualism are the only alternatives. These theorists see only individual behavior and claim that to discuss anything else entails jumping to the fantastical idea that there is a supraindividual entity and that everyone seeks the common interest. Discounting that possibility leaves only procedural individualism.

This perspective overlooks behavior that is neither narrowly self-interested nor altruistic. Goals and values may develop in consultation with others. The act of bargaining may change one's perspective. Reflection on strongly held values and ideals may modify attitudes and behavior. Individuals may internalize group norms; after all, people confront but do not create most of the norms and rules that surround them, a point these authors celebrate under the rubric of spontaneous order. If individual behavior is modified—and the modification is called a tradition, institution, society, or whatever—we are confronted with something new that is not reducible only to single individuals. Political and social institutions, unlike businesses, are not created to advance the interests of entrepreneurs, investors, or employees but have other purposes or missions. Moreover, self-interest is a motive, not a justification acceptable to others. Even if morality is a fig leaf for naked self-interest, people insist that self-interest be justified by appealing to a larger value. That there are rewards for advancing an institution's stated purpose, that individuals must conform their ends to the ends of the institution or tradition or be excluded from it, that they need the institution to achieve their own ends, that advancement requires behavior which seems to advance group norms—these counterassumptions mean that the node, or point, of interaction is important and must be analyzed in itself.

In asserting that all action is self-interested, these authors use self-interest in two ways. It means (a) any interest or gratification, including psychic income, and (b) tangibles—monetary, or occasionally power, gain. The conservative economists focus on the first when discussing general behavior and the second when discussing politics and government. By definition, the possibility of seeing political self-interest in terms of moral values is excluded by shifting the meaning of self-interest. Self-interest (b) excludes upgrading the common denominator, patriotism, and risking death in the armed forces. It prevents consideration of role playing, collective norms, and customs and depreciates structural limits on how an individual can pursue self-interest. If self-interest (a) were allowed into politics, internalization of group norms and guidance of self-interest by these norms would be possible. This would effectively undermine the political market concept because (a) allows the possibility of something other than coercively self-interested behavior. That would reduce the contrast between the political and economic markets. If only tangible self-interest is possible in politics, the economic market is protected from intervention, and politics should be drastically curtailed.

Even if politics is only self-interest (b), while (a) is possible in economics, and even if the conservatives adequately explained this difference, the model ignores the Aristotelian and Madisonian tradition of limiting political self-interest by pitting interest against interest, passion against passion. These authors make no attempt to explain why some actors do not define self-interest in terms of whistle blowing instead of competing to join in plundering the public or wealthy minorities. Yet the success of their political and constitutional proposals depends upon someone standing aside from the general scramble for place and plunder, seeing their and society's long-range interest and reinstating economic sanity. If people and politics are as these authors claim, it is unclear where the majority coalition to do this will come from – though a majority in support of their policies may not be necessary if high deficits, low taxes, and reduced popular participation destroy the resources necessary to support the welfare state. Moreover, it is left unexplained why and how these authors have overcome human nature, seen the truth, transcended the general chaos they describe, and avoided charges that their policies are tainted by self-interest. Either they stand above self-interested political struggle or their arguments express self-interest, not an abstract truth. Acceptance of the market may give this ability. Hayek states, "I am as certain as anyone can be that the beliefs set out in it [*Road to Serfdom*] are not determined by my personal interests."[42] If it is possible to transcend self-interest in this instance, why not others?

If people are solely rational utility maximizers as the conservatives paint them, the free-rider principle should apply in politics. Why should a rational economic man join a political group, or contribute to mosquito abatement or pollution control, when he will receive benefits whether he contributes or not, as long as others contribute? The linkage between voting or group membership and hoped-for rewards is even more tenuous in politics than in such public health programs. What is being "produced" and "purchased" is less obvious in politics than in the economic market. How votes replace dollars is unclear. Voting is extremely difficult to explain in individualistic terms. Presumably one weighs the costs of group membership or voting against the likelihood that membership or voting will directly affect the outcome in a way that is personally beneficial. If it is a large group (and in this model, despite Friedman, groups must be fairly large), individual action has little impact. It makes no sense to join a group even if membership is beneficial unless self-interest (a) is allowed,[43] and then civic virtue or ideals or group-think may be operating. To appeal to individuals by saying that if everyone behaved this way no one would get what he or she wants is irrelevant. That is a moral appeal, logically and functionally identical to "be a good citizen," "do your part," "win one for the Gipper," but given the conservative model this is irrelevant, perhaps impossible. Morality is often a cloak for self-interest,[44] a rationalization for the tangible self-interest of politics. Thus, either the conservative explanation of how groups act together is correct, or their picture of human motivation and the free rider are correct—but not both, unless people are irrational.[45]

As with God's will and fate, conservative self-interest is sufficiently broad to account for all behavior while not explaining it. At the same time, these authors reject the possibility of creating institutions to make narrow self-interest serve wider public goals and purposes. The market does this automatically, but it is impossible in politics. However, calling behavior self-interested solves nothing until one specifies how it is self-interested. Instead of a priori assertions, there should be empirical analysis to determine if this or that agency or policy can be shaped to channel self-interest into benefiting others. Regardless of whether conservative self-interest is a hypothesis to be tested or a metaphysical claim, it is presented as axiomatic and carries a heavier weight in shaping and coloring their argument and analysis than any of their other assumptions.

The issue of self-interest can never be resolved. Perhaps it is similar to the old question of whether the glass is half full or half empty. The answer is not important in itself—the glass is both[46]—but tells much about the answerer. How a person conceptualizes interest determines what policies he or she considers possible or legitimate. The conservative economists resolve the problem of self-interest by limiting politics and public policy. Self-interest shapes their image of order and the kind of polity that follows.

Order

Human nature, operating within the market, creates a natural, harmony producing, autonomous *order*. That self-interest here leads to coordination and harmony is based on the belief that this order exists, separate from human volition, immune from successful intervention or collective manipulation. In a fundamental philosophical assumption, the conservatives insist that instead of chaos, irregularity, or randomness, there is order, regularity, and identifiable causation which result from individual self-seeking behavior. This belief takes on mythic proportions, providing a basic explanation of reality. Despite a Hobbesian picture of human motivation, the market makes people naturally social. As with such nineteenth-century political-economy, natural-law theorists as Malthus, Herbert Spencer, and William Graham Sumner, the conservative economists believe that this order is both scientific and moral, setting limits to human desires and possibilities. It is an evolved order, not created by any single person or group, independent, and superordinate to politics. It is neither convention, model, nor metaphor and is not imposed by analysis.

The concept of an existing order to which behavior should conform is very old. Plato's forms, the medieval linkage between human and eternal law through natural law, and the concept of natural law as rational behavioral principles deduced from human nature sound a continuing, though disparate, theme in political analysis. Throughout its varied development, people making this argument have insisted that everything is not convention, that man is not the measure of all things, and that there are relations humanity cannot consciously change for the better.

The Physiocrats first developed the idea that the economy is orderly, forming a natural, independent operating system.[47] Adam Smith's invisible hand, where a person intending his or her own interest is led to promote the interests of others, and his assumption that the market tends to produce harmony of interests are based on the belief there is an existing order to which people contribute and conform. Malthus made the same assumption, but his order, though it summarized the essential idea of economic order until today, was not so benign. The ratio between food and population growth froze humanity into existing political-economic relations which could not be directly altered or ameliorated. Even political reform depended upon the poor accepting that government could not improve their situation. The natural order of things—including the distribution of property—decreed conformity and nonintervention.

Buchanan, Friedman, and Hayek agree that there is an order—a *spontaneous* order. This natural order is self-maintaining, in equilibrium in a fundamental sense. Hayek's concept of order is the most developed and serves as a model for the others. Though he does not consider economics to be as objective as Friedman does, he believes that spontaneous order in human affairs is an objectively true statement. It is the fundamental reality upon which he bases his political economy.

Hayek's spontaneous order exists "without having been deliberately created." It is characterized by self-correcting forces, a "self-steering mechanism," "regularities," and is "self-generating."[48] To Hayek, it is impossible for the conscious human mind to produce this kind of order and cooperation. "[T]he unconscious collaboration of individuals in the market leads to the solution of problems." Action is possible because the social and physical worlds are "orderly," but this order is "only partly the result of human design." Instead, it arises "from regularities of the behavior of the elements which it comprises" and, while affecting them, is "the unforseen effect of conduct that men have adopted" for their own ends. Human actions "take place within a more comprehensive spontaneous order" that rests "in part on regularities which are not spontaneous but imposed." Thus, it is "a spontaneous order of human activities of much greater complexity . . . than could ever be produced by deliberate arrangement," evolved by "individuals without their intending to create such an order." It is the nondeliberate and "unforeseen results of the haphazard activities of countless individuals and generations." Given human inability to understand complex wholes, this is "an order of much greater extent than we" could create by conscious manipulation. This order is the "outcome of a supraindividual process of evolution and selection." The *"discovery"* of this spontaneous order "provided the foundation for a systematic argument for individual liberty."[49]

Hayek's order is composed of abstract relations – actually a rationalist construction – though it is the basis for concrete policy recommendations, and "cannot be defined in terms of any particular observable facts . . . .not something visible or otherwise perceptible but something which can only be mentally reconstructed." It does not have a purpose but allows individuals to seek their purposes within it. General rules, equally applied, encourage the formation and maintenance of this natural, spontaneous order, but it is impossible to work out its details or force its development. As the product of long-run evolution and adaptation, the spontaneous order may not be the best that can be conceived, but it is better than anything man can deliberately create. Such an order "may persist while all the particular elements they comprise, and even the number of such elements, changes." General rules – stripped of reference to existing societies but discoverable through their behavior and evolution – allow people to adjust one to another "through the confinement of the action of each" to those rules. Each person is not assigned but creates his or her own position within this order. Thus relations develop without reference to any known, definite individual.[50]

The concept of order represents a reality superior and antecedent to individuals who must conform to the rules and needs of this order. As with Burke, it compensates for individual ignorance, providing answers for both individual and shared dilemmas. The assumed fact of the order's evolution is of crucial importance in conditioning acceptance of economic relations as natural, conveying an air of inevitability and creating a naturalistic standard superior to human will by which to judge behavior. This belief in order, evolution of order, and existence of an order of reality structures the thinking of other conservative economists. To Friedman, the development of "complicated and sophisticated structure . . . as an unintended consequence" of pursuit of individual self-interest explains not only the market but, as in Hayek, language, science, and social values. His monetarism cannot be understood apart from belief in underlying regularity and order. Friedman claims that an invisible hand promotes harmony in economics, while "scientific laws" guarantee failure when government interferes in economic affairs. Nothing can prevent it.[51]

Like Hayek, Buchanan claims that "discovery" of the spontaneous coordinating properties of the market in the eighteenth century provided concrete support for constitutional democracy, limited government, and economic analysis. This "untouchable" principle of classical political economy "combines freedom and order." Despite his interest in contractual creation of and limits on government, Buchanan rejects a constructivist position, claiming that the institutional structure and foundation of society are not consciously created, nor are outcomes "purposely directed." Order in the political economy evolves from the processes that generate it, primarily pursuit of individual economic interest. Order, a central element for each of these authors, has often developed in opposition to government.[52]

Despite differences with these authors, George Gilder repeatedly expresses faith in the compensating logic of the world and universe. The concept of order, natural relations, and natural systems permeates *Wealth and Poverty*. Increasing wealth for the rich benefits the poor because it is entrepreneurs who "know the rules of the world and the laws of God." There is a natural order in human affairs, with the wealthy on top and women in their natural, inferior position with regard to men. Poverty and inferior status for ethnic minorities result from interplay of natural forces. Though it is moved by creative entrepreneurs, not by Adam Smith's invisible hand, order exists.[53]

Spontaneous order has profound political implications, which are elaborated in later chapters. Along with self-interest, it is the key argument limiting politics and popular expectations. The concept can conceal political power under seemingly impersonal forces. Despite Buchanan's contractarianism, spontaneous order rejects the liberal tradition that a social contract is the basis of the political system. Government, a created not evolved institution, is suspect, based on ignorance, and likely to interfere in delicate relations no one fully understands. Spontaneous order limits political choice, setting large parts of public life off limits to political intervention. It considers social and class relations natural. It contends there is ultimate harmony between people. While its promoters avoid the word "equilibrium," their basic concepts and claims – monetarism, self-adjusting relations, the market as the best protection against market abuses, private gain leading to public good, adjustment of supply and demand –

assume order and equilibrium,[54] negating intervention. How could there be spontaneous order without belief in equilibrium? If people cannot direct outcomes to desired ends, all they can do is maintain the procedures that allow the natural system of spontaneous order to operate.

Order encourages the emphasis on procedures over outcomes that is seen throughout conservative economists' political theory, shaping their concepts of freedom, equality, democracy, justice, and the role of government. Hayek recognizes this. The key danger facing his order is revolt against impersonal forces and necessity—the unwillingness of people to accept "impersonal and anonymous" mechanisms. Conscious efforts to intervene, whether through planning, regulation, specification of collective goals, or vain attempts to impose "high ideals," inevitably fail—a theme constantly echoed in Buchanan and Friedman—leading to totalitarianism.[55]

This concept of order is a secularized version of natural law, embodying the authority and attractiveness of claims based on necessity and inevitability rather than human volition. It both describes and prescribes human behavior. Any theory that argues that people should follow a prescribed course of action because it flows from basic human nature or relations and is of universal application, is a form of natural-law thinking. Spontaneous order is natural in that it springs from innate human drives, human nature, and motivation but is independent of deliberate human design. Human actions generate relations and institutions, but neither consciously nor according to human wishes. Everything has some purpose and can be explained from within the system by those with knowledge.

The Market Is Spontaneous Order

While many spontaneous orders can exist, the quintessential one is economic, and conservative economists claim they have demonstrated its existence.[56] It is embodied in the *market*. The market is the single most important social interaction—a model for proper conduct and a goal of public policy. When free of government intervention, the market is orderly and order producing, distributing goods and services in direct proportion to each person's contribution to the self-determined welfare of others. With the exception of rare and necessarily transitory monopolies, no one exercises control. Each participant is equally subject to the same impersonal forces. Outcomes are not the result of any *one* person's or group's actions or will. The market is fair, just, spontaneous, and voluntary and coordinates self-interested individuals without coercion. It compensates for human nature by channeling self-interested impulses and correcting for limited knowledge and ability. This makes it much more efficient than any other possible means of organizing people. If the market is not working as it should, something external to the market, such as coercive labor unions or intrusive government, must be interfering to benefit some at the expense of others.

To Hayek, the market ensures "spontaneous collaboration" and order. If left free, the market operates at maximum efficiency, making more "available than could be done by any other known means." It assures "each will get for the share he wins . . . as large a real equivalent as can be secured." Since distribution is independent of "anyone's designs or intentions, it is meaningless to describe the manner in which the market distributed the good things of this world among particular individuals as just or unjust."[57]

Given a "stable monetary framework," Friedman's "market system is inherently stable," more so than any other system. It is characterized by equilibrium. Prices organize activity, provide incentives, and "determine who gets how much of the production—the distribution of income"—through operation of "an invisible hand." Pursuit of self-interest creates a "finely ordered and effectively tuned system, yet it is not deliberately created by men." It operates only when people voluntarily agree to trade, exchange, or interact. Everyone is free to enter. Competition peacefully coordinates behavior, prevents abuses, and distributes rewards. Distribution is fair because "market imperfections are not very significant," and there are fewer imperfections than in any alternative system. In the long run, despite any apparent difficulties, the market must be left to its own self-correcting, autonomous forces, because intervention ruins its intrinsic order. Past instability has "been produced by erratic and unwise government intervention rather than any inherent instability in the system itself."[58]

The market reconciles "autonomy . . . with coordination and continuity," or "spontaneous coordination." "The market is the classic example" of order produced by "decentralized processes."[59] It creates voluntary cooperation through competitive pursuit of self-interest without coercive imposition of common values. Friedman claims it "permits unanimity without conformity" and allows peaceful collaboration while each person "goes about his own business." Emphasizing each separate, distinct exchange, rather than the exchange framework and those who may be affected by that exchange, everyone involved benefits from a transaction, or else it would not occur because each person is allowed to choose with whom he or she will exchange.[60] In the absence of government intervention, market relations are "the institutional embodiment of the voluntary exchange process."[61]

These claims are reflected in Buchanan's identification of the market with moral order.[62] Though admitting the market is not perfectly competitive, he asserts that it embodies consent and unanimity through free exchange, is created by cooperative behavior developing over time, ensures that "owners of inputs" receive rewards "commensurate" with those inputs, and prevents "unilateral action" by any one participant.[63]

These arguments provide the essential justification – an appeal to higher standards to confirm the validity of an argument – of the market. They are a mixture of naturalistic and utilitarian claims. The market is a natural system, resulting from human nature, that has evolved through gradual accretions of unconscious and nondeliberate inputs from millions of individual participants. Fortuitously, the market harmonizes interests, ensuring that pursuit of self-interest promotes rather than harms the interests of others and eliminating the need for exogenous value systems. The market is the model of what people should aspire to be and do as well as a limit upon what they can do and be. By definition the effects of a natural system must be better than those of any possible alternative. Belief in a natural system provides a powerful attraction, since "the order of Nature is unquestionable and good. . . . in order to lead a better life one must conform to the laws of natural necessity."[64] Mankind has no choice but to conform to this natural order. People cannot do all they can imagine but must learn to accept the market order as the best they can achieve.

The conservative theorists also make utilitarian claims – even though Hayek and Buchanan reject utilitarianism – that are potentially subject to empirical verification. The market produces long-term desirable results (over time, more people will benefit) and is more efficient than any other economic or political system. Though these authors rarely mention Pareto, their market is Pareto-efficient and cannot be improved deliberately without reducing someone's self-defined welfare. Because it is voluntary and noncoercive, the market promotes more freedom, justice, and equality than politics or governments. It overcomes human greed and limits the worst effects of human ignorance. This produces a form of rule utilitarianism. Regardless of individual impact or outcome, people must follow the rules embedded in the market. Though too ignorant to deal with problems on a day-by-day or even cycle-by-cycle basis, people have been given the primary rule for political and economic behavior in the economists' discovery of the principle of spontaneous order operating through markets. The hypothetical element in this claim is soon lost, and the market's rules and injunctions become the only possible (an empirical claim) and legitimate (a moral claim) means to promote welfare, efficiency,[65] and such political values as democracy. Even if some individuals, classes, or nations suffer from supposedly temporary dislocations, there are no remedies outside of the market framework. Winners and losers may be different, but the only hope for long-term improvement is to follow the rules and allow natural market forces to operate. Hardships and disturbances are transient, adjustments occur rapidly, and people are guaranteed the maximally efficient use of all resources.

As a natural, autonomous, noncoercive, self-equilibrating, spontaneous system, the market provides an excellent perspective from which to analyze and critique sociopolitical phenomena. This deterministic portrait is not open to debate, which forestalls any analysis of its value assumptions. If this is an objective description of reality – at least the way reality would be in the absence of public intervention into economic relations – policy conclusions follow with logical inevitability. Rational people cannot debate them. The image of order through the market is the final element in the philosophical foundation for the market critique and model of politics.

The Market as Analytic Model and Challenge to Politics

The market as a political concept consists of three elements: The market is a model for political and social analysis, the basis for interpreting political ideas, and a replacement for and alternative to government and politics. This section briefly examines the market as a means of political analysis, focusing on "political markets," while later chapters will take up the two remaining themes.

For at least two centuries, a single protean idea has guided liberal, and deeply affected socialist, thought: The market is a remarkable coordinating, information producing, and distributive agency. Economists debate its exact nature, extent, and contemporary importance, but it is at the center of most of their analyses – Friedman or Galbraith, Hayek or Keynes. The analytic and prescriptive value of markets is, therefore, the heart of contemporary non-Marxist economic thinking. Political science, on the other hand, has largely ignored the market.[66] That neglect now haunts our discipline, because the market alternative disputes the validity of our normative and empirical enterprise. Some economists, such as James Buchanan, are engaged in virtual economic imperialism[67] with their claim that an individualistic market model explains political behavior. It supplants traditional political analysis that emphasizes institutions, interpersonal and intergroup relations, power (which disappears in the market), authority, role playing, legitimacy, normative analysis, and so forth. In extreme market models, relationships are reduced to individualistic, utility-maximizing, exchange terms that explain "economic" and "political," individual, group, and institutional behavior. Groups hardly exist as separate entities.

The simplicity, apparent precision, potential quantification, and determinism of the market model have encouraged its application outside of economics. Though this book does not examine economic (i.e., market) analysis of law, family life, marriage, language, philosophy, crime, anthropology, and other areas,[68] the market metaphor[69] (though it is intended as much more than a metaphor) is widely accepted as a valid and accurate analytic tool and basis for policy prescription. In some cases, individualistic economic analysis has become the sole behavioral explanation and the exclusive input for public-policy making.

Buchanan is very explicit. Economists offer the most valid theoretical explanation of human behavior, which enables them to "unravel the most tangled sets of structural relationships among human beings." This allows the development of "a meaningful 'public philosophy,'" in part by undermining collectivist–welfare–policies and in part by "imposing reality upon man's natural proclivity to dream. The economist, almost alone, takes man as he exists." This requires that political science change its perspective to that of economics, a "shift from the organizational entity as the unit to the individual-in-the-organization" and his or her interactions with other individuals. The approach of "methodological individualism" thus brings necessary realism and rigor to political analysis. Focusing on anything other than individual, private behavior while participating in decision making simply leads to faulty analysis and wishful thinking. Political science lacks a tradition of analyzing and incorporating "a theory of human behavior into" its study of political processes—meaning its conclusions are prescriptive, not explanatory. Economics can contribute a theory to political science, but beyond gathering data, political science can offer little to economics.[70]

How has the 2,400-year-old tradition of political analysis failed? By ignoring the *political market*. The economists referred to in this book save their most intemperate language, and the full normative implications of the market approach, for their description of the political market.

Political and Economic Markets: A Picture of Politics

The conservative economists insist on dividing political and social phenomena into mutually exclusive alternatives with no stable resting place in between. This dualism is apparent in the contrast between the political and economic markets. In an extreme restatement of the classical liberal distinction between society and state, there are only two ways to organize people: voluntary cooperation through markets or coercion through politics. These alternatives are irreconcilable,[71] at opposite ends of the spectrum. Though ideal types, these two markets form the basis for conservative policy prescriptions.

The political market is the reverse image of the economic market, revealing the essentials of politics. For Buchanan, "[T]he political relationship is not commonly encountered *in its pure form,* that of abject slavery. . . . the economic or exchange relationship is, at least conceptually, visualized in its pure form and, in certain instances, the relationship actually exists."[72] Human nature explains the "success" of the economic market and the "failure" of the political market. Motivation—self-interest—and the process of exchange are the same in both the economic and political markets, but they produce distinct results because behavior constraints are radically different. The orderly economic market is the result of spontaneous growth where many individuals over long periods of time separately make decisions; politics is the area of constructivist, deliberate, conscious decisions by the few for the many. The economic market controls self-interest; the coercive political market allows it to operate unchecked. Free individuals dominate economic markets; coercive groups make up temporary, exploitive majorities that dominate the political market. The evolved economic market is supposedly competitive, decentralized, noncoercive, and responsive to individuals and promotes diversity. Unless they have formed contracts, individuals may enter or leave at any time, such movement being the essence of freedom. People act rationally in pursuit of self-interest, each checking the ambitions of others while producing spontaneous order and benefits to others. Relations are always voluntary and expanding sum because people enter a relation only if it is beneficial.

These conditions are absent from politics. In the political market there is coercion and limited choice. Rational pursuit of self-interest is detrimental because groups, not individuals, compete, which opens the way to potential abuses of power. Unlike the economic market which supposedly harmonizes egoistic individuals, politics provides no systematic spontaneous checks on self-interest. There is neither free exit, as in the economic market, nor noncoercive competition. The object is to gain power to force others to comply with one's will. The invisible hand of self-interest leads to dominance and conformity. Coercive groups—usually labor unions and welfare claimants—organize and compete to control decision making, forcing redistributive demands on productive individuals.

How does this political market operate? Western political institutions "threaten to destroy the market economy" by allowing excessive public spending with "a bias toward deficits." Competitive democracy encourages incorrect popular expectations. Vote buying and lack of fiscal restraint create "inherent and fundamental biases" for intrusive intervention which undermines natural economic processes and stability. Because governments "are collectivities of utility maximizers," whose freedom from market control permits self-interest to become exploitive, there is an inherent "propensity to truck, barter and exchange" at the expense of public good. The result is a systematic bias favoring growth in public services at the expense of the natural economic order.[73] This is inevitable, flowing from human nature, universal suffrage, weak political parties, Keynesian economics, and immoral exploitation of the affluent minority by redistributive majorities.

Why have governments allowed this? Given existing rules and institutions, nothing else is possible. Government as a collective noun does not exist. Government institutions are aggregations of uncontrolled, self-interested utility maximizers who do what is necessary to gain or retain power. Politics is an exchange system employed for private, not public, ends. Public policy serves selfish purposes. Universal suffrage requires responding to whatever satisfies temporary majorities of greedy voters. Politicians and voters act alike; neither sees their real interest. There are neither moral nor institutional restraints as politicians outbid each other by making more and more promises to voters. Electoral competition replaces competition to produce a better product. The political market is created by luring voters into spending their "political income"–votes (which would seem to be expenditure, not income to obtain coercive advantages). Self-interest ordains that politicians promise reduced taxes and increased expenditures, encouraging gullible and unthinking political consumers[74] to follow their natural propensity to demand something for nothing. Politicians literally buy their election–a universal tendency– with funds taxed from someone else. In Friedman's terms, there is a "policy of spend and spend, tax and tax [someone else], elect and elect." Frequent elections ensure a short-term perspective, where particular and narrow interests dominate the general interest of cheap government and free markets.[75]

Special interests and group pursuit of privilege are the obvious problem. A special interest is any interest–demands for welfare, redistribution, social security, aid to education–that does not accept market outcomes but seeks gains outside the economic market. Any extramarket gain, such as welfare or minimum wages, is privilege. It does not matter if recipients are rich or destitute; they are privileged if part of their income comes from government programs. Whatever the market distributes cannot be privilege, no matter how much wealth is gained or inequality generated.[76] Thus a welfare recipient or a person working for the minimum wage, if that is higher than wages in a competitive market, is privileged while a successful entrepreneur is not.

Majorities are collections of small minorities. In a model reminiscent of John C. Calhoun, "The majority that rules is typically a coalition of special interests." Choosing a number determined more by the needs of the theory than by any empirical analysis, each interest rarely represents more than "2 or 3 percent" of a constituency, but combined they form temporary majorities.[77] Democratic theory,[78] according to Hayek and Samuel Brittan, holds that whatever majorities wish is just, gives majorities unlimited power to satisfy every whim, and fails to distinguish between temporary and permanent majorities. Unlimited modern democracy hardly differs from totalitarianism. In both cases, a selfish minority (or minorities, or temporary majorities of minorities) rules the (real) majority, producing government, in Hayek's mind, that is "[c]orrupt at the same time weak: unable to resist pressure from the component groups . . . however harmful to the rest such measures may be." The competitive market in votes, to Brittan, means "liberal democracy inhibits government from tackling coercive groups."[79] There is no unity of purpose, except to plunder; no limit upon excesses, other than destruction of the economy; no morality, save self-interest; no moral order, only voters and politicians bidding for power in the political market. The result is that each government "must be expected to be generally engaged in operating against the long-term public interest by serving its short-term political advantage."[80]

Human nature produces the political market and determines that governments *must* fail when they attempt to satisfy popular demands for welfare, regulation, or intervention. This is inevitable. To Friedman, "[T]here is something innate in the political process that produces this result." Government must be inefficient; "scientific laws" ensure the bankruptcy of any market intervention. This is no accident but is mandated by the "use of bad means to achieve good objectives." Spending someone else's money guarantees it will be spent badly. Friedman's argument virtually duplicates William Graham Sumner's:[81] "A person who intends only to serve the public interest is led by an invisible hand to serve private interests which it was no part of his intention to serve." As with Adam Smith's invisible hand, this ghostly guide is self-interest.[82]

By denying efficacy to politics and raising the idea of a political market, these conservatives shield the economic market from criticism and intervention. The political market prevents government from either ending or mitigating economic problems. Even if the economic market fails—which is doubtful— politics cannot correct it. Because the political system is preordained to fail, there is little or no likelihood that it could cure market failure, if market failure existed. Apparent problems such as recession, unemployment, or falling living standards must be endured because spontaneous order ensures that correction will occur and intervention prevents natural corrective action. Even if one concedes a market failure with consequent political and social dislocations, this must be balanced against the certainty that collective attempts to address it will also fail, compounding the initial failure. To Friedman, "[P]olitical considerations prevent the effective use of the scientific knowledge we do have for the purpose of promoting stability." The burden of proof must fall on those supporting intervention—and these authors reject the macroeconomic theory that might allow this. To the extent that markets fail, it is more often because of government intervention in spontaneous relations than any market defects.[83]

The economic market is clearly superior, if only we have patience and limit political intervention. The choice is either consumer protection, diversity, and freedom in the economic market or conformity and collectivism in the political market. Allowing just a little intervention is similar to being a little pregnant. The essence of freedom is being able to "choose how to use our income" and resources, and that, according to Friedman, may be more important than occasionally voting. Politics is virtually defined as coercion, which is lacking in the market; therefore, government and politics are the major, perhaps the only real, dangers to freedom. These authors reject the possibility that consumer preferences might dominate in politics as they claim they do in economics. In politics, preferences—and people have only individual preferences, not considered and collective judgments—must be limited and restrained, because in politics coercive power is added to preference. Intervention concentrates power, and centralization of power increases coercion. Given its many participants—the word implies individuals—the market denies centralizing power to an administrative king. No one is in control, able to impose his or her will; no one person or group makes all relevant decisions; no one must subserve another. Thus, for the conservatives, limiting politics ensures freedom.[84]

While economics is variable sum, politics is zero sum and coercive. "If participation were voluntary, one would not observe negative-sum games, since the affected minority could always refuse to participate."[85] This follows from conservatives' peculiar definition of coercion and their claim that all market relations are and must be voluntary. Ignoring externalities, constrained choices, and the impossibility of avoiding all exchanges, the authors believe that one always must choose the market over politics or collective decisions regardless of apparent inconveniences. As noted above, government use of resources is and must be wasteful because officials use someone else's assets for their own ends. Thus Friedman charges that "[c]rime has risen not *despite* government's growth but largely *because* of government's growth." Given human motivation, aid to education, pollution control, unemployment compensation, and regulation have inevitably compounded the problems they sought to address.[86] Whether focusing on greed, interference in natural relations, or simple carelessness, each author claims intervention inevitably causes inefficiency.

Comments

Assumptions are crucial. Discussing damaging industrial smoke, Buchanan and Tullock argue: "If the externality is real, *some* collectively imposed scheme through which *the damaged property owners are taxed and the firm's owners are subsidized* for capital losses incurred in putting in a smoke-abatement machine can command the assent of all parties. If no such compensation scheme is possible . . . the externality is only apparent and not real." In defining costs, Buchanan and Tullock assign the burden of proof, and therefore the policy decision as to who should pay, not to the persons imposing the fouled air, but onto those who are affected by it.[87] A different starting assumption could easily conclude that the cost of air pollution control should rest on those who produce pollution and their customers.

These authors contrast the *ideal* of an economic market with the partial reality of politics. They discuss how markets should operate, not how they do operate; how politics must operate, not how it actually does. By definition, the economic market is impersonal. It cannot be oppressive, because oppression is a relation between identifiable persons, and in the market one can avoid such relations. While an unemployed, hungry person may miss the significance of this distinction, these authors are unconcerned with such people if their problems are not the fault of an identifiable other. In economic relations, constraint, lack of alternatives, and inadequate means are irrelevant to freedom.

The market critique of politics is deduced from the starting assumptions about human nature and markets and is presented as a universally valid principle. Though Buchanan, Friedman, and Hayek do not accept all of the assumptions in this chapter to the same degree – there is most divergence over the objectivity claim – each accepts the essential argument. Their most important agreement is over their vision of human nature, spontaneous order, and the market, as they frequently employ identical language to describe similar phenomena. This shared view of the world encourages them to develop similar political and social arguments and recommendations, all converging to limit political possibility.

The market vision is a powerful naturalist and occasionally rule-utilitarian justification for conservative politics. Philosophical justification serves many purposes. The most important one is to convince others, and perhaps oneself, of the validity and superiority of a political, social, religious, or economic position or proposition. A justification establishes principles that can serve as operational statements in policy areas. It may be a sanction for belief or action. The market model produces a presumption for the market and against politics and government. It justifies self-interested economic and social behavior, the minimal state, and little concern for the social-political impact of economic behavior. It narrowly defines fundamental political values, so that they conform to natural market relations. This model leaves aside large parts of social and political reality, especially behaviors that at least seem to involve more than individual preferences and simple exchange. As economists, these authors are attuned to instrumental behavior, yet noninstrumental[88] behavior is often an important reason for cooperation, political participation, and patriotism. How institutions survive over long periods of time, if they are simply bundles of utility maximizers and unarticulated rules, remains unexamined. Despite grievous problems, the market model defines the great issues of politics. It is the basis for the claims and arguments examined in the rest of this book and will become clearer as we study the role of the market in conservative political theory.

Part Two

Market-Based Politics: Revising Political Arguments to Fit Economic Theory

Chapter Three

Freedom

The generality of labourers in this and most other countries have as little choice of occupation or freedom of locomotion, are practically as dependent on fixed rules and on the will of others, as they could be on any system short of actual slavery.
—John Stuart Mill, *Principles of Political Economy*, bk. 2, chap. 1, sec. 3.

And effective freedom depends on power; it is freedom to use power possessed and has content only insofar as the person has 'means.'
—Frank H. Knight, "Abstract Economics as Absolute Ethics," *Ethics* 76 (1966):166.

Definitional Assumptions and Politics

Politics is uniquely linguistic. Even in authoritarian systems people ultimately control and manipulate others with words and ideas. Though using the same terms, liberals, conservatives, socialists, and authoritarians give them different meaning and content. Basic ideas and values, such as freedom, justice, equality, and democracy are "hurrah" words that are almost universally approved. Even the most ruthless dictators claim to be "restoring" the conditions for democracy. Each of us values freedom, but we debate its meaning: being left alone, or having resources for choice and/or self-development, or willing acceptance of necessity. Justice is always the basis of the good life. But as Aristotle noted in his *Politics*, there are many competing interpretations of justice, each arming its holders with some partial and legitimate claim to recognition. Socrates and Thrasymachus discuss justice in the first two books of *The Republic*, but mean radically different things by it. Realization of either conception of justice must annihilate the other.

It matters how people define or conceptualize important political ideas. Words and ideas are not neutral but have consequences and symbolic importance. We perceive, explain, and understand the world through ideas and concepts; they construct and may constrict reality. Words control what people consider to be a problem, legitimate means to address that problem, and acceptable policy options. Frequently, definitions are actually moral claims and assumptions about basic political values and provide the gauge to measure and judge behavior, people, and institutions. A policy or proposal may be exploitative, a threat to freedom, acceptable in a democracy, or unjust depending upon how one conceptualizes these values. Radically different policies, or entire political systems, result from different images of commonly held beliefs and values.[1] If others accept our interpretation of the essence of freedom or the meaning of democracy, we have gained significant control over their political perspective and behavior. Though normally definitions are useful,[2] given a particular purpose, and not necessarily true or false, conservatives' definitions follow from their economic assumptions and support their policy and political claims.

This and the next three chapters explicate the conservative economists' understanding and use of political ideas that have been contested for centuries; ideas that are pivotal in the history and operation of western liberal-democratic systems. Conservative economists attempt to monopolize public debate by recasting traditional political ideas to conform to their market model. They assert that their definitions are not convention or convenience but are given by nature or at least human nature, virtually a form of natural history.[3] Human nature and the political market reveal the meaning of key ideas; any other interpretation will replace the competitive economic order with coercive political conflict, destroying freedom and the most productive possible economy. Moreover, conservatives' definitional claims are interrelated, so that one opens or closes possibilities and alternatives for the others, forming an integral part of the economists' policy claims. For example, if democracy requires little popular participation or if it means choosing among rival elites, then people do not need extensive freedom or much equality. If equality is the right to attempt to compete, then one does not need more freedom than the right to compete.

These definitions have consequences for political discourse and control the range of legitimate policy options.[4] In C. B. Macpherson's term, market economics sets "the inescapable *requirements*, of the political system." Though starting from a significantly different perspective, Milton Friedman claims the free market "defines the role that government should play in a free society."[5] The conservative economists' definitions are inescapable. If they are successful in convincing the public that freedom means being left alone, especially in market relations; that democracy has little to do with political participation and that currently low levels of participation should be further reduced; or that equality and inequality are the result of natural economic processes into which the public cannot constructively intervene, then their policy proposals and government model follow logically. These redefinitions, which flow from the view of human nature and economic and political markets discussed in chapter 2, set the framework for understanding the conservative economists' challenge to public provision of welfare, regulation, and intervention into the economy and are the basis for reconstructing contemporary liberal-democratic welfare states.

Debating the Meaning of Freedom

Freedom is one of the most important and contentious concepts in western political discourse. Even within the same normative tradition, such as liberalism, there is unending controversy over the content and meaning of freedom as well as what factual situations promote or retard freedom. In defining freedom differently, rival economists either condemn or applaud the welfare and/or interventionist state; limit or expand the scope of government and group action; and attack or defend democratic politics and equalization policies.

The perception of freedom has never been static. It has continually expanded to include more people and areas of life, adapting to problems, challenges, and opportunities. Freedom may refer to rights, liberties, powers, immunities,[6] national independence, or being left alone. For the ancient Greeks, freedom pertained to the polis and its independence from foreign rule, not the individual—a meaning it still retains in many twentieth century national liberation movements. Early modern theorists such as Locke emphasized the relation between the individual and government in defining freedom. Nineteenth-century theorists such as John Stuart Mill added oppressive social situations, majorities, and holders of economic power as dangers to freedom.[7] During the 1930s, freedom in the United States increasingly came to include protection against economic disaster and concentrations of economic power.[8]

It is a virtual truism that no value, not even of life, is absolute, uncompromisingly dominating and overcoming all other values in all circumstances. Freedom's meaning is no different. It too is hedged in by other values, beliefs, traditions, and interpretations of what constitutes an obstacle that should be overcome for its promotion. The question is not whether there will be any limits to freedom—classical theory always emphasized that freedom is possible only under the law—but rather what encompasses and constrains freedom, what trade-offs are legitimate between freedom and other desirable values, and what policies are likely to implement whatever one conceives as freedom. Such limits must be defended and justified in one of several ways. Limits may be imposed to protect another desirable value, as when the conservatives protect their economic freedom by criticizing democracy. Or, limits may be based on the claim that people are not yet ready to enjoy the value–such as Lenin's assertion that the proletariat was not ready to revolt or govern and therefore needed strict party leadership to enforce success. Limits may also be imposed on the ground that the value does not mean what it appears to mean, such as the frequent eighteenth-century claim that the political equality implied by widely accepted natural-law arguments did not include women, the poor, or slaves.

An adequate theory of freedom must address a number of questions: what is the general meaning of freedom; what are its source and justification; to what areas of life does it apply; if there is conflict between different arenas for freedom, which is dominant and by what criteria; is freedom a negative or positive concept, or both; who has freedom–individuals, groups, or both– and under what circumstances; what are the obstacles to realizing freedom and why; and what is choice.

Conservatives' Freedom

Freedom is the conservative economists' primary value and central idea. It trumps all other values, confining their meaning and application. The conservative economists reject the claim that the meaning and content of freedom continue to change and expand. Freedom has a specific content, the same as it had for liberals in the eighteenth century[9]: being left alone and using your property as you wish. Within a liberal-democratic framework developed over the last three hundred years, the conservatives have chosen the historically narrowest meanings of freedom, equality, democracy, and justice, forcing these concepts into the constraints of an idealized market economy while claiming to maximize them. (In this context, "narrow" means the fewest legitimate options, the smallest range of alternatives, the least chance for expansion, the most tenuous interconnections between politics, economics and society, and a focus on procedures, not substantive content or outcomes.) The result is that although these theorists claim that their economy is, or should be, autonomous, political and social relations must conform to their economic model.

The conservatives' depiction of human nature, the market, and market requirements provides an absolute barrier to expansive conceptions of economic or political freedom. Each of their values and proposals is structured upon, limited by, and required to conform to individualistic pursuit of self-interest as the essential component in freedom. A simple picture of human nature encourages a simple picture of freedom, its necessary conditions, and its value. Conservative freedom is grounded in human nature rather than an appeal to contract, rights, or transcendent standards. Though the economists write extensively about freedom, they are not concerned with related philosophical and political questions. They have no developed theory of rights. Freedom is their ultimate standard, but they justify it in negative, weak utilitarian terms.

Hayek defends freedom as the consequence of fundamental, "necessary," "irremediable," and "inevitable ignorance" that all people confront.[10] This primordial ignorance is not a reason for intervention but is the basis for rejecting intervention. People must be left alone to take their course in the market. No one can possibly have an adequate understanding of another's immediate situation, and no one can measure the consequences of the actions of millions; therefore, to maximize efficiency, production, and satisfaction, people must be allowed to choose, unhindered, in their immediate situation and take the consequences of their choices. In this formulation, freedom's justification depends upon the functioning of the economic system. Given human nature, freedom is *absolutely necessary* for achieving all that we want, but it is still an instrumental good, justified not in and for itself or even as a means to individual expression, development, or self-determination, but as a means to largely material-productive ends.[11] As such, it lacks the philosophical grounding these authors seek for their policies and is potentially open to refutation if the preferred ends can be achieved by empirically verifiable alternatives—though they believe this is not possible and reject all contrary evidence.

Freedom is a process and condition summarized by the absence of coercion, especially government intervention in one's affairs. The primary meaning of freedom is economic, negative, and individualistic: being allowed to attempt to use one's resources as one wills, in competition with others. It is an economic concept in the narrow sense of exchange relations in a market, not in a wider meaning of maximizing output or minimizing potential resource waste. Any political or social connotation is derivative and legitimate only if it supports the principle economic meaning. The market is, therefore, the absolutely essential arena for the exercise of freedom. Moreover, the requirements for freedom determine the role of government and the obligations citizens owe to one another. Freedom in the market allows people to promote self-interest, but giving equal (same) freedom to everyone prevents concentration or exercise of power. Thus market freedom is the best expression of human freedom and simultaneously limits the potential for abuse of freedom.

For Friedman, freedom means allowing each "individual to pursue his own interests so long as he does not interfere with the freedom of others to do likewise." This involves seeking one's ends, giving the "opportunity for the ordinary man to use his resources as effectively as possible." It has nothing to do with maximizing opportunities or being successful. Though Friedman believes that freedom is indivisible, with each component contributing to the others, he is most concerned with economic freedom—allowing the individual to pursue his or her economic interest.[12] To Hayek freedom is the opposite of slavery. It means "a state in which each can use his knowledge for his purposes." Freedom exists when people may act on the basis of their "own knowledge and in the service of their own ends," though this applies mainly in the market. Each of the conservative economists agrees with the argument that freedom involves the elimination of "coercion by the arbitrary will of another." The key word is "arbitrary." Coercion does not exist in the market. Only government can arbitrarily coerce people, making government the major threat to freedom. Thus, to Buchanan, "[A]n individual is at liberty or free to carry on an activity if he or she is not coerced from so doing." Freedom for Hayek does not guarantee "any particular opportunities, but leaves it to us to decide what use we shall make of the circumstances in which we find ourselves." Freedom does not include agency;[13] means or power to satisfy wishes; extensive choices; collective efforts to change circumstances; or any guarantees beyond protection from physical force and being allowed to attempt to do what one wishes. Freedom is not affected by the conditions under which one operates, the results of unsuccessful competition, perceptions, or the inadequacy of means to operationalize one's freedom.[14]

The Market and Freedom

Given these notions of freedom, how is the market related to freedom? The conservative position is clear. Freedom depends upon and is generated by the market. The market is the primary area of freedom, an absolutely essential means of protecting freedom, and a necessary support for freedom. Without a free market, political freedom and democracy could not long survive. Even if it does not operate perfectly, the market encourages freedom, especially in the long run. The conservative claim focuses on being allowed to act rather than broadly conceived conditions for the exercise of freedom.[15] To the extent that these authors relate freedom to self-development or self-realization, it is exclusively economic self-realization – pursuing one's ends – through a competitive market.

Though Hayek is less inclined than Friedman to claim that the market always defends freedom, he believes that it usually does and that it is absolutely essential to freedom. The preexisting spontaneous order is the basis for freedom; freedom grew as the spontaneous order developed. Thus, discovery of natural order in human relations "provided the foundation for a systematic argument for individual liberty."[16] As the spontaneous order is primarily economic, a market order is a functional, logical, and sequential prerequisite for the development of all freedom.

For Friedman, economic freedom "is itself a component of freedom broadly understood . . . an end in itself . . . . [and] an indispensable means toward the achievement of political freedom." Economic freedom means being allowed to choose "how to use our income" and "to use the resources we possess in accordance with our own values." There is no difference in freedom for those with large or small income, property, or resources. Regardless of contrasts in wealth—I have one dollar, you have one million—everyone is equally free as long as no one coerces another in the use of his or her resources. This freedom includes owning and using property; entering any chosen business or profession, without limits or licensing requirements; and voluntarily buying and selling in any market.[17] It means that freedom cannot be enhanced by acquisition of new resources through government redistribution or protection.

The conservatives equate free with voluntary. In another example of either/ or thinking, voluntary behavior is the opposite of being coerced. All behavior that is not coerced is free, voluntary, and self-chosen. Though the market is not the only arena of voluntary behavior, only voluntary behavior occurs in the market; only the market guarantees voluntary behavior. Equal formal access to the market, therefore, is the essence of freedom. Pursuit of self-interest ensures that voluntary relations are neither coercive nor uniformly one-sided. Voluntary, for these theorists, is a very broad concept, including situations where a person has little choice and may face substantial constraint.

This image of voluntariness transforms the market into the realm of consent, and consensual, noncoercive relations. Because market relations are voluntary, they are entered freely and deliberately: "[B]oth parties must benefit . . . so long as the exchange is voluntary and there is no force . . . both people are better off." Even if it is not a sufficient condition, "voluntary exchange is a necessary condition for both prosperity and freedom." Though in *Capitalism and Freedom* Friedman notes that "[e]xchange is truly voluntary only when nearly equivalent alternatives exist," this qualifier disappears from his later work. Because, by definition, force cannot take place in the voluntary market and in the absence of force freedom is preserved, government should not intervene in economic relations.[18] Any intervention *must* diminish freedom.

The "ethical attractiveness of voluntary exchange" becomes an important part of the defense of markets, even though analysis excludes concern for non-forceful coercion.[19] It assumes that each person in an "economic" relation is an autonomous, self-directing actor and views freedom from the perspective of the person acting, not the person acted upon. The notion of being acted upon—by manipulation, compulsion, subliminal suggestion, or passive receipt of externalities—hardly exists in this thinking. People outside market transactions are not considered.[20]

Other conservatives expand upon this position. William Hutt sees the market as both free and democratic, where "each person's vote" is weighed in proportion to his contribution "to the common pool of output"; that is, his contribution "to the well-being of the rest." This free and democratic system depends on private property, and its democratic content is not abridged by participants having different numbers of votes. As in classical political economy, property is a key element in the definition and defense of freedom. Protection of property is not a threat to individuals, even those without property, but is the basis for civilization, freedom, and the spontaneous order. For Ludwig von Mises, "Private property creates for the individual a sphere in which he is free of the state." Hayek agrees that we need such autonomous spheres to prevent coercion. Property, liberty, and law "are an inseparable trinity." The condition of propertylessness, however, does not compromise freedom, because those without property are free (allowed) to choose for which property owner they will work. To Murray Rothbard, freedom depends upon property and using property and talents as one wishes. Such "freedom leads to economic development" which encourages further scope for individual action and freedom.[21]

Economic and Political Freedom

Conservative and liberal economists agree that economic and political freedom are interdependent, but disagree over the meaning of economic freedom, the nature of its relation to politics, and whether freedom is an extensive or narrow idea. Liberals envisage an intimate, two-way linkage. Economic freedom may promote or harm political freedom. Both are necessary values, and neither should be emphasized to the detriment or exclusion of the other. Under a wide variety of circumstances, such as poverty, unemployment, unequal access to employment, or lack of educational opportunities, political intervention can expand economic freedom, whereas poverty and economic instability can destroy the conditions of political freedom. On the other hand, conservatives see a strong causal link from economic to political freedom. Economic freedom is prior to and necessary to political freedom, but economic freedom cannot be expanded by any public intervention. Indeed, the spontaneous order of economic freedom may flourish even in the absence of effective political freedom. There is no evidence that the conservatives contemplate any conditions where economic freedom could undermine political freedom or stability.

Friedman exemplifies the conservative position. "Economic freedom is an essential requisite for political freedom." "Restrictions on economic freedom inevitably affect freedom in general, even such areas as freedom of speech and press." The market limits government and reduces "greatly the range of issues that must be decided through political means," and anything that limits or diffuses government power increases freedom. Thus the market prevents concentration of political and economic power, which is the only alternative to free markets, thereby serving "as a check and a counter to political power." It does this by providing a wide variety of services, removing an important area of life from government, creating a polycentric system as opposed to a concentration of power in politics, and providing an economic base from which people who are not acceptable to the government may be able to advocate dissident ideas.[22]

Friedman makes no effort to explain to whom holders of economic power are responsible if they have the ability to check government power. The word "responsible" literally has no meaning in the market, as he and the other conservatives deny that there is any private, economic power because it dissolves in the market. Efforts to enforce "responsibility" must always be destructive. Market power is a positive contribution to political freedom for two reasons. First, one can always find another buyer, seller, employer, or employee; therefore, no single buyer, seller, and so forth can have any coercive control. Second, since coercion is the only danger to freedom, politics is coercive, and since the market is an impersonal mechanism that can never be coercive—a point upon which Hayek repeatedly insists—the market protects freedom. It provides "a system of checks and balances" which "enables economic strength to be a check to political power rather than a reinforcement."[23] Thus its limitations on government, even on popular majorities, always promotes freedom.

Economic freedom has virtually created political freedom. According to Friedman, political freedom in ancient Greece and Rome, as well as in the eighteenth and nineteenth centuries, "clearly came along with the free market and the development of capitalist institutions." By creating polycentrism, the market encourages diversity of opinion and reduces the areas of life where politics is dominant.[24] Hayek agrees: "Economic freedom is thus an indispensable condition of all other freedom," necessary to and resulting from personal freedom. It is "the prerequisite of any other freedom." He links planning and government intervention in economic affairs with "the disappearance of all personal freedom [including "spiritual freedom"] and the end of justice." Individual and political freedom have never existed and cannot now exist except under his version of economic freedom.[25] Buchanan also links economic to individual and political freedom, claiming that markets are less arbitrary and more likely to support freedom, justice, and equality than is politics or government. Markets "tend to maximize freedom of persons from political control," and it is in systems with free markets that freedom in general is best protected.[26] The conservatives' causal link between economic freedom and overall freedom is a deductive necessity rather than a hypothesis offered for evaluation. The conservative economists' choices are simple: unrestrained economic freedom, essentially laissez-faire capitalism, which is the *only* system promoting freedom; or centralized control, something close to the Soviet model. A stable mean does not exist.

The lack of a stable alternative between complete market freedom and a totalitarian system helps explain the conservative reluctance to support active measures to curb racial discrimination. Freedom to buy and sell in the market, as well as freedom to exit undesirable market situations, replaces the need and desirability for political action. In *Capitalism and Freedom,* Friedman argues that only coercion should be subject to public policy because discrimination is simply the refusal to trade with someone; efforts to address that kind of "'harm'" always "reduces freedom and limits voluntary co-operation." Antidiscrimination policy means arbitrary use of government power. Though discrimination *can* be an obstacle to freedom, Friedman argues that the market provides the only climate within which minorities can be free and that minority progress can be attributed to free, capitalist markets. Impersonal markets prevent arbitrary exercise of power, financially hurt those who discriminate, and provide a safe haven for minorities. Conversely, if the market does not eliminate what appears to be sex or race discrimination, this means they are in some sense natural. For Friedman, the market "protects men from being discriminated against in their economic activities for reasons that are irrelevant to their productivity." To Hutt, "the free market is colour blind." Profit incentives ensure the best worker will be hired, regardless of race. Assuming rationality and profit maximization as the primary goal, people would not discriminate if governments would only end minimum-wage laws and similar artificial supports for market imperfections. George Gilder sees racism as a myth and believes that minorities must work harder than they did in the past and that antidiscrimination policy has become the great enemy to minority progress.[27] In the long run, the market eliminates discrimination despite past inequalities and discrimination.

Discrimination is not an issue of morality but of efficiency and productivity, typical of any other exchange. Given ignorance and natural market relations, this position accepts the nineteenth-century ideal of free competition. Yet past discrimination has probably prevented people from developing their talents, so that minority workers may not be "the best" available. Except for Buchanan, who allows limited intervention,[28] the authors regard the conditions within which market freedom can end the results of discrimination as a nonissue. To admit it as a problem would open the possibility of legitimate public intervention which in turn must undermine the economic freedom necessary to political freedom.

The conservative economists deeply value all forms of freedom, including political freedom. Buchanan, Friedman, Hayek, and others repeatedly warn of the dangers that public economic intervention holds for democratic politics and political freedom, using prewar Germany, the Soviet Union, and Salvador Allende's Chile as examples. "Political freedom means the absence of coercion of a man by his fellow men."[29] Beyond the absence of coercion, what is the content of political freedom? The conservative economists do not provide a ready answer, though one can be construed from their view of politics and the political market, their emphasis on economic freedom, and their evaluation of democracy.

Political freedom requires limited government, not a particular form of government. Political freedom is dependent upon, secondary to, and in the long run probably less important than economic freedom. For example, in *The Road to Serfdom*, Hayek admits that in early modern Europe, growing political freedom encouraged economic freedom, yet "political freedom has never existed" without economic freedom. Friedman concurs: "[T]he ingenuity of people, acting separately, in the economic market in finding ways around governmental restrictions has been far more effective in maintaining a relatively free society than the good sense of citizens acting, jointly, in the political market."[30]

Since the economic market requires impartial application of law and relieves the political system of the burden of such divisive policies as redistribution or antidiscrimination laws, citizens have more protection and need a smaller range of political rights than in a system with extensive or active government.[31] Consequently, political freedom is a narrow, procedural concept, centering upon the essence of economic freedom – nonintervention. It contains a limited notion of political equality, which includes identical treatment by the law and acceptance of the principle, if not always the letter, of universal suffrage. Classical liberals such as James Mill claimed that participation to protect rights and interests is the heart of political freedom. But when government has little power to affect interests, there is not much need for extensive political participation. The market supplements and in some cases supplants civil and political liberties; indeed, dependence on welfare may be a proper ground for reducing a person's liberties.[32] Political freedom has nothing to do with antipoverty programs, socio-economic status, equal information, similar impact on formulating the political agenda or policies, or widespread public influence on government. In fact, the latter may be a danger, and many of these authors would curb citizen access to and influence on government.

Based upon their arguments about the dangers of concentration of political and economic power, the conservatives accept freedom of speech and the press, the right of people to organize – though they mistrust interest groups – and probably the right to dissent from public policy.[33] Other forms of freedom are possible. Friedman, for example, more consistently libertarian than the others, has opposed the draft, supported creation of a voluntary army, and argued for decriminalization of drugs.[34] These are normally seen as separate elements in freedom, rather than supplements to political freedom.

The conservatives' concept of political freedom discounts the possibly adverse impact of economic dislocation, poverty, unemployment, or depression upon political freedom or politics. If people are not allowed to demand that government address such problems, then these difficulties cannot trouble political stability. As such, they are not obstacles or dangers to political freedom or democracy. It is only when people attempt to force governments to intervene into the spontaneous economic order that economic, and therefore political, freedom become threatened. Given this rationalist construction, economic problems can never trouble the polity, because freedom requires that politics be divorced and removed from economics.

Though no one can deny that all control in the hands of one person, group, or government would constitute a condition for tyranny,[35] this does not mean that all types of economic freedom are necessary to political freedom, or that one cannot draw any line short of destroying a free economy.[36] There is no logical or historical reason for believing the market always protects freedom. Market failures, economic instability, and maldistribution undermine the conditions necessary for people to exercise their rights and encourage development of extremist movements. People will not ignore great inequalities, even if all inequalities were economically efficient, which they are not. People experiencing unemployment, sexual harassment at work, few or no job alternatives, or a declining regional economy understandably—even if, from the conservative perspective, erroneously—mistrust spontaneous forces. They may believe that their situation is accounted for by identifiable decisions of identifiable persons and expect some public aid to resolve their problems. When a person may be called free therefore depends heavily on what is an obstacle to freedom.

Obstacles to Freedom

Determining the obstacles to freedom—what makes a person unfree, takes freedom away, diminishes freedom, or creates conditions under which one is not free and/or able to do what one wishes—also defines the nature and scope of freedom by demarcating its parameters. Which obstacles an author considers "natural" and which are due to controllable human agency affects what he or she believes must be accepted, even if its results are undesirable—such as the inevitability of poverty and starvation to Malthus—and what may be purposefully changed. Thus if market distribution is "natural," this produces a different relation between freedom, politics, poverty, equality, and employment than if market distribution is controlled or at least deeply affected by some participants.

The question of freedom's context is, therefore, very important. It enables us to understand what authors mean by a value and what policies they consider suitable to implement it. Where liberals emphasize context and conditions, the conservatives depreciate most environmental considerations, focusing on the individual and his or her currently available choices. In looking at limits, they emphasize formal freedom. This has important policy results, because if freedom is a negative concept, there are fewer limits on it than if it is positive, requiring aid and support. The conservative economists emphasize the definitional fairness of starting "ground rules" rather than conditions, ability, "end states," or results.[37] Like individualism, equality, and democracy, freedom is a procedural concept. With this understanding, how are coercion, power, unemployment, the role of government, and the range of choice potential obstacles to freedom?

The conservative position is startlingly simple. *Coercion* is the only significant obstacle to freedom. The absence of coercion is a sufficient condition for freedom because individual choice is possible in all circumstances except under coercion. Only governments have consistent power to coerce. Therefore only government is a danger to freedom. How is this conclusion reached?

In a position accepted by Buchanan and Friedman, Hayek claims that "'freedom' refers solely to a relation of men to other men, and the only infringement on it is coercion by man." It does not involve being able to fulfill plans and is not limited by the range of available choices. Coercion is force, "arbitrary violence," *and* the intention to shape others' behavior. Thus losses in the market are never coercive, and in a definitional argument, coercion does not occur in the market if government leaves it alone. Coercion means "control of the environment or circumstances of a person by another that, in order to avoid greater evil, he is forced . . . to serve the ends of another."[38] The meaning of "greater evil" is narrowly conceived–withholding needed supplies and even imposing severe limits is not coercive–thus voiding the possibility of intervention to protect freedom.[39] Private property, equal application of the law, and the market provide the conditions which prevent coercion. In the market, one finds only "voluntary cooperation," making the market free.[40] The possible coerciveness of private property, compulsion, necessity, or few open possibilities is defined away.

The restraints some people see in the market are only apparent and trivial and do not affect being free (allowed) to attempt to act. The market is non-coercive because it is impersonal and spontaneous and its results are unintended, unforeseen, and undirected by any one person. Unlike politics, no one has direct control or power over another, therefore no one is forced to serve the end of any identifiable other. In a virtual caricature of Rousseau's General Will, it is no infringement on freedom that one must be dependent on all for the conditions of life. Every *one* is deprived of arbitrary power.[41] Existing restraints are not arbitrary but rather provide "narrow limits on the potential for exploitation of man by man."[42] Such restraints are natural in that they are "imposed under the 'democratic' form . . . consumers' sovereignty."[43]

There can be no rights against a natural, spontaneous order. Since the market is natural, it cannot be an obstacle to freedom. Even "[t]he threat of starvation" is neither coercive nor a violation of freedom if it results from normal market relations because "its effect on my freedom is not different from that of any natural calamity." For Hayek, the market prevents coercion by ensuring "that nobody has to be dependent on specific persons for the essential conditions of life." Only under the rarest monopoly over absolutely essential supplies, such as water, would it be possible for one person to coerce another in the market.[44] Without coercion, which can be sustained only with government support, monopoly is extremely rare and short-lived, because in a free market, monopoly prices encourage others to invest, thereby reducing the would-be monopolist's profits. If no one invests, it proves there are no monopoly profits to attract other investors; thus there is no monopoly and no one's freedom is endangered.[45] Under all other circumstances, even if the situation may be painful, freedom is protected because each person may seek another supplier, employer, or customer.[46] The absence of coercion becomes the necessary, and in most cases sufficient, condition for freedom.

The conservatives argue that businesses have no real power and that property is not normally a source of control because relations are voluntary, enterprises are private, and power is dissolved in the market which controls a firm's behavior and guarantees alternatives for consumers. This means that in any politically relevant sense, there is neither an economic elite nor economic power. Business decisions are private not public decisions. The potential ability of business leaders to reject public policies of which they disapprove is unimportant, is not an exercise of power, and is a wholesome limit on government.[47] Size is unimportant because it does not give real power if there is any competition. It simply means an enterprise has been successful in meeting consumer demand.[48]

Control over people in the workplace is thus not meaningful power or an obstacle to freedom, because, in Hayek's words, it is "never power over the whole life of a person."[49] If everything one does is for self-interest and if market relations are voluntary and mutually beneficial, no one has any reason to complain if results are unsatisfactory. Participants are always allowed to leave or find other employers or consumers; therefore, no one can control another without his or her agreement, meaning that there is no private power in the sense of controlling a person against his or her will. Thus, where theorists such as Heilbroner and Galbraith see control and subordination, in addition to voluntary behavior, in the market, Buchanan, Friedman, and Hayek see only voluntary behavior.[50] Business has no influence over employees or government. If it does have influence contrary to market theory, that is the fault of excessive government and its arbitrary power to benefit special interests. The power of business is a dangerous myth that can be employed to attack freedom.

Even work rules do not affect worker freedom. Hayek argues that freedom means taking the disadvantages of employment choices along with the benefits. Disadvantages from selling one's labor include doing "the bidding of others." This does not make a person unfree, because he or she may always quit, even if leaving has very high costs.[51] People choose to work for others. It is a voluntary agreement between individuals for their own benefit.[52] Only labor unions have coercive power; strikes are the only example of "private use of coercive power . . . an intolerable infringement of human freedom." Hutt claims that boycotts and strikes are not significantly different from the use of physical violence.[53] Neither hierarchical relations and dependence, which are never discussed, nor differences in wealth, status, position, and socio-economic benefits affect freedom because they are not coercive. Although private ownership is asserted as a necessary counter to governmental power, there is no real private power in the market. Thus the market can never endanger freedom, and there is no need to regulate the market or attempt to curb the "power" of large corporations. Indeed, there is good reason not to, because intervention concentrates more power in the hands of the shifting majorities who control government for their own selfish ends, or gives power to corporations they would not otherwise have, or both, thereby destroying freedom.[54]

Liberal economists do not accept this argument. They see more impediments to freedom than coercion or force. Market conditions such as constraint, availability of real choices, and inequality, whether intended or not, affect freedom. Racial discrimination[55] is a serious impediment to individual freedom and the efficient operation of markets. Freedom requires recognition that the market does not dissolve power and that many groups exercise market power, coupled with development of mechanisms to limit that power. Thus power is a more inclusive term and pervasive reality for liberal economists than for conservatives.

For Galbraith, power is "the ability of persons or institutions to bend others to their purposes."[56] Given this broad concept, power includes "condign, compensatory, and conditioned power."[57] Condign power is similar to the conservatives' physical coercion but also includes painful emotional situations. Conditioned power—which changes belief through education, persuasion, manipulation of perceived alternatives, appeals to common values, and even advertising[58]–does not exist for the conservatives. Where they see voluntary action, such as responding to an advertisement or popular acceptance of business goals, Galbraith sees conditioned power. Conditioned power is analogous to legitimate authority, but the conservatives exclude authority from their analysis. Compensation–the offer of positive rewards–is also missing from the conservative argument as either a form of or a means to exercise power. Rather, for them, it ensures voluntary cooperation. Where they see selfish farmers and coercive labor unions harming freedom, Galbraith sees countervailing power to that of what he calls the planning system. Great inequalities of wealth, therefore, mean that many exchanges are only formally free and that one or some parties have little or no choice but to accept an offer.

These different perceptions of the meaning of power are significant. For Galbraith, property, organization, and size are sources of power.[59] For the conservatives, property is natural and necessary to freedom; there is or should be no moral or political difference between the corner grocery store and General Motors–both are controlled by the market. Galbraith believes this is nonsense. Not only are the members of the planning system independent of the market, but, as Lindblom claims, they have influence and control over government. This includes expectations that they will be consulted by governments and the conditioning of popular and elite beliefs to accept corporate goals as national goals.[60]

This situation results in "the organic inequalities of bargaining power in a market where the many face the few." Power protects the large and well organized by enabling them to control and regulate markets.[61] Both Lester Thurow and Galbraith consider the neutralizing market a myth that disguises power, making its exercise easier and more effective; people see price increases, production decisions, wage offers, and so forth as dictated by the market, not as exercises in power. This, in turn, defends corporations from charges that they are acting against the public interest. If power to affect welfare, wages, and working conditions does not exist, government intervention to protect freedom is unnecessary.[62]

Power is not the only problem. Liberal freedom is more than not being coerced, and government is not the only danger to freedom. Liberal economists agree with Knight and Mill that conditions affect both freedom and its effective exercise. Unlike the conservatives, unintended consequences are not the equivalent of natural forces, nor is the market the result of the same kind of evolutionary processes that produced language or common law. The unregulated market does not guarantee freedom because freedom includes some ability to act, meaning that unintended consequences of market behavior can be as much of a limitation on freedom as are monopoly and intentional obstructions. For the liberals, freedom can be compromised even if there are no specific or identifiable actors or beneficiaries. Lack of material resources and inability to act are obstructions to freedom, therefore, maximization of freedom, consistent with other values, requires removal of as many obstacles for as many people as possible. Compulsion, vulnerability, discrimination, severely restricted opportunities, large inequalities, and what Galbraith called the "nerve-wracking problem of insecurity"[63] are all relevant to freedom.

Is *unemployment* related to freedom? That depends upon one's concept of freedom. If freedom is simply being left alone to use one's resources as one wills, the answer is no. If freedom has any positive content, even as little as having some means to employ one's resources or to take advantage of opportunities, the answer is yes. From Keynes onward, liberals have viewed unemployment as one of the most important conditions compromising effective exercise of freedom. They reject the claim that people are free as long as they are allowed to seek employment, whether or not they find it. For the conservatives, unemployment is neither a public problem nor an issue for freedom. Involuntary unemployment is impossible in a free market; all will find work, and if all have the opportunity to work, freedom cannot be compromised. For Galbraith, full employment, guaranteed income, or welfare reduce compulsion because they eliminate starvation as the alternative to exploitative employment.[64]

Governments can play an important role in promoting freedom and welfare only if the liberal position is correct. Otherwise governments can do nothing directly to promote freedom or, in the long run, people's welfare. This is the core of the conservative idea about the *role of government* in freedom. Government may be necessary, but it is always the chief danger to freedom. For Friedman, "to limit the government" is to free people.[65] Governments can do nothing to expand freedom except stay out of the market, avoid other coercive intervention, and enforce laws which apply equally to everyone. Anything else limits freedom. Redistribution does not increase the freedom of recipients, even if it provides them with more choices. It decreases the freedom of taxpayers and, by undermining incentives, reduces production. By interfering in natural market relations, governments are always the cause of poor economic performance.

Policies such as affirmative action, equal-pay requirements, guarantees of employment, minimum wages, welfare, and worker participation do not expand freedom and are unnecessary and dangerous. Thus for Friedman, "The growth of government at all levels . . . is destroying freedom, liberty and prosperity." Curbing government growth must augment individual freedom. Hutt says that any intervention cripples "these very humane social forces" which automatically harmonize interests and promote freedom. Stigler believes intervention undermines freedom, not only in terms of denying people the use of their property but also by replacing private expenditures; limiting private charity; deflecting private research and gifts to universities; creating barriers to employment; controlling licensure over television, liquor, and so forth; and, through "censorship of tastes," trying to protect consumers.[66] Friedman lists government spending, fear of the Internal Revenue Service, welfare, monetary controls to solve balance-of-payments problems, and even national parks and the National Science Foundation as dangers to freedom. Every intervention in spontaneous market relations is dangerous: "[F]reedom is one whole . . . anything that reduces freedom in one part of our lives is likely to affect freedom in other parts."[67]

Intervention, regulation, and welfare attack freedom in all its forms. To Friedman, welfare engenders "childlike dependence," takes away recipients' and taxpayers' freedom, and compromises freedom in general by giving discretionary power to public officials. Resources are wasted without any compensatory increase in freedom for anyone, and morality is undermined. To Hayek there is no logical stopping-place once extensive publicly supported welfare is introduced; it is a virtual code word for socialism and must lead toward that freedom-destroying result. As a multifaceted danger to freedom, public welfare must be eliminated. For Friedman, the only legitimate way to help those who fail is through his proposed negative income tax—which would eliminate the welfare bureaucracy by ensuring a minimum yearly income to people at a fraction of the poverty level—or preferably "voluntary action."[68]

The relation of *choice* to freedom also depends on one's basic concept of freedom. For the conservative economists, the number and scope of choices is irrelevant to freedom. Although the choices presented by the market promote freedom, freedom does not require that all or any of these choices be open. More important, government intervention, which by definition is coercive, cannot permanently increase choice. Even if it could provide more choices, coercive behavior cannot promote freedom. In all cases, intervention expands the role of government while crippling the freedom-producing market. Choice, in terms of directly expanding the number of options available to people, is simply not an aspect of freedom. Market maintenance, rather than individual choice, is the prime goal.

The conservatives claim that only their market promotes choice.[69] Although the title of Friedman's television series and one of his books is *Free to Choose*, in what sense are people "free to choose"? They are allowed to pick from what is offered in the market, if able to afford it, without government interference. The conservatives seem concerned with promoting freedom by expanding the number of choices only in areas where the market may profitably substitute for government services. Private mail delivery, Friedman's school vouchers, and Hayek's denationalization of money would end what they consider to be unnecessary and inefficient restrictions upon consumer choice, but there are no areas within the market where they seek to expand the number of choices.

Hayek identifies claims that choice is necessary to freedom with wishes to have power to do whatever we want, such as fly, and with deliberate attempts by socialists to confuse the meaning of freedom and destroy individual liberty. Demands for expanded freedom are the same as the desire to be released from "necessity" (meaning the market and its results) and from "the compulsion of circumstances." If freedom requires expanded choice, this inevitably leads to demands for equality and redistribution of wealth, which must destroy the true meaning of freedom. He argues "that the range of physical possibilities from which a person can choose at a given moment has no direct relevance to freedom." Freedom does "not depend on the range of choices" but on whether a person can act according to "present intentions" without coercion or manipulation or, in Friedman's terms, whether a person is allowed to enter "into any particular exchange." Focusing on the "given moment," "present intentions," or "particular exchange" means that freedom is not informed by long-term intentions and is not affected by the inability to carry out projects, no matter how one cherishes them. Freedom is not a function of context, of the total environment, or of all restraints upon a person. All that matters is the immediate situation (though this does not apply to defending the market against public intervention). Freedom means only "the absence of a particular obstacle – coercion by other men" – not the assurance of opportunities that allow one to take advantage of not being coerced.[70] In essence, the individual is protected from any *one,* but not from all.

As in their discussion of discrimination, a person is free if no identifiable other coerces him or her to hold a particular job,[71] live in a particular place, or shop at a particular store. As long as there is no coercion, external circumstances are irrelevant to freedom. One can always say no and accept the consequences. Hayek argues that even if one must pay "a cruelly high price," choice is available, making the market superior to any alternative.[72] Ignorance, lack of awareness of potential choices, poverty, necessity of taking a job at any wage, acceptance of costly alternatives against one's preference, and lack of nonharmful choices do not affect freedom, and public policies to ameliorate ignorance, poverty, and so forth do nothing to increase freedom. Collective choices, especially those altering the structure of the system and the choices offered by it, must be resisted in the name of freedom.

Choice is integral to the conservative view of freedom only when discussing coercive power. Since people are not coerced in the market, they have choice and freedom. In any nonmarket context, such as politics (except perhaps in elections), choice is not a component of freedom. People may choose between freedom as either noninterference or its negation, the destructive attempt to do all one can imagine. By setting up these alternatives, these writers defend their concept of the market but confuse their rationalist ideal with the realities people confront. People may be free from coercion but unable to experience the value[73] or worth of freedom because they are constrained. However, such factors are unimportant. Friedman, for example, claims that what is done with freedom, is an individual ethical problem.[74] But conditions and constraints do affect one's ability to make viable choices. Actual people face constraints—including life and death decisions about working conditions, insufficient health care, mental retardation caused by malnutrition, care for children or work outside the home—that are not neutralized by comparing them with the desire for the impossible. Economic distress erodes the ability to participate in politics and support for democratic politics. To expect people to value the conservative picture of freedom so highly that they must be willing to suffer great deprivations—such as exiting an undesirable market situation into worse conditions but not protesting or expecting public aid—presents citizens with too few alternatives. And that is the choice people face in the conservative model. Their freedom of choice does not include the idea that there will, or should be, a tolerable alternative,[75] though there is always the existential choice between life and death. If the market does not provide an acceptable (however minimally defined) option, then people must either endure what the market offers or do without, regardless of what they may be required to forego. The free individual is content to accept his or her fate whenever it comes through the market.

These beliefs about choice illustrate unspoken assumptions about *determinism:* that individuals always seek self-interest, that much of the political-economic world is beyond human will or control, and that individuals are fitted into an ongoing system. There is much more determinism in the conservative picture of freedom than in the liberal economists'. Individuals are subject to a necessity they do not create. For the conservatives, the natural market, guided by its internal law, adapts itself through an invisible hand to changing circumstances. Individuals discover but do not deliberately create it. If left alone, the system automatically produces efficiency. Individuals may do as they wish within their range of options as determined by the autonomous market, but it is improbable they will do anything except follow narrowly defined self-interest.

Given the conservatives' view of human nature, the individual is at least partly determined; Hayek uses iron filings and a magnet as an example of natural ordering principles.[76] As with Edmund Burke, Hayek says that individuals need not know much, not even the rules they follow, "in order to be able to take the right action."[77] In this context "right" means system supporting. People make few actual choices. They *must* choose only from the options available at the moment. Individually they may try to expand these within market rules, but collectively nothing can be done. They *must* act according to natural propensities. People respond to tax cuts by increasing expenditure; to opportunities by risk taking; to unemployment by accepting lower wages; to government intervention by reducing output.[78] The deductive logic of the system and human nature mandate that this will occur unless there is coercive interference from labor unions or governments. Thus the less each individual is coerced, the greater the degree of system-level determinism. The more people attempt to control, rather than accept, the macro system, the more they reduce freedom at the individual level. Acceptance of the necessity of nonintervention is a prerequisite to freedom.

In spite of their ostensible individualism, these theorists emphasize system needs. Ultimately it does not matter what happens to individuals as long as their behavior is system enhancing and the system is maintained. In discussing markets and coercion, for example, they lose sight of individuals and focus on the system. Occasionally they write as if the market has an aim or purpose and employ functional language, asking what does a person or group contribute to the spontaneous order. Individual welfare is less important than how people act within and contribute to the spontaneous order. For example, each author would reduce public assistance to force more people to work. Gilder is concerned with how religion and traditional sexual mores support capitalism. Entrepreneurs need freedom to "perform their role . . . . collectively." For Hayek, "Freedom means that in some measure we entrust our fate to forces which we do not control." Freedom is necessary if a businessman "is to perform his functions." That freedom is found in "submission to the impersonal forces of the market." The total order is much more regular "than the individual facts" that make it up.[79]

There is also an element of determinism about politics in the conservative definition of freedom. People cannot shape political relations as they wish. The human mind may imagine a better system, but idealism is impossible because human nature, the political market, and the dictates of freedom allow nothing better to develop. For Buchanan, Gilder, and Hayek, society, morals, and politics evolve. The pace of evolution cannot be hastened, though we can encourage those political institutions that, by conforming to human nature and the needs of the market, reflect underlying human drives. Market freedom, economic needs, and human nature delimit the range of permissible behavior, the nature of justice, and the duties, policies, and scope of legitimate government. Neither governments nor human willfulness can successfully intervene into or change the patterns set by economic relations. The rebellion of mindless children through destructive constructivist intervention is possible, but that is virtual suicide.[80]

Negative or Positive Freedom?

At the most obvious level, both conservatives and liberals espouse a negative concept of freedom, that is, a notion of freedom which emphasizes that people have or should have an area within which they are exempt from control by or interference from others. The debate focuses on what is interference, what is an obstacle to freedom, whether someone is free if no identifiable person coerces them through force, or if freedom requires being able to carry out some or many permitted behaviors. A broader notion of negative freedom is plausible, one requiring a good deal of regulation and intervention to prevent people from being subject to compulsion. Thus economic intervention, public education, antidiscrimination policies, provision of welfare, and so forth can be defended as negative freedom. They expand the scope or area of life where one is protected in what one does—in the sense of having more choices, opportunities to act, and doors open[81] and being protected from a wider range of potential interference than coercion defined as force. This does not include positive freedom conceived as real will, living up to a higher self, or obeying a true self.[82] On the other hand, if positive freedom is defined as legally guaranteed "rights to assistance of some sort,"[83] as rights to be supplied various goods or services, as creation of a framework within which people can achieve their negative freedom or expand autonomy, or even as assistance for fulfilling self-chosen ends, then many liberals accept a version of positive freedom that conservatives cannot accept.[84] Indeed, the conservative economists verbally reject all elements of positive freedom.[85]

Debate over the correct meaning of positive freedom is not directly relevant to this book. However, although the conservatives emphasize negative freedom, their argument sometimes resembles a concept of positive freedom.[86] While there is no real self in the conservative picture, except that real self-interest can be achieved only through competing in the market, freedom involves accepting necessity and the world as it is. Freedom is defended by and is possible only within the market. People who reject the market cannot be free, and one purpose of government is to prevent people from abusing or forcefully leaving the market—in a sense forcing them to be free. People will be free when they stop rebelling against the limits imposed by human nature and no longer want what the market cannot provide. Rational people do not attempt to alter market relations but try to "understand"[87] their necessity and operate only within them. That means accepting results—distribution, reward, equity—which, even if they are the product of human behavior, cannot be constructively changed by deliberate intervention. The market gives a single formula to end all economic and most political and social conflict, one that encompasses all value. Although people may have many, separate ends, the market reconciles them by placing a price on everything and provides the means to achieve them. Within this context liberals such as Galbraith and Keynes, who accept a plurality of values and the possibility of value conflict, are closer to the principles of the classical liberal tradition than are theorists such as Buchanan, Friedman, Hayek, or von Mises.

Implications

This picture of freedom has powerful implications for the meaning and construction of other political values and public policies. The conservative economists repeatedly celebrate the limitations their concept of freedom places upon government, politics, and public policy. Although these are discussed in the next several chapters, a few examples can illustrate the conservative view.

Liberal economists have long argued that the market does not operate as conservatives claim, neither protecting freedom nor promoting welfare. In Keynes's phrase, liberals accuse the conservatives of "regardlessness of social detail."[88] This charge is true, but irrelevant from the conservative perspective. From Malthus and Ricardo until today, the conservative position has claimed that economic efficiency and freedom are primary goals; that the natural, free market best achieves these goals; and that poverty and inequality, although undesirable, are the unchangeable result of natural, beneficial economic forces—forces with which we cannot interfere without destroying freedom, morality, and efficiency.

Two positions taken together prevent much conscious change. If a person does not like his or her employment, supplier, or customer, he or she can always find another position, supplier, or customer. However, given self-interest, conditions in the market are generally as good as they can be. Individuals are allowed to seek a better situation, but considering the market and profit-seeking employers, conditions are essentially the same for everyone offering the same services or product. Individual action produces little or no change in the absence of many other individuals acting in the same way, but combined action is illegitimate and inefficient. The result is that little or nothing can be done to increase freedom (or equality or democracy or justice) beyond what is allowed by the market.

Spontaneous order demands that governments stay out of autonomous economic relations. Public policy can do nothing positive to permanently reduce or eliminate poverty or the unhappy effects of market forces. Even if interpersonal comparison was possible and intervention increased happiness, taking resources from some to aid others must reduce freedom to use one's resources as one chooses and enlarge government. Requests for intervention based upon claims of collective needs mask partisan interests. Government should be small and inconsequential. In the name of freedom, the conservatives accept only those policies that narrowly support the market: impartial laws that are "neutral" between classes; protection of private property; defense; some limited provision of public education and welfare; enforcement of contracts; and so forth. Anything more undermines the interdependence between market and freedom.

Along with the assumptions in the previous chapter, this picture of freedom is the basis upon which the conservative economists build their politics. Their primary value is negative freedom, particularly economic freedom conceived as noninterference in the use of talents and property. There is only the actor and the absence of any coercive agent. Ability to act is incidental to freedom. Conservative freedom rules out conflict with other desirable values, since it always takes precedence. Thus there is no need to balance conflicting claims. Economic freedom is superior to all other political and social values, the basis for achieving whatever is good, and a condition of free and democratic governments. Any other concept of freedom must, in the long run, destroy freedom and democracy. The conservatives' policy advice follows from this picture of freedom and is designed to support it. As with individualism, equality, democracy, justice, and other fundamental values, they have selected the narrowest possible interpretation—requiring the least amount of government and holding the least possibility of expansion, particularly by collective or public intervention. The primary role of government in freedom is to leave it alone and enforce the law. A wider meaning for freedom or coercion cannot be admitted, because that portends a larger role for freedom-destroying public intervention.

This freedom follows from the conservative understanding of human nature. People promote their own interests, but by ensuring equal (the same) freedom to others, the market prevents the exercise of freedom-destroying power. Market freedom is the best expression of human freedom and at the same time inhibits its abuse. Noncoercion is the limit of duty regarding another's freedom. Within the spontaneous and benign forces of free markets, everyone has freedom, and the free individual is content to accept his or her fate, never asking government for protection from the inescapable vicissitudes of natural economic relations. It is within these relations that both freedom and equality develop to the maximum extent possible, given human nature.

This is an attenuated freedom that makes no provision for actual ability, resources, or opportunity to act. In its definitional rationalism, it is too limited to address the complex problems of contemporary societies. Absence of coercion is central to all individualistic conceptions of freedom, but there are many forms of coercion—including deception, invasion of privacy, manipulation, psychological abuse or pressure, and in some circumstances, compulsion – and more limits on freedom than only government and physical restraint. Although considering themselves classical liberals, these economists define coercion in narrower terms than Mill did in his most libertarian book, *On Liberty*. Mill listed as "compulsion and control" not only physical force but "the moral coercion of public opinion," "social stigma," and popular opinions which are "the eye of hostile and dreaded censorship"; he also noted that people whose actions are disapproved of "may be subjected either to social or to legal punishments." These economists have no room for Mill's concern for social liberty and majority or "social tyranny," which may be more difficult to escape than an oppressive government.[89]

Conservative freedom is action-oriented because one is allowed to act, but it does not require any action because the requirements for freedom are satisfied by the fact of being allowed. If one cannot carry out a permitted action, freedom is not compromised. Friedman frequently states that the world is not fair, but it is superficial to ignore cruel choices or to pretend that people have all possible freedom in the face of extremely difficult decisions. If freedom does not include some ability to do what is permitted, then it borders on nonsense – given the conservative picture of human motivation – to expect people who do not succeed in the market to support it. In fact, their support may not be necessary. Hayek, for one, believes that because the masses do not exercise economic freedom, they do not see its importance, making them a threat to freedom.[90] This perspective is too limiting. Public policies, such as public schools, health and sanitation programs, and income support, may expand freedom[91] and the range and number of choices, making people more satisfied with the economic and political system. These are not important considerations to the conservatives. Whether freedom actually exists or not is secondary to maintaining the necessary condition for freedom – limitation of government coercion.

Despite the claim that the market benefits everyone, it is difficult to understand how there can be popular support for freedom if outcomes of supposedly free processes are irrelevant and if freedom does not include at least some means for people to do what they are not prevented from doing. Even Frank Knight, whom Buchanan and Friedman acknowledge as an important teacher and mentor, noted that "'effective' freedom depends upon the possession of power as well as mere absence of interference."[92] Though the conditions for freedom are different from freedom itself, conditions are relevant to freedom's exercise, and more than noncoercion is needed to protect freedom and encourage individuals to take advantage of what they are permitted. One person's freedom may interdict another's; one form of freedom may limit another.[93] Freedom is multidimensional.[94] Political freedom may prove impossible if economic conditions do not permit a broadly based sense of safety and satisfaction.

The proposal that the market should become the final arbitrator of economic and much political freedom leaves too many areas of significance to too many people unresolved. For example, is the market–as presently constituted or as possible with the elimination of most welfare, regulation, and intervention–or freedom the primary value to be maximized? These authors claim both: that freedom can be realized only through the market. However, that means accepting as freedom enhancing whatever results from the market. If one really wished to maximize freedom within a market model, he or she would encourage more competition through rigorous antitrust policies, similar to a Jeffersonian ideal. But these authors refuse to push freedom that far.[95] Freedom does not require giving up a little market efficiency and corporate dominance. The conservatives ask that nothing be sacrificed for freedom, except the ability to be free if the market does not perform as promised. They present an either/or choice. Accept the market with market freedom or have neither markets nor freedom. Defense of market freedom must "be dogmatic."[96] There is no safety valve; no means to draw off pressure and reduced social trust; no way to enhance support for the political-economic system; no means to disarm discontent. In a crisis pressures may build up, as Keynes feared in the 1930s, and threaten the existence of both freedom and the market.

Even if the conservative picture of market operation is correct and their model took cognizance of large corporations and international trading, they offer little evidence to support it. Concern for social and political stability requires moving beyond a policy of doing nothing supported by a strong police. Leaving economic relations alone may undermine the freedom of people who do not have effective opportunities, resources, or alternative employment, multiplying the real power of those who possess alternatives and resources. People may be vulnerable[97] to more than just physical coercion. Rights may be more dependent upon what one's employer does–the Bill of Rights applies less in the workplace, and courts in the United States limit government employers more than private business in areas such as drug testing, electronic surveillance, and invasion of privacy–than what the police on patrol may do. Individual freedom requires more than a choice between accepting and rebelling, between conforming to what is offered and literally having no livelihood.

Consider the claim that employers have no power because employees (or suppliers or customers) have other opportunities from which to choose, therefore they are free. If this is a definition of freedom, it is not possible to argue with it except to ask for a broader concept of freedom. As a description of freedom, of what many people experience, sufficient conditions for freedom, the basis of changes in human lives, or a guide to public policy to foster freedom, however, this statement is incomplete even within economics, unless at least three conditions are met. There must be something close to full employment so that people have a viable opportunity to find alternative work. Positions of similar pay and satisfaction should be available. Costs of changing employment (or customers or suppliers) must not cause greater deprivation than is tolerable to the reasonable person celebrated in law. The higher the opportunity costs of changing, the more constraint there is against changing, thereby increasing the ability of employers, suppliers, or customers to enforce undesirable conditions. The person who has no choice, or extremely limited choice, is not free in the sense of being able to act. Everything that occurs in the market is not voluntary and, even if voluntary, may not be freedom enhancing. Even Adam Smith, writing about bank note issuance, acknowledged that it may be necessary to limit "the natural liberty of a few individuals, which might endanger the security of the whole society."[98] Experiencing freedom requires the opportunity and in many circumstances the means to implement freedom. Intervention may enlarge the opportunity to be free by removing obstacles to action or by expanding the range of available choices.

What meaning we give to the abstract concept of freedom is important because it involves the shape, direction, and guiding philosophy of politics, as well as who can and should benefit from public policy. Freedom is closely linked to equality, which the conservatives also claim develops in and is limited by the market. In the conservative world view, they are interchangeable.

Chapter Four

Equality

The weaker are always anxious of equality and justice. The stronger pay no heed to either.
　　　　　　　　　　　　　　　　　　　　　　 —Aristotle, *Politics,* bk. 6, chap. 3.

Equality is a traditional concern of normative political theory, but economists dominate contemporary policy debate over its meaning, scope, and specification. Conservative, liberal, socialist, and Marxist economists offer opposing policy prescriptions, basing them on incompatible conceptions of equality— who is or should be equal; what will be divided according to the accepted principle of equality; when persons are equal; how relative equality is evaluated; whether equality is an extensive or narrow, system-sustaining or individually oriented, group or individual idea and policy;[1] and what the conditions for and obstacles to equality are. Discussing the same issues analyzed by political theorists and philosophers, economists have had more influence than they have on public perceptions and policy in such areas as welfare, the role of government, taxes and the meaning and nature of justice. Conflicting conceptualizations of equality support rival pictures of the scope of legitimate political activity, attacking or supporting welfare programs, affirmative action, civil rights legislation, participatory democracy, and intervention into and regulation of the economy. From Plato to the present, the questions who is equal and under what circumstances are basic to a theorist's or politician's picture of legitimate equalization programs.

Defining the Meaning of Equality

Equality, like all important political ideas, is a protean concept that includes rival philosophical claims, debate over which policy may implement it, and conflict over whether a particular situation is relevant to it. Equality richly illustrates how words and concepts do not necessarily mean what they appear to mean. Equality is normally stated in universal terms, as in Jefferson's assertion "that all men are created equal," but few people suggest that the words are to be taken literally. There are always qualifications, limits, emendations. What is equality? Does it mean that all men are the same? Or are all people or persons the same, even though throughout most of history women were not people in a politically or legally relevant sense and slaves under the Constitution were persons but not part of "We the People"? Most people state that equality does not mean everyone is identical; opponents of equality focus on the obvious fact that people are different to discredit it as an ideal. Rather, there is some relevant sense or arena in which people are presumed or claimed to be similar, or the same, or requiring identical respect or consideration.

Is equality achieved through identical treatment in all areas, especially economics? Most people would say no, at least if that implies the same rewards or income. We have been taught that it is unjust and discourages effort to treat people the same or ensure identical income despite differences in effort, ability, or contribution. The constituency for such a concept of equality does not exist in western democracies, though there may be support for treating people according to needs in areas such as education, medicine, and welfare.

Perhaps equality does not mean equality, but equal opportunity. In the United States, one can almost visualize heads nodding approval—surely equality connotes equal opportunity, in which inequalities develop based only upon differences in effort and ability. But what is equal opportunity, and why must equality be narrowed to that? What is necessary and/or sufficient to have equal opportunity? To what and where does it apply? Does it mean to allow people to compete? to provide some resources, whatever these may be, to make it easier to compete with something approaching similar chances? to handicap some to make all compete evenly? to promote some sameness of result or outcome, and if so how much and where, to allow more equal competition? Is it measured by absence of formal restrictions on competition or by the results of competition? By looking at individuals or at groups? Where should competition by allowed? Everywhere? In the economy? By what means in the economy?

Many people emphasize political equality, where the popular meaning implies treating all alike. If the accepted assumptions and patterns of behavior are the obvious, natural meaning of equality, then equal opportunity as applied to politics requires some identical treatment. But political equality is not obvious. What is it, and why should it be valued? Is it equal or the same political power or identical influence? Most people say no, emphasizing the impossibility of creating a political system embodying these concepts—though Rousseau's General Will may have proposed it among that portion of the community who were citizens. Thus theorists do not normally claim that everyone should have equal or identical political power or influence, though it should be alike in some sense.

Perhaps political equality refers to rights (a common argument accepted by the conservative economists) but which ones, and does everyone have them? Does it mean simply possession or the ability to actualize those rights? Many people emphasize voting rights, but that reduces political equality to the equal (that is, the same) right of citizens, though not all persons, inhabitants, or potential members, to vote. For many, it refers only to the opportunity (regardless of how effective) to vote, not actual voting and, for the conservative economists, certainly not voting in such a way as to actively influence public policy.

Each of equality's meanings supports and is supported by rival views of human nature, justice, public order, and democracy. In application, equality is a tangle of possibilities. Equality may apply to political, social, moral, or economic relations, encompassing debate over what is to be divided and how. It can be a statement of fact about shared characteristics, a claim that people are alike, an assertion of hope, or a desirable but unachievable ideal. It can involve rights, equality before the law, political equality, equality of opportunity, equal respect, equal treatment, unequal treatment to equalize people, or equal result. It relates to distinctions based on age, sex, race, religion, class, ethnicity, income, education, nationality, status, and political standing. Equality may be inclusive or narrow, applied to everyone or to special categories of people. It may refer to human relations, moral worth, sameness before God, a common essence behind all differences, or an ideal future state. It encompasses formal procedures, such as allowing everyone to try, and substantive results, such as redistribution. It involves disagreement over the causes of inequality, justifications of policies that foster inequality or equality, what are acceptable inequalities, whether equality is an individual or group concept, and legitimate policies to achieve whatever one conceives as equality.[2]

The quest for equality and equalization is determined by what is perceived as an obstacle within such givens as human nature, what people conceive as being subject to successful human intervention, and goals. Each component may be further divided, as in the debate over what *is* equal opportunity and where is it applicable. The important point is that authors rarely mean by equality what an alien observer would assume it to mean by examining the word separate from context, tradition, and power relations. Equality has multiple meanings, especially when it appears to conflict with other goals, values, and purposes such as freedom or property. Tension is resolved by placing one value in ascendance, defining one value in terms of another, redefining equality, setting limits to its meaning, confining equality with other values and beliefs, claiming that people do not want "pure" equality, or stating that equality undermines efficiency. In this dance of reduction, authors must give good reasons or justifications why a seemingly universal value does not mean what it appears to mean.³ Their answers determine much of their view of the government's role in a society. Clearly, equality policy is not autonomous from other considerations, such as the nature, structure, and purposes of markets.

Liberals of all varieties have been more concerned with freedom than equality. They often define equality in terms of freedom: equal political rights; equal access to the market; equal educational, employment, welfare, and other opportunities; economic equalization to promote freedom.⁴ Having said this, however, we have not said much. Though the meaning of liberal equality is bound to liberal freedom, there is no single, simple meaning of liberal freedom. The interrelation of equality and freedom is a complex creative tension where changing notions of freedom and equality have modified, enriched, and limited each other. In the same way, to define freedom as conservative economists do, in negative economic and political terms, limits the scope and application of equality.

In discussing the meaning of equality, I will follow the conservative economists' pattern of concerns. To conservatives, equality denotes sameness, uniformity, and mathematical equality. Despite great differences between people, equality means that there is no difference in treatment. Whether in the context of economics, politics, or society, A is the same as B. Like freedom, equality is a procedural concept, satisfied if people are allowed to attempt to carry out their purposes. It refers to individuals and formal relations and is neither a public good nor a goal of public policy. Any attempt to apply it to groups or to consider the conditions for equality, beyond identical treatment by the law and equal right to attempt to compete in free markets, is illegitimate and must destroy freedom. Beyond these narrow limits freedom and equality are mutually exclusive. Emphasis on achieving equality must destroy freedom, while emphasis on freedom produces inequality *and* the only legitimate kind of equality, which allows everyone to use whatever resources they possess as they wish and to get ahead if they can.

Potential conflict between freedom and equality is resolved by defining equality as freedom or by claiming that equality is satisfied by equality before the law, which is essential to freedom. Otherwise freedom and equality become alternatives that must conflict whenever intervention or redistribution are attempted.⁵ When the two values do clash, freedom trumps equality. Not only is economic freedom more important, it also produces more equality than any other policy. For Friedman, people have "an equal right to freedom" and opportunity, nothing else. Egalitarian policies come "sharply into conflict with freedom; we must choose." Unfortunately, demands for equality are part of the "spirit of the times" and must destroy freedom. Such policies for Hayek are fundamentally immoral and "the opposite of freedom." Buchanan sees government-enforced transfers as the functional equivalent of theft. To Friedman, "A society that puts equality—in the sense of equality of outcome—ahead of freedom will end up with neither equality nor freedom."[6] In the long run, though great differences will remain, freedom challenges wealth, leading to natural as opposed to forced redistribution between families and classes. Conceived as sameness in all spheres and relevant only in a narrow range of relations, equality has limited application.

Equal Opportunity

Conservative claims center on a rigid distinction between equal opportunity versus equal results or outcome: Treat people alike or make them the same. Again they present dualistic alternatives. Equal opportunity and equal outcome are the only possible meanings of equality but are mutually destructive, incompatible options. Hayek's choice is equality before the law or "material equality," "the same material portion," or "the same material position," but in any case it means treating everyone alike. Equality before the law is simply due process. "Equal treatment . . . has nothing to do with . . . results that are more favourable to one group than to others." Buchanan contrasts the policies of individualists, who see the solution to inequality in extending individuals' capacity to compete and in promoting market-based solutions, with collectivists, who are concerned with equalizing such outcomes as consumption and advocate nonmarket solutions. Friedman agrees that equality means similar circumstances and treatment. Given that, one must choose between "equality of outcome" or "equality of opportunity." In the early years of the American Republic, equality meant "equality before God," not irrational efforts by intellectuals opposed to the successes of a free economy to impose uniformity or "equality of results."[7]

Society cannot move along a continuum of possibilities. If it goes very far beyond narrowly defined equality of opportunity, a disastrous jump occurs to equality of outcome, destroying capitalism, freedom, and democracy. Anything other than equal opportunity or equal treatment by the law is incompatible with freedom because it requires the same outcomes for each person, forcing everyone, regardless of differences, to be and act the same, rather than, in Hayek's term, leaving "each individual to find his own level." For Buchanan the principle of "equal treatment for equals" is absolutely necessary in a community "that makes any claim to fairness," but his equality means "identical." Hayek attacks "the fundamental immorality of all egalitarianism" except identical treatment by the law, regardless of differences in circumstances. For Brittan, "The ideal of equality . . . . has now turned sour" and has become a "disease" because of attempts to apply it to economic and social relations. For Friedman, "[t]he end result" of redistribution "has invariably been a state of terror." For Gilder, egalitarianism destroys family, community, and real chances of improvement.[8]

What, then, is equal opportunity, which, along with identical treatment by the law, is the only legitimate form of equality? Within an individualistic perspective, equality of opportunity may range between formal procedures allowing each person access to, or a chance at filling, available positions, to compensatory equality of opportunity, that is, attempts to equalize starting points through expanded or similar educational or job opportunities, some equalization of material conditions, and affirmative action. The first possibility is most compatible with assumptions that individuals are self-interested and solely responsible for themselves, while the second assumes a larger social component in individual behavior and success and can fit either an individual or group emphasis in equalization policies.

Conservative equal opportunity is a formal, procedural concept, applicable to individuals and summarized by the ideal of careers open to talent based on natural abilities, rather than on distinctions such as class, race, religion, or sex. Despite professed methodological and policy individualism, the conservatives do not support a very extensive equality of opportunity. Individualism is satisfied if minimal conditions (the same as for negative freedom) are present: no coercion, that is, no arbitrary (nonmarket) distinctions and no laws preventing people from making of themselves whatever they can, given their natural abilities, inherited resources, and the choices presented by the market. It is an ideal of "competitive equality,"[9] or the right of each person to compete against others for position, status, and wealth. "Competitive equality" does not imply a similar probability that everyone will attain desirable statuses, and the necessary means to compete are very limited. Except for coercion, actual conditions facing an individual are of secondary concern.

Friedman confines equal opportunity largely to economics; it is virtually equivalent to market economics. It means "equality before the law," "a career open to talents," and allowing "no arbitrary obstacles" such as birth, sex, color, or religion to coercively prevent anyone from exercising his or her abilities. It requires neither leveling, antidiscrimination regulations, direct intervention, nor limitations on inherited wealth. Equal opportunity "is not to be interpreted literally." Such sameness is impossible because of "what nature has spawned." Thus wealth, inheritance, parental care, and social position are irrelevant to each individual's attempt to employ his or her resources. Friedman questions whether "from an ethical point of view" there is "any difference between" inheriting wealth from parents and inheriting the genes that make people talented. In matters of equal opportunity, government can only address coercive arbitrariness, not these natural differences. Even its role in providing education is limited. Although primary education may be necessary, though not solely in public schools, public support for vocational and higher education is anti-egalitarian because it transfers resources from the lower classes to those profiting from college or training. Advanced education builds human capital. Its benefits are purely private and contribute to no larger social good, and individuals should pay for it themselves.[10]

Hayek's position is similar. Educational equalization does not improve the many but drags down the few. Calls for more educational opportunities are due to "[e]galitarian agitation."[11] Hayek's equal opportunity is realized by being "allowed to try [not] . . . an equal start and the same prospects." There is no need to level the starting points from which people compete. Equal opportunity is satisfied "only by treating them [people] according to the same rules irrespective of their factual differences, leaving the outcome to be decided by those constant restructurings of the economic order which are determined by circumstances nobody can foresee." Though primary education may be provided for minors, Hayek believes that "real equality of opportunity" would require complete government control of all external conditions—"the physical and human environment of all persons." There is no middle ground. Anything else, including limits on inherited wealth, produces "enforced equality," giving advantages and privileges to some by taking them from others. All advantages cannot be eliminated. Parental differences cause "undesigned and unavoidable inequalities of opportunity" but must be accepted since they result from a putatively natural and spontaneous process. There is no need to provide the same chances to all, nor is there any difference between inheriting wealth and receiving good childhood care or inheriting genes for intelligence.[12] Thus wealth, popular prejudices, and environment are distinctions as natural as native ability. Equal opportunity is compatible with extreme inequalities of educational opportunities, status, inheritance, and even reward for effort.

Buchanan varies in detail, in that he sees fewer inherent differences between people and his equal opportunity is not as limited as that of Friedman, Gilder, or Hayek. He agrees with them that equal opportunity means careers open to talent. It includes "fair chances," where the economic value "assigned" to each person is "determined by elements within himself" and by the kinds of "chance factors" which affect all people. It does not and cannot mean assuring identical chances to employ talents or equivalent results to people with similar talents. Most starting differences between people are irrelevant. Only those differences affecting economic performance need to be considered, and even these do not require that everyone be able to compete for each position. To believe that everyone should have the same starting capacities is a "narrow interpretation" of equal opportunity, one that a rational or fair society need not consider. Indeed, such an interpretation would transfer power and responsibility to governments which, given inherent limitations and the self-interest of governors, will be abused to the detriment of freedom and equality.[13]

If governments are incapable of adjusting for differences between people and markets are best able to do so, can anything be done to address initial differences that may affect ability to compete? Buchanan asserts that it is possible to "take some of the more apparent rough edges off gross inequalities in starting positions" though significant differences will always remain. As with John Stuart Mill (but not with Friedman or Hayek), Buchanan argues that individualists may propose reforms that tend to equalize initial endowments and the ability to compete. Buchanan emphasizes essentially negative means – the reduction of obstacles to competing, not direct aid – to reduce large disparities; these include taxes on inheritance and publicly supported, though not necessarily provided, education. Unlike Friedman and Hayek, he sees a morally relevant difference between human and nonhuman resources and believes that inheritance of wealth is not equivalent to inheritance of genes. Buchanan considers it ethically superior to encourage equality through market-type mechanisms which increase a person's ability to compete, rather than to equalize results through redistribution after competition. Moderate intergenerational transfer taxes and educational opportunities stress individual abilities; therefore, they may be legitimate – but they are also the limit of what should or can be done to promote equal opportunity. Thus, the emphasis is on the potential for long-term changes, not on policies to address inequalities between people currently competing. Direct transfers for purposes of equalization between current competitors must be arbitrary – i.e., nonmarket – and hence destructive of an open society, though limited redistribution may be necessary.[14]

The conservatives' position and policy recommendations stand or fall on their absolute distinction between equal opportunity and equal result. Based on the obvious fact that people are different, they conclude that there is no way in which people can be equal except before the law and in their right to compete. Thus equality means being identical, but one looks in vain for any major theorist – including Marx[15] and Rousseau – who conceived of equality in this way. Calling people "equal is not to say that they are identical," only that there is some relevant sense in which they are, or ought to be, treated alike.[16] The question becomes what are the relevant ways in which people are similar and dissimilar. Real sameness of result is not a significant or legitimate option in countries such as the United States[17] but there is near unanimous support for equal opportunity, whatever that means. The debate over equality should focus on meanings and applications – Buchanan moves in that direction – but it does not. Instead these conservatives assimilate socially conditioned differences that are embedded in a specific legal-political-social environment – such as political culture, property, and family status – to inherent distinctions and natural ability.

This position fails to acknowledge that equality and equalization are different. Equalization[18] means movement toward equality and reducing inequalities, not that people are identical or will be made the same. Equalization may raise the bottom; it need not remove the top. It is an ideal and an approximation. Providing a minimum standard for everyone does not produce uniformity but may save people from the uniformity of want and degradation. Freedom is the conservatives' chief value, but none of them defines it as license or lawlessness. However, applying their conception of equality to freedom would turn freedom into license. In the same way that freedom is defined and limited by values, social obligation, and *equal* freedom for others, equality is also limited. Equality is not uniformity or sameness, nor are equal opportunity and equal results as opposed as these authors claim. Equal opportunity invariably includes some equal treatment or results.[19] Equalization presents a continuum, not either/or alternatives. Values, not inherent economic limitations, determine our position on that continuum. Which equalities are legitimate depends on one's picture of individualism—whether it too is procedural or means autonomy—and what is natural (such as the market) or what is subject to conscious change. These authors, however, are concerned with procedures. Equal opportunity is satisfied if no one stands coercively in the way of another as he or she attempts to compete. That view does not address the conditions within which equal opportunity may operate or its worth and value. If people are convinced that uniformity is the only alternative to procedural equality of opportunity (especially when there is widespread disapproval of equal results), that competitive procedures are neutral, and that outcome is irrelevant to equality, then there will be no need to worry about equalization policies.

The Market and Obstacles to Equality

As with freedom, defining an obstacle to equality delimits equality's meaning and scope and the kinds of policies which promote it. The conservative economist theorists see few obstacles. Racial and sexual discrimination is not an obstacle, or at least would not be in a free market. Conversely, anything interfering in free-market operation is necessarily an obstacle to equality.

The conservatives believe the market is egalitarian. It produces equality by even-handed treatment of people who have identical motivations. Equality is satisfied by allowing people to compete in free markets, whether or not they have the resources to compete effectively. Anything beyond equal competitive opportunity invades the operation of a natural economic market and destroys freedom, upon which equality depends. As with freedom, noncoercion is the necessary and sufficient condition for equality. According to Friedman, active pursuit of equality destroys freedom and therefore equality. "On the other hand, a society that puts [economic] freedom first will, as a happy by-product, end up with both greater freedom and greater equality."[20]

This means that deliberate efforts to encourage equality must fail and that governments can do nothing positive to foster more equality. Extramarket obstacles in the form of attitudes and preferences may exist but are of minor importance, are "by no means insurmountable," and should be immune from public intervention.[21] The mistaken and fanciful belief that there are relevant obstacles to equality other than coercion, and that government can remove them is therefore the major impediment to realization of equality through market relations. The primary dangers to equality are active governments and the greedy majorities that support them and demand equal results through such misguided and interfering policies as antidiscrimination rules, affirmative action, welfare payments, aid to families with dependent children, farm price-support programs, minimum-wage laws, promotion of labor unions, and redistribution efforts. Once these policies are eliminated, the natural operation of free markets will create both freedom and equality.

Justifying Inequality

The economic theorists believe that both economic and political inequality are desirable and necessary. They share the common conservative fear that equality upsets natural order by eliminating variety and leveling natural distinctions. This claim joins a long procession of similar arguments in political theory. Economics-based defenses of political and economic inequality have typically employed a negative justification—defense of property. Aristotle argued that democracy was an undesirable form of government—though it was the best of the bad forms—because egalitarianism risked unjust seizure of property and dragged the best people down to the lowest common denominator. The latter concern was echoed in Alexis de Tocqueville's *Democracy in America* over two thousand years later.

Concern for protecting property runs throughout modern political thinking. The first serious attempt to distinguish political rights from property rights occurred during the English Civil War of the 1640s, and that attempt was unsuccessful. Both Locke and Burke saw property and the protection of property as primary considerations, overriding in Locke's case other natural rights such as political equality. The dominant argument throughout the seventeenth and eighteenth centuries claimed that despite natural rights and natural law, economic inequality was natural and that equal political rights would undermine property. Even Thomas Jefferson did not call for universal adult male suffrage but held that any man who paid taxes or served in the militia was entitled to vote. In nineteenth-century Britain, successive reform acts gradually enlarged the number of potential voters to include most male holders of property; complete male suffrage was not achieved until this century. In the United States, the last vestige of property-based justification for unequal political rights was not eliminated until Supreme Court decisions in such cases as *Baker* v. *Carr* (1962) began to require equal electoral districts and the Twenty-fourth Amendment to the Constitution removed the poll tax for federal elections. Throughout this long dispute, the defenders of inequality echoed the words of General Henry Ireton at the Putney Debates in 1647: "All the maine thinge that I speake for is because I would have an eye to propertie."[22]

The economic theorists mistrust equality but deny being anti-egalitarian. As self-proclaimed liberals, it is neither fashionable nor expedient to condemn equality outright. Inequality must be shown to be valuable and beneficial, while equality is narrowed and proven harmful. Instead of God's will, tradition, or nature, as in classical conservatism, their justification of inequality is essentially utilitarian, based on their view of the market and their analysis of its operation.

Justification of inequality requires a standard by which to judge. Once again, the market and freedom provide that standard. Inequality is an inevitable, natural, and necessary consequence of freedom and equal opportunity to compete in free markets; egalitarian policies retard progress and destroy freedom. For Hayek, "[E]quality before the law which freedom requires leads to material inequality." Friedman contends that freedom necessarily produces inequality and whatever equality is possible. Even if people were equal in any significant sense, the market rewards them differently for unequal services to others. Buchanan notes that the assumption of inequality in endowments and utility functions is common in economic theory.[23]

Inequality is desirable because equality is often a positive political danger. In another either/or argument reflecting the inevitability of the political market, equalization policies create a new class of privileged bureaucrats and millionaires; undermine respect for law; force the best, most productive people out of a country; increase taxes; destroy freedom; and lead to tyranny. Economic inequality helps preserve political freedom by reducing the role of government in economic and social relations, by protecting minorities, and by preserving dissent. Friedman and Hayek believe that in free-market systems, the rich may act as patrons for unpopular or new groups and ideas. Radicals "have typically been supported" by wealthy persons. Almost all new movements began when someone with wealth was enlisted to help propagate or publish the idea. Thus, in an egalitarian—by definition, "socialist"—or in a noncapitalist regime, there can be no significant opportunities to disagree with government policy. No one can dissent because of the impossibility of raising funds to promote ideas or groups. Economic inequality therefore becomes one of the important necessities for preserving political freedom. That economic inequality may discourage participation, cause conflict, or be employed to crush dissent is a non-problem, because, by definition, only free-market systems provide the means to protect dissidents and radical movements.[24]

The conservatives' market generates both equality and inequality. Inequality is necessary for equalization. The market creates inequality because it rewards people differently, but reward has nothing to do with power. This argument is simultaneously and inextricably empirical and moral, definitional and circular: only in the market do people get what they deserve, and what they deserve is what they get. As the market is not and cannot be coercive or arbitrary,[25] it judges everyone by the same criterion: satisfaction rendered to others. When free, it rewards people according to their contribution to the welfare of others. Like contributions are rewarded the same; unlike contributions, differently.

According to Friedman, competitive markets encourage three objectives: "political freedom, economic efficiency, and substantial equality of economic power." Markets are not the cause of poverty but improve the position of the poor and produce all the equality possible because no one receives more or less than he or she produces.[26] By encouraging effort and eliminating government coercion and preference for favored groups—namely, anyone receiving direct aid from public programs—the market ensures rewards proportionate to impersonally determined contribution and value to others.

Buchanan believes that market rules are fair, enabling distribution of benefits to people based upon differences in their "natural talents." Simultaneously and conveniently, market performance provides the means to discover an individual's natural talents. For Friedman, the market determines how much each person should receive. Hutt believes that individuals earn according to their skills and their contribution "to the well-being of the rest," ensuring that some earn much more than others. Hayek concedes that because market rewards correspond to the value of services to others, this gives more to those who already have the most, but this is the market's "merit rather than its defect." Given individual ability, effort, and luck, Hayek's impersonal market ensures that "each will get for the share he wins . . . as large a real equivalent as can be secured." The result of a "truly free market," for Friedman, would be "far less inequality than currently exists."[27] Only coercion allows anyone to arbitrarily receive more than their marginal value to others.

The argument that differential rewards are the natural result of freedom and the unequal contribution to the welfare of others is only part of the economic theorists' justification of inequality. There are several additional justifications, weighed differently by separate authors but, taken together, forming a consistent critique of equality: desert,[28] incentive, investment signals, choice, benefits to others, inheritance, luck, and the nature of the market. These justify narrowing equality in economics and politics.

Conservative justification of inequality is often based on efficiency claims. Inequality advances the common good. It is a necessary *incentive* to work and invest. As such, inequality produces more wealth which benefits everyone, though time frames are left vague. This claim is the basis of supply-side demands to reduce taxes and public welfare spending. A successful economy requires growth in the number of wealthy people. Concentrations of wealth create wealth, not poverty; therefore, if society increases the stakes and rewards, more wealth will be produced. As producers of wealth, the wealthy deserve "their rewards." This is part of Gilder's lyrical "enriching mysteries of inequality . . . the multiplying miracles of market economics." Thus the same policy that helps create inequality by shifting resources to the wealthy also encourages investment, which produces the wealth that benefits the less creative. Inequality spurs those on the bottom to work harder and promises the productive rich that they can keep the profits of their creative investment efforts. Conversely, equality undermines wealth and enterprise.[29]

Economic inequality, according to Friedman, Hayek, and Buchanan, is frequently the result of *choices, tastes, and willingness to assume risks*. Their claim neglects the fact that people are not equally able to refuse to take chances or enter lotteries; that often the level of risk varies between rich and poor (i.e., monetary versus life threatening); and that the poor have a much smaller surplus they can risk. To these writers, much economic inequality is due to deliberate choices. People use their freedom to deliberately take risks and satisfy others' tastes thereby earning large rewards. Gilder claims that inequality results from risk taking and that greater wealth is the reward for risk taking.[30] "Material progress is ineluctably elitist: it makes the rich richer and increases their numbers, exalting the few extraordinary men who can produce wealth over the democratic masses who comsume it. . . . Material progress, though democratically demanded, is procedurally undemocratic."[31]

The poor actually benefit from increasing inequality that enables the rich to expand investment, which is the key to ending poverty. Thus, "A successful economy depends on the proliferation of the rich." These wealth producers are mankind's "greatest benefactors." It is the creative, investing few who "are fighting America's only serious war against poverty." Using property to create large enterprises, the economically successful—in a version of William Graham Sumner's entrepreneur dragging the less able up the evolutionary ladder—freely give a better life to the rest.[32] Because inequality is essential to growth, deliberately increasing inequality helps the poor. In the absence of monopoly, which cannot exist in free markets, those who earn the most "are contributing most to the well-being of the rest."[33]

Inequality has other positive advantages. It is essential to the *progress of civilization*. According to Friedman, it encourages progress, diversity, and freedom. Growth requires a creative elite: "[E]conomic and social progress do not depend on the attributes or behavior of the masses." To von Mises, "[I]t stimulates everyone to produce as much as he can and at the lowest cost."[34] For Hayek, inequality is necessary "to achieve any sort of social organization." Rapid economic advance results from and is impossible without inequality. The wealthy, through high-level consumption, "perform a necessary service." Common goods and services are available today because the few who were able to afford them pioneered their development, allowing them to percolate down to the rest of society; new goods and services will arise in the same way. Progress requires inequality in order to produce goods "too expensive to provide for more than a few. . . . new things will often become available to the greater part of the people only *because* for some time they have been the luxuries of the few." Future welfare depends on "the unequal distribution of present benefits." In both production and consumption the poor benefit from inequality which spurs their effort while encouraging elite experimentation. This applies between nations. The developing states receive the same benefits from the north-south gap as do the poor inside wealthy nations.[35]

Inequality is also justified by the moral legitimacy and utilitarian value of *inheritance*. As the only link between generations, inheritance drives parents to work harder to provide for the next generation. Without presenting any evidence, Hayek asserts that it is not a significant obstacle to equality of opportunity. He claims that society will "get a better elite" if wealth accumulates across generations and if everyone is not required to start from the same level. Wealth is hardly separable from the nonmaterial advantages that families can pass on. Though inheritance increases inequality between individuals, it is not arbitrary or a question of "unmerited benefits"; therefore, those who do not receive bequests cannot claim to be harmed by those who do. Inheritance also maintains independent centers of power which are crucial to freedom. Friedman agrees that inheritance reduces the scramble to find a place for children that must occur in the absence of inheritance. He adds that inherited capital maintains gains across generations, preventing them from being wasted, thereby increasing output and total wealth. As noted previously, Friedman contends that there is no significant difference between a financial bequest and inheriting genes; such a "distinction is untenable." By linking inheritance of property and other advantages to nature, he disavows any ethical difference between inheriting real property as defined in the law and genetic inheritance. Economic inequalities are as natural as genetic distinctions.[36]

Having hard-working parents from a preferred cultural group, along with superior genes and a good investment portfolio, is just a matter of luck, and in a fair economic game, no one can interfere with the results of luck. *Luck,* seen as random good fortune for an individual, has little or nothing to do with sociopolitical relations and cannot be compensated for by public policy without making everyone alike and harming freedom. The social component is ignored in this argument. Luck simply happens. It occurs in the context of everyone pursuing their own self-interest and has no larger reference; therefore, no one other than lucky recipients can legitimately claim a share in windfalls. Whatever we receive for our efforts results from "choice and chance,"[37] and one result is not ethically superior to another.

This argument is the weakest element in the conservative defense of inequality. That something resulting from random good luck properly belongs to the beneficiary assumes a rights-based justification that the economists do not attempt. There is little concern for why some identifiable groups, such as ethnic minorities, seem to have less luck than other identifiable groups. Luck is not randomly distributed among individuals or groups. The rich, the middle groups, and the poor are exposed to different risks and opportunities. Luck in the market—especially in the productive part of the economy as opposed to sports[38]—more frequently depends upon socially derived position than any truly random occurrence.

Several other arguments also justify inequality. Egalitarianism is destructive, because it is frequently based on envy[39] and "tends to promote greed"[40] — an argument that necessarily follows from human nature and the political market. There is no real equality, and the overwhelming number of people prefer a system of opportunity and inequality to equalization. Egalitarianism violates "one of the most basic instincts of human beings"—the effort to improve one's condition—expands government power, and undermines respect for the law.[41]

Ultimately, inequality does not require separate justification. As in traditional conservatism, the basic principle of order—here, the market—necessitates and legitimates inequality. Equalization is inequitable and inefficient, a distemper attacking the fundamental structure of order. Inequality is part of the market system; as an integral result of impersonal forces in that system, one cannot exist without the other. Instead of condemnation, that is high praise. Rewards are unrelated and irrelevant to moral worth or even physical effort. Because their good fortune is the result of luck or is the reward for satisfying the needs and wants of others, people cannot be rewarded according to intrinsic merit,[42] even if that could be established. The economic game is played by all, for each person's own benefit, and outcomes are not controlled by any one person or group. On the whole, everyone's chances will be improved in this system, and that is justification enough.[43]

The decisive source of inequality, for the conservatives, lies in ourselves – in human nature and how each chooses to act. Much inequality comes from freely made, individual choices, not personal capacities. As such, it comes from individualism and the choices and preferences embodied in institutions, especially the market. To a large extent, individuals shape themselves according to market choices. Guessing or choosing wrongly is our mistake and cannot be rectified by exogenous intervention. Because the market is freer than other areas of life and encourages equality, inequalities cannot be eliminated by attacking the market.[44]

Little can be done outside the market to remove inequality. Equalization requires arbitrary and coercive political interference. Given the coercively self-interested political market and the need to organize such interference, Buchanan believes that interventions are dangerous and even in good causes "will be perverted for use in situations where they simply do not apply," thereby damaging efficiency and fairness. Hayek also urges restraint in having government help "the least fortunate," on the grounds that "benevolent motives" and charity "inevitably" cause violation of equal treatment by the law, arbitrariness, and expansion of power. Intervention is legitimate only when inequality is due to injustice, but the injustice must be recent to be eligible for correction. Long-standing injustices (how long is left unstated), even when they cause inequality should be treated "as due to accident"; they should not justify the dangerous expedient of helping identifiable groups. Regardless of purpose, treating people differently is unequal treatment that leads to arbitrary government, retards society's evolution, and undermines the spontaneous market.[45]

This argument for preservation and expansion of inequality stands in marked contrast to the claims of liberal economists. They contend that while differences in earnings and position are desirable, existing inequalities are inefficient and freedom destroying, and there is no economic or social justification for increasing them. They reject each of the conservative justifications for inequality: that large savings are needed for investment; that people are paid according to their marginal productivity; that inequality supports democracy; that in the long run market inequality generates more equality; and that intervention must undermine the economy. For them, the market is not neutral; it rewards equal effort unequally and many inequalities are due to position, inherited wealth, and market power.

Though liberal economists reject extensive equalization – despite the mythical critique of their opponents – they argue for a wider and more inclusive equality than conservatives do. Equality is a matter of relative standing that can be improved, not an either/or state. Liberals would actively promote equality for more individuals and groups, taking into account differences in situation and utilizing a more extensive image of equal opportunity and some redistribution.[46] Keynes set the general tone for subsequent liberal arguments. His *General Theory of Employment Interest and Money*, for those who accepted its arguments, removed economic validation for great differences in wealth. The traditional justification of inequality–"social injustice and apparent cruelty as an inevitable incident in the scheme of progress"–stemmed from bad economic theory, characterized "by the lack of correspondence between the results of their theory and the facts of observation." Keynes emphasized demand and consumption. Without demand there was no incentive to invest, and inequality depressed demand. Progress required increasing "the propensity to consume by the redistribution of incomes or otherwise," not relying on the rich to invest. Without investment opportunities, the wealthy were likely to waste income through saving or nonproductive consumption. In conditions of low demand and unemployment, "the growth of wealth, so far from being dependent on the abstinence of the rich . . . is more likely to be impeded by it. One of the chief justifications of great inequality of wealth is, therefore, removed." Some inequality is acceptable, but not for reasons of increased investment: "[T]here is social and psychological justification for significant inequalities of incomes and wealth" to channel off potentially destructive drives and passions, "but not for such large disparities as exist to-day." If investment is inadequate to ensure full employment, itself an equalizing policy, "the duty of ordering the current volume of investment cannot safely be left in private hands" but instead requires more public direction of investment and accumulation.[47]

Contemporary liberals reflect Keynes's sentiments. Galbraith claims that the wealthy may be taxed because "investment of saved income" is "mercurial" and "not an especially efficient way to promote capital formation"–a point echoed in Lester Thurow's observation that most industrial investment is made out of retained earnings, not invested private savings.[48] High taxes do not retard growth. Indeed, in an argument opposite to the conservative claim, they may increase work effort. In either case, the United States' most successful competitors have higher taxes, more regulation, and less economic inequality than does the United States. Galbraith adds that "the thesis that the rich have not been working because of too little income and the poor have been idling because of too much" (implying different motivations at the top and bottom of society) is "justification at an unduly primitive level."[49]

Keynes believed distribution is "arbitrary and inequitable." Where the conservatives see impersonal market determination of income, Galbraith sees "human agency" hidden by "the fiction that compensation is decided impersonally by outside forces." Thurow claims that "the world is not as deterministic" and that impersonal market forces do not reward effort or distribute income as the conservatives claim. Most large fortunes are the result of "stochastic processes," chance, and "economic lotteries rather than . . . individual characteristics," gradual reinvestment, or accumulation. The conservatives employ this insight to defend individual accumulation, but Thurow sees it as undermining an individual's exclusive claim to benefits. "Each individual is not paid in accordance with what he produces, and equals to not have equal *ex post* incomes." Marginal productivity does not determine income. Lower taxes have not "unleashed work effort and savings by increasing income differentials. Indeed, they have done directly the opposite." Increased production, even if inequality could generate it, cannot solve equity or equality problems.[50]

The conflict over equality "is also a clash over ideas, over the nature of the just society."[51] Though equality may be a component of equity or justice, they are not synonymous. The liberals claim that the market is not neutral between individuals and groups, ensuring that economic analysis has a large valuative component. They insist that economics impacts politics and society, requiring that economic relations be measured by a widely accepted theory of equity or justice. Choice is imposed upon us. "The Issue Cannot Be Avoided," according to Thurow. Both efficiency and equity require conscious decisions about distribution and acceptable relative standing. "To have no government program for redistributing income is simply to certify that the existing market distribution of resources is equitable. One way or the other, we are forced to reveal our collective preferences about what constitutes a just distribution of economic resources." The decision to allow or increase inequality is a political decision, not one imposed by economic necessity. Economic regulations "are designed to raise the income of someone (and therefore lower the income of others)." Only an independent theory of justice can determine whether "a regulation is good or bad."[52]

It would be easy to multiply quotations, but the essential liberal claim is that purposeful intervention and direction are necessary to ensure equalization, social justice, and economic efficiency. It is impossible to overemphasize the intensity of the conservative rejection of this argument, starting with Hayek's criticism of Keynes in the 1930s and 1940s. Root and branch, on moral, political, and economic grounds, they attack this position as unjust, inefficient, illogical, and destructive of freedom and equality.

Equality and Justice

Normative discourse has repeatedly linked equality and justice. Conservative economic theory severs this link, denying that justice is relevant to equality when discussing market relations and concurrently asserting that nothing positive or direct can be done to promote equality. This position is shaped by the conservative pictures of human nature, the political market, and the impersonal, autonomous economic market. The character of the market ensures that equity questions about market distribution cannot arise. If the market rewards people according to their contribution to others and if this determination is made impersonally, then it is illegitimate to inquire into market rewards or harms.

Hayek typifies this position. Only conduct can be considered just or unjust, never results. "Nature can be neither just nor unjust," and he and the other authors liken the market to nature. Only those "situations which have been created by individual human will," not anything resulting from the natural, spontaneous market, are relevant to justice. Wages and prices "determined in a free market" must be considered just because they are impersonally generated.[53] For a liberal such as Thurow, "Economic destruction in industrial societies is caused by identifiable human action that can be controlled" (whether or not control is desirable), which raises equity questions. For Hayek, no *one* controls the market, and "no single person or group determines who gets what"; thus, justice does not apply where "no human agency is responsible," and justice and equity issues "ought to be confined to the deliberate treatment of men by other men."[54] Even if the market does not fit one's preferences–and people have only preferences, not considered judgments–about equalization and justice, efforts to impose preferences are counterproductive, making the market immune from rational political assault and guiltless of adverse impact on society.

Fuller discussion must wait until chapter 6, but some ramifications of this position on justice directly relate to equality. The conservative view terminates debate over distribution and saps economic equalization. Justice connects with equality only as identical treatment by the law. Wage policy, antidiscrimination rules, social security, welfare, adjustment of taxes to achieve social ends– all are swept away by economic determination of political possibility. Laws treating people differently for the purpose of equal treatment are unjust, expand government, attack freedom and equality, and undermine creativity. As such they stand condemned on moral and efficiency grounds. All government can do to encourage equalization is maintain equal laws, property rights, and a stable monetary framework; enforce contracts; and get out of the market's way.[55] The attack on an extensive role for government is, therefore, a direct assault on most equalization policies, whether or not redistributive. This attack causes a shift in beneficiaries of public policy–claiming that all will be treated alike regardless of differences–deliberately increasing inequality and making impossible expansion or even continuation of the welfare and interventionist state.

Equality in Politics

The proper relation of the spheres of economic and political equality is an ancient issue and is integral to any discussion of democracy, as I elaborate in the next chapter. Most theorists have worried that political equality would threaten property and economic inequality. Only with the rise of liberal democracy did such people as Thomas Jefferson, John Stuart Mill, T. H. Green, and Louis Brandeis begin to address the possible impact of economic inequality on politics. Liberal economists such as Keynes reflect the latter concern. Conservative economists strongly endorse the older perspective and are not troubled that economic inequalities may undermine democracy or political equality. They unanimously deny that economic equalization is necessary to political equality. Business has no direct power to intervene in politics, and wealth buys influence only when free markets are subverted. Economic inequality promotes democracy by furnishing some people with the means to resist government and, as noted with Friedman and Hayek, supposedly provides support for radical ideas which would find no backing in a socialist system. Buchanan regularly refers to the "fiscal constitution" necessary to democracy, a model that calls for less participation and, of necessity, less political equality. He believes that his perspective requires "*ex ante*" political equality but not equal political influence.[56]

Political and economic inequality are regularly considered conceptually distinct, embodying different meanings of who is equal, how, and under what circumstances.[57] Limited political equality is acceptable to the conservative economists, but the idea remains suspect and potentially dangerous because of its possible spillover into economics. Political equality always implies equal opportunity *and* treating people alike; its ideal is sameness of influence and results, even when limited to voting. Debate centers on how much opportunity and how much equality of results are sufficient for political equality.[58] The conservatives argue strongly for equal treatment by the law–which is different from political equality–and accept universal suffrage as a principle, but more than anything else, they emphasize equal opportunity as the right to attempt to compete. If translated into political terms, this would be equivalent to ensuring everyone's right to run for office while disclaiming the need for an equal vote, voting districts, or rights protective of political participation.

The conservatives challenge the ideal of political equality from their economic perspective. Political equality is most important when government has a large, active role. When its role is confined to treating everyone identically, and when the market restrains it from expanding beyond this central duty, there is less need for political power or political equality. As the role of government is reduced, political equality is narrowed mainly to voting in elections.

It is political equality beyond the right to vote, combined with Keynesian economic theory, that encourages and demands expansion of government into economic relations. Since political equality can lead to an effective demand for more economic equalization, a stable economic system requires a minimizing redefinition of equality and democracy. Democracy's egalitarian thrust provides the basis for the conservatives' contention that the only way to protect the economy is to limit liberal democracy.

Summary and Some Conclusions

Equality is a complex idea made simple in conservative political economy. Equality for the conservatives is achieved by leaving people alone to struggle. It envisages a narrow meaning, content, and arena for equality. Rather than a complex of interrelated and conflicting issues and questions, equality is sameness and is not desirable except with reference to treatment under the law. Only the market promotes equality, and it determines who should benefit from neutral public policy. Equal opportunity, defined to exclude any equalization of results illustrates this point that we must accept market results. It is not a continuum of possibilities that require reducing differences to ensure that individuals with similar abilities have similar chances but a single possibility and policy: allowing people to compete without coercive interference. Equality is a by-product of and synonymous with freedom. Only this meaning eliminates conflict between freedom (the primary value) and equality, by reducing each to a single formula—participation in the market. Otherwise, antinomy exists between freedom and equality.

The conservative economists claim that the sole obstacle to both freedom and equality is government-enforced inequalities through preferential treatment—broadly defined to include most welfare measures, intervention, and programs such as affirmative action. Given human nature and the political and economic markets, equalization policies always produce effects different from their purposes. Treating people differently to treat them alike strengthens government, weakens respect for the real law, undermines creativity, destroys freedom, and prevents legitimate equalization through personal effort or luck in the market. The market is the only arena within which equality may be achieved and then exclusively through individual efforts. There is no other way to play a capitalist game, and an economic polity cannot be made to conform to exogenous beliefs about equality, equity, or desirable outcomes. Even when inequality is the result of luck, inheritance, radically different opportunities, and education, the conservatives see no reason for government intervention or for claims of unfair and unequal treatment. Gender, power, ethnicity, and class status are irrelevant to achievable equality, which is that produced in a completely free market. People must learn to accept inequalities resulting from natural processes, such as the market or genetic inheritance.

Contemporary United States politics illustrates the impact of economic theories on public policy and on perceptions of what is politically necessary and possible. One result is that equality has been deflated as a legitimate public goal. All of the rich complexity of equality in western thinking is missing from the conservative argument. Because people have the same motivation, they are fundamentally alike. Because the individual is the sole judge of what is important, no one can make equality decisions affecting another's property or interests. Under no circumstances can public policy distinguish between people. The conservatives take the economic system as given and make equality, politics, and social relations conform to market necessity. Equality becomes indistinguishable from freedom: isolated self-evaluation, competition, and keeping one's own property. Once again, the market defines permissible public policy. Government must not intervene in either the market or resultant political-social-economic inequalities.

Equality for the conservatives depends upon the actual existence of a neutral market, where there is no private power, coercion, or reward separate from random luck and/or individual contributions to the welfare of others. Or, it depends upon a believable promise that such a market could exist under necessary and attainable conditions. Absent one or the other of these circumstances, the conservative argument becomes another justification and plea for special interests and self-interest, to protect the haves from the have-nots. As a political theorist, not an economist, I do not intend to comment on the second possibility, and by the conservative's own admission, the first does not exist, even if they base policy advice upon it. I believe, along with liberal economists such as Keynes and Thurow, that the ideal neither exists nor is attainable at an acceptable cost, a belief that is compatible with support for private property and capitalism. Whether or not it is a viable possibility, this vision has political and social implications that demand consideration.

The claims about the operation of randomness in the market are also of doubtful validity. Hayek, for example, states that a particular rule and the market in general are legitimate because, ignorant of future outcomes, "we can assume it to increase everyone's chances equally." Statistically, someone must be on top and someone on the bottom, even if picked at random.[59] Hayek employs an obvious statement—that there must be a top and bottom in any ranking—to support a controversial claim—that in our ignorance we must believe the market is neutral between people and accept existing inequalities. Justification based upon chance or random good luck assumes that success is truly indiscriminate and not affected by power or position, that everyone has the same opportunity to achieve good fortune. But the market and market processes are not random in this simple sense. Existing property distribution, educational and cultural advantages, political culture, popular prejudices, and plain political power ensure that people are not picked in a fully random fashion. Ignorance of future positions is not the same for all actors, and people are not in the same situation with respect to knowledge, risk, property, or connections. For the system and its rules to be truly neutral between individuals, one would have to ensure the same starting point for everyone or draw lots for all positions—a concept of equality that most people reject. Since this is not acceptable, the economists conclude market distribution is justified.

Because equality is not a question of either/or states[60] but a continuum of possibilities and an approximation to a moral ideal, equality is always conceived in terms of purposes.[61] To the limited extent equality implies uniformity,[62] that uniformity is determined by purposes, such as the ideal of blind justice rendering all equal before the law. If our purpose is to maximize political participation, we will attempt to make the conditions for participation more equal. If it is to promote individualism (defined as developing individual talents, opportunities, and personality), we will emphasize support for people to grow, experiment, learn, and choose. If it is to justify existing power and property relations, we will limit equality to the minimum acceptable under existing political conditions. But at all times, purposes and perceptions condition the meaning and content of equality and the focus of equalization efforts.

The content of equal opportunity also reflects purposes. Although it is always dangerous to impute purposes to authors in the absence of their explicit statements, the conservatives' equal opportunity is not an expansive idea. Though its original eighteenth-century formulation was progressive in denying the relevance of anything other than talent, we have moved beyond the situation where people of equal talent are denied positions solely on class grounds. Today we are confronted with the common situation where persons of potentially equal ability do not have the opportunity to develop their talents. The conservatives would address this problem by allowing market competition to remove differences between men and women, minorities and favored groups, rich and poor, but that requires elimination of minimum-wage rules and other protections and a rational, profit-maximizing man, unmoved by other considerations. Such a creature may not exist in sufficient numbers.

In an effort to deny that self-interest is simply economic, the conservatives' themselves have testified that profit maximization may be a secondary consideration to desire for esteem, power, labor peace, prevention of boycotts, or personal satisfaction. If that is correct, and I believe it is, and if inequalities are cumulative, equal opportunity viewed as careers open to talent is insufficient to allow people to develop potential talents and to compete based on their ability. The conservatives cannot have it both ways. They cannot continue to claim that except for luck, differences and inequalities are the product of variations in tastes and choices *and* that the market promotes freedom and equality for minorities despite tastes and preferences among dominant groups that reduce real opportunities for minorities. Moreover, to the extent that inherited property gives some people greater life chances than those who have none, the ideal of careers open to talent will be subverted. This is especially important because advantages from property can accrue without any action on the part of recipients, while talent and ability require years of study, work, and development coupled with a receptive social environment before they benefit their possessors or society.[63] In this situation, the market claim to treat equally all who enter will remain unfulfilled.[64]

Equal opportunity remains for conservatives what it meant in the eighteenth century. That does not make it wrong, but conditions and purposes have changed; if one believes in equal opportunity, it becomes imperative to expand its meaning to reduce more economic and social barriers. Family and subcultural environment which prevent acquisition of basic skills and knowledge during childhood,[65] deficient educational opportunities, and continuing racial and sexual stereotypes are nearly as much a prison to talent as is coercion, and they leave affected individuals equally helpless with no one to rally against. Despite their shared claim that the market is a spontaneous process resulting from evolution, the conservative market marks the bounds of evolution. It can go no further. In that sense, history has ended. Self-seeking economic man is the apex of evolution and limits evolution of political and social institutions. Equal opportunity cannot be anything more than it was two hundred years ago, because human passions and drives subvert public policy designed to encourage equality beyond what the market allows.

Conservative claims about equality (and freedom, justice, and democracy) are vague regarding the time period in which equalization might occur. Aside from Buchanan's partial dissent, what is, is the best that can be at that particular point in time. Faith in the spontaneous forces of the market allows no other conclusion. This is an ahistorical model for an ahistorical world of determined beings who react like elements in an atomic table, not a contingent world of historical accident. I do not deny that market systems have become more equal over time or that they frequently offer more to people than nonmarket systems. However, everything is set in the eternal present, under the premise that current inequality will produce as much future equality as there can be; that is, inequality now promises to produce some or more equality in the future – but there is never a word on when, except for an amorphous "long run." In an individualist, as opposed to an organic, system, this promise could make sense only in a stationary state. In a dynamic system, one that requires inequality to generate ever more technology and capital, equalization must continue to be postponed. In a dynamic system, the justification for inequality pushes achievement of equality into the future, unless it is defined by the circular argument that equality is what the market can achieve. If liberal economists are correct that economic efficiency requires more economic equalization, and if political equilibrium also requires more economic equalization, then stability and democracy are postponed into the indefinite future.

Chapter Five

Democracy

Poverty is the cause of the defects of democracy. That is the reason why measures should be taken to ensure a permanent level of prosperity. This is in the interest of all classes, including the prosperous themselves.

—Aristotle, *Politics*, bk. 6, chap. 5.

Democracy is one of the most used and abused ideas in the twentieth century. Since the end of World War II, virtually everyone has claimed to be a democrat and to be supporting, working toward, or preserving democracy. Denominations include liberal democracy, constitutional democracy, participatory democracy, direct democracy, representative democracy, economic democracy, social democracy, elite democracy, majoritarian democracy, mass democracy, limited democracy, and people's democracy; there are military juntas claiming to restore democracy and theorists attempting to curb democracy in the name of preserving it. Sometimes these terms overlap, and often they are incompatible, but there is still virtually universal agreement that democracy is good. All claims, however, cannot be equally correct. What then is democracy? Where does it apply? What conditions are necessary to have whatever we decide is democracy? What are obstacles to democracy? How theorists respond reveals much about their social-political-economic preferences and models.

The conservative economists agree about democracy. Democracy is acceptable, but democratic theory and practice do not meet the needs of a modern economic system. This economic censure focuses specifically on democratic politics, not economic democracy or demands to democratize the economy. It contends that democratic theory and practice must be radically altered to become compatible with a free economy. These theorists assert that contemporary democratic politics interferes with efficient operation of the economy

Parts of this chapter appeared in "Conservative Economist Critics of Democracy," *Social Science Journal* 21, 2, pp. 99–116, and are reprinted here with permission.

and that unless this trend is reversed by limiting government's economic role and reducing popular expectations, both democracy and the free economy upon which it depends are doomed. As with freedom and equality, the analysis of and prescription for democracy are based on supposedly empirical economic analysis but are actually a form of normative political theory prescribing major political and social goals and modifications. The assumptions in chapter 2 provide the basis for an attack on Keynesian and welfare economics and, through them, on liberal democracy. Democracy is condemned as a form of majoritarian excess with an inherent bias toward intervention and deficit spending. This critique is associated with a picture of democracy as a limited, procedural, and purely political phenomenon having no particular aims or superior values. This chapter examines the economists' theories of how democracy does and should operate, the implications for democratic theory and practice, and related policy proposals that illustrate the basic normative argument.

Economic-based criticism of democracy has a long history and is closely related to criticism of equality. The current attack reproduces many traditional charges: democracy undermines property and property rights; it engenders mob rule, instability, and demagogues; democracy is despotic imperialism where the masses impose their ignorance on the elite; the mass public cannot appreciate the complexities and long-range nature of economics; and political equality is separate and distinct from economic relations. Aristotle stated the essential criticism. Democracy meant rule by the poor—government for benefit of men without means. Though the best of the undesirable forms of government, democracy was unsatisfactory because it allowed the many to rule in their own interest, not the common good. Aristotle feared that democracy always included the danger of lawless mob rule, where, in the name of equality, the *demos* would use "their numerical superiority to make distribution of the property of the rich" or to confiscate "the property of the rich and less numerous." Conversely, the majority was endangered by the rich attempting to despoil the people. The best system, his polity, combined elements of democracy and oligarchy. It limited the rival claims of both numbers or citizenship and wealth for preference in participation, giving a large role to the middle classes on the assumption that they had sufficiently broad interests to protect both property and wide, though not universal, participation. The good polity, however, protected property, even at the cost of limiting political participation.[1]

Concern for the problems of mass participation was echoed by nineteenth- and twentieth-century economic theorists. Much of the current conservative criticism is similar to the arguments of Malthus, Spencer, and Sumner. Though authors such as Knut Wicksell, Anthony Downs, and Kenneth Arrow fall outside the framework of this book, they illustrate the contemporary theoretical context and background to the conservative criticism of democracy. Despite

Wicksell's (1851–1926) decidedly liberal political and social preferences, Buchanan repeatedly asserts that Wicksell inspired his work. He considers his discovery of Wicksell's 1896 thesis as "[o]ne of the most exciting intellectual moments in my career." Though Wicksell did not employ these arguments to directly limit popular participation, Buchanan found in Wicksell an early statement of some of his most important views: politics and economics as exchange mechanisms; emphasis on the importance of rules in understanding policy outcomes; and concern for unanimity or near-unanimity in fiscal decision making.[2]

Downs accepts an individualistic perspective in analyzing how democracy operates, but he is not as overtly political as Buchanan, Friedman, and Hayek. Downs begins with a similar assumption—that people are self-interested and that their behavior is directed "primarily towards selfish ends." Individual motivation is the key to understanding politics. As with Arrow, analysis starts with individual utility calculations. Democracy behaves like a political market in which parties compete for votes and candidates are rational utility maximizers whose primary purpose is election or reelection. This leads them to attempt to satisfy the largest number of voters possible—and voters to choose the party promising the most. However, in Downs's model, consistency and ideology limit political promises in a way absent from that of the conservatives.[3]

Arrow made the first systematic statement of public choice theory. He too assumes individual pursuit of self-interest. Arrow illustrates that when individuals have a set of rankings among alternatives; when social outcomes are positively correlated with individual preferences; when removing one alternative will not change the order of preferences; when citizens' choices are not limited so that a preference cannot effectively be expressed; and when no one is allowed to dictate a decision, then there will not be any one social decision that can satisfy or reflect all individual preference rankings. This calls the efficacy of majority decision making into question, because simply voting will not satisfy everyone's preferences—although if bargaining is allowed beforehand, more individual rankings may become congruent.[4]

Theorists such as Arrow and Downs are distinguished from Buchanan, Friedman, and Hayek because they are less explicitly and deliberately normative and political. Though their analyses provide the basis for questioning liberal democratic theory and assumptions and can lend themselves to the politically limiting arguments of the conservatives, they do not draw the political and policy conclusions made by the conservatives, for whom popular democracy is dangerous.

Democratic Subversion of the Economic Constitution

Conservative assumptions about self-interest, spontaneous order, the political market, and the inevitability of government inefficiency form the starting point for a significant criticism of contemporary democracy. They are the basis for attacking Keynesian political economy and, through it, democratic values and practice.

Democracy is in trouble because it has abandoned traditional economic behavior and embraced Keynesian economics. These authors present both a political and economic criticism, each of which is essential to understanding their economic position. Buchanan, Wagner, and Tollison claim that under "The Old-Time Fiscal Religion," balanced budgets were the norm in the United States and Britain, and this "significantly limited the size of the state." This older discipline imposed fiscal restraints upon the natural "proclivities of ordinary politicians." The budgetary process produced surpluses in good times and deficits in bad times such as war, but these tended to balance. At all times the role of government was strictly limited. A balanced budget prevented excessive government spending and regulation. Governments could not collect sufficient taxes to meet all demands, nor could they shift payment onto the future, because an unwritten "fiscal constitution" prevented systematic deficit spending, ensuring limited government and limited extraction of resources from society.[5]

A balanced-budget rule formed the major part of this "fiscal constitution," defined as "a constitutional constraint . . . a fixed set of principles antecedent to and controlling the operating institutions of government." The fiscal constitution was superior to ordinary public policies, majority decisions, or temporary governments. Though it may have been unwritten,[6] "it nevertheless had constitutional status" and "was an extra-legal rule or custom that grew up around the formal document," presumably like political parties or judicial review. The fiscal constitution regulated public spending and financial decisions and required that government spending be balanced by tax revenues, not borrowing. It was as fundamental as any political institution or rule.[7]

The use of constitutional language to refer to economic policy indicates that fiscal affairs are more primary than political rules and decisions. This language elevates the status of economics by contending that deficit spending is essentially unconstitutional, contrary to the rule of law, and perhaps subversive. Limitations on government economic power become essential to the restoration of the rule of law. Such limits are more important than mere statutes or temporary majorities and are justified by an appeal to a higher rule; the natural economic order. Because balanced budgets existed in the past, conservatives can point to their occurrence as a paradigmatic moment when people behaved properly, making it easier for them to demand, in the name of restoration, curbs on contemporary democracy. In this theory of history, democracies have been seduced to abandon the old fiscal religion and embrace an economic heresy congenial to the "inherent tendency"[8] of democracy toward deficit spending and fiscal ruin.

The devil behind this seduction is, of course, the English economist John Maynard Keynes (1883–1946). He is condemned as the justifier of interventionist and welfare policy.[9] Buchanan, Friedman, Hayek, and Wagner all assert that Keynesian theory "may represent a substantial disease"[10] in democracy because it has released politicians from the limiting fiscal constitution. Keynesian economics is a dangerous construction, placing human will above the natural, spontaneous market process created by evolution. They claim that his macroeconomics and desire to reduce unemployment have taught democratic politicians that budget balance is undesirable and that interventionist government is necessary to save the economy from the disequilibria which the conservatives attribute to intervention. Buchanan and Wagner believe that Keynes "has turned the politicians loose . . . [and] destroyed the effective constraint on politicians' ordinary appetites." Politicians may now ignore all fiscal restraints on their natural propensity to spend and spend their way to reelection. With all spending restraint gone, such "Keynesians" as Lyndon Johnson and Richard Nixon could enlarge an already "bloated public sector." Keynes is charged with elitism, concocting a corrupting political economy, undermining fiscal responsibility, and causing a "shift in paradigm" that has led to most current woes. These disorders include a "bloated" budget and public sector; inflation, which cannot be solved as long as we retain current democratic theory and practice and is a "clear and present danger to the free society"; and unconcern for the future.[11]

This tendency is especially severe in democracies. Keynesian political economy supposedly requires elite or authoritarian government because democracies, unlike authoritarian systems, are uniquely susceptible to the lure of deficit spending. "[D]ebt is more dangerous for democracies." It is "particularly insidious for democratically organized governments" because voters, taxpayers, and politicians have no collective image, no concern for their future selves. Instead, they want the quick fix–the easy answer which must inevitably lead to default.[12] According to Hayek, democracies cannot even create an adequate monetary system.[13]

Conditions would be better if Keynes's ideas worked, but the conservatives contend that intervention and the provision of extensive welfare benefits are necessarily doomed to failure. Intervention in the market cannot work because it undermines economic freedom and the operation of natural, self-adjusting economic systems,[14] decreases total wealth in society, and assumes that governments can successfully intervene in economic affairs. Government can do nothing to "permanently stimulate employment," and its efforts usually go wrong. The result of heeding popular demands for intervention is to grievously weaken political democracy and the economy.[15] Why? Because Keynesian intervention is incompatible with spontaneous order and is a major obstacle to realization of democracy. Either intervention or democracy must give way. Although it is obvious to the conservative theorists that Keynesian and welfare economics must be eliminated, democracy does not fare well either, because of the claim that democratic institutions hinder the efficiency and rationality of the natural economic order.

The Critique of Democracy, Briefly Stated

Who will benefit from which public policies—i.e., the issue of distribution—lies at the heart of the debate over democracy and economics. Given their assumptions about freedom and the nature of markets, critics such as Friedman, Hayek, Buchanan, and Brittan have framed their questions so as to indict democratic politics for modern economic problems. In shifting from economic assumptions to political prescription, their position is simple: "[T]here is a fundamental flaw in the Constitution of the United States and of other constitutional democracies."[16] In answer to the question "whether there is something self-destructive about the process of political democracy"[17] in the area of economic policy, these authors say yes.

Contemporary democracy is the major obstacle to democratic government. The conservatives present a picture of democratic man similar to Plato's: blind, ignorant appetite rules. Citizens demand more than, in the nature of things, government can supply. "Excessive expectations"—anything that is outside their market, such as demands for security, welfare, protection, reduced pollution, readily available medical care, publicly funded retirement systems—are at fault. People in democracies are peculiarly prone to short-term thinking because they find it difficult to employ cost-benefit analysis and want only the benefits. Ordinary democratic politics is too weak to control fiscally damaging demands without constitutional props. Unrestrained democracy cannot resist special-interest claims or apply a balanced budget over a period of years, because it attempts to satisfy majority and group demands which, given human nature and the political market, can never be satisfied.

Budget deficits are the natural result of democratic politics. They grow unmanageable, undermine investment, cause inflation, and destroy a productive economy. As a result, the money supply is manipulated by electoral politics, special interests rule, and the danger of major tyranny grows. Too much of a redistributive burden is placed upon government because democracy requires prior agreement on a nonpolitical method of distribution. If politics decides who gets what, its decisions are always arbitrary and disputable, leading to renewed and unending distributive conflict.[18] A dangerous dilemma remains. Democratic man must be disciplined, or the economic system will collapse in an orgy of disastrous intervention, destroying in turn the freedom necessary to democracy.[19]

Both the public and the government are unwilling to accept the economic system as natural and settle for less in the short run with the promise that the spontaneous economic order will produce more in the long run. Politicians naturally wish to remain in office and so attempt to meet demands regardless of eventual consequences. Thus "the temptations to encourage false expectations among the electorate become overwhelming to politicians." This is inevitable, given the political market and its "inherent and fundamental" bias toward meeting demands, the "lack" of fiscal restraints, and "governments [that] are collectivities of utility maximizers" who do not represent any mythical collective or common interest. These economists assume that each official bargains and trades, based on pure self-interest, to improve his or her position, regardless of long-term effects. They doubt "that government can be safely trusted to operate in the public interest . . . on the contrary, it must be expected to be generally engaged in operating against the long-term interest by serving its short-term political advantage."[20] As a group, these authors do not discuss role playing, the constitutional position of counterelites, or the limiting impact of values. Instead, they assume that each official maximizes personal utility— reelection – by tempting uncomprehending and greedy voters with promises of more and better fiscal goodies plundered from the creative minority. This behavior corrupts democracy, undermines freedom, and violates the rule of law, creating a bias toward intervention, deficits,[21] and inflation because only deficits can finance intervention without raising taxes and deficits are the major cause of inflation. The electorate comes "to expect too much from government action at too little cost," expectations fed in large part by "competitive vote-bidding."[22]

The economic theorists usually speak of politicians and the government as general, undifferentiated terms. On the rare occasions when they mention parties or party competition, they assume that the self-seeking and shortsightedness that characterize individuals typifies group behavior. Indeed, parties are no more than aggregates of self-seeking individuals who have no corporate identity except their shared loyalty to advancing self-interest.[23] Unlike its efficacy in the economic market, competition in politics is disastrous. Parties compete for support, each attempting to become the monopoly supplier of public goods, and the winner is the one who makes the most extravagant promises. Ideological differences mean nothing.[24] Such buying of votes and support is an inevitable result of elections.[25]

As with many traditional conservatives, universal suffrage, while accepted in principle, is seen as part of the problem. Majority voting leads to "overexpansion" in such areas as the social insurance budget.[26] "[T]hose with the lowest incomes use the political process to increase their income" through coercive redistribution. Universal suffrage thus "increases the number and proportion of voters who favor redistribution."[27] This a priori argument, so reminiscent of Aristotle, appears plausible but has little connection to reality. The poor tend neither to vote nor to participate politically in any other way. In the United States, for example, the poor are the most politically alienated, voting less than any other group.[28]

As these economists see it, part of the problem is that the United States has changed from a pattern of liberal democracy, where the duties of government were strictly limited by a fiscal constitution and a confined notion of the rule of law, to corrupt, undisciplined majoritarian democracy. Democratic majorities readily transgress any limits, claim exclusive power to define what is right, ignore the rule of law, and modify constitutions at will. Democracy degenerates into a search for pure equality that refuses to recognize economic differences. According to Buchanan, contemporary politicians believe that it is legitimate to implement any policy "so long as 'democratic' procedures prevail." To Hayek, democratic majorities reject all limits, claiming the right to settle issues howsoever they please. They insist "that whatever they desire is just," yet the thirst for unattainable "social justice" leads to greater and greater abuses of power. Buchanan claims that except for "procedural guarantees," majorities have come to believe they can do as they please and that this is the "essence of 'democracy.'" To Brittan, contemporary majorities believe that they have a right to impose their will and are limited only "by the fears of physical resistance or a collapse of business confidence."[29]

Though his criticism is based less on economics per se than the others, Hayek best summarizes this position. Separation of powers has broken down. Legislatures no longer pass general rules equally applicable to all regardless of status or position but claim unlimited power to govern and change the rules of governing. Modern governments and the temporary majorities that support them decide limits to their own power. Unconstrained by acceptable constitutional rules, they literally are lawless. Without recognized limits, coercion, compulsion, and political pressure are seen as cheap ways to force (largely wealthy) minorities into conformity, shifting economic burdens to the creative and productive few. Inevitably governments serve special interests.[30]

These majorities, however, are not real majorities—majority rule being impossible—but are shifting coalitions of minorities in temporary alliance. Group politics are the bête noire of conservative criticism. Fear that legislatures will focus on special or partial interests dates to at least Adam Smith, Edmund Burke, and James Madison and was part of Aristotle's and Cicero's concern over democracy. Interest group selfishness helps explain why the older fiscal constitution has been abandoned. Though Hayek believes that the barriers to "arbitrary use of power" were breached for "benevolent" reasons, efforts to help the less well off inevitably create conditions for the exercise of unlimited, arbitrary power by temporary coalitions of coercive groups. Friedman charges that efforts "to promote" the public good inevitably lead to promotion of "special interests."[31]

Unlike those political scientists who consider competing groups to be a democratic, stabilizing factor, most of these economists believe that "the group pursuit of self-interest may be inherently unstable" in contrast to individual pursuit of self-interest.[32] Self-interested individuals, acting rationally, produce market competition while groups – usually labor unions or welfare seekers – pursuing the politics of compromise, accommodation, and intervention destroy competition. Indeed, government regulation, which always promotes monopoly and transfers wealth to groups able to influence government, results almost exclusively from lobbying against the public interest. The greater the omnipotence claimed by democratic government, the more groups will organize for both protection and plunder, and the more government will be forced to *buy* their support. Legislative majorities *must* meet sectional demands or be replaced by other, more compliant temporary coalitions.[33]

This situation flows from the inferiority of the political market to the real, economic market. A market model explains both democracy and its problems for these theorists. The economic market is supposedly responsive and responsible to individuals; it is competitive, free from coercive power, and allows little or no manipulation and no real monopoly. Individuals are free to enter or leave at any time, free to accept or reject any transaction, with few or no restraints. The "democratic political marketplace," however, is characterized by coercive "near monopoly of power," limited choice, and the necessity for losers to accept what winners want. Unlike the economic market, choice is severely limited, and the political market cannot provide different services or policies to meet individual needs. Centralization forces the same products on everyone. If government could meet separate needs, that would give public officials dangerous discretionary power. The nature of politics as a zero-sum game encourages further group competition and exacerbates the democratic dilemma.[34]

Not only is the economic market superior in general terms, some authors claim it is necessary, in a causative sense, to freedom and political democracy. Democracy requires that people have free and complete control over private property, with this autonomy in turn limiting government. Any invasion of private property rights or market freedom upsets the equilibrium within which individuals find room to attempt to develop and compete. Once upset, this equilibrium must be restored by limiting government power to intervene in economic relations, or both the market and democracy will be destroyed. The choice is simple: capitalism and democracy or socialism and tyranny. A mixed or nonmarket society cannot be democratic and free.[35]

The conservatives also claim that the market is the real realm of democracy, superior in every way to political democracy.[36] The market's "ballot" is preferable to the political "ballot" because it leaves more room for individual choice and freedom. This makes the market more democratic than the political system. Friedman claims that "the economic market is a more effective means for achieving political democracy than is a political market." As a voluntary alternative to inefficient coercion, it gives people exactly what they wish. It permits "unanimity without conformity . . . proportional representation."[37] Thus proportional representation is not applicable to politics, and its superiority in the economic market condemns politics.

Other conservative economists also see the market as both free and democratic in a way that politics can never be. For Gilder, it is "ultimate democracy." Hutt says that its inegalitarian aspect is a virtue. In the market, each person's dollar is treated as the equal of any other person's dollar, ensuring that those who are valued most by others will have the most votes. To the extent that there are restraints in the economic market, they limit the ability of one person or group to coerce another and are natural in that they are "imposed under the 'democratic' form . . .[i.e.,] consumers' sovereignty."[38] Equal formal access to the market guarantees that market relations are voluntary, entered willingly and consciously. This turns the market into the true realm of consensual, noncoercive relations, whereas politics and the so-called political market remain the realm of nonconsent and coercion.

The political market, which emphasizes once and for all (for a particular time period) elections, does not fit with the conservatives' previous picture of interest-group activity within democracy. The economists correctly imply that democratic politics is a continuing process of conflict and accommodation, a process much closer to their view of an economic market than they will admit. Yet they reduce the "political market" to zero-sum elections where the individual has little voice, choice, or role. The concept of a political market leaves no room for consensus building, the nonrational and irrational in politics, or the educational role of participation in democratic politics. It denies the place of manipulation and limited choice in economics. Everything is reduced to a simple exchange, and these exchanges are not intrinsically better in a democratic system than in a dictatorship. In both they are made for selfish, individual purposes. There is no moral difference between types of exchanges unless they involve redistribution or intervention. Unfortunately, it is not clear why these are significantly different from other exchanges. By reducing democracy to an exchange procedure—one which, by their evidence, usually involves selfishness and corruption – democracy is stripped of any significant moral content and of its traditional claims to moral superiority over other forms of government. All that distinguishes democracy from dictatorship in this model is democracy's allowance for "peaceful change of government," and given the economic problems peculiar to democracy, that is temporary and precious little.[39] If democracy is justified only as a procedure for peaceful change of government, does not hereditary monarchy receive superior justification on the same grounds?

The Economists' Picture of Democracy

The economic theorists never quite explain what democracy is, but they claim that excessive popular demands and participation coupled with Keynesianism undermine and pervert democracy. The same critique is repeated over and over with little variation. Current democracy is described as mass man seeking through coercion his own immediate self-interest. The massively selfish and ill-informed electorate demands the impossible, producing a built-in, inherent bias toward intervention, deficits, and inflation. Budget surpluses are virtually an accident. They can develop on a regular basis only with conscious decisions to raise taxes and/or lower spending, but such decisions alienate some voters and are difficult to make. Democratic politicians decide policy only according to what they can gain from a choice in terms of voter support.

This is a picture of pure majoritarianism drawn from Rousseau's dreams and Calhoun's nightmares. It contains every charge made against popular government since Plato. Majorities refuse to be guided by fundamental law. They decide what is just and what is law. Regulation, welfare, and intervention are solely in response to lobbying by special interests against the public.[40] These theorists share none of the pluralists' image of government as a balance between competing claims; nor Galbraith's image of it as a counterweight to private power; nor Keynes's premise that government intervenes to promote the stability of capitalism. Rather, the political market and human nature make such hopes futile. Under democracy, intervention aids only special interests. Nothing accrues to the general advantage. There can be no long-term improvement.[41] Welfare policy, redistribution, and intervention simply take from one group and give to another, and in general, the recipients have no legitimate claim to the wealth confiscated from productive individuals.

The conservative critics agree about how democracy should operate. They do not repudiate democracy, as traditional property-rights theorists often did. Instead, they redefine, modify, and limit democratic theory and practice. Democracy has neither goals nor purposes,[42] except peaceful change of governors.

Conservative democracy is a procedural and instrumental means – confined to voting or choosing from a limited number of alternatives – for majorities to select governors and affect the general direction of public policy. Claiming that it has another aim or purpose indicates a belief that there is a truth superior to individuals, which may be legitimately enforced by coercion. Democracy is functioning badly because of mad attempts to give it positive content.[43] As a procedure, it is limited to politics, and these authors consider it perverse to attempt to expand democracy to other areas.[44] Because pluralism and interest-group politics lead to fragmentation and government involvement in the economy, the conservative economists favor a democracy similar to Joseph Schumpeter's, which would limit popular input and the range of political decisions. Thus democracy is legitimate if it is not too responsive to popular economic demands. Its survival depends upon an unrestrained market. To intervene in the name of democracy, as suggested by Keynes, Thurow, or Galbraith, undermines the underlying economic reality necessary for a successful democracy – market freedom.

Proposed Solutions

There are two essential criticisms made by these authors. Intervention subverts economic efficiency and freedom. Contemporary democracy encourages intervention. What is to be done in the midst of this fiscal and moral[45] decay? Like an errant child, democracy must be disciplined – i.e., made to conform to correct economic theory – if it is to be saved. Since democratic man is incapable of controlling himself, he needs a guide and limits: a return to pre-Keynesian public policy. How? Through a "'constitutional revolution' . . . to preserve liberal democracy." We must rescue "the true ideal" of democracy and "protect democracy against itself," through "modification of the institutional structure" and limits on the power and resources of government. For Hayek, contemporary democracy must lead to socialism, which inevitably leads to totalitarianism; therefore, it is legitimate to deprive democratic governments of the power and resources that allow intervention and regulation even if these "may generally be regarded as good purposes."[46] This involves imposing limits on democratic government, because it is less able to "exercise self-restraint" than "an autocratic government." Current "unlimited democracy may well be worse than limited governments of a different kind." Thus, "*all* government, but especially if it be democratic, should be limited."[47] This is accomplished by reducing government's scope, size, and activities; depoliticizing distribution by placing most economic issues off limits to politics; stripping democracies of the resources that allow intervention, regulation, and welfare; restricting participation; and modifying majority rule.

Given the shortcomings and irresponsibility of democracy, where will the constituency develop for reform? Since there is no acceptable agreement on political-economic values and approaches, and since these critics do not trust normal democratic politics or the mass public (Buchanan and Wagner consider the hope that voters can be educated to support better policies to be "a tiresome relic"[48]), correct economic policies must be imposed by incorporating them into constitutions. Conservative economic theory must be elevated to the same, perhaps superior, constitutional standing as basic political rights and the structure of government already a part of western constitutions. Given their political market, these conservatives may believe it is easier to generate one-time support for constitutional change than to maintain support for limits on a year-to-year basis.[49]

A balanced-budget requirement is one of the most common proposals for depriving majorities of the means to violate the economic constitution. Most of these authors support a balanced-budget amendment[50] ending deficit spending, to contain what they consider democratic fiscal excesses. Friedman has actively campaigned for such limitations as California's Proposition 13. For Buchanan and Wagner, "Budgets cannot be left adrift in the sea of democratic politics." Citizens must be forced to recognize the full implications of spending.[51] Some authors prefer that budgets be balanced each year, regardless of the business cycle, except in a clearly defined situation such as a war or a major economic crisis. Even then, it would require a qualified majority – for example, two-thirds of the legislature – to override the balance mandate. Similar requirements have been called for in both the United States and Britain.[52]

A balanced-budget amendment is one of many proposals designed to limit government spending, government's share of the gross national product, intervention, and provision of welfare. Because majorities abuse their power, and the budget and size of government are "bloated," a balanced-budget requirement must be supplemented by constitutional provisions to limit taxing and spending power, thereby shifting resources to private control, even if this would have no impact on the size of the economy.[53] Each of these authors prefers individual to public spending of resources. To Friedman, "The deficit in the federal budget is only a symptom of a more deep-seated malady: the size of government spending."[54] Even if there were no deficit, public spending would harm freedom and the economy. Proposals for reducing the size of the public sector include[55] curtailing monetary growth, perhaps to a rate similar to growth in real gross national product (GNP); a requirement that legislative budget decisions be made by a qualified majority, such as three-quarters of the entire legislature; tax and expenditure limitations; and even a return to the gold standard, though this is very much a minority position.[56] Each recommendation is designed to restrict what democracies can do in socioeconomic relations by reducing the resources upon which they draw.

It is now easy to see why all of these authors reject tax increases. Although tax increases to curb inflation and end deficits were the standard remedy of pre-Keynesian economists, the conservatives hold that balancing the budget by increasing taxes would enable democratic government to continue to redistribute resources and intervene in the economy. In an increasingly popular but unsubstantiated charge, these theorists assert that as long as resources are available, democratic majorities will continue their selfish and destructive activities. Raising taxes simply gives democracies more resources to spend and waste and cannot lead to any long-term reduction in the deficit.[57] Friedman believes that it is better to run large deficits—perhaps in the hope that these will generate opposition to spending—than to allow government the means to expand through higher taxes.[58] Some economists also propose such constitutional limitations for Britain, wanting Parliament to impose rules on itself to restrain the rate of monetary growth, combine spending and taxing proposals, and adopt a balanced budget.[59] Brittan proposes limitations on majorities, electoral reforms to weaken party control, and proportional representation[60]—all to confine the power of majorities to spend for social welfare and/or intervene in the economy.

However, more radical remedies are suggested by a conservative scenario in which separation of powers has ended and representative institutions have failed. Modern legislatures have acquired too much power, making them prime targets for shifting majorities and interest groups seeking to aggrandize themselves. Given the inevitable pursuit of self-interest and the political market, legislatures claim immunity from constitutional limits. Self-interested majorities support them, pushing aside constitutional rules and traditions. The legislature's power, however, is fragile. It must be used to serve these abusive, special interests, or it will be given to someone else.

This situation requires "basic alteration of the structure of democratic government,"[61] particularly the power, function, and scope of legislatures, to conform to conservative economic theory. Hayek's solution reflects the pre-Madisonian concept of balance familiar to eighteenth- and early nineteenth-century constitutionalists. In that model, part of the legislature would be insulated from the mass public, and each interest would have a role in government such that it could virtually veto legislation inimical to itself. Hayek would do the same by ensuring the independence of one body from the public at large.

Hayek proposes a distinction between the legislature and the government or governing body, thus creating two different legislative bodies. One, the governing body, would be elected by existing democratic procedures. The other, the legislature, would pass fundamental rules equally applicable to all, that guide, limit, and bind the governing body in carrying out particular acts to enforce the general rules. Significantly different electorates would choose the legislature and the "governmental body." In an extension of Schumpeter's logic, the legislature would ignore party divisions, group interests, and popular pressures, following its own opinions of right, wrong, and the permanent interest of the nation. Moreover, to curb popular influence and to insulate this body from public pressures, legislators would be elected for a fifteen-year term and would be independent of parties. One-fifteenth of this legislature would be elected each year. Candidates would be eligible at age forty-five and would be elected by people of the same age. One would vote for these legislators only once in a lifetime. To help ensure their independence while in office, members would be guaranteed an honorable and lucrative position upon retirement at age sixty. Such legislators, having independence from the electorate, political parties, interest groups, and public opinion, would presumably limit government to obeying the law, enforcing contracts, providing justice, and keeping out of the way of the economy. Other new governmental units, such as a constitutional court, would help ensure observation of these limits while arbitrating differences between the legislature and the governing body.[62]

Buchanan, Friedman, and Hayek repeatedly claim that these proposals foster reestablishment of the *rule of law,* a rule that has a large economic component. Since the rule of law is desirable and since they represent the rule of law, anyone who disagrees with their position opposes the rule of law. People who differ with these far-reaching proposals are dismissed as acting in ignorance, bad faith, or narrow self-interest. Buchanan sees opposition to constitutional change as rooted in "constitutional illiteracy" or pure economic self-interest. In either case, opponents are worthy of no further consideration, because there is no principled, moral opposition to these irrefutable proposals.[63] This argument ignores that much constitutional debate is over what should or should not be included in a constitution, such as recommendations to grant constitutional status and protection to some welfare rights. That proposal must be dismissed as special-interest pleading, since all out-of-market proposals fall into that category. It is, however, common to try to have preferred policies incorporated into the Constitution—examples include the equal rights amendment, welfare rights, anti-abortion proposals, school prayer, and limitations on child labor—but economic conservatives claim something that these examples do not: an empirically valid analysis of political and economic reality that trumps all objections and is also good moral theory.

Implications

The political element in this economic critique is illustrated by what is excluded from analysis. Although this chapter centers on democracy, democracy is not the full picture. Conservative theory shifts the focus from economic failure to a critique of political participation and government. There is little or no discussion of technological change, corporate mismanagement, macroeconomic cycles, or the possibility that natural systems do not exist. There is little or no concern for social welfare, the social and political impact of conservative economic policies, or how these policies benefit the already affluent. These authors pride themselves on analyzing political economy in its institutional setting, yet that setting is limited to an extremely narrow range. There is no systematic discussion of why older economic values were abandoned. The entire focus is on misguided greed, mass selfishness, and political failure. Corporate and private market power are dismissed as impossible in a free market. With the exception of Friedman, none of these authors examines who is demanding what from government. OPEC, international trade and investment, and foreign policy are rarely mentioned. Defense spending is a great lacuna. Though it involves direct economic intervention, allocation of a large part of the GNP, nonproductive consumption of an increasing portion of national resources and a disproportionate share of scientific and engineering talent, no attempt is made to measure its impact on the free market. Only civilian spending is a danger.

Economists such as Brittan, Buchanan, Friedman, Hayek, and Wagner believe they can save democracy from itself. The cure for the ills of democracy is less democracy, not more, which requires substantial changes in democratic theory and practice to make them conform to and support correct economic theory. Conservative proposals are based upon unquestioned assumptions discussed earlier: human nature, evolutionary development of natural order embodied in the economic market, and the political market. The implications of this perspective for democracy depend on one's concept of democracy, as well as its goals, purposes, and possibilities. Instead of reviewing the many conflicting theories of democracy, we can measure the implications of conservative arguments against six common elements found in every theory of democracy. There is no single, agreed-upon conception of these elements, nor can they be considered in isolation one from another. Each element modifies and correlates with the others, producing a unique perspective on democratic theory and practice, depending on how each element is conceived. These common elements are the extent and type of democracy, equality, rights and freedom, participation, majority rule, and consent.

The *type and extent of democracy* refers to whether a theory emphasizes direct or indirect democracy; whether democracy is a process or is directed toward achieving a goal or purpose; and whether democracy is (primarily or exclusively) political or if it is applicable to economic and/or social relations. Questions of this type are deeply contentious, for they involve conflicting views of the purpose and structure of both government and society.

The conservative critics would save democracy by limiting the instruments that make intervention possible: the scope and resources of government. Clearly, they reject democratizing the economy, if that means more equality or having a voice in governance, since that would destroy free markets and the spontaneous forces which generate them. Democracy does not apply to industry, economic relations, worker decision making, cooperativism, public ownership, codetermination, greater equalization, or any proposal for industrial or economic democracy. Democracy is limited exclusively to politics, unless one accepts the disingenuous claim that free markets are exemplars of real democracy.

The economic theorists also limit the scope of democracy by claiming that it is only an indirect procedure for selecting governors and a method "for determining governmental decisions." It is not designed to achieve anything. It does not involve "putting into effect the people's will" but is simply a competition for votes and, through the ballot, a limited system of elite accountability. As such, it has neither aim, goal, nor purpose.[64] Because politics is merely the pursuit of self-interest, even within collective goals, its only purpose is to protect that pursuit. This means that traditional democratic goals such as social justice, developing a community of feeling and civic awareness, citizen education, and a shared good beyond individual goods disappear. There is no social justice; it is a "mirage." There are no social values, only the values of separate individuals. Community, equality, and distributive justice cannot be public goals, nor do they have anything to do with democracy; rather, they destroy economic freedom, personal responsibility, and the rule of law.[65]

Limiting democracy to political procedure weakens egalitarian claims and reduces the scope and potential power of government. Starting with Plato and Aristotle, opponents and supporters of democracy have agreed that *equality* (of some sort) and democracy are closely related. Traditional conservatives criticized democracy because of this link. Whether democratic equality referred to an equal right or opportunity to participate, an equal voice in government, equality before the law, or economic equalization to support participation, it upset the natural order. The economic critics believe democratic efforts toward equalization are a "disease"[66] that has gone too far and must be curbed. A large part of the conservative criticism of democracy is that political equality allows and even promotes demands for more economic equalization.

Political equality is satisfied by equality before the law and, generally, an equal right to vote.[67] Everyone is not equal,[68] and these theorists interpret public efforts to expand political equality or improve social and economic status as an attempt to impose equality of income and outcome on society–an attempt that must destroy efficiency, freedom, and achievable equality through personal effort. As democracy is simply a procedure–voting and competition for votes–and has no higher ends or purposes, reduction of economic disparities is not necessary to democracy. Democratic equality requires no more equality than whatever is needed to attempt to compete in economic markets. It is fulfilled politically when people have an opportunity to vote. Friedman speaks for all these authors when he claims that organized efforts to reduce inequality undermine the economic freedom necessary to democracy.[69]

Freedom and *rights* are integral to democratic theory and practice. Along with equality, freedom and rights are part of the historical criteria defining democracy. Whereas socialists and radical theorists have emphasized equality as essential to democracy, liberals, starting in the late eighteenth century, began to identify democracy with preservation of freedom. Many people continue to define democracy in terms of freedom. As we noted in chapter 3, the conservatives' primary value is freedom, not democracy, but political and economic freedom are narrow concepts. Economic freedom–being left alone to use our resources and property as we wish–is claimed as essential to political freedom and democracy. Redistribution cannot increase the freedom of those made better off; it only decreases the freedom of taxpayers. Poverty, few opportunities, and working for others cannot limit freedom under free-market conditions and are irrelevant to democracy. Since the conservative theorists believe that the market is free, not coercive, they are unconcerned that economic differences or control over economic resources may affect political and economic freedom and, through these, democracy.

The limited notion of freedom has profound implications. Determining how much freedom is necessary depends upon one's conception of the extent and content of democracy, what can be expected from people,[70] how they participate, and so forth. If the people and government have a reduced role, if intervention, welfare, and regulation diminish freedom, if political activity is inherently coercive, then it is not necessary to have an extended area of freedom and rights. The notion of social and economic freedom–positive freedom, affirmative action, worker participation, improved education, equal-pay requirements, protection from private power, guaranteed access to employment, minimum levels of maintenance–becomes unnecessary, dangerous, and irrelevant to democracy. In short, these theorists believe that demands for social, economic, and broader political freedom or rights undermine economic freedom, destroying the basis for democracy.

The same limitations apply to *participation*. Having a voice in determining the affairs of the community is one of the oldest, most contentious elements in democratic theory. Equality, the nature and necessity of consent, the type and extent of democracy, the range and limits of majority rule, the purpose of democracy, and the scope of freedom shape participation. In keeping with their individualist pursuit of self-interest and the political market, the economic critics have a minimal, purely instrumental view of participation, applying it exclusively to politics. It is hardly different from plebiscite democracy, where the public is allowed to vote on issues or candidates presented to them but have little input in shaping or choosing them. The purpose of participation is to ensure the legitimacy of government through popular selection of the ruling elite and perhaps to protect self-interest. Participation has no other role. It does not create or educate[71] the citizen, decide issues, determine common interest, or serve to integrate the community. Not only do the conservative economists undermine arguments for more participation, such as those of Thomas Jefferson and John Stuart Mill and of contemporary theorists such as Benjamin Barber, Robert Dahl, C. B. Macpherson, and Carole Patemen, they call into question pluralist[72] and interest-group politics.

These economists reflect the traditional conservative argument that human reason is limited, successful intervention is difficult, and people do not know their real, long-range interests. The logic of this position is to limit political participation to voting and even to call for reduction in the level and intensity of voting participation because it leads to intervention in the market. Hayek questions whether government employees, "old age pensioners, the unemployed, etc." should be allowed to vote. The belief that it may be legitimate to restrict voting rights for such classifications of people reflects the underlying assumption that self-interest is primarily economic, that people sell their votes for more government goodies plundered from others, and that politics is a secondary concern and phenomenon.[73]

Because politics is the realm of coercion and the mass public cannot be trusted, participation must be limited to limit coercion. Full citizen participation and involvement in politics introduce too much ignorance, resistance to the dictates of the market, short-range thinking, and destructively self-seeking behavior into the political system. Once again, these theorists present an either/or situation: either extensive participation and pressure on government, accompanied by destructive intervention, or reduced participation and protection of the free economy. Hayek's once-in-a-lifetime vote for the more powerful legislature, as opposed to the governing body, exemplifies this duality.[74] Friedman seems to see voting as the only legitimate form of political participation, but it is not very important. Participation in the market is superior to political participation. In politics, "Once I have voted, I have done my duty," but there is continuing participation in the economic market. In politics, little or no incentive exists to vote or choose with care or to attempt to follow up on outcomes. Instead, there is incentive to combine in order to plunder those less efficient in combining for plunder.[75] Though the other authors rarely discuss participation as such, their criticism of interest groups, responsive government, and the "political market" illustrate their mistrust of mass participation. In terms made familiar by Albert Hirschman, the conservative economists employ the more passive economic argument of exit from an undesirable situation rather than the more active political voice—that is, complaint and deliberate efforts to change an undesirable situation.[76] If government does not or cannot do very much, self-interest is protected, and it is unnecessary to participate extensively in government's limited decisions. As man is an economic not a political animal, the need for political participation is further reduced. A chastened government also limits the scope of popular choice and reduces the impact of participation.

The inconsistencies in this criticism of participation escape the economists' notice. Given self-interest and their political market, voting, much less more complex forms of participation, must be for narrowly self-interested reasons. Group membership, patriotism, appeals to common interest, and citizen education cannot be reasons for participating, though people may delude themselves into believing they are. The problem is that with any nontautological conception of individualistic pursuit of self-interest that can be made operational, participation is irrational nonsense for the maximizing individual, especially if the free-rider principle holds. If people pursue self-interest as these theorists claim, then there is no way to explain why they take the time to combine with others or why they participate, other than that people are irrational and incapable of seeing that individual participation is a waste of time given the unlikelihood of having an impact. That may be a defensible argument, especially within a simplistic individualistic perspective, but it is not the argument that these theorists make. Instead, they claim that there is excessive participation, that individuals combine to pressure and plunder the economy, and that this behavior must be disciplined by constraining constitutional devices.

All forms of democratic theory associate *majority governance* with democracy, but there is significant disagreement over the nature of majorities, who or what is a majority, and what are the limits to majorities. Majority rule is often justified on the Lockean principle that in a community of persons with equal rights, each person is to count as one and only one in decisions affecting that community, making majority decisions the only legitimate means to bind people consistent with their rights and equality.

Majority rule rarely means that a majority actually determines the day-to-day activities of government. Rather, it can signify either that a majority of representatives who have been elected by a majority of voters actually rules, or that the majority is more entitled to rule than a minority, or that governments must maintain support or approval from the majority, or that the majority is entitled to determine what government will do, given minority rights. The majority is often limited to certain categories of people: citizens, male citizens, or land-owning citizens. In all cases, the ruling majority is smaller than the number of persons or inhabitants subject to it, without apparent conflict with the fundamental principle. What proportion of those entitled to compose the majority is sufficient to constitute its voice or decision is also hotly debated, as is the question of what limits majorities.

Although the majority principle is accepted by these economic theorists, majority rule does not fare well. As noted before, they characterize majorities as greedy coalitions of selfish minorities. As with Aristotle, they fear that majorities may act foolishly and unjustly. Not only do these conservatives restrict the scope of majority decision making through limiting constitutional amendments, but the majority principle is dispensable in many circumstances. "[T]here is nothing hallowed about the simple-majority rule." "The principal fallacy. . . . [i]n our age . . . is occupied by the principle of majority rule." "Majority voting is a convenient *decision rule;* but it has been wrongly elevated into a fundamental moral principle" which allows "elective dictatorship" and rapacious majorities to impose any costs on a minority. Friedman finds majority rule to be "an expedient rather than itself a basic principle." Buchanan believes that majority decision making might be inserted into a constitutional agreement, but there is nothing "sacrosanct" about what is only "one among a set of plausibly acceptable decision rules, any one of which might be chosen with equal validity." In agreeing to a constitution, majority rule must give way to unanimity. Hayek repeatedly states that he is not opposed to majority rule, but majorities are usually bought and do not exist in any real sense; therefore, majority rule must be limited to prevent arbitrary–nonmarket–behavior.[77] Majorities required for addressing economic questions should be greater than 50 percent. Legislative majorities of two-thirds and three-quarters are proposed for fiscal affairs.

This call for increasing the power of minorities is often based on the idea that there is "a true majority view" that gets lost in vote trading, bargaining, and legislative maneuvering.[78] This view assumes the existence of a criterion for distinguishing a true from a false majority, and these authors represent the real majority, or what a majority should want and must be required to accept for its long-term good. But such a majority is more likely to develop if a large number of groups are required to enter a consensus, especially one that involves economics. By focusing on the power of 50-percent-plus-one to oppress minorities, these theorists ignore the possibility that minority vetoes are a major problem preventing majorities from making necessary hard decisions. The conservative proposal to limit majorities to force compromise increases the power of veto groups, especially those with great wealth. Until they, like Calhoun, give an adequate explanation of permanent minorities needing protection through frustration of majorities, one can only assume their limiting principle can be employed by any minority seeking to oppose majorities.[79]

There is a still more significant problem with the conservatives' view of majorities. Buchanan especially, though the others concur, argues that the individual is the source of value.[80] If individualism and individual freedom are considered primary values, there are only two possibilities for government: rule by unanimity (which as a practical matter is impossible) or the majoritarian principle, perhaps with limits consistent with the preservation of those values. If some principle other than equality or individualism is the basis of value, then majority rule (plus consent and individual rights) becomes less important. Given the procedural nature of conservative individualism and freedom, the market becomes *the* extra-individual value source. Preservation of the market model is the primary goal. Despite the description of fair rules as those that individuals decide upon, or accept, because they evolved, these rules must conform to the market. The market becomes the only arena for and supplants individual value-creation, individualism, and equal freedom, subordinating them to market needs. Thus subordinated, it is illegitimate and impossible for individuals to exercise equal freedom and individualism to join majorities demanding limits to market behavior. Majority rule is inferior to the market.

If participation and majority rule are unimportant, then the last common element in theories of democracy, *consent,* loses its value. To the extent that democracy includes governance by the people, there is no way to avoid consent. Even if one does not link obligation to consent, the essential notion of democratic rule, governance, approval of leaders, or dialogue between governed and governors implies that in some sense the public can or does give consent and that its consent is necessary to legitimize government. In general, consent refers to public or citizen agreement to and/or approval of government, and/or its policies, and/or the system of rules and institutions under which decisions are made. Consent is a quintessential liberal concept, one that expresses an individualistic ethic that governments and majorities receive legitimacy from and are limited in their power over individuals.

There is much disagreement over the meaning and adequate expression of consent, but it is unnecessary to review that debate. Except for their claim that the market is the realm of consensual relations, the economic theorists simply do not deal with consent.[81] It is a nonissue. This lack of concern for consent is puzzling in authors professing individualism and occasionally a contractual source of obligation. But the economists' procedural individualism, lacking substantial content, coupled with their emphasis on spontaneous order, system needs, and fitting individuals to the system, is a weak support for consent. Given Hayek's and Buchanan's picture of institutional evolution—an inherently organic as opposed to individualistic concept—and each author's emphasis on the development of spontaneous order, consent does not confer legitimacy. Why people should be obligated to obey, especially when there is so much potential for losing many of the benefits they have gained in the last hundred years, remains unexplained.

Some Conclusions

These economists propose to create a free market, and this requires redefinition and remodeling of democracy. For them, existing democracy is objectively antidemocratic. It is neither pure nor strong enough to resist the popular policies which destroy it. Both the outcomes and procedures of contemporary democracy must be changed, because it is those procedures which make possible the responsiveness to temporary majorities that these authors find so repugnant. Economic theory sets the limits to what is possible. Liberal democracy must be replaced with a different model, one that compensates for self-interested human drives and safeguards conservative economic theory.

Though these theorists sincerely profess support for democracy, they display no awareness of how their language, attack on, and depreciation of democracy undermines democratic legitimacy *and* the legitimacy of democracy. Point by point, on all the great issues of normative democratic discourse, the conservative economists choose a minimal answer. Their theory provides a minor role for the public, which should be passive, quiet, obedient to leaders. Moreover, the power of leaders need not be limited by the selfish public, because there are more efficient restraints in market and constitutional prohibitions. Participation has no intrinsic value; it is instrumental and confined to voting with little government responsiveness. There is no notion that democratic participation educates citizens. Expansion of the "private" sphere and reduction of the area of public discourse weaken any sense that democratic government is a shared activity involving common citizenship, loyalty, or community. Among all of the many theories of democracy, this is a truly limited and limiting theory, a consumer model[82] in which the public may choose from what is offered within the limits of the fiscal constitution but cannot attempt to change opportunities or have an active voice in formulating possibilities.

The analogy between economy and polity also breaks down. Politics is not simply buying or not buying something to consume but has always included changing options and behavior, both as means to ends and ends in themselves. Protest, with the purpose of participating in a decision, characterizes politics and is an essential difference between politics and economics missed by these authors. For twenty-five hundred years, principled democrats have attempted to expand the number of people who have a role in deciding for the public. This disappears in the conservative model. With the public reduced to the accidental coincidence of the private, man the citizen disappears.

This theory also requires the reduction of popular political, social, and economic expectations, pointing to the next two chapters. As democracy is only a procedure, citizens should not expect much from it. Democratic man must accept the claim that many political-social-economic concerns such as social justice, employment, poverty, and private power lie in an area of natural and exclusively personal relations, outside the scope of collective effort or concern. Problems are not the fault of any identifiable person. Government cannot successfully intervene. This leads to the claim that public policy can be neutral, and those who lose from the economic theorists' policies should be willing to play by their fiscally limiting rules. Since economic relations are natural and political intervention is not, these theorists subordinate social, political, cultural, and aesthetic goals and values to narrow economic concerns. As such, this model accepts monocausality in human affairs, constricting the range of important human interests to the economic and private while failing to apply the self-interest hypothesis to its own analysis. Concurrently, an economic theory is elevated to the same constitutional status as free speech and distribution of power.

The conservative emphasis on democracy as procedure can be a useful corrective to dreams of unity and solidarity in achieving the one true goal that makes us democratic, but it is an incomplete picture. First, the argument is not consistently procedural. The market functions as the one true goal to which everything is to be subordinated, as illustrated in the next two chapters. For these writers, the market is superordinate to any other consideration, as it functions to achieve those political goods people desire—freedom, equality, democracy, justice, morality, community. Second, procedures do not legitimize themselves. They must have some goal or purpose. If procedures are self-justifying, any outcome of that procedure is legitimate. No principle would exist to limit extension of democratic procedures into other activities, a conclusion these authors reject. Operating rules embody values. They are means to an end. A procedure is chosen in part because of expected outcomes. There is no rigid distinction between constitutional order and results. To the extent that one is actually chosen, a constitutional order is chosen with ends in mind.[83] For example, no matter how far we fall short of reality, traditional defenses of popular government include protecting the interests of citizens, limiting the power of the aristocracy, educating citizens, and conferring dignity on the common man. Popular participation and limited government are means to these ends, not abstract procedures randomly chosen. Democracy is both procedures and goals. Goals may properly be debated, but it is not possible to deny the legitimacy of goals by claiming that democracy is simply a procedure. If it is only that, if it does not promise a better life, at least in terms of more responsive governments than the brutalities of history, if people are not practiced in these goals and procedures, then there seems little reason for the inevitable losers to maintain a democratic system.

There is much wrong with our democracy, but the conservative picture of the operation of democracy is superficial and inadequate. Madison in *Federalist* No. 10 saw two cures for the inadequacies and dangers of popular government, paralleling the two cures for the dangers of fire. One is to end danger by destroying the element within which it exists; the other is to control its effects. The conservative cure and defense of democracy destroys the air in which democracy exists. If their view of how the economic market operates is wrong in any substantial component—if there is significant private power, if the costs of exiting an undesirable situation are very high, if self-correction extends beyond the lifetime of a person or a nation, if competitive self-interest produces in the economic market half the harm these critics claim it produces in politics—it would leave political control in the hands of unchecked elites and the public with little effective power.

Even if these critics were correct in their assumptions, and even if their political conclusions were logically necessary (both controversial and doubtful possibilities), that would attenuate neither the normative component of their supposedly objective and empirical critique of democracy nor the possibility that welfare, redistribution, and/or intervention are necessary to political stability, economic growth, and a popular sense of satisfaction and legitimacy. These authors exclude from their analysis defense spending; private and corporate power; the fact that the United States has nearly the lowest taxes of any industrialized democracy; comparative analysis of Japanese and European experience since World War II; considerations of foreign policy; and the defects of the old "fiscal constitution." Had they included all these elements, they would still have presented an incomplete prescription for democracy. But this is not simply an economic theory. It is a political theory, though based on economics, with deep implications for politics. Given the popularity of this critique and its probable ramifications, democrats must ask for more, for this is a conflict over the scope and guiding philosophy of a democratic system, including the shape, direction, and beneficiaries of public policy.

Chapter Six

The Good Society:
Justice, Morality, and Community

We are firmly convinced, and we act on that conviction, that with nations, as with individuals, our interests soundly calculated, will ever be found inseparable from our moral duties.
    —Thomas Jefferson, Second Inaugural Address, 1805.

Where this school of public spirit does not exist, scarcely any sense is entertained that private persons . . . owe any duties to society, except to obey the laws and submit to the government. . . . The man never thinks of any collective interest, of any objects to be pursued jointly with others, but only in competition with them, and in some measure at their expense. . . . Thus even private morality suffers, while public is actually extinct.
    —John Stuart Mill, *Considerations on Representative Government*, chap. 3.

All social philosophies, social myths, political theories, and most religions are concerned with justice and morality within a community. Justice, morality, and political community are closely interwoven, each delineating the others. Sophisticated analysis of their meaning and interconnection began when the ancient Greeks invented systematic political speculation. For Plato and Aristotle, justice defined the nature of community and made the good life possible. Then as now, contending systems of justice and community shared a common goal: to regulate interpersonal relations in a way satisfactory to whoever counts—citizens, gods, the warrior class—by whatever standards—utility, natural law, philosophy, will—that could command sufficient accord. However, attempts to achieve agreement on the meanings of justice and community, and warfare over the failure to do so, has been continuous throughout human history, because rival pictures of justice support incompatible political, social, and economic systems. Viewed from the outside, justice, morality, and community are highly problematic, but from within systems that claim objective truth, they present few difficulties. The firmer the belief that one's system furnishes inescapable answers, the less apparent need there is for discourse, for weighing and balancing rival claims, or for admitting the possibility of alternatives. In that case, justice and community are ensured by following the system's rules and procedures.

This chapter samples the conservative economists' arguments about justice, morality, and community, briefly noting policy implications. For these theorists, the market provides answers to questions that have animated public discourse for millennia. In a seemingly positivist argument, they claim that there are no applicable exogenous sources of justice or morality and that the market defines the scope of community and common interest. As in other theories postulating a system independent of human wishes—such as Marxism—proper behavior is determined by system needs. The conservative economists' concepts of justice, morality, and community are indivisible from their pictures of spontaneous order and human nature. People are separate, with few ties, and generally follow narrow self-interest. Justice and morality are defined by and limited to behavior necessary for spontaneous market order. Community flows from this order, and human nature prevents development of truly common or collective purposes. As with freedom, equality, and democracy, justice and community putatively lack substantive content, being limited to marketlike procedures.

This perspective contrasts strongly with traditional concepts of justice, morality, and community. The National Conference of Catholic Bishops' pastoral letter, *Economic Justice for All*,[1] is a contemporary example of traditional religious-based arguments about justice, morality, and community within political economy. Based on Aristotelian and Thomistic philosophical assumptions,[2] and extending papal encyclicals dating to 1891, this letter represents an argument that was once common in western religious and philosophical thought.[3]

The bishops claim that market and economy are not separate, autonomous spheres of morality. Rather, "[M]ost of the policy issues generally called economic are, at root, moral and therefore require the application of moral principles." Given the market's importance, the bishops assert that it is legitimate to analyze and criticize economic relations from an external moral perspective: "to measure this economy, not only by what it produces, but also by how it touches the dignity of the human person." Economic relations are morally significant because they have profound social and political impact, deeply affect human interaction, are sources of conflict as well as accord, structure people's ability to develop, can frustrate and isolate or fulfill individuals, and shape family life. People are not equally able or free to act or not act in the economy, ensuring inequality of bargaining position and uneven results. "Serious economic choices go beyond purely technical issues to fundamental questions of value and human purpose."[4]

The bishops assert that human dignity is one of the most important moral components of the economy. Although wholeheartedly agreeing with conservative critics that poverty destroys dignity, the bishops reject the claim that market relations are always fair and must be accepted. Human dignity means treating people as ends, not means. Human dignity requires economic and social justice, community, respect for persons, solidarity with others, promotion of human rights, participation, and protection of the poor and vulnerable. Material and spiritual well-being are interrelated. Each sustains the other and coalesce into a pattern of supportive community. A sense of citizenship, a common good beyond individual pursuit of self-interest, and a justice embodying more than ensuring that people keep what they earn in the market develop only within such a supportive community.[5]

Socioeconomic arrangements are neither inexorable nor inherent in a natural economic system. Public policies are not neutral. People can choose how to interact. A free economy and negative freedom are valuable, but people must "recognize the inescapably social and political nature of the economy." This requires accepting responsibility for all actions, even those filtered through markets. If economics is not autonomous, it can and must be judged and guided by customary moral criteria and commutative, distributive, and social justice. The bishops insist that traditional religious values require economic justice beyond procedural safeguards ensuring people the right to compete. The economy communicates and embodies morally significant values and has an impact on fundamental human relations. Social and political results are morally significant and must be considered in evaluating economic policies. Community and common interest do exist, and although they include individualism, they cannot be reduced to self-regarding pursuit of self-interest. The bishops propose numerous policies that might realize their norms of justice and human dignity. Whether domestic or international, there is a "fundamental moral criterion for all economic decisions, policies and institutions" which requires that "[t]hey must be at the service of *all people, especially the poor.*"[6]

Most traditionalist arguments agree that work is an integral part of human development and that external criteria must guide socioeconomic relations. These arguments share with classical liberalism the belief in "a law beyond the law," that is, a standard to which all rules and behavior must conform.[7] Thus from the same perspective as the Catholic bishops, Richard Regan insists that the justice of modern economic systems must be judged by "the general acceptability of distributions, and the compatibility of distributions with the human development of all contributors," as well as by the gross national product.[8] From a different conservative perspective, Russell Kirk insists that social justice exists and must enter into calculations, though he tends to identify it with charity rather than active government. Kirk claims that economic liberalism—meaning conservative economics—has degenerated to the point where its economic abstractions endanger real freedom, community, and the myths by which people live and interact. In part, he calls for efforts "to humanize the industrial system" to the extent possible, reducing monotony and lack of pride in work.[9] Graham Walker wants to accept Hayek's economic arguments but finds himself deeply troubled by rejection of the transcendent.[10]

Buchanan, Friedman, and Hayek do not seem to have directly addressed the bishops' letter, but the anguished denunciation of the document by other economic conservatives is compatible with their position.[11] These authors' rejection of the bishops' claims is founded on the effort to give economics scientific status and goes back to the origins of classical political economy. Although it is not possible to measure accurately the influence of classical and neoclassical theorists on Buchanan, Friedman, Hayek, and other conservative economists, early writers provide a background against which current political-social ideas may be explicated. Classical economics and its descendants attempted to create an objective system of analysis, based upon deductive statements about real-world relations, that denied the relevance of and would not depend upon transcendent principles, moral criteria, or prescription. That it was only partially successful is shown by Malthus's assimilation of the laws of political economy to the laws of God; that is, his claim that intervention in socio-economic relations based on popular pictures of morality or justice offended both nature and God and his denial of the need for moral choice and responsibility for others outside one's own family.[12]

Malthus exemplifies a widespread tendency among social-political-economic theorists. Moral judgment often enters description and analysis.[13] Whether individual theorists explicitly embrace it or not, political economy has a long-standing concern with justice and morality. Smith, Malthus, Marx, Alfred Marshall, Keynes, and the authors in this book illustrate that political economists persistently employ the language of good, bad, moral, just, and so forth in reference to political-economic relations. Marshall (1842–1924), arguably the most important of the neoclassical economists, believed that economic science should be employed for moral ends and purposes.[14] This belief may have influenced Keynes's claim that economics is also a moral science because it prescribes behavior and people choose outcomes. The essential point is that economists often make claims that have moral content, involve justice, or employ the language of more traditional concerns.

Simultaneously, these and many other theorists have attempted to make economics a positive science or at least base it on objective criteria. This effort to establish the autonomy of economic analysis from philosophy and morality reaches deep into the history of political economy. Classical theory, and the later, more refined neoclassical theory, emphasized relations thought to be based on fundamental human motivation—adjustment of prices to marginal costs and changes in purchasing power, self-correcting mechanisms, full employment of resources, naturalness of economic relations, and the autonomy of economics. Following Malthus, Ricardo, and Mill, William Stanley Jevons (1835–1882) attempted to reestablish economics on what he considered an exact, scientific foundation, stressing collection and analysis of statistics, in an effort to move economics from the moral to the natural sciences.[15] Knut Wicksell (1851–1926) modified the classical approach to marginal analysis, emphasized that money and credit affected the level of economic activity, and influenced Buchanan's analysis of government operation. The eight editions of Marshall's *Principles of Economics* trained two generations of economists and provided a virtual syllabus of research concerns. Vilfredo Pareto (1848–1923) was even more influential in shaping how social scientists view moral issues.

Pareto is perhaps most famous for the socioeconomic concept of Pareto optimality. Advocating public policy requires value judgments and interpersonal comparison, but efforts to make political economy into a science decry the use of moral criteria. Pareto optimality apparently answers this dilemma. Given strong individualistic assumptions and accepting the existing economic distribution, this concept states that it is not possible to determine which social alternative is better, in the absence of unanimous agreement, without violating someone's rights. To avoid these alternatives, Pareto and subsequent theorists proposed that it is legitimate to proceed with policy changes making some people better off without harming anyone or making everyone concerned better off. This allows a ranking of political-social-economic alternatives without using interpersonal comparisons. If someone or everyone benefits, and no one is hurt, we may presume that everyone consents to a change in the status quo. Pareto optimality is reached when it is no longer possible to improve anyone's situation without making someone else worse off. Because of its limited application, the concept has been extended to legitimize changes where beneficiaries compensate, or potentially can compensate, losers.[16] Though they rarely refer to Pareto, Buchanan, Friedman, and Hayek make Pareto-like claims about the market: It embodies fair procedures, benefits to all participants, and voluntary action, thus satisfying individualism, unanimity, and presumably Pareto-type criteria. They also claim that no one is blameable for undesirable market results, meaning that all outcomes need not be Pareto-optimal.[17]

Despite the long effort to elude normative conclusions, the concern for justice, morality, community, and application of noneconomic criteria to socioeconomic relations has persisted. In response, Buchanan, Friedman, Hayek, and others who accept and amplify the classical and neoclassical emphasis on individualism tend to solve problems of distribution, moral relations, justice, and community with an appeal to system needs. If the economic system is based on objective criteria – human nature, evolution, positive science, or a hypothetical contract—that lend an element of determinism to relations, then answers to social problems and concerns are justified by appealing to the system's needs and structure rather than to metaphysics. The system of spontaneous order provides answers and limits the number of problems involving justice and morality. This makes it possible to dismiss exogenous claims, employ something similar to Pareto optimality, and ignore the moral content of one's argument. The wish, therefore, to divorce political economy from external criteria such as that detailed in the bishops' letter combines with objectivity claims *and* the normative criteria of individualism and economic freedom to produce the conservative economists' conclusions about justice, morality, and community.

Conservative economics is a belief system encompassing public and private morality, justice, and common interest. Hayek, Friedman, and Buchanan deduce complete models of justice, morality, and community and propose social policies consequent to their starting assumptions about human nature, order, and the market. Justice is defined and circumscribed by the market. Morality and moral relations are shaped by economic relations, so that the morality implicit in the conservative economic system excludes all exogenous systems of morality as irrelevant to economics. Community in this vision contains neither public good, common good, nor community except as each is embodied in the individual interests of each separate person.

Justice

Justice is the oldest and perhaps most common concern of political theory. Ancient Greek political thought viewed justice as the moral cement holding a community together. Plato aspired to create a just society and polity in conformity with transcendent standards; Aristotle attempted to reconcile rival views of justice in order to find general rules, acceptance of which would produce political stability. Their discussions illustrate the common concern of all theories of justice: treating individuals correctly, according to a knowable standard; maintaining social stability and order; and attempting to reconcile conflicts of interest between individuals and groups. Even when addressing nondistributive concerns, discussions of justice retain the difficult Greek emphasis on ensuring stability while giving to each person his or her due. The perennial problem is determining what is owed to each person and by what standard. Ideologies respond to these seemingly eternal questions with radically different answers. Finding an acceptable one becomes especially difficult when addressing the interrelation of economics and justice[18] to the political system.

Previous chapters discussed issues relevant to justice: market distribution, self-interest, discrimination, equality, equal treatment, and freedom. While closely related, equality, freedom, and community are not identical to justice. Though it is a fundamental value of all normative theories, the spirit and content of justice is always shaped by a system's assumptions and purposes.

The conservative economists are most concerned with justice conceived as ensuring that people retain free-market winnings. As with individualism, freedom, equality, and democracy, their picture of justice appears to be procedural and lacking in substantive content. It claims that fair procedures establish justice, not outcomes. If fair procedures – determined by evolution, agreement, or freedom – are followed, the result is just. There are no other standards, and the market embodies such procedures. Government and politics are not founded on justice but are generally detrimental to it. Because government permits unrestrained pursuit of self-interest, any occurrence of fairness or justice is frequently an accident. Transcendent standards are irrelevant. Even if they exist, disagreement over content encourages the use of coercion to make people conform. As repeatedly seen with other values, however, protection of the market and marketlike relations is a primary consideration, so that little that might interfere with pure market relations can be considered just. Like equality, justice is virtually identical to market freedom – keeping and using the resources one earns in the market. Within the market-constrained concept of law, justice means equal treatment by and conformity to the letter of the law.

Hayek discusses justice more than does Buchanan or Friedman (who hardly considers it at all). Hayek allows more room for traditional values, but he too portrays justice as a process: conformity to fair, marketlike procedures and uniform rules. Justice "has nothing to do with the question whether the application of such general rules in a particular situation may lead to *results* which are more favourable to one group than to others: justice is not concerned with the results of the various transactions but only whether the transactions themselves are fair." Rules of justice reduce uncertainty and conflict; what people receive is determined by competition. Moreover, justice has nothing to do with the Aristotelian notion of balancing rival claims, particularly in specific cases. That introduces human intervention and manipulation and produces unjust results. On the other hand, an undesirable outcome resulting from the operation of natural, spontaneous forces is not unjust and therefore is not subject to intervention. Justice refers only to intentional actions that directly affect an identifiable other; it can never apply to an impersonal process. Spontaneous orders such as nature, society, or the market can never be unjust because "nobody has the responsibility or the power to assure that these separate actions of many will produce a particular result for a certain person."[19] Irremediable ignorance therefore frees people of the responsibility upon which the Catholic bishops insist.

Buchanan agrees that justice is determined by the nature of the process, not by final distribution. Though his model of justice is more contractarian than Hayek's, and though he also is critical of utilitarianism, he too accepts the rule-utilitarian reasoning that emphasizes maintenance of general rules to the exclusion of particular results. Justice therefore involves fairness, and fairness means "that all persons are effectively required to play by the same rules"– those supporting the market. Government discretion and distinctions between individuals and groups, except for limited promotion of equal opportunity, cause injustice.[20]

Buchanan occasionally links his argument to John Rawls. Buchanan claims to be a contractarian and bases part of his argument on the possibility of constructing a hypothetical social contract that can be employed to decide the justice or fairness of political-economic policies such as intervention, taxes, and welfare programs. Justice becomes the evenhanded application of rules to which a contractarian would agree. This exercise is based on his radical individualism, which assumes that the individual is the source of both values and valuations; that there are no outside sources; that the possibility and content of justice are limited to what self-seeking individuals will accept in the pursuit of their own self-interest; and that the market embodies the essence of procedural fairness, including equal treatment of equals, and individual agreement, meeting Rawls's equal liberty requirement. Given these assumptions, Buchanan judges rules and laws by asking if they could have emerged through agreement "in an authentic constitutional convention"–presumably one allowing full rein to egotistical individuals. In a Rawls-like argument, Buchanan claims that self-interested people, ignorant of their interests, will choose general political and social rules that guarantee free competition and retention of most earnings. General rules protect property, life, and rights and mitigate against fraud and coercion while disallowing redistribution against one's will. Because fundamental rules are based on individual valuation, there is no supra-individual value that can bind people; therefore, general rules are those procedural rules to which rational, egoistic individuals would agree to protect the pursuit of their self-interest. Whereas Rawls stresses both maximum equal liberty and the possibility of redistribution, Buchanan emphasizes rules that maximize competitive freedom. Because these are rules supposedly acceptable to an individualist seeking his or her self-interest, and because there are no other motivations upon which people can consistently rely, maintenance of these procedures is the substance of fairness–"fairness is defined by agreement"–and thus justice.[21]

Though the conservatives are seemingly most positivist when discussing justice and morality (claiming to be descriptive, neutral, and objective), their argument is as normative as the Catholic bishops' distributive-justice claim. Government's responsibility for justice is placed in the same category of duties as the provision of weights and measures. The entire tradition of justice as a higher value is abandoned, as it must be, given radical individualism, self-interest, and individual valuation. By eliminating politically and socially relevant conflict over distribution, the market obviates the problem of justice,[22] except for criminal justice. Because the market reflects a spontaneous order, extramarket concepts of justice are not applicable to it; the individualistic, rule-bound market is always fair and efficient, ensuring that equal contributors are treated alike and guaranteeing to each person the full value of his or her service to others. For Friedman, the market protects people from arbitrary action. Moreover, market distribution and ownership are as natural as the inheritance of genes. Therefore, "The ethical principle that would directly justify the distribution of income in a free society is 'To each according to what he and the instruments he owns produces.'" As such, the market is a theory of equity and justice, setting the parameters of justice.[23]

Hayek's argument is more elaborate. Speculation over nonmarket economic components of a just society is absurd and even dangerous. Distribution cannot be evaluated by any external criterion, nor can the existing, market-determined distribution be deliberately changed without violating general rules of justice. Given his picture of spontaneous versus created order (that is, organizations), justice has virtually no application to market (spontaneous) relations, though ideas of justice bind governments because they are not spontaneous and their actions directly affect others. The results from a spontaneous process "cannot be just or unjust." To Hayek, when the market is free, "no single person or group determines who gets what" and questions of justice do not apply where "no human agency is responsible." "To demand justice from such a process is clearly absurd," because people do not directly intend or control outcomes of market processes. Questions of justice are relevant only to deliberate treatment of one person by another or to clearly foreseeable results of one's actions. Thus, in a free market, "considerations of justice just do not make sense." Wages and so forth are not related to desert, personal goodness, or any single individual's decision but are the workings of the freely entered free market.[24] Even if market results do not fit *preferences* about justice, efforts to impose such preferences are dangerous and destructive.

Buchanan accepts the logic of this position but adds a stronger statement of individualism. Unjust rules or institutions are those "that would prevent . . . [one] from making mutually advantageous trades." Though Buchanan allows more scope than Friedman or Hayek for adjustment of the market through transfer taxes and limited intervention to promote equal opportunity, justice essentially means maintaining the distribution results of freely entered market relations.[25]

The deductive, definitional nature of conservative theory is illustrated by its claims about the market and justice. It exonerates the economy from responsibility for such unfortunate circumstances as low wages, poverty, unemployment, and related problems. Given the idealized, always competitive market, each party benefits, or thinks it benefits, or else neither would enter into an exchange; therefore, it does not matter if benefits from a voluntary exchange are unequal. Thus the market epitomizes justice. Market distribution becomes an ethical precept and a statement of what people deserve. As a natural system, a scientific principle, and an ethical norm, the market cannot be questioned. Nonmarket standards endanger self-interest-driven free exchange, making nonmarket standards inapplicable to economic relations. At the same time, because the market-generated concept of justice reflects fundamental human nature, it legitimately judges politics and government.

The Catholic bishops, some traditional conservatives, and many liberals argue instead for *social justice*. Social justice implies an exogenous distributive standard by which to judge both the procedures and results of economic exchange. Liberal economists assert that it is both possible and necessary to combine efficiency and nonmarket equity concerns. The idea of social justice permeated Keynes's work. He was deeply concerned with the economic causes of political and social upheaval and believed that stability required creation of a widespread sense of social justice within which people would be assured of jobs and minimum standards. A notion of social justice is required to maintain free institutions and the broadly based spending power, cooperation, and sense of fairness necessary for economic efficiency—as well as to alleviate the destructive impact of single-minded pursuit of self-interest.[26]

The conservative economists consider such notions of justice irrelevant, and attempts to implement them are destructive nonsense that violates freedom, individualism, modern morality, and efficiency. Hayek is most emphatic.[27] Justice is applicable only to relations among identifiable individuals, not to groups; only individuals are moral, not groups or government. The general pattern of distribution can never be discussed in terms of justice, because, again, no one directly controls the market. Social justice is a dangerous myth, a "mirage," a "primitive" concept, the result of "naive thinking," "a quasi-religious superstition," "empty and meaningless," "a sign of the immaturity of our minds," "intellectually disreputable, the mark of demagogy or cheap journalism . . . dishonest," and "destructive of moral feeling." Social justice "is at present probably the gravest threat to most other values of a free civilization." It presupposes the power to order values or rewards and "can be given meaning only in a directed" system. It has "an anti-ethical effect," by destroying "the feeling of personal responsibility" and freedom.[28] Evolution of a workable concept of social justice is impossible. Continuation of the market order requires abandoning social justice to prevent socialism and totalitarianism.[29]

Buchanan and Friedman concur in rejecting the existence of social justice. Because of pervasive self-interest, social justice is impossible for Buchanan. Separate valuations, as opposed to a nonexistent common good, make redistribution illegitimate. Though justice requires evaluating starting positions when considering distribution, perceived maldistribution can be addressed only by promoting the ability to compete and requiring uniform, though limited, antidiscriminatory policies from business. Otherwise, involuntary redistribution is the virtual equivalent of theft, and thus clearly unjust.[30]

Since there is no social justice, business has no "social responsibility." Hayek alludes to this, but Friedman is explicit. "Moral responsibility is an individual matter." Social responsibility for business, as with the broader idea of social justice, is "a fundamentally subversive doctrine." It can "undermine the very foundation of our free society" by creating power which free markets prevent business from having. If business has any social responsibility, one person or group must determine what it is. This would subject business to central control and probably lead to the appointment of businessmen by government, bringing the political market and concentrated power into the economy. Social responsibility is opposed to the reality of a market economy—"a fundamental misconception of the character and nature of a free economy." In "a competitive market [no participant] has appreciable power to alter the terms of exchange." Given their resources, people must accept the position in which they find themselves. Each participant "is hardly viable as a separate entity." No one has the power to significantly alter pay rates, working conditions, or hiring practices set by the impersonal spontaneous market. Coupled with claims that the market restrains our worst behavior, this assertion shifts attention from firms to individuals. That no person has the ability or means to alter the terms of economic relations ensures that no one has responsibility, freeing business people from accountability for the impact of any legal activity. What responsibilities do market participants have? The primary duty of "corporate officials . . . [is] to make as much money for their stockholders as possible . . . .making maximum profits." Second, they have the responsibility "which is shared by all citizens to obey the law of the land and to live according to its lights." This includes staying "within the rules of the game" and engaging "in open and free competition, without deception or fraud." Labor has the same responsibilities. Only monopolists could have any strict social responsibility,[31] but in a free market there is no monopoly.

Important policy conclusions follow. If justice is solely an attribute of relations among individuals, specifiable only in that context, then it is illegitimate to discuss public policies to encourage justice for groups. In fact, groups as such do not exist. Composed of self-seeking individuals, they may signify identifiable categories but have no corporate identity. Progressive taxation and public policies to encourage consumer protection, equalization, or redistribution are also spurious. Speculation on nonmarket components of the good society is futile and perhaps dangerous. Justice considerations require direct, personal responsibility for outcomes, and the market absolves people of direct personal responsibility. If outcomes are unsatisfactory, people must accept them as natural and inevitable and even change their concept of justice to conform to necessity. Once again, politics is deflated and downgraded, as the customary political role in the creation and promotion of justice is taken over and reduced by the market. Though law enforcement remains, the state neither encompasses nor actively promotes justice.

Emphasizing procedures, the conservatives avoid the possibility that evenhanded application of rules may cause injustice. Beyond limited expansion of equal opportunity, they cannot imagine that seemingly acceptable procedures may lead to terrible outcomes, or that terrible outcomes require reevaluation of procedures and rules. Ostensibly having no substantive measure by which to judge the justice or morality of outcomes, their market supplies this standard. Because the market embodies justice, anything in conflict with the market must be unjust. Once again, their procedures are not simply neutral but lead inevitably to an overwhelming conclusion: The market embodies and promotes justice; justice requires the market; and there is no real justice beyond the possibilities and limitations contained in the market.

Morality

Most of the conservative economists' arguments apply equally to justice and morality in that they reject traditional theories and substitute an individualistic, market ethic. Self-interest and the market determine morality—including truth telling, promise keeping and not harming others—in the same way that they shape justice. Though people may dream of broader, more inclusive relations, the self-interest that creates the market ensures that moral behavior cannot extend beyond prudential self-interest.

These authors do not attempt to specify the meaning of morality as they did for justice, although they freely label as immoral such policies as high taxes. They would deny that they are offering a moral theory on the ground that these are empirical deductions, which makes their conclusions not a matter of moral choice but of necessity. Only Buchanan attempts to explain how he employs morality, and his use is eclectic. Buchanan employs the concept in three ways: to describe unscientific thinking, as a term of approval, and in reference to what he calls traditional morality.

Buchanan's first usage virtually identifies morals and morality as those aspects of life that cannot be predicted. In a position Amartya Sen identifies as harmful to economists' ability to analyze and understand reality, Buchanan states: "I define *moral philosophy* as discourse that embodies an explicit denial of the relevance of scientific explanation." This conception—his major attempt to specify the meaning of moral—is simultaneously too narrow, in rejecting the factual basis of moral theorizing; too wide, in fitting many things that are not moral philosophy; and factually questionable. Though it does not explicitly deny the relevance of moral considerations, it alludes to an unspecified middle ground "between empirical science and moral philosophy," leaving the strong implication that the one does not inform the other. Whereas theorists such as Sen insist that a closer linkage is necessary to the development of both, Buchanan limits the arena of morality with what he considers to be empirically valid propositions.[32] Given Friedman's insistence that economics is or can be a positive science, we may assume that he agrees with this conception of morality. If moral concerns do not or should not inform recommendations based on empirical science, then it is not possible to analyze or criticize the conservative argument from a moral perspective.

In its second sense, "moral" is a term of approval emptied of normative content. Buchanan claims that political economists operating as political economists are "ethically neutral."[33] As with other political normative terms, "moral" is drained of widely accepted and traditional meaning, leaving an unspecified term for which one can expect approval. Thus Buchanan entitled one essay "Moral Community, Moral Order, or Moral Anarchy," in which "moral" is informed in each case by the second term and seems to mean any area of interaction and agreement. "Order" is Buchanan's preferred term, conceived as policies that support his concept of a market. What function does the addition of "moral" serve over the bare use of "community," "order," and "anarchy"? Moral embodies the favorable connotations with which it is typically associated, but Buchanan avoids specification by claiming his usage is not normative. Although he asserts that his essay has no moral content, he provides no clear explanation of how, or even why, he employs the word. It serves no function except to provide a warm and fuzzy feeling of approval. "Community," "order," and "anarchy" do carry a freight of meaning, but as patterns of interaction with limited substantive content.[34]

Buchanan shares his third use of morals and morality with the other authors. He states that it is necessary to deal with and be concerned for moral questions that arise from economics, but it is an odd morality, not concerned with "social costs and social benefits."[35] Occasionally, he claims to be employing morality in its traditional, unspecified meaning to attack policies of which he disapproves, such as debt financing. Agreeing with Hayek, Buchanan believes that moral standards evolve over time, but, as with Schumpeter, rationally constructed ideas undermine these standards. Deficit spending is an example of the destructive constructivism that causes traditional morality to break down and is itself immoral because it destroys capital.[36] Buchanan's specific contention, however, is less important than his willingness to construct and then appeal to neoclassical economic arguments as the embodiment of morality. Whatever its content, traditional morality justifies restrictive public policies because interference in the market is immoral. Nonmarket morality cannot be employed to criticize either the content or result of market relations because the market does not raise moral questions. Appeals to previously existing moral rules seem legitimate only in support of the conservative vision.

This attempt to empty morality of normative content while employing the term is in marked contrast to broader concepts which emphasize guiding behavior through autogenously developed normative rules. Morals and morality refer to images of what people believe to be good, desirable, and of value in influencing behavior. The essence of moral rules lies in the provision of a standard to guide people when they confront choices. Any issue is a moral one when it involves choice among values, especially when there is the possibility of harm to others. Though moral issues frequently involve questions of humanity's relation to God, even these often entail the specification of norms for interpersonal conduct. From this perspective, one cannot escape moral choices in either politics or economics because there are no truly neutral policies. For our purposes, therefore, morality refers to attempts to regulate human behavior, based on an appeal to a standard higher than temporary convenience or even prudence.[37]

A deterministic, lawlike system has scant room for moral issues. The conservative economists solve and transcend moral questions by defining problems away. Their market produces harmony and eliminates the possibility of deliberate economic decisions affecting others in a morally significant sense. This removes responsibility for outcomes, obligation on anyone's part to address problems, and concern for persons and future generations who are not part of current bargaining. The system itself sets the requirements for, parameters of, and limitations upon morality. It is impossible to exceed system possibilities; therefore, as with justice, limits of morality are set by nature – expressed in a particular political-social-economic institutional arrangement and interpreted by conservative economists. Coupled with an emphasis on procedures, the market settles all seemingly moral conflicts over distribution.

Is this a *moral theory?* Yes. Its basic ideas carry moral overtones, and moral values are inherent in the system, which functions as a guide to behavior and provides answers to questions that many people label as moral. As such, it is a remarkable belief system providing assurance on disturbing issues of distribution and interpersonal relations. It contains three basic claims: There are no exogenous sources of morality by which to judge market relations; the market is moral or is the realm of real morality; and interference with the market is immoral. Assumptions about acquisitive human nature and harmony of interest provide strong ethical justification for the market.[38] The claim that individuals need not be good or have good intentions, that differences are reconciled and bad motivations neutralized, implies a moral structure. Despite frequent claims to be value-free, this economics is founded on a metaphysics, in the sense of accepting and employing a description and explanation of underlying reality, including human nature. At minimum, emphasizing individual ends and individual pursuit of self-interest, though not individuals or satisfaction of individual ends, implies a theory of morality.

Frequent attacks on taxation and debt financing as immoral indicate the belief that conservative economics is not only efficient but a superior form of morality. Buchanan claims that Keynes was a "Moral Revolutionary." Echoing Hayek, he asserts that by allowing debt financing, Keynes's economic theories encourage reversion to "tribal morality." Fiscal virtue has eroded under Keynesian tutelage, producing moral anarchy and putting "traditional" morality under seige. Government spending is "partially responsible for the erosion of the traditional moral order in the United States." Restoring moral order requires reducing the size and scope of government. Buchanan also contends that there are "Ethical Limits of Taxation." This limit is specified by what individuals will rationally allow in pursuit of their self-interest. A right of secession measures this limit. If an actual or theoretical right of secession was allowed, then the costs of peacefully leaving a community would set upper limits on the amount that a community was morally justified in extracting from individuals. In proposing an "ethical limit on taxation," a limit coterminous with what self-interested individuals will tolerate, Buchanan again employs a normative term stripped of its commonly accepted content. The moral limit on taxes has nothing to do with mythical common interest or nonmarket morality but is rather ethical egoism. Individually determined self-interest is the limit of individual moral requirements.[39]

Friedman seems to believe that the conclusions of "positive economics" should take precedence over normative values if these conflict.[40] He, Buchanan, and Hayek all label as immoral policies with which they disagree, claiming that active government induces immorality. Intervention, such as wage or price controls, is "deeply and inherently immoral" because it substitutes "the rule of men" for what Friedman considers "the rule of law and voluntary cooperation in the marketplace." Given the nature of individualism, social goals do not exist apart from those people who find it to their advantage to proclaim such goals. Appeals to values like patriotism are irrelevant to pricing decisions, while efforts to influence such decisions are both immoral and destructive of the fundamental values upon which the Republic was founded.[41]

Hayek also contends that government intervention, including measures to promote egalitarianism, is immoral. Although he stipulates that a free society needs strong moral convictions and standards, he fails to specify the content and meaning of that morality beyond the evolved behavior that maintains individualistic market relations. Because democracy leads to the growth of government, the expansion of modern democracy is a threat to morality and peace. Welfare demands undermine morality by stealing resources from producers, destroying freedom, and eliminating responsibility for personal conduct.[42]

Hayek and Buchanan equate nonmarket-based concepts of morality that call for intervention, an extensive welfare system, or collective responsibility with primitive morality: the morality of the tribe instead of that necessary to a great society. They are not concerned with taking popular notions of moral and community relations in contemporary society and creating an economics to accommodate them, but rather with claiming that ideas—such as the Catholic bishops'—of morality, justice, solidarity, and needs satisfaction in economic relations are wrong and destructive.

In making this argument, Hayek has invented an anthropology to explain social evolution. The morality of small hunting bands, struggling for existence in a hostile world, has evolved into morals appropriate for a modern, impersonal market society. He claims, however, that primitive morals became and remain part of human instinct. Hayek postulates that the premarket values, sentiments, and behavior appropriate to a tribal, face-to-face society are being applied with destructive results to contemporary society, where size and anonymity prevent caring and responsible relations. These instincts are inappropriate in a spontaneous order because they introduce human will in place of the rule of law—i.e., the invisible hand. Thus for the ignorant masses, "it is necessarily their prejudices which would determine" demands for government intervention. Though motives may be "benevolent," such demands are inevitably destructive. Social evolution has left behind primitive desires for social justice, solidarity, and a sense of duty to other members of society. Such instinctual "moral feelings" evolved during the long millennia of human development and made sense "in more primitive conditions . . . [when directed] toward the fellow members of the small group." All that modern society requires is conceding to others "the same protection of rules of just conduct," that is, rules and procedures conducive to market relations. "Our inherited or perhaps in part even innate moral emotions" are "inapplicable" in a modern, open, market society that will lead man to a "great moral adventure," a "new morals" in which obligations and moral relations are limited to market rules, under which "we generally are doing most good by pursuing gain." Here, Hayek allows constructivism to intrude, because in transcending the state of primitive morality, "we make our rational insight dominate over our inherited instincts."[43]

For Buchanan, humanity's "Tribal Heritage" is the cause of deficit spending, necessitating limits on the role of government. "Biologically, we remain tribal animals . . . our natural instincts have not evolved beyond those that emerged" in the primitive small group. What is called moral thinking usually reflects this early behavior, a "communitarian sense of loyalty to fellow members of the tribe" and hostility and willingness to exploit those outside the tribe. This is in contrast to the culturally evolved morality of his moral order – the market.[44] A moral case for a market economy is common among other conservative writers such as Robert Nozick and George Gilder.[45]

What is the result? Nature in the sense of humanity's caring self is not a guide to human goodness when discussing morals, but human nature – radical individualism – is a limit on morality, justice, and community because the early essay of morality is no longer applicable. Greed is more evolved than compassion, as concern for others releases destructive passions. In rejecting primitive morality, Buchanan and Hayek are selective. Altruism and solidarity are rejected; long-standing concern for truth telling and promise keeping are not. The relation between humanity's "primitive" instincts to care, share, and promote solidarity and continuing self-interest remains unexplored. So also does the possibility that "compassion has been a key to human survival."[46] Ultimately, the invention and criticism of primitive morality repudiates claims that capitalism undermines traditional moral relations and social structures.

Buchanan identifies the behavior needed to support markets – "moral order" – with Hayek's "great society." For both, this is the system of evolved rules which guide people in pursuit of self-interest. Reflecting Nozick's distinction between the minimal state, utopian efforts to create a redistributive state, and anarchy, Buchanan's moral order differs both from what he calls moral community, where individuals identify themselves with a community and lose their separateness and individualism, and from moral anarchy, where people are completely apart and lack mutual ties. In a moral order, people place minimal requirements on one another but agree to follow the same procedural rules. Government in such an order is drastically reduced from that in moral community – a point Friedman also makes – where it would have the impossible task of fulfilling primitive moral expectations.[47]

This eliminates the nation as the focus of morality or loyalty, and cultural evolution can never make it such. Moral feelings and behavior can never apply to a large unit which is sustainable only with minimal rules for conduct – again, primarily those of the market or those convenient for supporting the market. The market becomes the primary example and embodiment of moral relations. It exists independent of human will, and behavior should conform to it. Attributing a higher stage of moral development to the market helps account for the vehemence of attacks upon those who disagree with the conservative world view: they are outside the pale. Demands for extensive welfare, economic justice, redistributive taxation, women's liberation, or corporate responsibility are virtually moral outrages violating a natural order.

These authors do not always specify the justification that would allow equating economic recommendations with morality. Hayek identifies "our moral obligations" with "benefiting from an order which rests on certain rules,"[48] but it is difficult to imagine anything that this could not justify. Normative criteria enter through claims that people's real interest entails accepting market order rules. A partial answer to why people should obey or accept market rules is found in the conservatives' sometimes contradictory pictures of the source of morality.

Discussing the hypothetical source and nature of morality, Hayek rejects all rationalist, supernatural, and transcendent explanations. He claims that morality is a product of the gradual evolution of individual behavior in a marketlike process, with superior morality being that behavior which has survived. There is no criterion for moral rules other than their survival, yet Hayek opposes changes in these rules. Given human nature, morality cannot evolve beyond market behavior. He asserts that his evolutionary position is antirationalist, not based on any construction of morality but rather on acceptance of the process by which people gradually learned to adjust to one another. Despite individualism, however, people are obligated to this order. Individualism is the key to morality—there is neither "goodness nor badness" outside of individual responsibility—but individuals conform to rules they have not made. These rules have developed gradually from individual confrontation with problems and "have proved more successful than those of competing individuals or groups." Morality, law, political and social institutions, intelligence, language, writing, and the market all result from a similar evolutionary process, propelled in each case by self-interest.[49] In rejecting the possibility of either deliberate change or spontaneous growth beyond these rules, Hayek ignores the role of cooperation and force in the development of rules and the expansion of groups.

Buchanan also argues that "[a]bstract rules . . . have evolved unconsciously," and while they cannot be restored when abandoned, it is possible to create functional equivalents in formal, "rationally chosen constraints" on immoral behavior, such as a balanced-budget requirement. Morality therefore grows and evolves and is not grounded in or justified by higher standards. Like Hayek, Buchanan believes that rationally constructed ideas can undermine this morality. However, the overriding point is that he accepts moral and social evolution.[50] Friedman concurs.[51]

Buchanan is also a contractarian. Although he does not assert that a hypothetical contract will be compatible with evolved values and morals, it probably will be. In terms of justification, evolution and contract are never integrated. There is real potential for conflict between Hayek's and Buchanan's evolutionary argument and Buchanan's contractarianism. First, people may agree to something other than the conservative market. If one asserts that human nature requires the market or that alternatives are impossible, a contract adds nothing to the discussion. If human nature is not so deterministic, contractual arguments allow the possibility of alternative arrangements and would then be in agreement with individual valuation. If not, individual valuation also adds nothing. Second, a contract holds contracting parties responsible for outcomes, making it no longer possible to claim that outcomes result from natural behavior, and thus relieve individuals of responsibility–though one may still claim that the contract fits basic human drives and allows one to reach conscious agreement.

Moreover, it is difficult to reconcile acceptance of moral evolution up to but not beyond the market, with either Buchanan's proposal to create functional equivalents of abandoned rules or individual valuation. Buchanan describes two sources of morality. Though both limit redistribution and reflect the market, they are not consonant. The first source of morality is culturally evolved norms, which appear to develop from self-interest *but* apply to everyone. The second, and apparently favored, source lies in the individual, especially in self-interest. Buchanan claims that there are only two possible sources of value: "supra-individual" norms–something like Rousseau's General Will–or the individual. Since there are no supra-individual sources, all that exists "are the separate and several objects of the individuals." Individuals "are the ultimate sources of valuation." Politics, for example, should allow "individuals to express their own values, the only values that exist." This position depends upon "criteria that are internal to the individuals. . . . It becomes illegitimate to invoke external criteria for evaluating either processes or end-states."[52] The market maximizes individual values, while politics imposes conformity, again making the market the primary arena of public moral relations.[53]

Hayek does not make individuals the source or purpose of morality to this extent, although he believes that morals and morality are always a question of individual conduct, having no collective content even if collectively they create a moral system. Society simply does not "behave morally." To a greater extent than Buchanan potentially allows, however, individuals must work within accepted rules and behaviors. In an argument reminiscent of Burke, Hayek contends that the gradual development of rules "greatly reduces the extent to which the private moral judgment of any individual" can improve upon established rules.[54] Friedman hardly raises such issues, but the general tenor of his ostensibly positivist argument is consistent with this position. He too believes that rules of social intercourse do not come from God or traditional natural law but are preferred rules created and accepted through individual interaction.[55]

There is unresolved tension between Hayek and Buchanan—and between evolution and individualism—not because individual behavior cannot propel evolution, but because these authors do not allow individualism to develop beyond the point already reached by evolution. Buchanan's contractarianism contains the theoretical, if unrealized, possibility of judging the process by which rules are or were made, thereby evaluating the justice and morality of both rules and their results.[56] Hayek's emphasis on evolution of rules and morals—and the extent to which Buchanan and Friedman employ evolutionary language—undermines this possibility. Individuals are the source of values, but human nature prevents further development of common morals. In either case the *result* is the same. Intervention into socioeconomic affairs is impermissible because it violates fundamental evolved rules of justice and morality. Society must acknowledge these rules because evolution beyond them is impossible, and heeding them is natural when a truly individualistic—nonmajoritarian—contract is employed.

Thus these theorists draw no radical conclusions from seeing the individual as the source of value. Individual valuation is a variation on negative freedom. Although individuals may be the source of value, this involves neither conscience nor valuing individual purposes outside market competition. An individual is the source of value when functioning in the market in conformity to valuations and the behavior of others in the market. Morality is what rationally self-interested people do, or agree to have imposed upon them, and nothing more can be said. Individuals are not, however, the source of justification. That lies in the market, because once again the market is the standard beyond individuals which defines and embodies morality and acceptable rational self-interest.

What does economic morality include? It is largely rules that allow market competition without fraud or deception and negative freedom—staying out of one another's way. There are no positive duties, no obligations to groups, and no higher justification than avoiding jail and following long-term interest in maintaining the rules of the game. If self-interest is the only passion that can be relied upon, can we have a socially viable or politically relevant morality? Or does an emphasis on self-interest lead to and encourage only self-interest?

This question cannot be answered here. Perhaps there is no answer. Friedman tends to identify morality with independence in a market economy. The market is "a mechanism for the development and not merely the reflection of value judgments." Individual cooperation helps establish "common values."[57]

Gilder believes in the "redemptive morality of capitalism."[58] For each, most questions and choices that seemingly involve morality are decided by the market: obligation, freedom, equity, harmony, and desert.

Hayek seems to believe something more is required of morality. Given these theorists' image of psychology, however, it is difficult to see how there can be a shared morality. If one is guided by individual preference, rejects the possibility of aggregating and upgrading preferences, and denies intersubjective validation of preferences, then how can collective preferences be enforced? These authors confront a dilemma. They want traditional morality,[59] but their nominalistic psychology, definition of freedom, and economics will not allow it. Their psychology is more atomistic than classical liberalism—Adam Smith allowed a role for sympathy—ending any possibility of internalizing morality. They claim that people are independent in choosing and developing their preferences. They assert that morality is often a cloak for self-interest or for imposing upon others. As such, are cheating, lying, or insider trading wrong? Each would answer yes, but that answer is separate from their analysis. The market does not justify its own morality or answer why it is wrong to harm others if one can get away with it, and individual pursuit of self-interest, even if limited by others' pursuit of self-interest, is not morally coherent.

This does not deny that morality exists in economic relations. My claim is narrower, limited to the statement that *this* theory lacks a basis, model, or justification for wider moral behavior. Failing to link moral justification of the market to its other values, this position finds the moral value of the market in the market, but the moral value of the market must come from another value.[60] Moral questions, in the sense of prescribing behavior and choosing outcomes, disappear. There is no more room for them here than in any other natural system following its own laws. There is no higher purpose, moral end, or social cement other than allowing each person to pursue self-interest. Arguing that the conservatives make moral claims raises basic normative questions which these economists put aside. Admission of choice and morality acknowledges that people face ethical and political questions,[61] bringing up the possibility that welfare, intervention, social justice, and equalization may be legitimate. These theorists cannot accept such a possibility. The spontaneous order relieves people of personal responsibility for unpleasant side effects of their market behavior because everything is treated as an individualistic, voluntary exchange. Taking advantage of another's desperation is not immoral. People are morally responsible for only a narrow and unspecified area of personal behavior and for following system rules. By regulating behavior, the market's neutral, natural criteria legitimize distribution and determine obligations and duties. Self-interest guides us to serve others. Any attempt to introduce other considerations, such as those in the Catholic bishops' letter on the economy, runs counter to human nature and is immoral because it allows full reign to individual self-interest, enabling passions from the political market to enter economic relations.

This perspective eliminates political or public morality, because all public acts are reduced to individual motivation. Civic and social morality cannot and do not exist. Self-interest ensures that there will be neither common interest nor community beyond the self-defined self-interest of egoistic individuals.

Community and Common Interest

Individual pursuit of self-interest coupled with limited morality, justice, and social responsibility eliminates the possibility of an expansive concept of community or common interest. Though there is harmony and order in the conservative model, these are achievable only through competitive markets.

The Catholic bishops' and similar arguments assume the existence and reality of *society* as distinguishable from each individual composing it. This is not an organic concept but a claim that the community as a whole can and does have responsibility, for example, for human dignity, human rights, and the poor.[62] In traditional conservatism, as exemplified by Burke, society is a partnership in all that is good, and community represents continuity across time, in which imperceptible ties link together the innumerable levels of society. Reform liberals such as Keynes or Galbraith have a simpler image, emphasizing individuals, but their arguments for social justice and shared responsibility for outcomes indicate concern for society and common interest.

The conservative economists strongly reject this approach. They identify the economy with society. Buchanan believes that "[t]he implications" of spontaneous order "for social philosophy are straightforward". It combines freedom with order, creating society, without the need for deliberate, conscious planning or strong public direction.[63] For Buchanan and, to a lesser extent, Friedman and Hayek, individuals enter voluntary market relations, producing all the order and harmony possible given human motivation. Community is a place to live; corporate bodies reflect the self-interest of individual members, not a collective or shared identity; each person pursues self-interest; and, with few exceptions, people have limited ties. They are alone in the crowd, the mass man that more traditionally minded conservatives of the 1930s, including Jose Ortega y Gasset and Walter Lippmann, warned against.[64]

According to Hayek, society does not first exist and then create law; observing common rules creates society. The former view is an "erroneous" example of destructive "constructivist rationalism," which ignores the individualistic evolution of society and law. Whether or not people are naturally social in a classical liberal sense, order and change are possible because the "elements" (individuals) possess "capacities to follow rules"[65] developed while pursuing self-interest, which produce society. These are abstract rules that do not refer to any person, group, or outcome. They make it possible for people to peacefully pursue separate ends, especially "monetary impulses." There is not, however, a single society but a "network of voluntary relations" defining an individual's associations. Pursuit of self-interest does not isolate people, because they follow shared rules, even if they do not understand them: rules that derive ultimately from individual pursuit of self-interest but take on the character of traditional morality in defining and limiting the self-interest that is their source. Society therefore consists of individuals pursuing self-interest within a framework of rules that each individual takes as given, even while shaping those rules in conformity to the market.[66]

Friedman's society is more minimalist. It is nothing more than a "collection of individuals." Individual freedom is the primary objective of social arrangements, and anything abridging that freedom is harmful. Friedman agrees with Buchanan (despite his contractarian approach) and Hayek that society does not develop out of a mythical social contract or central direction. Ordered society is neither planned nor created but is the unintended consequence of pursuit of self-interest, evolving out of the activities of millions of people pursuing their own interests in marketlike situations.[67]

The individualistic market theory and its picture of human nature is also a theory of *community* disguised as an economic argument. Community is limited. The desire for close, supportive association is a primitive emotion having no validity in a large society. Empathy and understanding do not curb self-seeking. Communities are created by and based on voluntary exchange which produces cooperation. Consistent with the market, no one has general responsibility to others. Individuals have few duties, certainly none to look after the welfare of others. The group is simply individuals in association—whose only tie is following common, evolved rules—each pursuing self-interest. Size limits the arena in which community can command personal loyalty or ethical behavior; regions and nation-states, much less the world, are too large to encourage moral identity or behavior.[68] There are no public or common purposes, goods or values apart from individual purposes and the total of separate individual goods.

Political theory has traditionally attempted to find some common ground that could be called the *public interest* or *common good*,[69] though Buchanan's interpretation that such theories claim everyone seeks the common good is simply wrong. Common good may benefit each person not in their separate capacity but rather as a member of a community, in their shared or corporate capacity. The conservative economists reject both the possibility and legitimacy of that enterprise. Ignorance and self-interest doom attempts to identify and secure common interest. Individualism and common interest are dichotomous concepts. A separate, recognizable public interest does not exist. To claim that there is a common interest beyond the interests of distinct individuals is to claim the existence of a separate, exogenous, supravalue or supra-individual. But these theorists accept only the interests of individuals.

Wagner and Tollison, two of Buchanan's collaborators and associates, claim that "[p]ublic interest is an outcome of the pursuit of personal interest within a given institutional framework." Friedman believes that "[t]he sum of all the private goods is the public good, but the sum of what all the people *think* to be in their private good is not necessarily the public good." Efforts to deliberately promote the common interest necessarily serve only special interests. Under a free market, however, private interest creates the public interest. Buchanan asserts that the market "allows the transformation of private interest into 'public interest.'" The search for a distinct public interest, however, is equivalent to a belief in the general will, an "organic conception of society." For Hayek, social ends are the "coincidence of individual ends" and do not exist apart from them. Appeal to a common interest indicates lack of agreement.[70]

According to Buchanan, "[E]xpansion of government's role under the folly that some national interest exists" has undermined the moral order of markets. Only self-interested allegiance to market rules and the political system that polices them unites people. For Friedman, a "country is the collection of individuals who compose it." There are no national goals except the sum of "goals that the citizens severally serve"; no national purposes except "the consensus of the purposes for which the citizens severally strive."[71] Given self-interested human nature, public purposes are reducible to private self-interest in the market. Public interest and the common good do not and cannot exist apart from the individual purposes of which they are composed. Common good is nothing more than widely sought ends.

These theorists accept the logic of Kenneth Arrow's[72] limits on interpersonal utility comparisons. Starting with strong individualist assumptions, when a group of people choose by rank ordering their preferences it may be impossible to arrive at a consensus or a majority. Indeed, it is probably impossible to reach a common preference because no collective decision can satisfy everyone's preference order. For the conservative economists, individual valuation, pursuit of self-interest, and lack of common interest create incommensurable individual valuations and preferences. Social values cannot be constructed from these elements. Thus government has no role in meeting or fulfilling such fictitious collective preferences, or individual preferences that may clash with the market—the real preference-satisfying mechanism. Given this situation, the ideal polity must work toward achieving unanimity. Happily, the market already functions to create unanimous agreement.[73]

It is not quite accurate, however, to say that no common good, common interest, or national interest exist. Rather, they exist in a special way—in conjunction with and in the market. This argument incorporates a hidden picture of *real* private good, weakening the claim that individuals are the source of value. Private good does not mean doing anything that will advance one's self, if that implies hostility to the market. Private, and therefore public, good is contained in and must be advanced through the market. To the extent that there is a common good, it is satisfied by maintaining spontaneous order: the procedures for pursuit of individual interest. Common good requires maintaining property and the conservative market system, regardless of harm to particular individuals or groups.

This world view eliminates higher purposes, moral ends, and the moral cement holding society together.[74] Morality and justice do not set goals and boundaries for proper conduct but are defined and limited by self-interested human nature. Indeed, there is nothing to check self-interest except others' pursuit of self-interest in a virtual war of each against all.[75] The age-old question of the nature of the just society is answered obliquely, as competitive individualism—as each person defining his or her own good in conformity with the market. Wider public order is relegated to a supportive backdrop. Indeed, a picture of public order hardly exists.

Buchanan, Friedman, and Hayek employ several justifications in reaching these conclusions. Though claiming to be based on scientific and empirical theory, they offer a combination of naturalist philosophy and claims based on evolution, contracts, utility, and positivism, with little attempt made to sort out or reconcile inconsistencies. Each author rejects any appeal to transcendent standards, and except to the extent that rights may be the same as negative freedom, this is not a rights-based claim. In appealing to their common version of human nature, each offers a naturalistic argument. In addition, Hayek constructs a hypothetical evolution, one that Buchanan and Friedman accept. Buchanan adds the possibility of social contract. Friedman emphasizes what he believes are conclusions from positive science. Each author criticizes utilitarianism but makes utilitarian claims that the market is the primary means to achieve human ends and freedom. Though employing sometimes incompatible justifications, each reaches the same political-social conclusions—justice, morality, and community result from relations among self-seeking individuals, and intervention in market relations is inefficient and immoral.

The social context and impact of economic relations is missing from this model. Social and political dislocations and other consequences of economic activities are discounted for the present and the future. These theorists ignore Frank Knight's warning that trustworthiness and a sense of responsibility for others are necessary to the functioning of society.[76] They will not recognize

Robert Heilbroner's point that economic relations are also "a social act."[77] They refuse to see interconnections between behavior that cannot be captured by individuals in the market because all moral and social connections dissolve there. People must accept their fate with slight expectation of help from others. If people are individualistic, self-interested, and have only contractual, market ties, then society is a congregation of local interests—a conglomeration producing a limited-liability corporation, not a nation. If so, many people are excluded from full participation in both polity and economy. Those who have little to offer in the market are lesser members of the community, set apart from full membership. Their nonmarket needs and demands must be ignored. Without civic or public virtue to guide them, with only each individual's small stock of private virtue, winners and losers have little stake in the system and less reason not to pursue their own image of self-interest.

Human nature, the market, freedom, justice, and the nature of community and common interest set limits to the scope and duties of government. They determine that active, interventionist government is both impossible and dangerous. We turn now to the conservatives' image of government.

Chapter Seven

Conservative Economists' Theory of Government

In this present crisis, government is not the solution to our problem. Government is the problem.
—Ronald Reagan, First Inaugural Address, 1981.

[M]an is by nature a political animal.
—Aristotle, *Politics,* bk. 1, chap. 2.

It is a political truism that conservative economists want limited government, but it is not clear what that means. Upon what is their argument based? Why should government be limited and to what extent? What may government legitimately do and why? How do these economists propose to limit modern governments and what follows from their limits?

The conservative theory of government is based on the assumptions examined previously. Two are of crucial importance: the conservatives' picture of human motivation and their distinction between economic and political markets. In the first instance, these theorists portray individuals as utility maximizers who cooperate solely for self-interest in marketlike situations. Pursuit of self-interest in the market produces spontaneous order. In the second assumption, the economists create ideal types of political and economic relations and then employ them to explain and criticize reality. The economic and political markets are mirror images in which market good is reversed into political harm. The spontaneous economic market compensates for human limitations by controlling and channeling self-centered impulses and correcting for limited knowledge and ability. Politics is dominated by the political market, where the invisible hand of self-interest leads to coercive conflict, dominance, and conformity. Political pursuit of self-interest is harmful because there are neither spontaneous limits to potential abuses of power nor systematic checks on self-interest. Vote buying, manipulation, and lack of fiscal restraint create "inherent and fundamental biases" for intrusive intervention which undermines natural economic processes and stability. Governments "are collectivities of utility maximizers" whose freedom from market control permits self-interest to become exploitive, creating an inherent "propensity to truck, barter and exchange" at the expense of the public good. This generates constant growth in public services, so that western political institutions "threaten to destroy the market economy."[1]

These starting, metaphysical-like assumptions provide the basis for good order and restrict the proper scope and content of political and governmental activity. They create the requirements for politics and government, shape essential government duties, and determine what governments may and should do. They ensure that very little political or governmental activity will be legitimate beyond a narrow range of activities that support the economic market and correspond to the conservative economic view.

A Theory of Government Failure

The conservative model of government is based upon a theory of government failure and private, market efficiency. As in the classical liberal distinction between society and government, the value of government is drastically reduced when people have a natural, spontaneously generated virtue–here the market–which tends to produce order.

This position must be stated unequivocally. The conservative economists are not claiming that government *may* fail. Rather, government *must* fail. The certainty of failure is infinitely more important than the remote possibility of success. These authors mistrust both the competence and motives of government. They are in complete agreement that government is inefficient, ignorant, coercive, and driven by selfish passions that necessitate inevitable government failure in any attempt to intervene in socioeconomic affairs, harming freedom in the process. Government failure is always more common and destructive than market failure. The market is inherently stable and self-equilibrating. It needs no intervention, and if it did, governments are incapable of providing it.[2] Even when performing acceptable duties, governments are less successful and efficient than private business performing the same activity. This is not a hypothesis advanced for discussion, but an unassailable, a priori truism, based largely upon anecdotal evidence and definitional presuppositions, uttered with certitude akin to a religious fundamentalist's belief in God or a Marxist's conviction in the dialectic. This act of faith provides a powerful explanatory paradigm for rejecting all socioeconomic intervention and drastically limiting the scope of legitimate government activities. The government-failure theory makes four claims: All behavior is self-interested; when free from market checks, self-interested behavior inevitably becomes corrupted; intervention undermines the market; and intervention harms freedom. There are no circumstances under which expansive government can succeed.[3]

To the conservative economists, government must fail because human passion is uncontrollable in politics. Unchecked pursuit of self-interest undermines natural market relations and human freedom, which is ultimately dependent upon the conservative market. Without carefully examining the meaning and manifestation of self-interest, these authors make it the key to government failure. For them, it is inconceivable that public policy can serve anything other than narrow self-interest. If everything follows from individually defined valuations of self-interest, then all intervention must serve self-interest. Thus government cannot achieve publicly stated ends and mythic common interest because it will be subverted to serve the individual self-interest of those running a program.

In this image of political behavior, nothing is done for the public interest because it does not exist in a politically or socially significant sense. To Hayek, "*Government* cannot *act in the general interest.*" Government, for Friedman, is "literally uncontrollable . . . feeding on itself–and us–and getting larger and larger like some enormous tumor." Without explaining what these emotive terms mean, or suggesting empirical and/or comparative evidence of actual behavior, government is simply "excessive" or, in Gilder's argument, "overweening" or, in Buchanan's frequently repeated term "bloated."[4]

Echoing their criticism of democracy, the economic conservatives assert that legislative decision making is always "characterized by a short-term horizon."[5] Popular governments are incapable of long-term thinking or planning but always serve the immediate interest of acquiring and holding power. Without competitive market control, there is no independent test of efficiency, guaranteeing egotistic pursuit of self-interest accompanied by coercive, inefficient, and often corrupt use of resources. Even if people intended to do good, fragmented power, the need for bureaucracy, the large size of government, and concentrated interest groups guarantee the failure of altruistic purposes. Stated colloquially by Friedman and more elegantly by Buchanan, without market controls and cost allocations to identifiable individuals, bureaucratic use of someone else's money ensures that it is wasted. The ostensible purpose of public programs is always subverted to serve the interests of those initiating or administering the program, while taxpayers and supposed beneficiaries at best receive no real benefits and in most cases lose freedom, dignity, and the chance to participate in competitive markets.[6]

The chief conservative indictment of government is that intervention interferes with the operation of the spontaneous market. Conditions in the market are the best that can be because individual self-interest impels people to make the most efficient possible use of resources to further their self-interest. Intervention cannot improve people's lives. Though government may rob some to reward its supporters, redistribution and intervention are harmful and inefficient. In all cases, intervention destroys the freedom to use one's property as one chooses, decreases work effort, and destroys resources.

Government is always the problem, rarely if ever a solution. Intervention explains why the market does not operate according to market theory and why the ideal market system does not yet exist. Uncomprehending people demand intervention, which worsens the situation. Failure perpetuates the abusive cycle, as government-induced market failure sparks demands for still more intervention. In all but the simplest cases, government is always the enemy, always serving special interests, always crippling the spontaneous forces which sustain the market and freedom. To Hayek, any interference in a spontaneous order impedes the operation of that order. In a simultaneously empirical and moral claim, he states that intervention must create disorder and be unjust, removing some grievances by causing new ones elsewhere. Buchanan believes that fine tuning the economy or relations within it is impossible. Public policy is incapable of adjusting for differences between people. The market does not require it, and government cannot make such adjustments. The reason, says Friedman, is because public policy forces identical services onto everyone, which is unjust. And services cannot be different because that is also unjust. Hayek believes that giving public officials discretionary power to attempt adjustments between persons subverts the rule of law, freedom, the constitutional order, and the spontaneous economic forces that sustain them.[7]

Friedman addresses this specific issue more than the others. Once a problem is defined or discovered, government is induced to address it; inevitably the problem grows worse, which is the fault of the government's intervention. The logic is irrefutable, even if the empirical connection is asserted rather than investigated, as in his claim that the quality of education in the United States has deteriorated because of increased federal spending. Whether discussing schools, consumer protection, inflation, labor unions, unemployment, monetary policy, or welfare policy, public intervention has worsened problems by providing resources for self-interested individuals to seek their interests unimpeded by market limits. In each case, taxpayers and the supposed beneficiaries of these programs would be better off—in some ultimate, undefined sense—if the public programs created to address these problems had not existed. Beyond the limited duties noted below, Friedman sees no benefits from government spending. Though he concedes that there are occasional market failures, most instability is caused by government, resulting in more harm than if government had not intervened. Even inflation is a government phenomenon. "The real obstacles to ending inflation are political, not economic."[8] In contrast to liberals such as Keynes and Galbraith, Friedman, Buchanan, and Hayek agree that the Great Depression was caused by government failure, not by any intrinsic propensity or problem in spontaneous market forces, and efforts to deal with it compounded and deepened the crisis.[9]

The certainty of harmful government failure is a commonplace among other conservative economic theorists. George Gilder, Ludwig von Mises, David Stockman, and William Simon all assert that government inevitably forces a decline in economic progress. It cannot increase aggregate demand, positively aid the private sector, successfully intervene into socioeconomic relations, or permanently increase employment, and it is always at fault when the market falters or economic problems develop. In each case, public intervention is not the answer to problems but the cause of worse ones.[10]

Each author agrees that the inevitable failure of government means that Keynesian efforts to stimulate aggregate demand and promote employment are bad economics and worse policy advice, necessarily causing more severe problems than they attempt to address. Intervention is harmful not only to the economy but also to government, robbing it of the resources and time required to perform its legitimate functions. Thus these theorists would have no problem in rejecting calls for government aid in, for example, development of high-resolution television: Government is inefficient and must fail; all intervention promotes individual self-interest; all interests are private and only individuals have interests, therefore promoting an industry cannot be in the public interest; and if a profit is to be made, private industry will make the necessary investment. Hayek concludes that with such policies, "decent government is impossible."[11]

The damages from inevitable government failure are compounded by the crippling impact on the spontaneous forces that sustain freedom. Intervention is the cause of authoritarian government and is inevitably unjust. If, as Buchanan claims, "abject slavery" is the "pure form" of political relations while economic relations are free and cooperative, then government must always endanger freedom while "markets tend to maximize freedom." For Friedman, taxes, such bureaucracies as the Securities and Exchange Commission, National Endowment for the Humanities, or the National Science Foundation, and the power to intervene in business are destructive of freedom. Hayek believes that government may be unjust, but not spontaneous order.[12] Government's inability to do anything positive to aid freedom reinforces the conservatives' empirical-like claim of inevitable government failure.

Intervention, regulation, and welfare are distinct policy areas, but if government must fail, all are impossible. Welfare illustrates this argument. Welfare is a broad concept for the conservative economists. It extends beyond aid to families with dependent children or income support to include unemployment compensation, social security programs, all transfer payments, education subsidies, farm price-supports, and any program where people – "special interests" –

receive aid or services outside a market framework. Limited provision for those who fail or are incompetent is acceptable, but welfare must be kept to a minimum. Why? Because *any* transfer payment violates freedom and individualism. Self-interest and natural economic relations do not allow extensive aid. Political and economic freedom and equality are not enhanced by welfare, which is viewed as morally,[13] politically, and economically destructive.

Welfare supposedly promotes the behavior it attempts to eliminate–dependence–because it is in the self-interest of recipients to not work, of politicians to buy votes by providing welfare, and of bureaucrats to expand the welfare budget. The conservatives believe that in a free market, most welfare measures, especially income support such as unemployment compensation, would be unnecessary. Moreover, Friedman asserts that welfare programs undermine the ability of the United States to finance defense and that "[t]he traditional functions of government have been starved by the rapacious appetite of the welfare state." He sees the Soviet Union as a lesser threat to the United States; "[t]he real threat is the welfare state." Friedman and Hayek agree (though Buchanan disagrees) that welfare spending is another guise for collectivism and socialism, destroys initiative, and forces people into identical molds. It causes "loss of self-government and freedom. . . . financial crisis leads to a loss of self-government."[14]

A major conservative economic attack on welfare, if it can be separated from the political emphasis on freedom, is that social welfare programs are obstacles to equality because they sabotage efficient labor markets and freeze people into inferior status by discouraging initiative. The argument is true by definition. If economic self-interest motivates people, welfare payments discourage work. In a market free of minimum wages and income support, everyone could find a job; there could be no involuntary unemployment. Poverty is caused by personal failure–unwillingness to work and compete–that is compounded by welfare. As with the nineteenth-century liberal Malthus, the greatest kindness is to force people to work, not to give them aid. That is why Gilder attacks the welfare system and argues that "the current poor . . . are refusing to work hard." If they did work hard–and to overcome their poverty, they must work harder than other groups–they would not be poor.[15] "The actual outcome of almost all programs that are sold in the name of helping the poor . . . is to make the poor worse off."[16] Thus intervention creates conditions that cause more demands for welfare.

In proclaiming one law for all and no special categories of people, the conservatives state that public policy should treat everyone alike and ignore individual differences. Individualism and equal treatment by the law preclude welfare. What can be done? A minimum income floor is acceptable, but charity is superior because it is private, voluntary, local, and discriminatory and reduces the need for coercive public involvement.[17] (By definition, anything that is voluntary is free and does not involve coercion.) To claim that welfare is a right subordinates individuals to the group, but the group is simply the sum of individuals, each pursuing his or her own interest. Welfare thus subordinates individuals to the purposes of other individuals. People have very different preferences, and community membership creates no obligation to maintain the poor. Therefore, no one can have an obligation to another unless it is freely accepted.[18]

Friedman proposes a negative income tax as a "transitional" program until welfare and the social security system can be eliminated entirely. This proposal would replace most welfare programs with a direct cash grant. After determining minimum incomes necessary for a family, those who fell below this level would be subsidized for up to 50 percent of the calculated minimum. Thus, if a family had no income, they would receive half of the minimum, with the difference presumably coming from charity. The program would not reduce payments on a dollar-for-dollar basis with earnings until the combined total of earnings and negative income tax equaled the minimum income. This proposal is acceptable to Friedman because it involves less intervention into the market, would be administered by the Internal Revenue Service (reducing the need for bureaucracy) and encourages individual responsibility.[19]

The conservative argument leads to an inescapable conclusion that if welfare, regulation, and intervention must fail, socialism of *any* type is absolutely unworkable and undesirable. Again, the reasons focus on government failure, ignorance, and freedom. Goods and services cannot be allocated on any rational, planning basis. Human nature makes socialism unattainable. According to Buchanan, Marxism's greatest shortcoming is "its failure to construct its analysis within an individualistic frame of reference." If it had, neither Marx nor socialists could have believed that people who are individual "rational utility maximizers" could "behave so as to further the interests" of their class. Inevitable pursuit of self-interest always overwhelms collective decisions, bending them to the interests of individuals and dooming planning, central control, and presumably cooperation.[20]

Hayek goes further. Planning, mixed systems, and the welfare state inevitably lead first to socialism and then totalitarianism. High ideals do not guide behavior. There is a stark choice: capitalism and limited democracy, or the welfare state and eventual totalitarianism. As with Friedman's invisible hand of self-interest that always produces harm in politics, efforts to shape the future according to "high ideals" "unwittingly" and relentlessly yield "the very opposite of what we have been striving for." Both self-interest and human ignorance make successful planning impossible. Planners serve their own interests and can never know enough. Human ability is too limited to make production and distribution decisions without the autonomous market. Thus socialism is impossible and represents a return to "primordial instincts." Socialism violates freedom, the rule of law, and treats people not according to their worth as determined in the "self-forming" impersonal market but according to unachievable abstract concepts of merit and morality.[21]

This is a common theme. Gilder believes that socialism is morally bankrupt, static, and dead. Capitalism is morally superior, the only creative system and the only form of organization providing the drive to grow and change. Human ignorance and the need to strive for "initiative, sympathy, discovery, and love"– in the economy–prove that socialism cannot fit the human condition, that it is forever a fond dream denying the best in humanity for a faulty insurance against risk and life.[22] Von Mises insists that we must choose between private and communal ownership, but that given human drives and the need for freedom, socialism is impossible. It is a scientific "fact" that conservative capitalism and its requisite, a limited political system, are the only possible form of social organization.[23] Friedman sees "an intimate connection between politics and economics," such that all combinations of political and economic systems are not possible. Specifically, democracy is inseparable from capitalism. Extensive control of economic activities–"detailed central economic planning"–puts "ordinary citizens . . . in political fetters," produces "a low standard of living," and ensures that people "have little power to control their own destiny."[24] In all cases, the political system is absolutely incapable of managing or successfully intervening in natural market relations.

The Role of Government

Given the political market and human nature as negative limitations and the economic market's positive role in rewarding and organizing people, there is little that government can or should do. If the market is the premier harmonizing mechanism, government should be reduced to the minimum necessary to support the market. The conservative economists propose an automatic political system parallel to their automatic economic system, one without discretion, intervention, or extensive public choice. The market furnishes the unquestionable criteria to determine if "the intended results" of a policy "are ones that it is proper for government to seek and, further, whether the action will in fact achieve these results." The market "defines the role that government should play in a free society."[25]

Adam Smith provides the historical base for the conservative position, though their argument is closer to those of Malthus,[26] William Graham Sumner, and Herbert Spencer. Smith believed that the duties of government depended on the state of economic development, and he did not advocate uncompromising laissez-faire. A primitive level of development required smaller expenditures for defense, a legal system, public works, and education than a more developed society. Though this opened the prospect for more extensive government as societies industrialized, Smith did not project his observation into the future, and subsequent laissez-faire writers have ignored this possibility.

On the surface, the duties of government were quite simple and

> plain and intelligible to common understandings: first, the duty of protecting the society from the violence and invasion of other independent societies; secondly, the duty of protecting, as far as possible, every member of the society from the injustice or oppression of every other member of it, or the duty of establishing an exact administration of justice; and thirdly, the duty of erecting and maintaining certain public works and certain public institutions.

Government was, therefore, instrumental. It had no grand goal or purpose. Government's primary duty was to facilitate market relations but not to interfere in exchanges with any preference or restraint when individuals were competent to advance their own interests. Defense and justice were valuable to all members, though some of the expenses of justice could be borne by litigants. Smith viewed a limited number of public works as legitimate, that is, those advantageous to the whole society but unprofitable for any individual or group to undertake. This duty of government depended heavily on the state of development—as did the next duty, education. Some public support for education was essential, especially for the lower orders in a modern society. Specialization and the division of labor could cripple people intellectually. "A man without the proper use of the intellectual facilities . . . seems to be mutilated and deformed." Requirement of minimal educational attainments and even some public provision of educational opportunities could go far toward addressing the stultifying nature of a modern economy and the rebelliousness of the lower classes unaware of the real source of their problems.[27] In this argument, Smith set a pattern for later claims that governments fulfill their primary duties by protecting property and enforcing basic rules, regardless of who gets what.

The conservative economists accept Smith's policies, if not his observation that the role of government varies with the level of the social economy. Government has little or nothing to do with responding to popular demands, pressures, or wants. Popular will is neither the measure nor the source of governmental duties. There is nothing in the conservative model to indicate that government is natural to people, as suggested by Aristotle or Aquinas; or that it is a punishment and corrective for sin, as in Augustine or Martin Luther;

or that it is necessary to curb our worst impulses, as in traditional conservatism—indeed, it magnifies them. Government cannot make society better, and there is none of Smith's implication that government may successfully achieve important things. Nor is there the liberal economists' role for government as a corrective to market failures or a counterweight to private power. Beyond reasserting Smith's policies, the conservatives, despite their vehement denunciations to the contrary, have not clearly thought out the role of government. Moreover, they add propositions that Smith did not imagine. Where he saw a *tendency* toward harmony through pursuit of self-interest, they see spontaneous order as established fact. Where he saw problems, they see absolutes: Government must fail, intervention always harms freedom, and the market is always more efficient.

The logical question for the conservatives is, why have government at all? Why not accept a fully libertarian or even anarchist position? Their answer is that although the market is the primary organizing institution, it cannot do everything. For von Mises, "Human society cannot do without the apparatus of the state, but the whole of mankind's progress has had to be achieved against the resistance and opposition of the state and its power of coercion." Hayek believes that government should render a narrow range of services which the spontaneous order cannot produce "adequately." Though it is "conceivable that the spontaneous order . . . may exist without government," there are insufficient guarantees that people will observe the rules; therefore, "in most circumstances the organization we call government becomes indispensable in order to assure that those rules are obeyed." However, this does not give government an exalted position. Its role "is somewhat like that of a maintenance squad in a factory"—to oil machinery and clean the floor but not to produce anything, determine what is produced, or intervene in running the productive apparatus.[28]

It follows that all intervention is not harmful, or at least some intervention is more beneficial than harmful, though how the need for government outweighs its inherent inefficiency is never discussed. The frequently used, emotive word "interference" implies a standard for proper public involvement, a clear demarcation of what is private from what is public. Some intervention is at least useful, and as with all utilitarian or quasi-utilitarian claims, the scope of exceptions to the primary rule—here, no intervention—should be decided by empirical analysis and not by a priori reasoning. Surely, if government is as bad as asserted, these theorists should be willing to give up some market efficiency to have less government. Private police forces and private court systems are conceivable, if the market lives up to its reputation for efficiency. Buried in a tangle of inconsistencies, exceptions to the rule of nonintervention are stated rather than justified. Government's role turns out to be the same as its traditional role among such late nineteenth-century theorists as Sumner: It provides the coercive apparatus to support the market, making the market into the natural standard by which to judge government.

Every normative political theory contains arguments for the proper role and structure of government. Conservative economic theory also spells out the purpose of government: to protect the spontaneous order from coercion and fraud. Government may do those presumably neutral things which narrowly support the abstract market. It may act where individual self-interests coincide, such as with road building, but may not attempt to forge a common interest. It can do nothing positive or anything that benefits specific persons. Government duties are simple: Get out of the way of the market; protect people from crime; dispense justice; maintain national defense; enforce private contracts; and provide limited support for public works, public welfare, and education—all things that individuals and voluntary groups cannot easily do by themselves. None of these elements has any other purpose than to ensure a framework within which individuals may attempt to pursue their self-interest through competition in the market.

Von Mises epitomizes an extreme form of this position. Government's primary duty is "the protection not only of private property, but also of peace," because "the task of the state consists solely and exclusively in guaranteeing the protection of life, health, liberty, and private property against violent attacks. Everything that goes beyond this," such as unemployment compensation or regulation of alcohol and drugs, "is an evil," in that it is inefficient, harmful to freedom, and, in attempting to protect people from themselves, treats them as incompetent.[29]

Hayek potentially allows government a wider range of responsibilities but in practice restricts legitimate public activity. As with Friedman, Buchanan, and others, his primary presumption is against government involvement in socioeconomic relations, with the overwhelming burden of proof placed on those who favor action. Hayek claims that the important issue is not what government does but how and how much it acts. An inactive but clumsy government would be a disaster while an active one that remained within its appropriate sphere might be legitimate and useful. He distinguishes between coercive functions, which include any activity that is enforced by the law, and service functions, where government administers "resources placed at its disposal" merely as one among competing organizations serving the market. Coercive functions, which include all taxation, must be kept to the absolute minimum, while service functions may expand if there is widespread demand and if government makes no attempt to become an exclusive supplier or to use tax money to provide those services. Exceedingly vague about the specific content of service functions, Hayek does not develop this possibility.[30]

Hayek distinguishes the state (the created realm of coercion) and society (spontaneous organization). The primary duty of government is to support the right of individual decision making within the market but not to intervene. The state, as one among many organizations, should "provide an effective external framework within which self-generating orders can form." "[M]aintenance of a spontaneous order . . . is the prime condition of the general welfare." Monumental ignorance prevents anything else. Government has no right or ability to attempt to plan for the entire economy, aid specific persons, control prices, limit who can enter a profession, determine the content of normal contracts, or redistribute resources. Such intervention puts human will in place of spontaneous economic relations, makes one person directly subject to another, is inefficient, and attacks freedom. What can government do? Only those activities that promote spontaneous forces: Protect people against force and fraud; enforce laws equally, including antipollution regulations and pure food laws; maintain roads; and provide services the market cannot easily furnish— such as weights and measures, building regulations, limited public works, some enterprises on the same terms as private citizens, education for the young, minimal welfare for the incompetent, and defense. Government issuance and regulation of money may not be required. In all cases, local taxation and decentralized government are preferable to national government, and private provision of services is superior to public provision.[31]

With the possible exception of limited public enterprises that would compete on the same basis as private enterprises and a preference for private monetary systems, there is little or nothing in Hayek's discussion with which Friedman or Buchanan disagree. Friedman also sees government as providing support for the market. Its primary duty is that of "Rule-Maker and Umpire"—something the market cannot do for itself—though the range of rules is narrow, supplementing and modifying custom and tradition. Government is to facilitate "voluntary exchanges," not any specific exchange. Government may do the same things that Hayek allows plus provide a stable monetary system. Indeed, that is its most important activity. Governments may also regulate to overcome the worst effects of "technical monopolies" and spillover or "neighborhood effects," but this power must be as circumscribed as possible. In *Free to Choose*, Friedman accepts government provision of a small number of public works, associating this with protection from neighborhood effects, but states that this "raises the most troublesome issues" of Smith's government duties. Friedman is quick to assert that this duty does not justify very much intervention because of the greater likelihood that government, not the market, will fail. He seems to assume that all harms can be compensated for and that compensation is less detrimental to freedom and the market than prevention. This argument supposes that only individuals can be harmed and that harm must be specific and readily identifiable, not a long-run statistical probability. If the market cannot identify those who pollute and compensate those who are harmed, government is even less likely to do so. As is usual whenever he concedes a role for government, Friedman trivializes it with a simplistic example to illustrate neighborhood effects or market failures needing regulation. His primary example of air pollution is a dirty "shirt collar." Such an innocent example misrepresents the health and environmental dangers of pollution, reducing the regulatory need to unimportance. Coupled with reiterations about government failure—government will make matters worse and impose "costs on innocent third parties"—such marginal concessions ensure that little will be done to regulate the market. As always, the overwhelming burden of proof must be on proponents of regulation, and given the incompetence of governments and the superiority of markets, there is little chance that a case for regulation will be made.[32]

If Friedman regards the provision of public works and regulation as the greatest problem in Smith's government duties,[33] perhaps he should have considered defense more closely. These authors see defense spending as a simple issue. It is not. If their picture of self-interest, human nature, and government operation has any validity, they should be deeply worried about defense spending. It is government spending, allocates a large part of the gross national product, and presumably should present the same problems of government inefficiency, danger to freedom, and failure as every other intervention. Government spending on defense arguably causes more distortion of private markets and has greater direct economic impact than any other government activity. In the United States, it consumes approximately 6.5 percent of the GNP. Because it involves direct public purchases of goods and services, rather than redistribution which allows beneficiaries to buy in the market, it entails authoritative public control—a virtual command as opposed to a market economy—over what will be produced and by whom. The decision to build a major new weapons system not only determines the fate of specific companies but also draws large amounts of resources, including capital, labor, and engineering skill, to an activity that is usually outside market control. In addition, defense spending is under the administrative discretion and direction of those much-maligned bureaucrats whose self-interest, according to conservative theory, impels them to serve interest-group clients, such as labor unions, corporations, military factions, and politicians, in place of the hardly existent national interest. Growing scandals and indictments in 1988–89 over defense procurement, bribery, illegal trading of information between defense contractors, cost overruns, and systems that do not work properly indicate the magnitude of the conservative oversight.

Defense spending, therefore, should be highly distressing for the conservative vision of market and government. It represents the ultimate form of coercion; consumes large amounts of resources; requires regulation of and intervention into the economy; is a major source of bureaucratic and government growth;[34] is filled with special interests cloaking themselves in an image of the national interest; may undermine freedom in the demand for conformity when confronted with perceived foreign threats;[35] and increases government power, especially the power of control and surveillance. Unfortunately, the analysis these authors apply to welfare spending or regulation of air pollution is never applied to the much larger area of defense spending. On the positive side, defense spending may stimulate an economy, as with Britain during the Napoleonic Wars or the United States during World War II, but this too does not fit the conservative world view and remains unexplored. Hayek, as did Smith, admits that *war*–which is very different from our current permanent war footing–is the great exception to laissez-faire, but he makes no attempt to analyze defense's impact on his political economy.[36]

Only Friedman discusses defense, and his sole concern is that public provision of defense is more costly than if it could be provided by the free market. According to Friedman, defense spending is not the chief cause of high taxes and deficits. As if it were somehow exempt from having an adverse impact, he makes no attempt to explain why defense spending is less harmful than other public expenditures or why it is unnecessary to worry about its economic impact. He overlooks the possibility that defense bureaucracies and related "private" businesses have a vested interest in expanding weapons systems and military spending, exaggerating threats, or perpetuating tension. Friedman accepts defense claims without subjecting them to even the simplest cost-benefit analysis. As if priority claims either excluded other claims or are self-explanatory, he believes that "defense must take priority over every other function of government" and that it is welfare spending, not the Soviet Union, that is "the real threat to our national security." Friedman would drastically reduce other spending to increase defense–a political decision having no economic justification in his model–and regrets that the private market cannot provide defense, though he does not explore any market organization of defense.[37] Surely, if the market promotes the values these theorists claim, they should be willing to sacrifice some military security for its advantages. They strive to limit the power of government, but they leave its greatest coercive power untouched and unchecked. This failure to address the criteria that presumably distinguish defense spending from other public spending undermines conservative claims about government inefficiency.

Given the generalities that these authors employ and their collective failure to specify concrete examples of legitimate public spending, their description of limited government duties sounds convincing to people raised in the liberal faith. That is one source of their attraction. These limiting and radical proposals are wrapped in platitudes and the commonplace of classical liberalism – without its expansiveness and concern for actualizing liberties – and repeated until they become a truth rather than propositions to be examined. It is only when one looks at actual people and the lack of concern for the losers from conservative policy that the full implications of their position become apparent. Instead of reviewing specific policy proposals, my discussion turns to *how* the conservatives would limit what governments may do. The conservatives intend to make impossible any repeat of the Great Society. They will do this in two closely related ways: by expanding the role of the market, and by stripping government of the resources and ability that allow it to respond to popular demands for welfare, regulation, and intervention.

Prescriptions: The Market as a Substitute for and Limit on Politics and Government

The conservative economists claim that the market is superior to politics and government. The free market is order producing, noncoercive, in accord with human nature, more efficient than government, and less likely to fail than public policy. This assertion has the status of metaphysical truth. The market must be more efficient because, by definition, government cannot test any of its proposals and is not subject to market discipline or limits on self-interest. Governments do nothing creative, neither producing material goods, positively assisting in their creation, nor evolving new arrangements and compromises that develop collective and individual welfare.

The conservative economists offer their market as the substitute for a wide range of current government activities. The market renders three services: It supports freedom, requires limited government, and provides countervailing power to that of government. The market does this by performing functions frequently given to government by people who do not understand their real interest or government's limited ability. It also defines what problems require government intervention (and few or no economic issues qualify) and legitimate policies to address those few problems susceptible to intervention, as well as policies on wider political-social issues. By taking over these tasks, the market can drastically reduce the area of politics and coercive conflict over distribution. Government failure does not doom western civilization. The free market can save it, but we must modify popular behavior and reduce expectations. For conservative economists, the market is omnifunctional. They push the market's frontier far into politics and public concerns. Not only does it explain all behavior, as with the political market, it can solve most public issues that require a solution.

Because government failure is the cause of most intervention demands, its failure and market efficiency encourage market expansion. Only the market can direct, limit, and control greed and self-interest,[38] producing cooperation. Expanding on Adam Smith, Buchanan's market is "a perfectible social organization" that channels self-interest to serve others. To Ryan Amacher, markets allow society to "minimize the need for 'good action' to solve social problems." For Friedman, unavoidable greed does less harm and more good under capitalism than in any other system.[39]

Whereas political scientists such as Charles Lindblom, Robert Dahl, and Benjamin Barber[40] see the removal of economic issues from public debate as weakening democracy, economists such as Dan Usher claim that this has positive advantages. Usher contends that popular governments need a nonpolitical system of equity, such as the market, to save democracy from the politically destructive and impossible task of assigning income. Political systems cannot determine incomes because that supposedly makes every issue subject to majoritarian decision making. The resulting conflict and tension destroy peace, stability, democracy, and the consensus upon which society depends.[41]

The conservatives expand upon Usher's argument, going far beyond economists' traditional view that the economy promotes peaceful conflict resolution among families and firms.[42] Market and government are irreconcilable organizing principles.[43] The conservative market has a specifically political function in depoliticizing socioeconomic struggle. The conservatives do not annihilate politics but turn numerous public decisions[44] over to the market, taking them off the agenda of public debate. The market replaces government in many areas and limits it in others. It can order a broader range of human relations than are assigned to it in most existing systems. Reducing the amount and extent of resources allocated by government and relying on the market to solve social and distribution issues decreases divisive conflict and inefficiency and fosters individual freedom.

The market accomplishes this in a seemingly automatic manner, distributing desired goods nonpolitically while avoiding face-to-face confrontation. Buchanan claims that it is perverse to argue for extension of democratic decision making to "previously non-politicized areas," presumably the market, because that will enhance "interpersonal and intergroup conflict." For him, "the principle of spontaneous coordination suggests" that the economy can peacefully reconcile separate interests, drastically reducing the scope of government. Hayek agrees. To even remotely replace "the ordering function of the market," governments "would have to co-ordinate the whole economy . . . from a single central authority." This would require arbitrary judgments in place of impersonal markets. One intervention must lead to another, and another, ending in chaos.[45]

Friedman is very specific. The market limits government by transmitting information, providing incentives, and distributing incomes, thereby lessening "greatly the range of issues that must be decided through political means." It diminishes conformity and concentrations of power by "reducing the area over which political power is exercised" and provides a counterweight to political power. By eliminating and distributing power, the market acts as "a system of checks and balances" upon government that decreases the amount of coercive power in society. "It enables economic strength to be a check to political power rather than a reinforcement." He does not explain to whom private power is responsible if it can check popularly elected government.[46]

Politics is again seen in zero-sum terms. Unlike the theories of Aristotle, Thomas Jefferson, and John Stuart Mill, political participation does not enlarge capacities and perspectives, encouraging understanding and the shared bonds and moral sensibilities that unite a nation. Political participation has no educational, citizenship-creating role. Politics means plunder, coercion, and conflict over basic values because it imposes uniformity upon people. Winners and losers must accept the same policies, regardless of preferences. As Friedman claims, "The use of political channels, while inevitable, tends to strain [never enhance] the social cohesion essential for a stable society." Instability is increased in proportion to the "range of issues for which explicit agreement is sought" and decreased when the political system makes few specific distribution decisions. Because the market requires much less agreement and is by definition voluntary, it "reduces the strain on the social fabric" by allowing people to fulfill their separate preferences, reducing conformity and conflict over conformity. The market relieves government from making decisions which no minority is willing to grant to a temporary majority, while these minorities are protected in and by the impersonal market. The choice is simple. Either limited government through the market or civil war.[47] That the market is not subject to direct popular control becomes a point in its favor.

Privatization – private sector provision of public services, including garbage collection, staffing airport control towers, running prisions, and the sale of such public assets as Amtrak, Conrail, parts of the National Weather Service, the loan program of the Rural Electrification Administration, public lands, parks, and naval petroleum reserves (or, in Britain, British Airways and British Petroleum) – is an answer that the conservative economists strongly favor. By definition it is better because the alternative is impossible and undesirable. Though this widespread proposal has had mixed results,[48] privatization simultaneously fills three desiderata: It expands the market; it shifts emphasis from public to private purposes; and it reduces the size of government by stripping it of the resources that allow regulation and intervention. In each case this putatively expands freedom while limiting the destructive aspects of the pursuit of self-interest.

Hayek argues that while government may provide a wide range of services, we must always look for alternatives to public provision. He quotes Richard C. Cornuelle: The market could produce jobs for everyone, end poverty, eliminate juvenile delinquency, replace numerous government regulations, take over the entire research effort, eliminate air and water pollution, provide efficient education to everyone, and end segregation. He favors Friedman's voucher plan for schools and argues that it could be expanded to other areas. Even money can be provided by the market. In all cases where government is necessary, the private market must be allowed to attempt to provide similar services.[49]

Friedman finds extensive public concerns that can be left to the market. These include provision of most education at the primary and secondary level and all postsecondary education, old-age security programs, determination of wage rates, industrial regulation, licensure, public housing, national parks, mail delivery, toll roads, consumer protection, and protection from inflation (though he believes that inflation is exclusively a government-caused phenomenon). Even crime would be reduced if there were fewer government programs. The overall result will be to decrease government power, which must of necessity increase freedom and efficiency. There will be no long-lasting adverse impact.[50]

Despite its Hobbesian view of self-interest,[51] conservative market theory assumes that competitive markets produce harmony because people must and will learn to accept their outcomes. The expanded market requires that distribution issues and all forms of intervention must always be excluded from political consideration and that people accept market distribution. This shift from a descriptive to a prescriptive statement further implies that the market is, or should be, the only legitimate harmonizing mechanism because it alone ensures and requires voluntary cooperation, not coercion. Peace, harmony, justice, and order through the market would exist if there were no government, no force, no coercion. However, these do exist, and the line between market and government remains undetermined. The market can be a conflict-reducing mechanism in the conservative sense only if people accept its distribution mechanism as natural or make an antecedent decision–or nondecision–to give it precedence over politics. As in the myth that public administration can be nonpolitical, depoliticizing issues requires a prior commitment–a constitutional decision–as to what will or will not be included in political debate. The decision to concede this power to the market, however, is not subject to discussion. It is not a conscious choice. Given human nature, evolution, and the political and economic markets, it follows naturally.

How could any rational person debate the necessity of reducing government in scope and size? The market, guided by the invisible hand of competitive self-interest, will take up the areas vacated by government, thereby eliminating conflict. If it does not, this means they were not problems to begin with.

Prescriptions: Limiting Government Resources

As created, not spontaneous, institutions, governments need to be greatly controlled. The conservative economists propose stripping governments of the ability and resources that allow them to respond to popular demands for intervention, protection, welfare, regulation, and aid, thereby placing these issues off limits to public policy. Taking away resources and power expands the market's role, preventing selfish majorities and ignorant political leaders from intervening.

These theorists claim that all existing political systems and constitutions are corrupt because they escape market constraints and market concepts of political legitimacy. Traditional limits on government power are not adequate, and even separation of powers "has not achieved what it was meant to achieve." Hayek accepts the aims of Montesquieu and the American founders, but "their means have proved inadequate." He believes that the "division of power" and modern representative government have failed because they do not protect economic freedom. Buchanan agrees that western democracies and pluralism have failed and that they undermine moral order, threaten freedom, and are headed for destruction. They are an out-of-control "Leviathan," ruled by "bias" for public spending, that must be constrained. Friedman contends that government power will always be abused. Power exists because "people are afraid to leave things alone." This causes "Tyranny of Beneficiaries," "Tyranny of Politicians," and "Tyranny of Bureaucracy" resulting in a "Tyranny of the Status Quo." The only way to end abuse of power is to eliminate power.[52]

If ideas, institutions, and constitutional rules are inadequate and destructive, it is not enough to elect good leaders. Friedman had great hopes for the Reagan presidency, seeing its opposition to large government as the harbinger of "a renaissance of freedom and prosperity." A little later he noted that "[u]nder the best of circumstances, a massive government cannot be reordered and reduced overnight" or "dismantled in one or two years," but Reagan failed to make sufficiently far-reaching proposals for reducing government. Ultimately, however, it does not matter who is elected. Individuals fall short, and policies cannot be changed unless institutions and constitutional rules are altered radically. Buchanan asserts that the Reagan administration had "a noble agenda, and one partially if not fully met," but too much had been expected of it. More important, it focused "on a prepared agenda" instead of attempting "a structural revolution" to modify "the basic structure of politics and government." It failed to change the Federal Reserve system, enact a balanced-budget amendment, or eliminate the Departments of Education and Energy – meaning that "the only opportunity to change the structure of politics" has been "forfeited." President Reagan's most important legacy will be deflation of the "Mass

Delusion" that politics and bureaucracy can accomplish great things. His constant opposition to government has illustrated that government is a failure, that it cannot positively improve people's lives, that Camelot is impossible. Friedman echoes this belief with his claim that the Reagan administration's policies have "altered [the] political atmosphere" so that the opposition's "political position" has been modified.[53]

Regardless of who is elected, good intentions are swamped by corrupt political pursuit of self-interest. The only hope, as noted in chapter 5, is a constitutional revolution to change the form, structure, function, and resources of government to prevent this corruption from reoccurring. If no passion other than self-interest can be relied upon, institutions to channel self-interest away from its current, politically destructive path must be created. For Buchanan, this requires major "institutional reform" providing "constitutional protection for a morally legitimized sphere of human activity"–market freedom.[54] Hayek calls for "new institutional invention" to replace discredited western governments with a new model of politics "which could be realized by the consistent application" of market principles.[55]

In the same way that the Bill of Rights is a limit upon government in the United States, depriving it of resources is also a limit. As with all theories, the proposed constitutional rules enshrine a theory of distributive justice; essentially negative, they forbid government from doing some things and remove the resources to do others. The conservatives expect much from this policy. Hayek sees it as a key to "The Containment . . . and the Dethronement of Politics" because "politics has become much too important . . . costly and harmful." Friedman wants to reduce the size of government, whether or not deficits and debt are problems. He believes that "[t]here is nothing wrong with the United States that a dose of smaller and less intrusive government will not cure." Writing in the context of his proposed balanced-budget amendment, he argued "to limit the government in order to free the people" and expounded the "importance of limiting government in order to preserve and expand individual freedom."[56] The primary idea is to eliminate the means and resources that allow economic intervention. As examples, I will briefly examine proposals for taking away resources, the concept of a fiscal constitution, government issuance of money, and the conservative notion of rule of law.

Taxation and levels of taxation are fundamentally political decisions. They shape distribution and limit public policy and the size of government. Tax rules reflect basic civic principles and help promote those principles. Debate over taxes and budgets is a debate over the philosophy of government–its chief beneficiaries, proper role, structure, functions, duties, and national priorities. Realizing this, conservative economists demand that taxes be reduced. Though the United States is one of the least taxed of industrialized democracies, lower taxes are more of a political and philosophical than economic issue for these authors. Without the resources for intervention, government can no longer accede to the public's demand for intervention. Friedman confirms that "the relation between taxes and the scope of government . . . reflects a political judgment rather than an economic judgment." Given their preference for consumption that is private—which they claim is more democratic and just—as opposed to public—which must deprive individuals of the freedom to use their resources as they choose—reduced taxation expands the private while curtailing the public sphere. This is important because all taxes are seen as coercive. Thus, Buchanan emphasizes that choosing a tax system is "analogous to the choice among rules or to *constitutional* choice." Analyzing this option within uncertainty about future individual economic status presumably leads to choosing a tax system that limits redistribution and ensures that individuals keep most of their earnings.[57] Friedman is more blunt about reducing government's ability to meet popular demands. "Truly simplify the tax system and all of a sudden a major source of patronage for politicians would disappear." With fewer resources, temporary majorities can no longer coerce governments into destructive, unworkable, and costly programs.[58] It is so important to reduce the size of the federal government that Friedman would "accept large deficits as the lesser of evils" compared to higher taxes.[59]

Reducing taxes and spending requires a criterion. The market provides the essential constitutional and moral standard through the conservatives' *fiscal constitution,* discussed earlier. The market is a mechanism for reducing conflict and government power only when a fundamental, constitutional decision has been made to exclude categories of economic issues—as was achieved in the political exclusion of issues respecting religion or the press—from normal legislative and administrative jurisdiction. The conservatives maintain that this decision has been made, though apparently many people who are, or should be, bound by it are unaware of its existence. The fiscal constitution is the rule of conduct, part of the rule of law, that "forbids" deficit spending and high taxes. In an often repated phrase, the "fiscal constitution"[60] is a "constitutional constraint" that bars such matters as redistribution, deficit financing, and steeply progressive taxation. Principles such as the fiscal constitution are not created but are "culturally evolved rules of fiscal prudence," unwritten rules that are the result of cultural and moral evolution. Adhered to in the past, this evolved standard limits intervention into the natural economy and is "a set of fixed principles antecedent to and controlling the operating institutions of government." A balanced-budget requirement is one of these constitutional norms to restrict intervention. More than separation or enumeration of powers, the fiscal constitution limited the budget and therefore the size of government. Repeatedly violated, it still "had constitutional status. For expenditures in excess of receipts were considered to be violations of moral principles." Although not written into the Constitution – most of these authors want it included – it represented a customary or unwritten rule having the same status as political parties, "the actual operation of the electoral college," and judicial review. Violation of this constitutional norm, made possible by Keynesian economics combined with democracy, eliminated limits on the size and scope of government, embarking western nations on their current suicidal path.[61]

For these theorists, interventionist and/or welfare government is not only impolitic, coercive, counterproductive, inefficient, and freedom destroying but immoral and unconstitutional. Conservative fiscal concerns are prior to and more important than normal political activity. Their economy equals fundamental political rules and values composing the constitutional order. Deficit spending and/or intervention are subversive of fundamental law – of the real constitutional order represented by "The Old-Time Fiscal Religion."[62] Reducing government's role implies restoration of a legal order undermined by the irresponsibility, greed, and democracy of the political market. As with Hayek's rule of law, this is spontaneously generated moral law beyond that written by legislatures responsive to temporary majorities. Thus the role of enlightened economists is to return the nation to the higher reality embodied in market relations.

This argument is flawed. The fiscal constitution is not simply a principle employed to explicate positive law but confuses positive law with social norms and what are claimed as moral rules. These theorists convert what they perceive as a fundamental principle to the legally binding status of positive law. It is not sufficient to claim that the fiscal constitution is a tradition or customary behavior similar to political parties; if it were, people would be aware of it. It is a moral rule, generated by the economy, and as noted in chapter 6, there are no exogenous sources of morality that can challenge moral rules generated by the economy. Making the fiscal constitution a moral rule differentiates it from other practices and institutions which custom and usage have elevated to constitutional status. The latter can be changed or modified by statute or constitutional amendment, but the elements that make up the fiscal constitution are prior and superior to the political elements of the constitution and therefore unchangeable – a permanent limit on government. Though supposedly based on the evolution of custom and tradition, no amount of evolution can change these fiscal rules.

If there is, or was, a "fiscal constitution" whose rules are at least as fundamental as human rights and the structure of government, the rest of the system must correspond to it. This claim justifies the demand for *constitutional amendments* to make government conform to economic rules and needs, allowing the spontaneous economic order to provide most of the goods and services that people wrongly expect from government. These authors have numerous proposals to limit resources and the power to intervene in order to make the political constitution conform to the fiscal constitution. Their most important shared proposal is a balanced-budget amendment, because it would eliminate deficit spending. As their political faith leads them to assert that democracies are incapable of adequately taxing themselves to pay for services, a balanced-budget requirement reduces the size of western governments, correspondingly expanding the role of markets. Friedman suggests additional amendments to limit government's role that are consistent with the position taken by the others: a flat tax; free trade; a presidential item veto; limitations on the growth of the money supply; forbidding wage and price controls; ending laws requiring a license to practice a profession; elimination of corporate taxes; inflation indexing of contracts; and termination of such policies as public housing and social security.[63]

For the conservative economists, these changes in the role of government embody the *rule of law*. The rule of law is a classical liberal principle designed as protection from arbitrary government action and limitation on the scope of government. It specifies the principles by which other rules are judged. The rule of law includes impartiality, removal of vagueness, nonarbitrariness, neutrality, and advance notice of new rules and rule changes. It refers to treating people by known standards and to constitutionalism—adhering to basic limits and rules. The idea of rule of law is favored by each of these authors but elaborated most by Hayek—and then more through repetition than detailed analysis of content and consequences. Moreover, this ideal is given a peculiar twist by these writers, to emphasize their version of proper economic relations as the key to freedom, limited government, and the good life.

Hayek and Friedman both express the desire for general rules and law to guide action and limit human will and discretion in politics, especially where it impacts on economics. Along with Buchanan's "fiscal constitution," which is the functional equivalent of Hayek's rule of law or "rules for just conduct," general rules are the essential means to maintain freedom and prevent excessively responsive governments from giving in to what these theorists call special-interest pleading for intervention. The rule of law is a standard superior to the mere will of majorities embodied in statutes, to written law, even to the written constitution, in that it provides norms of conduct to protect the conservative market, based on an underlying economic reality that orders other behavior.[64]

Hayek's rule of law limits what government and majorities may do. It stresses methods and procedures in the belief that these produce the best outcomes over time, not results to specific individuals or classes. It is another example of either/or thinking: People must choose between his notion of rule of law or tyranny. Hayek's rule of law offers general, established, unvarying rules, "fixed and announced beforehand," that allow virtually no discretion – the essence of tyranny – to government and no differentiation between people. Prohibiting discretion excludes intervention in economic or social relations because such intervention treats some people differently from others. Rule of law assumes that government and public policy can be impartial and neutral if they treat people identically and do not benefit any identifiable person. To do this it must follow those general rules which support the abstract market order. Governments are precluded from legislating for specific problems or persons. If it is possible to see the effects of a policy on specific persons, that policy is illegitimate, a violation of the rule of law. In no case is it legitimate to differentiate between people in the name of justice, equality, or freedom, because such differentiation must destroy freedom, justice, and equality along with the spontaneous market order upon which these depend.[65]

Formal equality before the law – identical treatment regardless of differences – is, therefore, the essence of the rule of law. "[E]quality before the law is in conflict, and in fact incompatible, with any activity of a government deliberately aiming at material or substantive equality of different people" (i.e., *any* aid or reward given outside the structure of the market) or at "distributive justice," which *must* destroy the rule of law and free markets. The market-based, natural-law-like character of this position is illustrated by Hayek's claim that constraining rules, like the fiscal constitution, need not be written or even apparently known to be binding. They include "not only articulated but also not yet articulated rules which are implicit in the system or have yet to be found." As in the development of capitalism, when people followed rules without expressing or even knowing them, evolved rules of the market set the limits to political possibility and legitimacy.[66]

In claiming that public policy cannot benefit identifiable persons, Hayek is referring to the impact of specific rules – say, welfare legislation, where it is possible to identify who will benefit. He wants general rules, like stop signs, which everyone must equally obey and of which everyone may attempt to take advantage. He is not referring to the socioeconomic environment where property owners, children of the affluent, or white males have built-in advantages in market competition or competition resulting from general rules. Hayek insists that such context must be ignored. Law cannot take cognizance of individual differences or circumstances. In short, it is not a violation of rule of law if, based on socioeconomic characteristics, one can identify beforehand particular likely winners. But it is a violation of rule of law if government attempts to aid likely classes of losers, that is, those people who lack the resources or ability to effectively compete.

As an abstract concept, the rule of law does not specify the content of rules but rather the form they must follow. To conservatives, however, the rule of law does have specific content: the rules of conservative political economy. It follows from spontaneous order and human ignorance, requiring that people comply with a form of rule utilitarianism produced by market needs. Anything that violates these canons, even if applicable to all, violates the rule of law. The measure of the rule of law becomes conformity to these economic rules (which specify the principle of neutrality), not its conformity to abstract rules of procedure, which to be made operational must be informed by moral judgments. Yet people and philosophers insist on such judgments to ensure that a decision that is impartial is acceptable. Their judgments might distinguish between people because of their different position in the socioeconomic lottery and would have to be justified in exactly the same way that conservative rules need justification.

Circumscribing government's ability to *issue money* is also an effective limitation on its scope and power. Friedman and Hayek differ on the best means—Buchanan does not discuss this option—but agree that the public ability to issue money must be constrained. Friedman's monetarism removes public discretion, so that issuing money becomes a seemingly administrative task, innocent of political involvement. Monetarism assumes that the money supply (quantity of money), not fiscal policy, is the key government support for the economy. Monetarism claims that long-term prosperity and stable prices can be ensured by creating an automatic monetary system under which the money supply grows 4 to 5 percent a year.[67] Friedman believes that this rate will prevent inflation by not providing money to finance higher prices and will have no undesirable consequences, at least in the long run.[68] Creation of a fixed monetary rule ends the possibility of discretionary intervention into economic affairs and supposedly removes the means of financing intervention and welfare. To be successful, monetarism requires an additional politically difficult policy: wage and price flexibility.

Hayek's proposal to reduce government's monetary role reflects his mistrust of government and his concurrent belief that the private market is superior to and is an effective limit upon government. Whereas Friedman supposes that government can be efficient enough to adhere to a fixed rule of monetary growth, Hayek doubts this. Instead, Hayek wishes to denationalize money; that is, take away government's exclusive power to issue money and allow private firms to issue alternative and competing currencies. Hayek claims that government has always abused its money-issuing monopoly. "[G]overnment power over money facilitates centralisation," allowing it to deliberately squeeze resources out of the public. "[T]here is every reason to mistrust government . . . there is no reason to doubt that private enterprise whose business depended on succeeding in the attempt could keep stable the value of the money it issued." A detailed discussion of this proposal is unnecessary. It is another example of attempts to remove resources which allow extensive welfare, regulation, or intervention. It is the corollary of the belief that the market is always more just, fair, and efficient than politics and that people must learn to passively accept market outcomes.[69]

Proposals to remove resources from government control require a radical change in the structure of government, its operations, and the public to whom government presumably responds. Politics becomes an adjunct to economic theory. The market restricts and defines the scope of government and the public sphere and introduces greater purity into politics. For example, public choice theory, which Friedman applauds, "offers the normative understanding necessary to lay down 'better' rules." Such theorists "should begin to advance their own versions of the ideal constitution for society." This includes "institutional reform" to fit man's "moral-ethical capacities" and "genuinely constitutional rules that will, to an extent at least, be immune from ordinary political pressures."[70] Change will take a fair amount of time, since the perceived corruption has sunk deeply into the political fabric.[71] But change will come, even though "new institutional invention is needed."[72] Hayek's proposals include a new legislative structure, with much reduced power for the branch that is subject to regular elections. To Friedman and Buchanan, there should be more local and less national government. For Hayek and Friedman, structural changes such as the line-item veto will shift more power to the executive.

The reasoning is simple. Either we have a free market and limited government or total government and a command economy. There are no intermediate possibilities. Inefficient and coercive, government must be limited to its essential duty of protecting the harmonizing market mechanism. Despite acceptance of a limited welfare system and Friedman's demand that government maintain a stable money supply, government duties are no greater than those listed by Adam Smith and, given vast socioeconomic changes since Smith, are proportionally less: internal and external security, a judicial system, defense of private property, enforcement of contracts, and provision of limited public works and minimal support for public education.

This model can operate best in a system that has little popular political participation, a passive or docile population, and few resources to support protest. Some of the possibilities and dangers implicit in the conservative position are illustrated by Friedman's comments on Hong Kong and Chile. Despite its limited local self-rule or political participation, Friedman considers Hong Kong as "[p]erhaps the best example" of government kept to its proper duties. It is a paradigmatic market society with neither tariffs, minimum wages, nor limits upon buying and selling, entering a business, or hiring practices. Though tiny, it is an example for the United States.[73]

Friedman's discussion of Chile is more naive and ominous. Friedman's initial support for Gen. Augusto Pinochet's dictatorship illustrates the conflict between his notions of freedom and the purpose of government and wider concepts of freedom, democracy, and legitimate government. Friedman visited Chile in March 1975, eighteen months after a military coup overthrew the elected president, Salvador Allende. The exact nature of his six-day visit is controversial, but while in Chile, he met a number of government officials—some economic advisers to the ruling junta were either former students or close adherents of the Chicago School of Economics—gave talks, and subsequently wrote a paper recommending spending cuts, sale of nationalized industries, and other steps to curb inflation.[74] Friedman did not ask if Latin American conditions made it difficult to apply his advice, or if cultural, political, social, and religious circumstances might affect a supposedly universally valid monetarist model.

Friedman saw in Chile what the United States and Britain can become if they continue to expand intervention and welfare. Thus, "[t]he present state of Chile [1977], in my opinion, is the end result of an expansion in the role of government" in socioeconomic problem solving, especially "an increase in government spending."[75] Presumably this is the ultimate cause of the 1973 coup. Because of his presupposition about the inevitably destructive impact of government, he was slow to attack brutality and violations of human rights and quick to praise the junta's efforts to return Chile to a "free" economy. Friedman advised what came to be called the shock treatment to curb inflation: drastic cuts in public welfare, services, and subsidies; reduced employment; a slower rate of growth in the money supply; and so on. His "only concern" was "that they [the junta] push it long enough and hard enough,"[76] though their method of doing so seems at first to have escaped his notice. He believed that "the economic policy adopted by the Chilean government has been well adapted to the problems it inherited from the Allende regime." That the policies he supported required political repression in Chile and could be imposed only under an authoritarian, antidemocratic regime seems not to have troubled him. Friedman said that though he deplored the political situation, the economic solution was absolutely necessary.[77] In response to critics, Friedman initially claimed that Chile was an exception, that strong government cannot normally impose a free economy, and that critics of Friedman and Chile are inconsistent in not also criticizing communist states. In the end, after much censure, he admitted that preservation of the free market requires restoration of political freedom.[78]

There is moral and political callousness in Friedman's early association with and later partial repudiation of the Chilean junta. Despite his protestations, Friedman's argument illustrates greater concern for the conservative version of a free economy than for politics or political freedom. I cannot attribute Friedman's position on Chile to other conservative economists, even if their starting economic and political assumptions are similar. They did not comment on Chile, and one expects that they too disapproved of the junta's political repression. Yet Friedman epitomizes a potential in the conservative economic contempt for government and politics: the belief that political and social relations must conform to economic theory, regardless of costs. The economist's purpose is to enforce the economic limits to politics, unlike the Keynesian claim that economists should attempt to find workable means to meet popular demands and reduce economic pressures on political stability.

Politics as an Adjunct to Economics

The message is always identical, repeated with persistent regularity. Politics is inferior to economics. Politics is a self-serving exchange mechanism. Politics is coercive. Politics is uncontrollable. Government is the enemy. Government power is always abused. Government always fails. Government failure is always worse than any imaginable market failure. Public support for correcting market imperfections through regulation, intervention, welfare, labor unions, most health and safety regulations, and so on must be terminated. In a caricature of Marxism, the political constitution must conform to the underlying economic constitution.

The conservatives' free market requires a particular political system, though not necessarily a minimal state. For example, Buchanan accepts some of Robert Nozick's arguments but considers the possibility of a minimal state to be a dream.[79] Hayek leaves open the possibility of active though limited government. Potentially, this state is minimal only in terms of its nonintervention in the "spontaneous" market order. A strong state may sometimes be necessary, but one responsible to a higher value than popular demands. Given the conservative view of self-interest and their failure to explain why people will accept losses when interventionist-regulatory-welfare government is dismantled, a strong government—and possibly a revamped, centralized educational system to teach acceptance—may be needed to control unrest and contain or ignore redistribution demands if consensus breaks down.

The conservatives seem to believe that all that is necessary is to remove the source of what they consider abuses, yet there will be losers from their proposals. Entitlements, most welfare, a wide range of business, price, and environmental regulations will disappear. There will be fewer opportunities for advancement, aid, and education for groups and individuals who fare poorly in the market. The conservatives' own picture of human nature warns that losers will not go quietly to their reduced position and status. Thus when an economic policy requires ignoring popular fears and demands and reducing popular impact on decision making—given the conservative picture of the political market and the place of self-interest in politics—suppression of dissent is probably inevitable. Losers must be forced so that they can be truly free in the market.

Moreover, the limitations these authors place on democracy and popular control of government and the deliberately reduced responsibility of government to respond to popular demands would leave modern governments unchallenged in foreign and military policy, areas that have increased the power of government more than have demands for welfare or economic regulation. A further result of limiting access to government would be to increase the influence of those who now have ready access that does not depend on popular pressure or voting, such as business executives who must be placated to fulfill much government policy.[80] This could lead to a greater asymmetric relation between groups to government than now exists. These theorists believe that their limits on the power of government will end all economic intervention, but the more probable result will be expansion in police powers, a shift in the beneficiaries of public policy, and more inequality, where traditional business claimants for public aid will become even more dominant than at present. There is, therefore, a potentially large role for government in maintaining internal order and other supports necessary to the market.

This possibility of a particular kind of strong state may not, however, be the entire story. As with all elitist theories, the conservatives assume that there is an elemental reality to which behavior must conform for justice and harmony to be realized. Despite conventional wisdom and the conservatives' own claims, two points support this contention. First, the system as a whole is determined, operating virtually as a natural order, and individuals have little impact on outcomes. Second, the conservative market is not a proposition put forward for debate and analysis but a true and objectively correct standard to which people should adhere. It functions for the conservatives in the identical manner as natural law and objective truth asserted by other systems. As in Plato's Republic, the criterion of good government is not political. Existential reality is inadequate. Mass wants reflect ignorance and are irrelevant to what should or must be. People must be made to conform to the disciplining/liberating spontaneous order. They must adopt a political system which reflects this reality beyond their desires; the political-economic system cannot conform to what people desire or how they actually behave. The underlying reality is not Plato's transcendent forms; these authors are good enough liberals to doubt the validity of that intellectual enterprise and to realize that it requires a morality different from their own. Instead, the foundation is the market, which is to be the arbitrator of politics and government. Polity must conform to economy. In the same way that a cancer patient must comply with a medical regimen (against his/her will?) to be cured, modern governments must observe and be limited by market discipline for order, freedom, and efficiency to prevail.

This rationalist picture is sorely lacking. Buchanan and especially Hayek defend the market as the result of evolution,[81] but apparently only the market can evolve. Since it has evolved in conformity with fundamental human drives, there is little or no likelihood for further evolution to social market systems or successful, close government-market partnership. Governments are created, and though they are also human institutions and important for solving problems and overcoming conflict, they are not capable of evolutionary growth or improvement. As government is a constructed system, these authors discount the possibility of political evolution. Thus it is no defense to say that the present range of public activities is the result of popular demand, or to claim that duties have evolved over time. That is irrelevant, because only the market provides the mechanism—competition—to propel evolution and curb both appetite and the natural political disposition to plunder whomever one can. If government evolved—in a sense, Buchanan's contractarianism, if it allowed other possible contracts—then it would have equal claim to consideration with spontaneous orders such as the market.[82] But this would undermine the idea that the market is natural and politics destructive.

Conservative evolution operates in and through the market, having as its goal protection of the market. It is employed as a descriptive and prescriptive concept. Evolution can proceed according to only one pattern: individualistic competition in spontaneous orders such as the market. Any other pattern is a blind end, a return to primitive emotions and organization and harmful to freedom. Institutional evolution of markets has stopped in that no amount of change or evolution can make the free market more free or efficient.

All evolution of tradition arguments share a common problem: Either one must be morally neutral and accept everything that develops, or one must abandon the argument in order to criticize recently developed political and social forms. The conservatives accept neither of these alternatives, leaving them with several problems they fail to address. First, if, as these authors believe, survival is the criterion of success, what is the time frame in which success is measured, within which one can determine if a practice is or is not the newly evolved norm? The welfare state is more than fifty years old in the United States and a century old in democratic Europe. Is it the path that social evolution is currently following? If procedures have simply evolved, it is not legitimate to argue for reinstatement of previous procedures because they evolved. Can there be dysfunctional evolution, and if yes, what are the criteria? It cannot be found in the process of evolution. Second, the conservatives seem to be asserting that history has ended, that evolution stopped with their political economy, that for example, the nineteenth-century fiscal constitution is the limit of sustainable evolution, given human nature. Why and how can this be? Are not the democratic practices and institutions these authors criticize also the result of evolution? Third, why and how has change occurred outside the acceptable evolutionary path? The answer—bad men and desires—does not address the failure of their tradition. Fourth, discussion of political, economic, and institutional evolution is of course a metaphor, because unlike nature, social evolution is not the result solely of chance. Even if people are as ignorant as the conservatives claim, reason, goals, purposes, and planning—as well as the force, power, and predatory practices ignored by these theorists—shaped and continue to shape the development of human arrangements. They may not produce the results people wish, but results are not independent of purposes. If people can understand the process, they may be able to direct or at least deflect it. Then the evolution argument ceases to be a naturalist argument and becomes a purely rationalist one.

All that is desirable is promoted through the market. What cannot fit will be ignored or suppressed. Because there are only individual interests, they can be made to mesh together in the market where an extended view reveals that the world is harmonious, orderly, coherent, and at bottom, one. This position fails to appreciate the sociopolitical dislocation that results from rational individual decisions that are harmful in the aggregate. It may be perfectly rational for an individual to ignore the long-term impact of actions but disastrous for society; examples include toxic waste disposal, use of chlorofluorocarbons, pollution, refusal to serve in the armed forces, discrimination, selling secrets to an enemy, ignoring interests of future generations, or Garrett Hardin's "tragedy of the commons."[83] Even if the market can address such issues, future generations cannot participate in *our* market and are therefore unprotected. The theory is unable to address harm that flows from sole dependence on markets when costs cannot easily be allocated to individuals or when people cannot adequately be compensated for harm but are protected only if the harm is prevented, as with acid rain or disease. The conservatives rightly insist that government failure is too often ignored in calls for regulation of market failure, but that should be a caution against expectations of perfection, not a reason for doing nothing. Instead, for these authors, that simple observation is magnified into the basis for an entire theory of government, one where government and politics are to conform to market theory, never to interfere into spontaneous order.

Because these theorists see politics and government as coercion, neither government nor politics have anything other than narrow instrumental value. They cannot accomplish great things, there is no creativity in politics, there is no value in unity or participation, and humanity will never share a common image of a common future. Government is condemned for being centralized and for failing to impose uniformity on public policy.[84] Power has no moral justification, except as it contributes to market efficiency. Legitimacy, legitimate authority, and ultimately popular control–despite claims that the market is the true realm of democracy–are missing. Traditional political concern with what is rightful, as in legitimacy, is reduced to individual rights largely in a market context. There is no attempt to account for obligation. The citizen is gone. Politics and participation are the pursuit of self-interest as determined outside a social or collective context, without debate, deliberation with, or concern for fellow citizens. High politics is never addressed. There is no sense for, reference to, or understanding of diplomacy, war, and peace, those concerns which a slightly older generation referred to as the great issues of politics. They are not missed, because the market will satisfy most issues formerly left to politics.

By limiting expectations, the market supposedly reduces conflict and solves problems that the democratic masses foolishly expect government to address. If people are convinced that the market is neutral, that inequality is necessary to its operation, that market outcomes are the best individuals can attain given their resources, and that such outcomes are natural, they may feel disappointed but not discontented. If, however, the power to affect outcomes does exist; if people are unwilling to believe that the market is neutral between men and women, black and white, poor and rich; if many people have little or no equal and effective choice about important exchanges; if inequality undermines efficiency; if welfare and intervention are the price of social and political stability; if large numbers are unwilling to remove issues important to them from the public agenda, then the market does not limit conflict but becomes a pivot for expanded conflict.

Leaving aside the rich tradition in normative theory that man lives not by bread alone but becomes fully human through participation, popular protests demanding democratization in South Korea in June 1987 and the subsequent election there (as well as popular demands for more democracy in the People's Republic of China in June 1989) illustrate that economic growth alone is not enough to satisfy popular aspirations, that people want a sense of control over their futures, that demands for political reform and some sort of democratic participation cannot be satisfied by the phrase that the market is the real realm of democracy because people can choose to buy whatever they wish, if they can. This reality will be lost on the economist theorists. With their preference for theory over existent reality, for making behavior conform to their economic model rather than altering their assumptions to reflect behavior, and for a unified solution to all dilemmas, they are unconcerned with the problems that confront individuals and governments. All that the conservative theory of government has to offer is the promise that in the long run, things will be right with the world; on the average, people will be better off or at least living as they should without handouts, intervention, or regulation to cripple their freedom; and that there will be more economic efficiency, defined as whatever results from their natural market process. Much is missing from this attempt to find a single answer for all public concerns.

Chapter Eight

Conclusions

What is still more important than even this matter of feeling, is the practical discipline which the character obtains, from the occasional demand made upon the citizens to exercise, for a time and in their turn, some social function. It is not sufficiently considered how little there is in most men's ordinary life to give any largeness either to their conceptions or to their sentiments. . . . If circumstances allow the amount of public duty assigned him to be considerable, it makes him an educated man. . . . Still more salutary is the moral part of the instruction afforded by the participation of the private citizen, if even rarely, in public functions.
    —John Stuart Mill, *Considerations on Representative Government*, chap. 3.

Every man will submit with becoming patience to evils which he believes arise from the general laws of nature."
—Thomas Robert Malthus, *An Essay on the Principles of Population*, bk. 2, chap. 2.

Ideas, belief systems, and operational concepts mold what people see and how they respond to events. Disagreement over the content and public definition of political ideas is a major part of political conflict. Within broad limits, ideas can control or liberate people, promote unity or conflict, or determine winners and losers in political-economic clashes. The authors whom this book examines are highly influential and implore us to accept a theory which seeks to transform western governments and widely held political and social values. Since their politics have received little discussion, I have attempted to explicate their political ideas and claims instead of making a detailed criticism. This chapter, however, points to some of the social and political difficulties inherent in conservative economists' political theory.

Despite contrary protestations, conservative economic theory is also a normative political theory that has serious implications for widely accepted ideas, values, and policies. The conservative economists are keenly alert to unintended results and implications of policies, theories, and proposals with which they disagree, as in their continual claim that even with good intentions, intervention is always harmful. Given this concern, it is proper to ex-

185

amine the implications and results of their political model. In the same way that economic analysis creates new possibilities for understanding politics, looking at conservative economic theory as normative political theory advances understanding of its meaning. It also produces an entirely different result from treating it (or any other economic theory claiming to be a guide to proper public policy) as empirical, verified, and purely economic. Such an approach makes the character of conservative theory more apparent and opens it to analysis and criticism.

Conservative economic theory is a political theory and ideology in that it provides a coherent view of man and human relations, one that explains reality to those who accept it, determines goals, furnishes adherents the means to measure and judge others, and provides a guide to action.[1] As a normative political theory, it attempts to subordinate and incorporate much of politics into economics; defines politics and government in narrow instrumental terms; determines the legitimacy of political and social behavior by its impact on economic efficiency and the spontaneous economic order; envisages human nature and the human condition so that public goals and purposes become impossible; and redefines individualism, freedom, equality, democracy, morality, justice, and community in cramped, procedural terms that strip them of substantive content and obviate their expansion. The result is a logical, deductive theory which solves complex problems by defining them away. In its fear of government power, it leaves people defenseless before private power; condones inequality; accepts social relations as given and immune from positive intervention; denies the relevance of traditional moral and ethical theories to political economy; reduces all relations to private relations; and sees humanity's highest good and true nature in the pursuit of private self-interest.

Conservative political economy is founded upon an optimistic and proud belief that it is an accurate, empirically correct, and morally superior model of how the world operates. The order-producing market promises that things will turn out as well as they possibly can, if people accept their fate and leave the market alone. Being optimists in a world where many things are going wrong, conservative economists offer the illusion of hope to people who must forgo public protection, cherished freedoms, and democratic practices to pay the costs for conservative ideas. Such sacrifices seem necessary because these theorists have virtually monopolized the public discussion and definition of social and political ideas, claiming that their limited political view is the only legitimate conceptualization of and means to reach the good society. In the process, they have shifted the language and focus of debate away from Keynesian, liberal, and social democratic philosophy to their revolutionary picture which emphasizes the inevitability of government failure; limited government, political participation, and public expectations; reduced welfare, intervention, and regulation; conceptualization of political and social concerns as narrowly economic; and the superiority of the private over the public aspects of human existence. Some of the political nature of this theory can be illustrated by what is missing.[2]

Neglected Issues and Concerns

Theories are like road maps, giving a schema of where one is going, what to expect, what one must pay attention to, and what can safely be ignored. As with maps, they are abstractions from reality that focus on some things and ignore others, that are useful for some purposes but inappropriate for others. Conservative economic theory, however, is like an abstract map for all situations, regardless of terrain, local landmarks, direction of travel, means of transport, and purposes. Despite pretensions to a universally valid psychology, the market theory of politics is a normative theory, a new version of natural law whose conclusions and prescriptions proceed from the conservative economists' image of unchangeable human motivation. This picture is not subject to debate but is "the *premise* on which debate is built."[3] Society and politics must be as asserted. Discrepancies must be ignored or made to conform. The theory claims to explain all domestic political behavior and offers elaborate political and social prescriptions. It is not, however, an adequate normative or empirical political theory. In its pursuit of a single explanation for all social phenomena, these theorists' shared political theory neglects too much behavior and has little room for the impact of widely held ethical and moral rules and beliefs on how individuals define self-interest. The theory overlooks the social nature of economic relations and fails to examine circumstances when general, abstract rules may discriminate against persons. Its impaired image of human motivation is too narrow to support a working political system or an adequate morality. Previous chapters noted specific missing elements, such as substantive content for individualism, democracy, freedom, equality, morality, justice, community, and inconsistency over defense. Here I note more general difficulties.

The importance of what I assert to be missing from conservative theory cannot be proven but represents concerns from contemporary political debate and historical political theory. These omitted elements have been considered important by traditional conservatives, theorists in the historical core of modern liberalism, socialists, and Marxists. Is it fair to criticize a theory for what it does not address? Yes, if that theory goes beyond manipulation of abstract symbols to recommend real-world institutional, value, and policy changes. When large numbers of people are concerned with certain issues and problems and a theory claims comprehensive and universal validity, that theory should address those matters, even if they are illegitimate, irrelevant, or unfortunate within its confines. At minimum it should explain why such concerns are unimportant. This is especially true for a theory which limits government and replaces political accommodation with the operation of a supposedly autonomous and automatic system. Instead, conservative political economy banishes these concerns to a category of nonproblems.

The conservatives correctly remind us that everything is interconnected and that to change one part or one relation in a system has an (often unforeseen) impact on others. Unfortunately, they apply this insight only to politics and government, not to the political-social changes resulting from the market or from their market-based advice. They have little concern for social equilibrium as distinct from market relations and act as if the stability and safety of the Republic have a narrowly economic base. For them, human systems and relations are derivative from and analyzable as economics. Areas that conservative theory inadequately addresses include: social costs, cohesion, political considerations, legitimacy, patriotism, public goals, participation, more expansive individualism, efficiency, class, transition to their political model, the nature of public alternatives, and problems of procedures without substance.

Keynes criticized neoclassical economics for "its general regardlessness of social detail."[4] This charge is applicable to contemporary conservative theory. *Social costs* and losses are not simply overlooked but, given procedural individualism, do not exist; therefore, the possibility of adverse sociopolitical impact is excluded from policy advice. Private and social costs and benefits coincide. Buchanan, for example, believes that economics should emphasize markets and exchanges, not "social costs and social benefits."[5] This is a defensible position, but it is incompatible with making sociopolitical prescriptions.

Though it is plausible to argue that the conservative defense of the market is based on its results,[6] these conservatives take a nonconsequentialist position when it comes to actual results. It is the economic order that matters, not consequences to specific individuals, to the social system, or to politics and government. These authors do not believe that conditions other than coercion prevent people from acting. Those who cannot compete are largely ignored, and the children of unsuccessful competitors present few problems for equal opportunity, long-term political-social stability, or justice. Because the system is seen as natural and neutral between people, there is no need to choose between groups and claimants. Each receives what he or she deserves. No one can have more without stealing from others. Market outcomes determine fairness. To the extent that this system exempts individuals and firms from responsibility for unintended consequences, it cannot address problems of ecological degradation or the imposition of small costs on many individuals.[7]

How the interests of future individuals can be protected is unexplored. People must learn to accept the results of market relations. All relevant social phenomena are expressed by prices.[8] People have no right to expect welfare or aid in adapting to adjustments and losses, which are natural. Given the conservatives' picture of man and politics, it makes sense to depreciate the social costs of economic failure, falling wages, or unemployment because these costs are purely individual. Efforts to address them through collective action must serve individual interest, not the common good.

The conservatives' world view prevents them from seeing the nature and relevance of common identity that many people take comfort from and which encourages cooperation. Procedural individualism, lack of a common interest except those interests that each person possesses, narrow self-interest, and freedom conceived as doing with one's possessions as one wishes encourages the slighting of *social cohesion*. This is absent from the conservatives' model. They make no effort to explain deference to the interests and concerns of others or not pushing one's self-interest when that is detrimental to others. Indeed, they have no way to account for such feelings and actions except as masks for self-interest or the mistaken understanding of one's real interest. These authors never discuss cooperation outside the market nexus, causing them to miss the cooperative element in much social, political, and economic interaction. They believe that cooperation is for narrowly self-interested reasons and can be bought. Learning curves, shared skill development, labor-management trust, job satisfaction, group loyalty, upgrading the consensus, pride, and satisfaction are merely components in individual self-interest that are captured by market prices and have no other relevance. Private ownership and pursuit of self-interest in the market are ultimately indistinguishable from cooperation, freedom, and efficiency.

Politics, political considerations, and *political stability* are also missing from the conservative model and policy advice. These authors ignore that the boundary between politics and economics is translucent, permeable, and located not in the nature of things but at man's convenience. They are concerned only with what they see as a one-way adverse relation – from politics to economics – and a one-way beneficial relation – from market economics to politics. The two remaining relations – the adverse impact of economics on politics[9] and the beneficial impact of politics on economics – do not exist in any significant sense.

For the conservatives, politics cannot have a positive impact on market economics, even by helping people achieve their goals or avoid situations such as the "prisoner's dilemma";[10] and economics has no harmful, destabilizing consequences for politics confined to its proper sphere. Economic discontent should not, therefore it does not, harm democracy and free government. They miss Jefferson's argument that relations of superordination and subordination in the economy can create conditions for political stability or instability, for a republic or tyranny. Keynes in the 1930s and Thurow in the 1980s repeatedly claim that economic dislocation encourages the development of despair and extremism. Keynes believed that severe unsolved economic problems could discredit democratic government, making destructive and radical changes inevitable. Most students of developmental politics and of revolution concur. The social and political impact of debt repayment by developing countries may soon provide a case study. That debt repayment is destabilizing for newly reestablished democratic regimes in countries such as Brazil or Argentina because it requires reducing already low living standards, causing social strain, political unrest, and a sense of loss of national sovereignty, is not discussed. Keynes addressed this problem for Germany in the 1920s, and the United States will face it in the 1990s, but the conservatives provide no advice except reduce popular expectations and let the market prevail.

The conservative economists are unconcerned with possible economic sources of political instability. Their political theory sees politics as static. They seem to assume that the political system will continue as before regardless of economic shocks. Problems are defined away as misperceptions of human possibility. This makes sense within their hermetically-sealed, deductive model, where people must learn to passively accept their fate. Political stability will then presumably follow, because the economic market is an unchallengeable standard of proper conduct. If allowed to function without intervention, and if people defer to economic forces, political freedom, equality, democracy, government, and apparently political stability will be the best that can be, given limited human ability. Deviation from the market destroys these goods. Economics is, therefore, separate from social and political concerns. As with Marx, economics is the fundamental reality, and politics is epiphenomenal. Political and social institutions must conform to the natural economic system, which needs no modification to fit political needs. Maintaining social and political stability, support and a sense of legitimacy through welfare[11] is immoral. The stability of the Republic depends only on an economic base.

This casual attitude to political order is illustrated by nondiscussion of *legitimacy* and *authority*. Legitimacy is a nonquantifiable, quasi-mystical concept (though hardly more than spontaneous order or efficiency) that reflects real attitudes without which no political or economic system can survive. It refers to popular acceptance of community, governmental institutions, rules and procedures for distributing power and status; public values; and/or the belief that public officials, who fill roles within the structure of rules and institutions, have the right to govern. The concept of legitimacy is captured in the distinction between de jure and de facto—the difference between proper, legal rule and the fact of ruling or having power to impose rule or will. The conservatives acknowledge only de facto power. Power and office as a public trust are impossible. They virtually duplicate Marx's claim that politics reflects the interests of the dominant class. Though the players are different—capitalists are the victims in conservative martyrology, since wealth does not produce political power—modern governments are still tools of group oppression. For the conservatives, majorities and special interests employ the political system to exploit and oppress unorganized minorities. Negligent of their long-range interest and ultimate dependence on the peaceful operation of spontaneous order, ignorant and selfish majorities disregard the law and follow temporary self-interest by imposing intervention and high taxes on the creative minority. Given the view of politics as coercion, a political system is legitimate if it conforms to the market but always remains suspect and open to destructive misuse.

No system can survive for long without a sense of legitimacy, at least among a regime's armed followers. Unlike Keynes, the conservatives do not discuss how democratic legitimacy is promoted by government attempts to address widely felt problems.[12] These authors cannot explain popular acceptance of a democratic system—especially if democracy is only a procedure—or, having stripped government of the resources with which it may attempt to address popular discontent, any means by which it can allay dissatisfaction with economic performance. Policies, intervention, or restrictions reducing the "efficiency" of free markets, no matter how much they might contribute to political stability and legitimacy, are suspect, dangerous, and forbidden.

These authors make legitimacy claims for and about their economy—for example, that market competition is the only legitimate way to distribute goods and status—and their economic system depends upon a popular sense of its legitimacy. However, they have no way of convincing self-interested economic losers that the system is legitimate or of defending it peacefully. Moreover, authority can be justified only on moral grounds, such as justice, common interest, public benefit, and so on, not by efficiency and system needs. The conservative model has no such justification. With its restricted individualism, celebration of pursuing self-interest, and assertions that public officials always seek their narrow self-interest and that public policy inevitably fails, conservative political economy deeply corrupts politics. It undermines feelings of legitimacy and rightful authority[13] while legitimating self-seeking behavior, because if one expects government to serve self-interest, one can safely conclude that it will.

The conservatives' clearest failure lies in not explaining why people, characterized as ignorant and narrowly self-interested, will accept the market system, especially if they lose from market relations. Clearly many people believe that they are not winners. People on the edge of poverty, those threatened with job loss, and those experiencing chronic insecurity often feel powerless, hope-

less, alone, defeated, and alienated. Family and social ties weaken and deteri-
orate. Child and spouse abuse, drug use, crime, and physical and mental illness
are normal correlates of these feelings. Buffeted by adversity and unable to improve their lives, they can become internal dropouts or the raw material for
movements of despair. Conservative psychology cannot explain why these people, who can have little personal self-interest in doing so, will support the
political-economic system. For example, Friedman's and Hayek's claim that people should willingly accept their fate, that because they experienced good conditions in the past they should accept adversity when it comes, or Hayek's admission that some must suffer during economic change, ignores their own
assumptions about human behavior and motivation. Except for Hayek's belief
in traditional rules which individuals neither understand nor articulate but
simply follow, there are no ties except self-interest with which to maintain
stability.

Why and how self-interest remains confined to the market, why it does
not lead to more and brutal expressions of self-interest and how even markets
can survive with only self-interest are questions answered by a promise that
the market curbs and limits self-interest. Why the inherent selfishness of those
who have not but want, *or* of those who have but want more, does not destroy
the social system remains unexamined and unexplained. If losers or winners
cease to see their self-interest as being promoted by the market, they are bound
by no other ties or moral rules in the conservative model with which to hold
society together, resulting in chaos and/or demands for a strong government
to repress antimarket behavior. Dedication solely to self-interest and private
affairs is more characteristic of authoritarian regimes than democracies.[14]

This does not imply revolution, though the conservatives occasionally warn
about the violence and rebellion that will result if their system is not enacted
or maintained.[15] The real danger lies elsewhere, in the destruction of the civic
virtues that hold society together—seen in the continuing decline of voting
in the United States and the accelerating unwillingness to consider the needs
of others. Anger, mistrust, discontent, breakdown in social ties and stable expectations, and noncooperation are sometimes harbingers of violence and extra-
constitutional changes. More often they portend a generalized loss of support
for social and political institutions, basic values, and authorities. The greater
this breakdown in social ties and consensus, the greater the probability that
Arrow's dilemma for democratic decision making will be realized and Buchanan's search for unanimity frustrated.

These observations apply also to *patriotism*. Patriotism can exist in the conservative world only as a response to external enemies, and there is little in
this for the average individual. Love of country, willingness to sacrifice, the
primal sense of belonging to something larger than oneself, identification with

something beyond self-interest, loyalty to an ideal, and what the founders of the Republic referred to as civic virtue ill fits the conservative world view. Indeed, with their model of human motivation and individually derived valuation, these attributes have no collective value and usually are masks for selfishness. Patriotism and the place of patriotism in social cohesion, political legitimacy, and cooperation would have to be discussed in terms of self-interested psychic income, and would otherwise be inexplicable within their psychology.

Throughout the centuries, political theorists, including individualists, have insisted that politics has a *larger goal* or *purpose* than individual self-gratification. The conservative economists dispute this contention. They have no concern for authority, consent, citizenship, nonmarket legitimacy, obligation, or public goods separate from individual interest. The customary purpose of politics and government—to promote justice and strengthen community and a shared order—is impossible. In making policy recommendations, they are concerned with narrowly economic ends. Other considerations are either unimportant or contained within, subordinate to, and identified with economic means and ends. Political science's long-standing concern for power, role playing, non-rational activity, socialization, and macrosystem relations is subsumed under individual self-interest. Moral issues have disappeared, and defining democracy, freedom, or equality as procedures eliminates moral concerns from politics—which is no loss to these theorists because those values are divisive and frequently disguised self-interest.

Participation integrates democracies, expands awareness, modifies old and develops new preferences, and encourages people to enlarge their interests and understand the position of others. It frequently encourages commitment—a nonexistent concept for the conservatives—to improving the system, as opposed to the market notion of exiting from an undesirable situation. Participation creates the citizen. Given their depreciation of politics and their fundamentally economic reality, the conservatives play down the significance of citizenship and participation and eagerly anticipate a drastic reduction of the political sphere. Politics is not an arena of extensive human choice and development. It is not a means to change individual utility functions, perceptions, and notions of interest. It is not designed to help people attain ultimate goals and the good life. It has no value in adjusting rival claims or reconciling differences. Politics does not fulfill human needs.

In conservative economic theory, the group is simply an aggregate of separate, distinct egos, having no other existence or identity. This perspective ensures that these authors cannot explain even the simple act of voting. In their model, people vote for politicians who promise the most plunder. But, as noted earlier, this violates the conservatives' own free-rider principle and view of human motivation. A simple cost-benefit calculation cannot explain either voting or differences in participation rates between economic groups within a country or differences between countries. In any large election, it is rational to not vote because one vote cannot affect the outcome proportionate to the trouble of leaving home, traveling, waiting in line, and eventually casting a ballot. Yet approximately half the eligible voters in the United States vote on a fairly regular basis, and the proportions are significantly higher in other open systems such as Britain, Canada, or France.

A completely self-regarding person would not vote. Cultural influences, ethical principles, and a sense of group membership or duty, however, can motivate participation. People routinely distinguish their private from their public selves, and behavior appropriate in one forum is not always appropriate in the other.[16] People may not want to see their private desires established as public policy applicable to the entire society; and they may support a measure that does no direct personal good because it is beneficial to society. A person's decision to support a tax increase to finance pollution control (though he or she will not live long enough to benefit from it), or a bond issue for schools, or a lower wage increase to shift funds to a university library may express seriously held convictions as a member of a community—as a public person—as opposed to narrowly self-interested behavior. Individuals live in two intersecting realms and have two persona, the private and the public. They may sometimes be in conflict and sometimes consonant, but one is not subsumed under the other.

Voting is different from buying in a market for at least three other reasons. First, in politics there is no equivalent to prices,[17] but there is a strong effort to eliminate the buying and selling of influence. Second, the economic market responds to unequal preferences expressed in dollars, pounds, marks, and yen, giving each person a different number of "votes." Political participation emphasizes formal equality and, when limited to voting, actual equality that at least occasionally upsets the plans of political-economic elites. Third, when purchasing an item for personal satisfaction, change in others' behavior is incidental. In participation, it is personal satisfaction that is often incidental and other-directed purposes that are paramount. Voting has many functions, from expressing community to inducing behavior changes so that people conform to a moral or political ideal. It is not simply a private act even if the motivation is private. The element of deliberately choosing *with* and *for* others makes this into a different sphere with different purposes and consequences than private, market behavior.

Theorists such as Buchanan or Friedman have one great truth: *self-interest and individualism*. Conservative individualism is both a starting assumption and an explanation. Individualism—"private behavior"[18], expressed by pursuit of self-interest—is the fundamental reality and motivation, accounting for all behavior; there is *no* motivation beyond personally defined self-interest. It explains the success of markets and the inevitable failure of politics and public policy. Public policy, customs, group norms, institutions, and traditions result from and exist exclusively in the motivations and behavior of individuals acting as individuals. Individualistic self-interest structures the conservatives' concepts of markets, freedom, equality, democracy, government, morality, justice, and public policy and determines their policy proposals.

These theorists have one great error: This is all there is. They look at groups and see only individuals acting as individuals, with only a single motivation. This image presents an inadequate, nonempirical, and incomplete psychology[19] which, because it does not, cannot, or refuses to specify the meaning of self-interest beyond asserting that whatever an individual does is in his/her self-interest, becomes a tautology unable to explain real-world behavior. Even if self-interest is quantifiable in an empirically valid sense, it is assumed and asserted in such a way as to prove whatever the authors wish. Institutions, public policies, political activity, and all forms of cooperation are reduced to individual purpose and explained in terms of individual motivation, with insufficient reference to the environment.

In explaining human behavior, these theorists leave little room for internalization of shared beliefs or social and cultural influences. Although institutions may be the result of individual behavior and exist only in the minds and behavior of individuals, reification is not the only alternative. One needs only to accept the conservative insight that outcomes and institutions may be independent of anyone's intentions to realize that individual self-interested behavior does not account for all outcomes. Even if people always pursue narrow self-interest, individuals are not completely free to choose their behavior or to blatantly seek self-interest within an institution. Behavior is constrained. Though institutions limit how self-interest is sought, most constraint on the pursuit of self-interest outside the market is missing from the conservative model. Their depreciation of participation leads them to ignore how concepts of self-interest develop with and are modified by interaction with others. Judgments change as people attempt to convince each other of the best course of action. In shared decision making, people modify, develop, and upgrade their perceptions and understandings of self-interest, frequently merging them with a perceived common good. At that point, explaining behavior in terms of utility-maximizing self-interest becomes so vague as to lose all explanatory value.

Moreover, self-interest is a motive, not a justification. It is advanced only through conformity to at least some of the rules, roles, and norms of the institution and values within which one operates—the environment within which we define self-interest and we respond to one another. There is a big difference in how people react to demands justified by "I want that"; "I want that because a voice told me I deserve it"; "I want that or I will bash your head"; "I want that because according to our mutually shared values I deserve it or it is mine"; or "I want that because it will be mutually beneficial for me to have it." The person who internalizes norms or pursues self-interest by conforming to a *found* set of rules and values—which seem to exist only in spontaneous order for the conservatives—advances self-interest in a very different way from the person who has no constraints. Unless self-interest is reduced to a tautological truism, rules and the behavior and beliefs of others affect how a person behaves. These writers overlook Mill's insight, in such arguments of his as the tyranny of the majority, that individuals are constrained and shaped by the ideas and behavior of others until they cannot imagine an alternative thought or behavior. In the real world—witness the conservative picture of a nonmarket society—people face limits which their self-interest must heed.

In terms of actually explaining behavior, little is gained by reducing all behavior to narrow self-interest. But the reduction is integral to the conservatives' project. Their concept of individualism and freedom eliminates concern for private power[20] and the fate of individuals and denies a view of individualism as encouraging individual development. If there is nothing but individual self-interest, there is no justification for public efforts to protect the losers from conservative policies. They can have no claim on the resources of others, because they too have acted from the same self-interested motives. If everyone acts from the same motives, has the same formal chance, and there is no power to discriminate against individuals in the market, then everyone deserves what he or she gets. No one is responsible for the fate of others. Collective, deliberate controls over selfish behavior disappear. Conservative markets, individualism, and freedom prevent active government and redistribution because maintenance of the market system is the highest priority to which individuals must conform.

The conservative economists consistently claim that the market is more efficient than government. Claims about *efficiency*[21] are closely related to self-interest, inadequate conceptualization of individualism, and individual valuation. Though Buchanan occasionally acknowledges that efficiency requires a criterion,[22] the conservative economists share a widespread misperception that efficiency is a neutral, obvious concept, yet they repeatedly employed it in a blatantly ideological manner. Because of its alleged scientific status, invoking efficiency often ends normative policy dialogue. Efficiency, however, is the start of a discussion, *not* its end. It is neither self-justifying nor meaningful in the abstract; rather, it is an instrumental value. Though efficiency considerations may help one choose between goals, they cannot determine desirability or tell which goal to choose.

The meaning of efficiency depends upon exogenously determined purposes. One must always ask, efficiency in terms of which goal or purpose?

What do people wish to conserve? Maximize? Achieve? Efficiency differs depending on what we wish to maximize: individual negative freedom, effective individual freedom, collective freedom, individual equality, equality between nations, class peace, social stability, maximum capital accumulation, building a pyramid, putting a man on the moon, or putting pyramids on the moon. To claim that there is an inherent conflict between freedom or equality and efficiency simply means that one has a goal other than freedom or equality, such as wealth maximization for some. To define efficiency as maximum output given available resources is insufficient until preferences among goods are specified – free time, washing machines, fine art, computer games, or nuclear missiles. Selecting the relevant time frame is also crucial, since what is efficient in the short run may not be so in the long run, as illustrated by concern over the cumulative impact of environmental degradation. Answers to these concerns are normative judgments.

The common conservative answer is that the market determines what will be produced based upon satisfying individual preferences, but this is an evasion. Individual choices are made only from options presented by the market, by those able to pay. The chain of reasoning runs as follows:

There are only individual choices, preferences, and evaluations.
Preferences have the same value; there is no legitimate way to distinguish them.
Preferences should be satisfied.
Preferences are to be expressed in the market.
Markets are accurate measures of individual preferences, are fair, and are the only means to measure and aggregate preferences.
Preferences are expressed through money, which is fair because people earn money (rewards) in proportion to individual contribution to the welfare of others. The market compels people to satisfy the wants of others and requires the most effective use of resources.
The market therefore guarantees maximum utilization of resources, even as it expands the given resource base and technology. That is efficiency.
The market thus guarantees efficiency, or, in a very short step, market results are efficient.
Intervention must be inefficient.

This argument confuses the goal (achieving the maximum amount of what is desired with a minimum of resources) with one means of reaching it (the market). It is a circular but effective claim that the widely shared value of efficiency can be achieved only in the market. The typical use of "efficiency" focuses on individual choices in only the most superficial manner. Efficiency does not mean preference satisfaction but satisfying preferences in the market. Efficiency and individual choice are frequently procedural concepts having nothing to do with individuals achieving their ends or with autonomously determining preferences and ends. Individualism and individual preferences are satisfied if people are allowed to *attempt* to choose and to *attempt* to compete without coercion. It does not matter if they actually achieve their ends. Advertising, inequality, demand manipulation (which is impossible given the picture of freedom), or a small number of choices are irrelevant, as long as the framework of procedures exists to allow people to try to achieve purposes or express preferences. Outcome is secondary to system maintenance.

All individual preferences are not taken into account in efficiency calculations, but outside the market, what can be done to help people achieve their goals and preferences? For the conservatives, the answer is little or nothing. To emphasize all preferences, not just those realized in the market, opens the unacceptable possibility of collective intervention or action to help people articulate and achieve preferences. Thus it is logical for these authors to criticize all intervention and popular political participation. Such policies as environmental impact statements invoke nonmarket concepts of efficiency. The original attempt at limited participation in community action programs illustrates a wider conceptualization of efficiency than market efficiency. According to the conservative economists, these efforts cannot be efficient, not because they do not achieve their purposes, but because the purpose achieved is illegitimate according to the market model. This is, however, inadequate. The economists' efficiency cannot be a model for and critique of politics and public policy until it is justified morally and specified in terms of an acceptable goal.

Much else is missing from the market model of politics—for example, *class*. Given individualism, the belief that everyone benefits from market exchanges, and the conservative picture of freedom, class, along with race, ethnicity, and gender, do not exist as relevant or legitimate policy classifications. They contribute nothing to understanding and are erroneous, divisive, and ultimately destructive concepts inviting disastrous intervention. Neither does *international politics* figure in the conservative model, except for an occasional reference to defense and a general preference for free trade. The impact of international events—which deeply worried Keynes—is missing. However, if government is to do nothing to intervene in the economy, this omission is logical, even though dangerous in its passive acceptance of possible external manipulation.

These authors seem unconcerned with how the *transition* will occur from the current chaos to their preferred system. Though very critical of existing conditions and providing copious comment on what must be changed, they are curiously abstracted from the actual, real-world, political process through which their desired transformation can take place. They do not explain how changes will be made, what existing elements can be built upon, or how a new coalition can be created. If human nature is as these authors claim, how will public behavior change to accept the conservatives' system? Surely there can be no motivational metamorphosis, no sudden awareness of common interest, no willingness to sacrifice one's interest for another's, no likelihood that politicians able to end this chaos can be elected, and no chance that constitutional amendments limiting the power of majorities will be passed by rapacious majorities. None of this can occur if the assumptions upon which these authors build are accurate. Is disaster the only way? Perhaps. Unremitting claims that government must fail, coupled with the destruction through deliberate budget deficits and tax reductions of the resources that allow intervention, could change popular expectations. But that is a dangerous game which could just as easily lead to policies rejected by those who counsel such expedients.

The conservatives' microeconomics encourages this lack of concern with other issues. Keynesian macroeconomics promised the possibility of successful intervention and manipulation to address economic dislocations. Conservative microeconomics emphasizes individual units and fatalistically assumes that the system as a whole will take care of itself. Paralleling their economics, there is no macrotheory of system-wide political behavior. This shifts responsibility for addressing problems away from government and restricts the size of the public arena by reducing politics to individual behavior. Each theorist seeks to reduce government discretion. Hayek's evolution and adherence to unknown rules; Friedman's monetarism; Buchanan's contractarianism; and the shared arguments about government failure, self-interest, constitutional reconstruction, and the rule of law add up to leaving the economy alone. By eliminating the resources which allow system-wide intervention and by narrowing the scope of public concern, they hope to make permanently impossible a recreation of Keynesian intervention or Lyndon Johnson's Great Society.

This micro-outlook is related to the conservatives' predilection to view the world in ideal-type, procrustean *either/or terms*. These men see few shades of gray. Given the certitude of their universally valid market and self-interest principle, they divide institutions, policies, and interpretations into legitimate – those that agree with the market model – and illegitimate – those that do not. These dichotomies are not merely useful "for organizing thought"[23] but are seen as categorically true statements about the world: either individualism or collectivist conformity, self-interest or impossible altruism, economic freedom or slavery, justice or distribution of property, limited government or slavery, and so forth. These are "alternative principles."[24] There can be nothing in between, no continuum between policies, no viable or stable compromises among different positions, no reinterpretation of policies to achieve agreed-upon values, and no evolution of policies and attitudes beyond those necessary to their market.

As with their either/or fallacy, the conservatives do not allow any substantive content for ideals such as democracy, freedom, equality, or individualism. These are merely means to an end: choosing governors or allowing market competition. Beyond supporting the market, outcomes are of little concern. This emphasis on *procedure*, however, is without substance. Procedures are not neutral "but [are] morally charged and therefore morally problematic."[25] No procedure, not even an evolved one, is self-justifying or justified separate from the results it encourages or allows. If procedures are, were, or could be self-justifying, the conservatives could not limit democratic decision making from extending into any area. Procedures and operating rules always aim at some goal or purpose and are usually chosen or accepted because people assume that they promote a desired outcome, such as popular participation educating citizens, protecting their interests, and limiting government. By arguing that widely accepted ideals are satisfied by following set procedures, the conservatives justify but refuse to accept the outcome of those procedures. Losers in market competition have no reason to complain, no recourse against outcomes, and no right to appeal to a value higher than competition, because they have "fairly" competed and competition is the real content of these ideals. This approach too is an evasion because these economists do have a substantive end–protection of the market to which everything else is subordinate and derivative. But to acknowledge this would require justifying the market rather than basing justification on the market.

Conservative Political Economy as Empirical Theory

The problem of missing political concerns is compounded by the nature of the theory itself. This book contends that the political theory of conservative economists warrants notice apart from the question of the validity of their economics. The conservative economists may be defended on the grounds that they present tested and testable hypotheses, propositions, and theories, not normative statements. That defense is unwarranted for two reasons. First, as this book has argued, these authors clearly make normative recommendations and arguments, which they may claim are derived from empirical propositions but are frequently asserted not analyzed. Second, their theories of political economy are faulty and deficient in explaining actual behavior. In this section, I briefly review some of the difficulties inherent in the conservatives' method.

No major economic theory has proven to have great predictive power, except in terms of general trends. Much of the prestige of economics is based upon quantification that may or may not have actual empirical reference and on the afterglow of post–World War II Keynesian successes. Whether talking about Smith, Marx, Keynes, or their successors, all leave out significant components of political, social, *and* economic reality, producing very loose fits between theory and perceptions.

One of the most severe problems is the use of economic models to explain all political behavior. In the history of political theory, there have been at least five great patterns of attempts to devalue politics by claiming that it has no autonomous existence or value, or that it is secondary to or derivative from some other underlying reality that explains and should guide politics and public behavior. These include the idea, expressed brilliantly by Plato, that it is possible for a gifted person to have true *knowledge* of the fundamental structure of the universe. True knowledge gives true virtue, and the person possessing such knowledge/virtue has an absolute right to rule. *Religion* may also provide a fundamental reality, as in St. Augustine's claim that God created government as a punishment and corrective for sin and in contemporary assertions that some possess special insight provided by God into politics. Burke emphasized *culture* and *tradition*: the notion that the gradual evolution, adaptation, and acceptance of customs, usages, and behavior enabled people to overcome their adversities while demonstrating the limits of political possibility. (Unlike Hayek's tradition-based claims, Burke allowed the possibility of tradition evolving beyond the current ideal.) Other theorists have claimed *psychology* is the underlying reality and most severe limit on politics and political theory, as in Robert Owen's and B. F. Skinner's ideal cooperative communities. The conservative economists—and Marx—find their fundamental reality in the *economic foundation* of society. Economic relations, as reflected in the development of spontaneous order, are the fundamental human relations. Politics is secondary and dependent; good government depends upon the reality beyond and behind the temporary shifts and flows of politics—having the right economic relations.

As with other monocausal explanations, the economic model of politics lends insight into politics, but it and its behavioral assumptions provide an insufficient explanation of political behavior and are unable to make politics an adjunct of economic theory. Economics can benefit political analysis as a useful model of behavior and/or motivation, as a pattern of analysis, and by suggesting areas needing more study. However, when used to displace political analysis, it can narrow and cripple effective understanding of and prescription for politics. While keeping much of the language of politics—if not political analysis—the market model changes meaning and content to conform to its needs. The distinction between politics and economics as means to achieving functionally different ends is obscured. Thus economics defines the good political order, the problems and legitimate solutions of politics, and the duties of government; conceives of freedom as competition and the right to use one's property as one wishes; reduces equality to identical treatment by the law and the right to compete; and eliminates concern for inequalities of power and political stability. The result is to limit government and discredit claims that government has anything to do with creating the good life.[26] In the process, important issues are relegated to secondary considerations.

The comparison of politics to the market can be relevant in some circumstances but cannot be used to explain all behavior. Smith's invisible hand in economics is a metaphor—and does not operate in all cases—but the metaphorical element and limited application are missing from the conservative model. This *is* how the world operates; there are no exceptions. The metaphor made concrete is transferred to politics, to prove that an "invisible hand" propels the political market to inevitable failure.[27] As with voting, it is problematic how politics is analogous to idealized economic markets. There are no goods or services for sale. There are no recognized currencies, prices, or legitimate transactions. Behavior is dependent on institutions[28] and changes from one forum to another. People and politicians do engage in rational discussion and analysis which alter and widen their preferences based on evidence and needs of others. It matters who is in office because their perceptions and preferences shape what they consider to be a problem, a legitimate demand, or acceptable policy. Role playing constrains behavior. Political leaders do not and normally cannot act from naked self-interest but often base their actions on their values and beliefs about the public interest and sometimes in response to their perceptions of the needs of those who are not organized.[29] Unless values are simply rationalizations of individual self-interest, reflect system needs, or are treated as psychic income—a largely meaningless concept that cannot be made operational in an empirically relevant sense even within the conservative model—they must be viewed as real motivations and constraints upon behavior. Indeed, actualization of the conservative model depends upon the reality of values and beliefs as motivation.

The conservatives claim that their economics acknowledges and compensates for irremediable human ignorance. Though occasionally stated in tentative terms, the resulting political-social recommendations are unequivocal[30] and inescapable consequences of their supposedly objective understanding of natural behavior. This position confuses scientific methodology and analytic principles with conclusions. Though potentially separate, ethical judgments, methodologies, principles, and policies are mixed together, presenting prescriptive rules as well as observations. This does not make conservative theory incorrect, but neither its assumptions nor its political-social conclusions are detached statements about an independently existing reality, neutral and thus exempt from analysis and criticism.[31] More important, many conclusions are not disinterested deductions but judgments where values and preferences play as crucial a role as "scientific" facts. An illustration is how decisions are made on the relevant costs of an economic policy, whether it is a viable policy, and should it be implemented. Answers depend on shifting conjunctions of possibilities and desirabilities. There is no rigid distinction between preferences and objectively derived considerations of feasibility. Evidence is evaluated through the beliefs and values brought to it. Values and ethics shape what is perceived as evidence. One provides substance for, interacts with, shapes, and informs the other in evaluating behavior and institutions.[32]

For example, even if democracies and democratic governments operate as claimed, that does not automatically warrant the conservatives' limiting conclusions. It is a matter of judgment to determine the goals, trade-offs, and the values that are promoted by such systems. It is credible that citizen passivity following from conservatives' recommendations outweighs the damage claimed from excessive participation. Whether or not this is correct (though I believe it is), whether or not democracies are performing as they should, are conclusions that cannot be deduced from claims about inevitability, objectivity, neutrality, efficiency, and methodology. These conclusions must be weighed, balanced, and analyzed in light of all relevant purposes and data. Messy facts about how people actually behave cannot be dismissed as inconsistent with underlying theory while that theory is employed as an objectively correct analysis and prescription.

Normative political theorizing is an honorable, ancient, and necessary activity. Conservative economists have a potentially significant contribution to make to an unending debate. They cannot, however, disguise their participation with the claim—along with Marx—that they have an objective, value-free comprehension of reality that gives them an exact understanding of politics. Although that is a good ideological argument, it is neither philosophy nor science.

Despite Hayek's and occasionally Buchanan's criticism of constructivism and their shared concern for observation and evolution, conservative political economy is a rationalist construction, emphasizing logical consistency[33] and imposed upon reality. Observation and behavior are to conform to already accepted principles. These authors define behavior, institutions, and values, deduce logical results from them, and insist that they have discovered an accurate explanation of behavior and a basis for prescription. Missing observations are supplied by hypothesis and then assumed to fit reality because they conform to underlying postulates, which in turn are used to evaluate behavior. Research presupposes the validity of starting assumptions and is frequently dedicated to finding evidence to support them. Phenomena—such as increased productivity due to wage security, expansion of the American economy under government direction during World War II, firms that do not maximize profits, seemingly altruistic behavior, or noncoercive constraints on freedom—that do not conform to assumptions are ignored, explained away, or contorted to fit the conservative model, as in the use of self-interest to explain all behavior.

The outcome when applied to politics and society is a long chain of deductive reasoning, producing a deterministic, untestable – including starting assumptions, definition of human nature, political values, and deductive policy conclusions[34]– nonempirical system in which causation is casually asserted.[35] Many political and social statements are true by definition and therefore immune to empirical refutation, counter factual evidence, or falsification. Contrary examples cannot invalidate the theory or basic assumptions, such as government failure. This applies to the self-interest postulate. These authors are not saying that they have examined all behavior and found it to be self-interested. Rather, they define all behavior as self-interested and the market as the only institution capable of containing self-interest. People necessarily desire their own self-interest, a proposition that cannot be disputed on empirical grounds. Therefore everything they do is to benefit themselves. From this, it is a logical deduction that if people are allowed (free) to seek their self-interest, they will do so, leading to the politically charged conclusion that losers deserve no special help and everything that governments attempt is for purposes of self-interest, ensuring its failure. Conversely, if the market is the only institution able to contain and turn this natural propensity to good results, the market is natural. As both a valuable and natural institution, it is insusceptible to rational intervention.

Conservative Political Economy as Theology

From the conservative point of view, it does not matter that so much is missing from this market model. It serves roles other than completeness. Despite its claims, the political and philosophical economy of conservative theory is not scientific in the sense of only offering hypotheses for examination. As with Marx,[36] it is a system to be accepted as a whole Truth – a life philosophy that does not respond or change under the pressure of events but serves to rationalize, explain, and guide them.

Ideologies fill many of the same emotional and psychological needs as religion. They are widely accepted because of their emotive ideas, vision, hope of a better life, messianic zeal, or promise of participation in creating a superior world. Theological truths aside, religions supply their adherents with an inclusive belief system that depicts how the world operates, their place within it, and a code of behavior. Conservative political economy provides these elements for those who believe and accept. It is a powerful, self-contained, natural-law-based belief system that functions like a religion. Gilder recognizes this, and Buchanan's references to the "Old-Time Fiscal Religion" express deeply held convictions on moral propriety.[37]

Comparing conservative political economy with the sociological functions of religion illustrates its normative content and impact. Its picture of evolution explains the world – past, present and, future – and integrates it into the self seeking its own ends. All behavior is understandable and evaluated from within the system. It contains a crude eschatology, a theory of human nature, an autonomous morality, an explanation of the sources of corruption, a demonology (Keynes and intervention), dualism, a promise of justice, rewards for following fundamental rules, and punishment for violating them. In explaining man's role and place in the world and the individual's relation to the group, it assures people that they are rewarded according to their intrinsic worth as determined by impersonal, transindividual rules in the market. As in all great systems of natural law, these rules have universal application, derive from human nature, are independent of any specific person or group, and guide people to proper conduct and a better life. In this way, conservative political economy explains the world, and the world explained justifies the theory, making it into an explanation of social reality and a call to transform the world.

Spontaneous order fully expresses this autonomous, automatic system. This notion captures all the dualistic mystery in the theology of conservative political economy: independence and simultaneous interdependence of individuals and groups; harmony and conflict; selfish impulses transfigured into cooperative behavior and benefits for others; an order apart from men yet immanent; freedom coupled with determinism; explanation of success and failure; reward and punishment; and the promise of a system that is separate from individual will yet operates for the best without intervention or even understanding. *Dualism* divides the world into the good and bad, the elect and the damned, based upon acceptance or rejection of the mysteries of spontaneous order. Though beyond direct human control, the invisible hand of spontaneous order overcomes human weakness and ignorance to guide behavior.

This order *promises earthly salvation and threatens punishment*. Rewards and punishments are determined by conduct. Those who patiently follow the natural competitive rules and prohibitions of the spontaneous order/market will be rewarded with as much of the good they seek as is possible given their worth. Though corrupt, self-interested people will not fill every want, they are assured by the very nature of this autonomous system that their individual rewards are as large as they can possibly be. Conservative economics promises more than material goods but assures that one's behavior is in conformity with higher standards. Although individuals may do quite well from government intervention, the conservatives believe that they are being false to their real interests; that they rob those who live by the market code; and that, in the aggregate, society cannot survive if people act in this way. Nations failing to follow the system's oughts and those who place human will and willfulness ahead of system morality and maintenance are automatically punished by the system itself. Intervention–putting human pride and individual morality above the impersonal yet just and universal rules of the market–destroys its delicate equilibrium, penalizing violators with poverty, economic and social failure, injustice, and public strife.

Existing reality and behavior are viewed as intolerable and in need of transformation. The political world is flawed and corrupt for not adhering to conservative theory. Fallen man is Keynesian man. Overweening pride in human ability to overcome inherent ignorance and learn enough about political-economic relations to improve society successfully is the corruption that has crippled natural market relations. Evil enters the market world when mutable men act on the debased constructivist notion that they can overcome the limits of their own natures–limits which are accommodated only within the rules of the market. Secular salvation requires repentance: abandonment of the original sin of human pride and a return to an earlier state of grace when people recognized and lived by revealed economic truth. Accepting the necessity of giving oneself up to the market order, rather than rebelling through intervention, is the key to proper living. Only acceptance ensures efficiency and the creation of a correct order, one that reflects the conservatives' perception of human nature.

Part of the appeal of conservative political theology is its claim to *transcend both politics and the need to choose proper conduct*. Real-world politics involves ambiguity, conflict, compromise, and uncertainty. Conservative political economy is an antipolitical search for a final answer that will overcome ambiguity and doubt. While emphasizing human ignorance, these authors claim to have discovered a fundamental truth to guide politics, reduce the impact of ignorance and pride, and give a pattern to human lives. That truth developed in and is revealed by the operation of the spontaneous market order. When accepted, it produces harmony, order, and certainty in the correctness of actions. Politics, on the other hand, inculcates temptation to interfere in this natural order. It may express an inherent human urge to pursue self-interest, but it also frees men from the market constraints which limit the harmful impact of self-interested impulses. As such, the market order is the answer to the problems people foolishly seek to address through politics and is the most effective limit on the use of power. Being attendants of truth, these economists do not wish to accommodate the passions to which fallen, political man is prey, or to find ways to meet popular hopes and demands, but to limit harmful and destructive passions by holding people to the realization of market truth.

How should people relate to one another? The needs of system maintenance answer that perennial and vexing question. The market has the character of a *moral absolute*. People who follow market rules are relieved of responsibility for everything except narrow personal relations. The system itself provides the answer for disturbing questions of justice, proper distribution, and correct relations: namely, to follow self-interest within the framework of the spontaneous market order. In guiding self-interest, the system guides and constrains behavior, determining what people owe to one another while providing ultimate harmony. One's highest duty is to pursue self-interest. Following that natural impulse within the rules of the transcending market purifies self-centered action into benefits for others. Altruism and deliberate efforts to help others through political action, however, are punished with ruinous failure when self-interest inevitably corrupts them.

An act of *faith,* or what George Gilder refers to as "faith . . . in the compensatory logic of the cosmos,"[38] underpins the beliefs that the market system is harmonious, autonomous, and just; that people deserve what they get and can do no better; that they must accept their place within the spontaneous order because that order reflects the fundamental reality of which they are a part; that economic competition is the only legitimate way to gain; and that those who have much have succeeded through their own efforts and factors which no person controls.

This political economy is riddled with acts of faith masquerading as scientific principles. One of the most basic is that the market can accommodate all changes. Of course this is true, but it is the truth of which all tautologies partake. It is true by definition, if people accept their fate and do not interfere in the natural spontaneous order. It is the truth of the medieval peasant faced with war or a sick person who lacks medical care—events will take their course, and everything will work out for the best. Real hardships, the rise and fall of nations and of men, and the impact on people who bear the costs are ignored. Conservative faith insists these costs must be slighted, or else the faith will be compromised and people will believe that they can do something through intervention, leading again to a fall from grace.

Emphasis on the long run parallels this secular salvation. Eventually the forces of spontaneous order will produce the optimum outcome. Though this cannot be proven, and indeed empirical proof is probably impossible, it is an article of faith. People will be saved (though this refers to society, not individuals) if they are patient, believe, and follow the market's just and spontaneous rules without complaint. But if people are as self-seeking as these theorists claim, this demand reduces to a moral appeal for which their model allows no room.

The religious nature of this argument is apparent from its appeals to *a power greater than men*: inevitability, the inexorable working-out of political-economic relations, and inescapable conclusions. As an ideological faith, there is no way to challenge these arguments. They are more akin to faith healing than science.

When it "works"—and whatever happens is what works—adherents take that as a sign of grace and believe even more strongly. When it fails—when what occurs is not as adherents hope—that is a sign of human failure. People did not believe strongly enough, or unregenerate man refused to accept that spontaneous order will reassert itself, or tampering with the conservative version of evolution upset the delicate, natural adjustment mechanism. In any case, there is always an external cause why things have not worked according to the theory. There is never any internal problem, never any accommodation of theory to the reality of popular government, labor unions, private power, sticky wages, social stability, and large-scale production. Solutions require radical, external changes to conform the world to the system's assumptions and conclusions. Faith, however, may offer insights into the human condition, but it is not enough to guide the destiny of great nations. Though great nations need a belief system to order and make sense of experience, conservative political economy falls short in its attempts to provide that system.

Conclusions

There are at least two fundamental critiques of conservative political economy. The first is broadly economic: The market model is an inaccurate and incomplete representation of reality, making it a poor basis for and justification of public policy. Keynes epitomized this argument for liberals when he claimed that classical theory assumes political and economic characteristics that "happen not to be those of the economic society in which we actually live, with the result that its teaching is misleading and disastrous if we attempt to apply it to the facts of experience." Such theory "follows not from the actual facts, but from an incomplete hypothesis introduced for the sake of simplicity."[39] Keynes and other liberals deny that the economic system is autonomous or self-regulating in the way claimed by the conservatives and assert that exclusive emphasis on private gain is unlikely to achieve either efficiency, satisfaction, or national safety. They also believe that common interest exists and that public policy may sometimes be employed to achieve it. This ensures a positive role for government while still mistrusting government.

The second critique, and the one this book examines, is that as a normative political theory, the conservative model is inadequate to fulfill its political aspirations. Conservative political economy attempts to employ economic concepts to monopolize political debate. Even if the economic theory is acceptable and even though its criticisms of democracy and politics are sometimes accurate, that does not automatically or necessarily validate its political theory or its radical reconstruction of political values and institutions.

Though this theory takes up deep problems in both the domestic and international political economy—indeed, much of its popularity must be attributed to its pledge to remedy current maladies—the deductive, definitional conservative model is not a solution to these difficulties. Because societies as a whole rarely die, it is often impossible to prove whether a theory is successful or not, but one can see if it addresses relevant problems. Conservative theory defines away many perceived problems. Issues such as private power and popular discontent should not exist and under the proper economy will not exist; therefore, policy advice need not be concerned with them. The theory is too simple, too monocausal, ignoring both real complexities of everyday life and its own extremely high social costs. It elevates a narrow range of economic concepts such as economic order, efficiency, and competition from an instrumental relation to freedom, equality, democracy, and justice into primary values. In the process, it narrows, downgrades, and subordinates these traditional ends, emptying out much of the content and meaning that has attached to them over the last two hundred years, weakening their legitimacy, making them dependent on economic success, and undermining the basis for liberal democracy.

This is an old issue, reenacted in a less conspicuously political form between Malthus and Ricardo and their critics, including the Owenite socialists and the Chartists; between social Darwinism and its critics, including populism and the social gospel movement; and neoclassical economics and Keynesianism in the 1930s. Though the exact terms of this debate have changed from one period to the next, the metaphysics have remained remarkably constant. Differences are as much philosophical as empirical. It is a debate over the nature of economic and political reality, rival views of the nature of order, and acceptable models and procedures in science. In its claim to possess correct answers to perennial political questions, conservative political economy raises many unavoidable normative issues: human motivation; proper conduct; limits of human possibility; relevant time frames when prescribing for society; the meaning and arena of freedom; the nature of community; the relation of individual and community; proper social and political goals; standards for determining goals; the nature, meaning, and location of power; and whether social systems are created or discovered or both.

These are not scientific questions, but they are the questions that political and social theories must ceaselessly explore. There is no single answer to any of them, just varying patterns of attempts to find an answer in which policies change in order to fulfill basic principles in altered circumstances. Conservative theory is not, however, content to explore these but insists it has absolutely correct answers. The claim is not methodologically wrong, but the answers exclude a large part of experience. The naturalness of the spontaneous order, whose premises are to be followed, not contested, terminates debate. When alternatives are impossible, it is futile to search for them. People experiencing distress will not turn to the political system for relief if they are convinced that their problems are natural or are the result of forces and arrangements over which no one has control, or that public action must fail. Even if dissatisfied, they will accept their fate. As with Orwell's "newspeak," the conservative view shrinks possibilities, cuts off options to the future, and ends the search for other arrangements. Without the belief that alternatives are available, neither the concept of nor desire for intervention can exist. If for some perverse reason it remains, it will be seen as unnatural, irrational, and illegitimate.

What is to be made of the conservative argument? These theorists raise serious questions about politics and public policy. They express the anguish and despair of people faced with the dislocations and uncertainty of our times but do not offer answers that include all problems or all actors. Conservative theory is an escape from real predicaments into a world where there will be neither public issues, public moral dilemmas, nor the perennial political problem of how to govern. Given the probable political ramifications of this economic model, we must ask for more. The issue extends beyond economics and is more than a contest for the soul of economic man. It also determines the activities of the citizen and the shape, direction, and guiding philosophy of politics. Though disguised as economics, this is a political question. This is political philosophy.

Notes

Chapter One. Introduction

1. John Locke, *The Second Treatise of Government*, in *Two Treatises of Government*, ed. Peter Laslett (New York: Mentor Books, 1965), secs. 27–50, 85.

2. Charles E. Lindblom, *Politics and Markets: The World's Political-Economic Systems* (New York: Basic Books, 1977), p. 8.

3. Friedrich A. Hayek, *The Road to Serfdom*, with a new preface by the author (Chicago: University of Chicago Press, Phoenix Books, 1976), pp. ix, 10–20; idem, *Studies in Philosophy, Politics and Economics* (Chicago: University of Chicago Press, 1967), p. 149; idem, *Law, Legislation and Liberty: A New Statement of the Liberal Principles of Justice and Political Economy*, vol. 2, *The Mirage of Social Justice* (Chicago: University of Chicago Press, 1976), p. 44. See also his often-reprinted essay, "Why I Am Not a Conservative," in Friedrich A. Hayek, *The Constitution of Liberty* (Chicago: Gateway Editions, Henry Regnery, 1972), pp. 397–411.

4. *Individual Freedom: Selected Works of William H. Hutt*, ed. Svetozar Pejovich and David Klingaman (Westport, Conn.: Greenwood Press, 1975), p. 12 n. 1.

5. Milton Friedman, *Capitalism and Freedom* (Chicago: University of Chicago Press, 1962), pp. 5–6.

6. Quoted in Sidney Blumenthal, *The Rise of the Counter-Establishment: From Conservative Ideology to Political Power* (New York: Times Books, 1986), p. 89.

7. John Gray, *Liberalism* (Minneapolis: University of Minnesota Press, 1986), pp. 37ff, 78–79; Robert Nisbet, *Conservatism: Dream and Reality* (Minneapolis: University of Minnesota Press, 1986), pp. 52, 97–98; David Sidorsky, ed., *The Liberal Tradition in European Thought* (New York: G. P. Putnam's Sons, 1970), pp. 260–72; Robert Lindsay Schuettinger, ed., *The Conservative Tradition in European Thought* (New York: G. P. Putnam's Sons, 1970), pp. 91–102; Russell Kirk, *A Program for Conservatives* (Chicago: Henry Regnery, 1954), p. 144; Hayek, *Constitution of Liberty*, p. 409. Kirk, *Program*, sees influence of Burke on Hayek, p. 154. This is essentially what Thomas Sowell calls the constrained vision in *A Conflict of Visions: Ideological Origins of Political Struggles* (New York: Quill, 1987). He too (p. 41) sees links between Burke and Hayek. William F. Buckley, Jr., ed., *American Conservative Thought in the Twentieth Century* (Indianapolis: Bobbs-Merrill, 1970), does not see a fundamental split in conservatism and includes Friedman and Kirk in the same volume; see pp. xv–xl, 205–12, 355–81. See also "A Symposium: What Is a Liberal–Who Is a Conservative," *Commentary*, Sept. 1976, pp. 31–113 (special issue).

8. George Stigler has no difficulty in calling emphasis on competition and the cooperative-regulatory role of the market "conservative." He also believes that the training

of economists encourages them to be conservatives. "The Politics of Political Economists," *Quarterly Journal of Economics* 73 (1959): 522–32. See also George Stigler, *Memoirs of an Unregulated Economist* (New York: Basic Books, 1988), pp. 138–40.

9. These authors accept formal principles similar to those of the conservatives—freedom, equality, individualism, self-interest as an important motivation, and limited government. Differences center on the content, meaning, and interrelation of these principles as well as policies to implement them, creating distinct approaches to politics and public policy even when both sides claim to be protecting and maximizing the same value.

10. See John Stuart Mill, *Principles of Political Economy*. The relevant passages are in Conrad Waligorski and Thomas Hone, eds., *Anglo-American Liberalism: Readings in Normative Political Economy* (Chicago: Nelson Hall, 1981), pp. 219–29.

11. Gray's reference to Burke applies here. He represents a form of "conservatism in which liberal values are preserved but liberal hopes chastened." Gray, *Liberalism*, p. 19.

12. See Mancur Olson and Christopher Clague, "Dissent in Economics: The Convergence of Extremes," in Ryan C. Amacher, Robert D. Tollison, and Thomas D. Willett, *The Economic Approach to Public Policy: Selected Readings* (Ithaca, N.Y.: Cornell University Press, 1976), p. 83. On p. 81 they associate Stigler with the public-choice school.

13. Don Patinkin, "Keynes and Economics Today," *American Economic Review, Papers and Proceedings* 74 (1984): 99.

14. See Jude Wanniski, "The Burden of Friedman's Monetarism," *New York Times*, July 16, 1981, sec. 3, p. 2.

15. *New York Times Book Review*, Feb. 24, 1980, p. 46. *Free to Choose* was a Book of the Month Club alternate selection and a selection by the Conservative Book Club.

16. See James Petras, "The Chicago Boys Flunk Out in Chile," *Nation*, Feb. 19, 1983, pp. 193, 210–11. Friedman also uses "Chicago Boys." See Milton Friedman, "Free Markets and Generals," *Newsweek*, Jan. 25, 1982, p. 59.

17. See Paul Lews, "A New Monetarism Sweeps the West," *New York Times*, Feb. 3, 1980, sec. 12, pp. 9 and 14. See also Milton Friedman and Rose Friedman, *Tyranny of the Status Quo* (San Diego: Harcourt Brace Jovanovich, 1984), where the dust jacket discusses influence; Rich Thomas, "The Magic of Reaganomics," *Newsweek*, Dec. 26, 1988, pp. 40–41, 44.

18. See Blumenthal, *Rise of the Counter-Establishment*, p. 15 and passim. On p. 116 Blumenthal claims Margaret Thatcher was "most influenced" by Hayek and Friedman and on p. 118 notes that in 1980 Friedman submitted a memo to the House of Commons supporting and criticizing some of Thatcher's policies. David Stockman, *The Triumph of Politics: The Inside Story of the Reagan Revolution* (New York: Avon, 1987), pp. 33–34, 42. Stockman also mentions Friedman as an influence.

19. Hayek, *Road to Serfdom*, p. v n. 3.

20. Gray, *Liberalism*, p. 38. See also Charles R. Morris, *A Time of Passion: America, 1960–1980* (New York: Penguin, 1986), p. 182.

21. Thomas Sowell, *Say's Law: An Historical Analysis* (Princeton, N.J.: Princeton University Press, 1972), p. vii.

22. Keynes is the only exception, as he was the occasion for much of the conservatives' writings and remains a target of their critiques.

23. I owe this phrase to Warren J. Samuels.

24. For some specific points see: James M. Buchanan, *What Should Economists Do?* (Indianapolis: Liberty Press, 1979), p. 275; F. A. Hayek, *Denationalisation of Money: An Analysis of the Theory and Practice of Concurrent Currencies* (London: Institute of Economic Affairs, 1976), pp. 64–65, 80, and passim; Friedman and Friedman, *Tyranny*,

pp. 99–100; George Gilder, *Wealth and Poverty,* (New York: Basic Books, 1981), esp. pp. 31, 37–38.

25. Buchanan, *What Should Economists Do?* p. 22; Milton Friedman and Rose Friedman, *Free to Choose: A Personal Statement* (New York: Avon, 1979), pp. ix–x, xx; Friedman, *Capitalism and Freedom,* preface.

26. George J. Stigler in William Breit and Roger W. Spencer, eds., *Lives of the Laureates: Seven Nobel Economists* (Cambridge: MIT Press, 1986), p. 108.

27. Buchanan comes closest to recognizing this when he notes that "it is in the realms of political philosophy that the struggle must be waged." *Liberty, Market and State: Political Economy in the 1980s* (New York: New York University Press, 1986), p. 67.

28. See Charles E. Lindblom, "The Market as Prison," *Journal of Politics* 44 (1982): 332. "Both as an institution and as an intellectual concept, it seems to have imprisoned our thinking about politics and economics."

29. See Thomas S. Kuhn, *The Structure of Scientific Revolutions* (Chicago: University of Chicago Press, 1970); Daniel J. Boorstin, *The Discoverers: A History of Man's Search to Know His World and Himself* (New York: Vintage Books, 1985); J. Bronowski, *The Common Sense of Science* (Cambridge, Mass.: Harvard University Press, 1967); J. Bronowski, *The Ascent of Man* (Boston: Little, Brown and Co., 1973); Stephen Jay Gould, *Time's Arrow, Time's Cycle: Myth and Metaphor in the Discovery of Geological Time* (Cambridge, Mass.: Harvard University Press, 1987); James Burke, *The Day the Universe Changed* (Boston: Little, Brown and Co., 1985).

30. Hayek seemed more aware of this in the 1940s than today. "This is a political book. . . . all I shall have to say is derived from certain ultimate values." *Road to Serfdom,* p. xvii.

31. For example, see Walter A. Weisskopf, "Hidden Value Conflicts in Economic Thought," *Ethics* 61 (1951): 195–204; *idem,* "The Method Is the Ideology: From a Newtonian to a Heisenbergian Paradigm in Economics," *Journal of Economic Issues* 13 (1979): 869–83; Robert A. Solo, "Value Judgments in the Discourse of the Sciences," in Robert A. Solo and Charles W. Anderson, eds., *Value Judgement and Income Distribution* (New York: Praeger, 1981), pp. 9–40.

Chapter Two. Starting Assumptions: The Philosophical-Economic Foundations for a Political Argument

1. From different ends of the political spectrum, Robert Heilbroner and Thomas Sowell employ the same concept: "visions." Robert L. Heilbroner, *Behind the Veil of Economics: Essays in the Worldly Philosophy* (New York: W. W. Norton and Co., 1988), pp. 7–8, 165–84, 196–99; Thomas Sowell, *A Conflict of Visions: Ideological Origins of Political Struggles* (New York: Quill, 1987). Hayek agrees that assumptions are often held "as self-evident truths." *Law, Legislation and Liberty: A New Statement of the Liberal Principles of Justice and Political Economy,* vol. 1, *Rules and Order* (Chicago: University of Chicago Press, 1973), p. 70.

2. J. Philip Wogaman, *The Great Economic Debate: An Ethical Analysis* (Philadelphia: Westminster Press, 1977), p. 39. Carol Leutner Anderson uses the term "the reality base" for underlying assumptions about "the structure of reality and the nature of man and the universe." "Economics and Metaphysics: Framework for the Future," *Review of Social Economy* 40 (1982):200. See also Robert E. Goodin, *Political Theory and Public Policy* (Chicago: University of Chicago Press, 1982), p. 18 and passim.

3. Milton Friedman, "Value Judgments in Economics," in Sidney Hook, ed., *Human Values and Economic Policy* (New York: New York University Press, 1967), pp. 85, 86. This is in marked contrast to the liberal position, represented by John Maynard Keynes. He regularly referred to economics as a "moral science." *The Collected Writings of John Maynard Keynes*, vol. 14, *The General Theory and After* (London: Macmillan, 1973), p. 300. See also Keynes to the Archbishop of York, Dec. 3, 1941, where he claimed that policy issues, as opposed to techniques, usually involve moral considerations. Keynes Papers, box 21, bundle 4, Kings College Archives, Cambridge.

4. Milton Friedman, "What All Is Utility?" *Economic Journal* 65 (1955):409.

5. Milton Friedman, "Nobel Lecture: Inflation and Unemployment," *Journal of Political Economy* 85 (1977):453.

6. Milton Friedman, *Essays in Positive Economics* (Chicago: University of Chicago Press, 1953), pp. 3–43.

7. Ibid., pp. 4–7.

8. Ibid., pp. 8–9, 16–21, 40–41, 21, 14. Hutt also claims, in discussing *Calculus of Consent,* that assumptions need not be realistic. *Individual Freedom: Selected Works of William H. Hutt,* ed. Svetozar Pejovich and David Klingaman (Westport, Conn.: Greenwood Press, 1975), p. 18.

9. Friedman, "Value Judgments in Economics," p. 88.

10. Sowell, *Conflict of Visions,* pp. 113, 180, 216ff, and passim.

11. James M. Buchanan and Gordon Tullock, *The Calculus of Consent: Logical Foundations of Constitutional Democracy* (Ann Arbor: University of Michigan Press, 1965), p. 29; James M. Buchanan, *What Should Economists Do?* (Indianapolis: Liberty Press, 1979), pp. 36, 84, 120, 136, 207; James M. Buchanan, *Economics: Between Predictive Science and Moral Philosophy,* comp. and with a preface by Robert D. Tollison and Viktor J. Vanberg (College Station: Texas A&M University Press, 1987), pp. 16, 174, 304; James Buchanan, "Toward Analysis of Closed Behavioral Systems," in Ryan C. Amacher, Robert D. Tollison, and Thomas D. Willett, eds., *The Economic Approach to Public Policy: Selected Readings* (Ithaca, N.Y.: Cornell University Press, 1976), p. 343. See also James M. Buchanan, *Liberty, Market and State: Political Economy in the 1980s* (New York: New York University Press, 1986), pp. 108–12, 123, 261.

12. Ryan C. Amacher, "Introduction," in Amacher, Tollison, and Willett, *Economic Approach,* p. 16.

13. Hayek, *Law, Legislation and Liberty,* 1:13, 64, 5; idem, *Law, Legislation and Liberty: A New Statement of the Liberal Principles of Justice and Political Economy,* vol. 2, *The Mirage of Social Justice* (Chicago: University of Chicago Press, 1976), p. 113.

14. George Stigler is more skeptical: "[W]here do economists get their ethical systems? . . . .wherever they can find them." *The Economist as Preacher and Other Essays* (Chicago: University of Chicago Press, 1982), pp. 19, 3.

15. Lester C. Thurow, *Generating Inequality: Mechanisms of Distribution in the U.S. Economy* (New York: Basic Books, 1975), pp. viii–x, 21–25, 54, 208–9; idem, *Dangerous Currents: The State of Economics* (New York: Random House, 1983), pp. 16, 18, 216; idem, *The Zero-Sum Society: Distribution and the Possibilities for Economic Change* (New York: Basic Books, 1980), pp. 16–17; idem, "Why Do Economists Disagree?" *Dissent* 29 (Spring 1982):176–82.

16. On this last point see Ludwig von Mises, *Epistemological Problems of Economics,* trans. George Reisman (New York: New York University Press, 1981), pp. 27–29.

17. This objectivity claim is often challenged. Cf. Piero V. Mini, *Philosophy and Economics: The Origins and Development of Economic Theory* (Gainesville: University Presses of Florida, 1974); Thurow, *Dangerous Currents;* Thurow, "Why Do Economists Disagree?" pp. 176–82; Wogaman, *Great Economic Debate,* pp. 2–3 and passim; Homa Katouzian,

Ideology and Method in Economics (New York: New York University Press, 1980); Martin Staniland, *What Is Political Economy: A Study of Social Theory and Underdevelopment* (New Haven, Conn.: Yale University Press, 1985), pp. 197–200; Donald N. McCloskey, *The Rhetoric of Economics* (Madison: University of Wisconsin Press, 1985); Heilbroner, *Behind the Veil.*

18. It may appear old-fashioned to speak about human nature because many people erroneously interpret it as a fixed essence, unaffected by culture. I employ the older term because it is a link with traditional political discourse, and the conservative economists often talk as if behavior is fixed and determined, their theory is of universal applicability, and social-cultural influences are of little consequence. Readers who prefer motivation, psychology, drives, genetic predispositions, or cultural determination may freely substitute these terms for human nature. We are discussing essentially the same thing: assumptions and images about why and how people behave.

19. To Pierre Samuel Dupont de Nemours, Apr. 14, 1816; quoted in *Anglo-American Liberalism: Readings in Normative Political Economy,* ed. Conrad Waligorski and Thomas Hone (Chicago: Nelson Hall, 1981), p. 95.

20. The quote is from Adam Smith, *An Inquiry into the Nature and Causes of the Wealth of Nations,* ed. Edwin Cannan (New York: Modern Library, 1965), p. 508. See also p. 324: "[T]he desire of bettering our condition . . . comes with us from the womb, and never leaves us till we go into the grave."

21. See Friedrich A. Hayek, *Law, Legislation and Liberty: A New Statement of the Liberal Principles of Justice and Political Economy,* vol. 3, *The Political Order of a Free People* (Chicago: University of Chicago Press, 1979), pp. 160, 163.

22. The conservative economists generally employ masculine pronouns or use "man" as a generic term. In Gilder, women clearly hold an inferior position.

23. This is a continuing theme in Hayek. See Friedrich A. Hayek, *The Constitution of Liberty* (South Bend, Ind.: Gateway Editions, 1960), p. 29; idem, *Law, Legislation and Liberty,* 1:11–15; Buchanan, *Economics,* pp. 5, 58, 64, 73, 79, 191; Milton Friedman and Rose Friedman, *Free to Choose: A Personal Statement* (New York: Avon, 1979), passim.

24. George Gilder's self-interest is somewhat different. His entrepreneur is the supreme individualist, breaking away from the masses and in the process creating civilization. As with William Graham Sumner, the entrepreneur drags the rest of us along with him, motivated not by greed but by the creative altruistic act of giving to others. Entrepreneurs work for spiritual reasons, not just material rewards, "impelled by their curiosity, imagination, and faith"; they deserve to keep the wealth they earn. Gilder, *The Spirit of Enterprise* (New York: Simon and Schuster, 1984), pp. 16–17, 254–55. See also George Gilder, *Wealth and Poverty* (New York: Basic Books, 1981).

25. Buchanan, "Toward Analysis," in Amacher, Tollison, and Willett, *Economic Approach,* p. 343. See also Buchanan and Tullock, *Calculus of Consent,* pp. 23, 25–26, 29. By definition, each person desires to maximize his or her utility, emphasizing economic self-interest. See Buchanan, *What Should Economists Do?* p. 275; Stigler, *Economist as Preacher,* p. 21.

26. Aanund Hylland, "The Purpose and Significance of Social Choice Theory: Some General Remarks and an Application to the 'Lady Chatterley Problem,'" in Jon Elster and Aanund Hylland, eds., *Foundations of Social Choice Theory* (Cambridge: Cambridge University Press, 1986), p. 48.

27. Friedman and Friedman, *Free to Choose,* pp. 108, 17, 19; see also pp. ix–x and 110. See Amacher, Tollison, and Willett, "The Economic Approach to Social Policy Questions: Some Methodological Perspectives," in their *Economic Approach,* pp. 24–25. Buchanan refers to a person choosing the highest alternative "on his preference order-

ing." *What Should Economists Do?* p. 42. See also Buchanan, *Economics,* p. 59; idem, *Liberty, Market and State,* p. 175.

28. Hayek, *Law, Legislation and Liberty,* 3:70; idem, *The Road to Serfdom,* with a new preface by the author (Chicago: University of Chicago Press, Phoenix Books, 1976), p. 125; idem, *Denationalisation of Money: An Analysis of the Theory and Practice of Concurrent Currencies* (London: Institute of Economic Affairs, 1976), p. 100; idem, *Law, Legislation and Liberty,* 2:145.

29. Milton Friedman and Rose Friedman, *Tyranny of the Status Quo* (San Diego: Harcourt Brace Jovanovich, 1984), pp. 38–39; Richard E. Wagner and Robert D. Tollison, *Balanced Budgets, Fiscal Responsibility and the Constitution* (San Francisco: Cato Institute, 1980), pp. 45–46; Hayek, *Law, Legislation and Liberty,* 3:120; Buchanan, *What Should Economists Do?* pp. 210–11.

30. See Gilder, *Wealth and Poverty,* passim; Milton Friedman, *Capitalism and Freedom* (Chicago: University of Chicago Press, 1962), p. 33. The family is the only corporate body that Friedman and Hayek recognize as having corporate rights, whereas traditional conservatives recognize many such bodies. These authors do not explain why the family is an exception to the operation of narrow self-interest. See also Miriam David, "Moral and Maternal: The Family in the Right," in Ruth Levitas, ed., *The Ideology of the New Right* (Cambridge: Polity Press, 1986), pp. 136–68.

31. Hayek, *Law, Legislation and Liberty,* 3: 65–70; idem, *Road to Serfdom,* p. 48; idem, *Denationalisation,* pp. 40–45.

32. Buchanan, *What Should Economists Do?* p. 35. See also Mini, *Philosophy and Economics,* p. 46: "[E]conomics recognizes no entity higher than the individual's consciousness."

33. See Buchanan and Tullock, *Calculus of Consent,* passim; Buchanan, *Economics,* passim.

34. See especially Buchanan, *What Should Economists Do?* pp. 70–77, 281–82, for limits on a narrow economic perspective and his growing awareness of the importance of institutions. Buchanan, *Economics,* pp. 305–6, from his Nobel Prize lecture.

35. See Buchanan, *What Should Economists Do?* p. 144. See also pp. 22–23, 120–21, 144–46, 148.

36. The quote is from Hayek, *Road to Serfdom,* p. 59. See also pp. 14, 32–42, 56, 59–60, 148; and F. A. Hayek, "Individualism and Economic Order," in Robert Lindsay Schuettinger, ed., *The Conservative Tradition in European Thought* (New York: G. P. Putnam's Sons, 1970), pp. 91–102, esp. 94–95. Hayek, *Law, Legislation and Liberty,* 1:33 and passim, 2:1, 33, and passim; idem, *Studies in Philosophy, Politics and Economics* (Chicago: University of Chicago Press, 1967), p. 232.

37. Gilder, *Spirit of Enterprise,* pp. 16–17, 254.

38. See John Stuart Mill, *On Liberty,* in Marshall Cohen, ed., *The Philosophy of John Stuart Mill: Ethical, Political and Religious* (New York: Modern Library, 1961), chap. 3, entitled "Of Individuality, as One of the Elements of Well-Being." Keynes was in this tradition of individualism. He wanted to purge liberalism of what he considered the excesses of laissez-faire individualism, protecting individualism's advantages: "efficiency . . . decentralisation . . . the play of self-interest," "personal choice. . . . the variety of life." *The Collected Writings of John Maynard Keynes,* vol. 7, *The General Theory of Employment Interest and Money* (London: Macmillan, 1973), p. 380.

39. Thomas Robert Malthus, in Waligorski and Hone, *Anglo-American Liberalism,* p. 198.

40. In *Conflict of Visions,* Sowell seems to admit this, especially pp. 141–71.

41. Sowell notes that the arguments of theorists such as Condorcet, Smith, Friedman, and Burke did not simply advance their self-interest; *Conflict of Visions,* p. 222.

42. Hayek, *Road to Serfdom,* p. xvii.

43. See Amartya Sen, *On Ethics and Economics* (Oxford: Basil Blackwell, 1987), pp. 81, 83. Alan Nelson notes that the "economically rational agent" might "feign agreement" to get a share but refuse to contribute. "Economic Rationality and Morality," *Philosophy and Public Affairs* 17 (1988):156.

44. See Friedman and Friedman, *Free to Choose*, p. x. Behavior is "determined by the interaction among persons pursuing their own self-interests (broadly interpreted) rather than the social goals the participants find it advantageous to enunciate."

45. Mancur Olson's "selective incentives" address this problem. These are noneconomic incentives that might mobilize a latent group. By not examining this possibility, the conservatives undermine their discussion of the free-rider principle and their analysis of interest-group membership. They tend to view the interests of group members as fairly monolithic and do not analyze appeals other than to narrow self-interest, whereas Olson does include them in his analysis. See Mancur Olson, Jr., *The Logic of Collective Action: Public Goods and the Theory of Groups* (New York: Schocken Books, 1971), pp. 60–65, 132–34.

46. Albert O. Hirschman, *Rival Views of Market Society and Other Recent Essays* (New York: Viking, 1986), pp. 156–57, notes that we must rely upon appeals to both self-interest and civic welfare. This was the position of the founders of the American Republic.

47. Albert O. Hirschman, *The Passions and the Interests: Political Arguments for Capitalism before Its Triumph* (Princeton, N.J.: Princeton University Press, 1977), pp. 93–94. See also Sidney Fine, *Laissez-Faire and the General Welfare State: A Study of Conflict in American Thought 1865–1901* (Ann Arbor: University of Michigan Press, Ann Arbor Paperbacks, 1964), pp. 6–8; Giuseppa Saccaro-Battisti, "Changing Metaphors of Political Structures," *Journal of the History of Ideas* 44 (1983):31–54.

48. This is a continuing theme in Hayek. Hayek, *Studies*, pp. 97, 162; idem, *Denationalisation*, p. 80; idem, *Law, Legislation and Liberty*, 1:xii, 36–37.

49. Friedrich A. von Hayek, *Freedom and the Economic System*, Public Policy Pamphlet no. 29 (Chicago: University of Chicago Press, 1939), p. 14; idem, *The Confusion of Language in Political Thought: With Some Suggestions for Remedying It*, Occasional Paper no. 20 (London: Institute of Economic Affairs, 1968), pp. 10–12; idem, *Studies*, pp. 97, 162–63, 241; idem, "Kinds of Order in Society," in Kenneth S. Templeton, Jr., ed., *The Politicization of Society* (Indianapolis: Liberty Press, 1979), pp. 504–7, 509, 516. See also Buchanan, *What Should Economists Do?* p. 205.

50. Hayek, *Law, Legislation and Liberty*, 1:104, 38–39, 120; idem, "Kinds of Order," pp. 515–17, 520–21.

51. Friedman and Friedman, *Free to Choose*, pp. 16–18, 183; Milton Friedman, *Adam Smith's Relevance for 1976*, Original Paper no. 5 (Los Angeles: International Institute for Economic Research, 1976).

52. Buchanan, *Liberty, Market and State*, pp. 254, 4, 20, 73–86, 267–68; idem, *What Should Economists Do?* pp. 205, 146, 130.

53. Gilder, *Wealth and Poverty*, p. 24 and passim. The quote is from idem, *Spirit of Enterprise*, p. 19. See also Ludwig von Mises, *Liberalism: A Socio-Economic Exposition*, trans. Ralph Raico, ed. Arthur Goddard (Kansas City: Sheed Andrews and McMeel, 1978), pp. xiii, 79, 198–99.

54. None of these authors accepts equilibrium as a return to optimum levels—an idea that characterized some pre-Keynesian political economy—but their ideas contain an equilibrium argument. Hirschman, *Rival Views*, p. 77, equates order with equilibrium as involving the same thought process. Hayek, *Law, Legislation and Liberty*, 2: 128, uses a clock analogy to describe the market and on p. 129 refers to "inherent principles." See also James M. Buchanan and Richard E. Wagner, *Democracy in Deficit: The Political Legacy of Lord Keynes* (New York: Academic Press, 1977), p. 25; James M. Buchanan

and Richard E. Wagner, eds., *Fiscal Responsibility in Constitutional Democracy* (Leiden and Boston: Martinus Nijhoff, 1978), p. 86. See the reference to "self-correcting forces" in James M. Buchanan, Richard E. Wagner, and John Burton, eds., *The Consequences of Mr. Kaynes: An Analysis of the Misuse of Economic Theory for Political Profiteering, with Proposals for Constitutional Disciplines* (London: Institute of Economic Affairs, 1978), p. 13.

55. This is a continuing theme. See Hayek, *Road to Serfdom*, pp. 5, 21, 201, and passim; idem, *Law, Legislation and Liberty*, 1: 42, 54, 2:106, and passim. Acceptance of necessity is another common theme. The questions remain as to whose necessity and what does the word mean?

56. Cf. Buchanan: People "require a vision of the social order," and economists can provide one "that is not chaotic, uncontrolled, and unplanned." *What Should Economists Do?* p. 76. Hayek, *Law, Legislation and Liberty*, 1:36–37, 68, 114–15, 2:4, 107, claims that economists have demonstrated the existence of this order and that only they fully integrate it into their analysis.

57. Hayek, *Freedom and the Economic System*, p. 13; idem, *Law, Legislation and Liberty*, 3:74 (an especially strong efficiency claim); idem, *Confusion of Language*, p. 30; idem, *Studies*, p. 167.

58. Milton Friedman, "Monetary Policy," *Proceedings of the American Philosophical Society* 116 (January 1972):193, 194; Friedman and Friedman, *Free to Choose*, pp. 5–6, 212; Milton Friedman, *There's No Such Thing as a Free Lunch* (La Salle, Ill.: Open Court, 1975), p. 210; idem, *Adam Smith's Relevance*, p. 15; Friedman, *Essays*, p. 271. See also Friedman, *Capitalism and Freedom*, p. 38.

59. Joseph J. Spengler, "The Problem of Order in Economic Affairs," *Southern Economic Journal* 15 (1948): 15; Buchanan, *What Should Economists Do?* pp. 81, 282.

60. Friedman, *Capitalism and Freedom*, p. 23; Friedman and Friedman, *Free to Choose*, pp. 1–5. See also Milton Friedman, "The Threat to Freedom in the Welfare State," *Business and Society Review* 21 (Spring 1977):15; idem, "Value Judgments in Economics," pp. 89–90.

61. Buchanan, *What Should Economists Do?* p. 31.

62. Buchanan, *Liberty, Market and State*, pp. 108–20.

63. Buchanan, *Economics*, pp. 16, 28–29; idem, *Liberty, Market and State*, pp. 167, 190.

64. Saccaro-Battisti, "Changing Metaphors," p. 34.

65. In connoting what is desirable, "efficiency" requires a criterion and is itself a normative concept—i.e., efficiency in terms of a goal or purpose.

66. With some notable exceptions. Cf. Charles E. Lindblom, "The Market as Prison," *Journal Of Politics* 44 (1982):324–36; C. B. Macpherson, *Democratic Theory: Essays in Retrieval* (Oxford: Clarendon Press, 1973), pp. 185–94; idem, "The Economic Penetration of Political Theory: Some Hypotheses," *Journal of the History of Ideas* 39 (1978):101–18; Robert E. Lane, "Market Justice, Political Justice," *American Political Science Review* 80 (1986):383–402.

67. See Thurow, *Dangerous Currents*, p. 31; and McCloskey, *Rhetoric*, pp. 76, 179.

68. Amacher, Tollison, and Willett, in *Economic Approach*, provide an excellent introduction, though their assumptions may be found in most of my references. See Friedman and Friedman, *Free to Choose*, pp. ix–x, 16–17; Buchanan, *What Should Economists Do?* pp. 199ff, 219–29; James M. Buchanan, "The Moral Dimension of Debt Financing," *Economic Inquiry* 23 (1985):1–6.

69. McCloskey, *Rhetoric*, passim.

70. Buchanan, *What Should Economists Do?* pp. 120, 91, 129, 157, 155, 148, 130, 123–26. See James M. Buchanan and Robert D. Tollison, eds., *Theory of Public Choice: Political Applications of Economics* (Ann Arbor: University of Michigan Press, 1972),

pp. 16–20; Buchanan, "Toward Analysis," in Amacher, Tollison, and Willett, *Economic Approach,* p. 344. See also Hutt, *Individual Freedom,* p. 15. The purpose of Hayek's three-volume *Law, Legislation and Liberty* is to combine the study of economics, law, politics, and ethics into one analysis dominated by the market model; see 1:4.

71. See Hayek, *Law, Legislation and Liberty,* 3:151; Buchanan, *What Should Economists Do?* p. 241.

72. Buchanan, *What Should Economists Do?* p. 168, emphasis added. Note the implication that politics is coercion. See also Buchanan, *Liberty, Market and State,* p. 127.

73. F. A. Hayek, *Economic Freedom and Representative Government,* Occasional Paper no. 39 (London: Institute of Economic Affairs, 1973), p. 9; Buchanan and Wagner, *Democracy in Deficit,* pp. 104, 118, 102–3; Samuel Brittan, *The Economic Consequences of Democracy* (London: Temple Smith, 1977), pp. 255–57; John Burton, "Keynes's Legacy to Great Britain: Folly in a Great Kingdom," in Buchanan, Wagner, and Burton, *Consequences,* pp. 73–74; Jesse Burkhead and Charles Knerr, "Congressional Budget Reform: New Decision Structures," in Buchanan and Wagner, *Fiscal Responsibility,* p. 134.

74. This term envisages humanity as passive. This passive and negative emphasis dominates the economists' discussions of freedom, equality, democracy, justice, and community.

75. Ryan C. Amacher, "A Menu of Distributional Considerations," in Amacher, Tollison, and Willett, *Economic Approach,* p. 262; Wagner and Tollison, *Balanced Budgets,* pp. 6–7; Friedman and Friedman, *Tyranny,* pp. 94, 45; Friedman, *There's No Such Thing,* pp. 59–60. See also Hutt, *Individual Freedom,* pp. 25–26; Buchanan and Wagner, *Democracy in Deficit,* pp. 50–51; Hayek, *Law, Legislation and Liberty,* 3:32.

76. See Hayek, *Law, Legislation and Liberty,* 2:129, 137, 3:73; Sidney Blumenthal, *The Rise of the Counter-Establishment: From Conservative Ideology to Political Power* (New York: Times Books, 1986), p. 220.

77. Friedman, *There's No Such Thing,* pp. 289–90; Friedman and Friedman, *Free to Choose,* pp. 290–91.

78. This is a false generalization. These authors ignore the history and wide range of democratic theories. Writing in the context of liberal democracies, they see pure majoritarianism.

79. Hayek, *Economic Freedom,* pp. 9, 12; Brittan, *Economic Consequences,* pp. 81, 288, 248; Hayek, *Law, Legislation, and Liberty,* 3:11.

80. Arthur Seldon, preface to Buchanan, Wagner, and Burton, *Consequences,* p. 9. That government is always the cause of problems and always interferes in natural economic processes are also continuing themes in Gilder, *Wealth and Poverty,* pp. 128–52 and passim.

81. For Sumner, welfare was always a case of A and B agreeing together what C should do for D. "The Forgotten Man," in *Social Darwinism: Selected Essays of William Graham Sumner* (Englewood Cliffs, N.J.: Prentice-Hall, 1963), pp. 110–35; or, "On the Case of a Certain Man Who Is Never Thought Of," in William Graham Sumner, *What Social Classes Owe to Each Other* (Caldwell, Idaho: Caxton Printers, 1974), pp. 107–15.

82. Friedman, *There's No Such Thing,* p. 233; cf. pp. 208, 210; Friedman and Friedman, *Free to Choose,* pp. 183, 87–88, 108; Milton Friedman, *The Invisible Hand in Economics and Politics* (Singapore: Institute of Southeast Asian Studies, 1981), pp. 11–12. Milton Friedman, *Tax Limitation, Inflation and the Role of Government* (Dallas, Tex.: Fisher Institute, 1978), pp. 7–8.

83. See Buchanan, "Toward Analysis," in Amacher, Tollison, and Willett, *Economic Approach,* p. 348. Here he cautions about applications of the market approach to politics. Mancur Olson and Christopher K. Clague, "Dissent in Economics: Convergence of Extremes," in ibid., pp. 75, 81; Friedman, *There's No Such Thing,* p. 233; Friedman

and Friedman, *Free to Choose*, pp. 9, 23, 83–115; Friedman, "Monetary Policy," p. 196; Jan-Erik Lane, ed., *State and Market: The Politics of the Public and Private* (London: Sage, 1985), p. 32.

84. Friedman and Friedman, *Free to Choose*, p. 56. See also Buchanan, *What Should Economists Do?* pp. 31, 33–34; von Mises, *Liberalism*, p. 57; Friedman, *There's No Such Thing*, pp. 294–95, 208–10, 258; Friedman, *Capitalism and Freedom*, pp. 15–16; Gilder, *Wealth and Poverty*, p. 38; Hutt, *Individual Freedom*, p. 25. The origins of this definitional model lie in seventeenth-century liberal distinctions between state and society and the beliefs that government was the source of most coercion and that man is naturally social. The conservative economists apply this latter idea only to economics.

85. Ryan C. Amacher, "Risk Avoidance and Political Advertising: Neglected Issues in the Literature on Budget Size in a Democracy," in Amacher, Tollison, and Willett, *Economic Approach*, p. 411. He identifies this position with Buchanan. See Buchanan, *Liberty, Market and State*, on "the positive-sum nature of the competitive economic process" (p. 30).

86. Friedman and Friedman, *Tyranny*, pp. 132, 143, and passim.

87. Buchanan and Tullock, *Calculus of Consent*, p. 91, emphasis added. See Friedman and Friedman, *Free to Choose*, p. 24, and Buchanan, *Economics*, pp. 9–10 for similar statements.

88. Albert Hirschman faults other economists for ignoring noninstrumental action; see *Rival Views*, p. 152. Jon Elster makes the same point in "The Market and the Forum: Three Varieties of Political Theory," in Elster and Hylland, *Foundations of Social Choice Theory*, pp. 103–4.

Chapter Three. Freedom

1. In the United States, belief in private ownership created the myth that the nuclear energy industry is private. President Reagan proposed launching satellites by private companies, though at the time there were no private launch facilities or any proposals for such facilities that would not depend upon publicly funded designs. All societies prohibit murder but often define it differently. The construction placed on the Anti-Ballistic Missile Treaty, the definition of income for programs such as food stamps, or a determination about taxable income have profound implications for millions of people. On the importance of definitions for the last two examples, see Dale Russakoff, "Government Alchemy: Turning Words into Dollars," *Washington Post National Weekly Edition,* Jan. 3, 1988, p. 33.

2. See David Spitz, *The Real World of Liberalism* (Chicago: University of Chicago Press, 1982), p. 92.

3. This term is from Joan Robinson, *Economic Philosophy* (Harmondsworth, Eng.: Penguin, 1962), p. 7.

4. "Definition" includes the understanding and meaning people put into a concept in viewing, evaluating, and attempting to change the world. Words and definitions are not the issue. They are means through which people express how they want themselves and others to live.

5. C. B. Macpherson, "The Economic Penetration Of Political Theory: Some Hypotheses," *Journal of the History of Ideas* 39 (1978):103; Milton Friedman and Rose Friedman, *Free to Choose: A Personal Statement* (New York: Avon, 1979), p. ix.

6. Lawrence C. Becker, "Individual Rights," in Tom Regan and Donald Van De Veer, eds., *And Justice for All* (Totowa, N.J.: Rowman and Littlefield, 1982), pp. 201–2.

7. David Spitz, *Real World of Liberalism*, pp. 92–93.

8. See Michael Kammen, *Spheres of Liberty: Changing Perceptions of Liberty in American Culture* (Madison: University of Wisconsin Press, 1986), pp. 148–50.

9. See Friedrich A. Hayek, *The Road to Serfdom,* with a new preface by the author (Chicago: University of Chicago Press, Phoenix Books, 1976), p. 159.

10. F. A. Hayek, *Law, Legislation and Liberty: A New Statement of the Liberal Principles of Justice and Political Economy,* vol. 1, *Rules and Order* (Chicago: University of Chicago Press, 1973), pp. 12–13; idem, *The Constitution of Liberty* (Chicago: Gateway Editions, Henry Regnery, 1972), p. 29. Hayek intensely dislikes Bentham.

11. Buchanan does not wish to focus solely on utilitarian goals but believes that people want freedom in order to become whomever they want to become. *What Should Economists Do?* (Indianapolis: Liberty Press, 1979), p. 112. This occurs primarily within the market.

12. Milton Friedman, "The Goldwater View of Economics," *New York Times,* Oct. 11, 1964, sec. 6, p. 35; idem, "Value Judgments in Economics," in Sidney Hook, ed., *Human Values and Economic Policy* (New York: New York University Press, 1967), p. 90; idem, "The Threat to Freedom in the Welfare State," *Business and Society Review* 21 (Spring 1977):8–16.

13. Amartya Sen, *On Ethics and Economics* (Oxford: Basil Blackwell, 1987), pp. 41, 58–59.

14. Hayek, *Law, Legislation and Liberty,* 1:55–56; idem, *Constitution of Liberty,* pp. 11, 16, 19; idem, *Law, Legislation and Liberty: A New Statement of the Liberal Principles of Justice and Political Economy,* vol. 2, *The Mirage of Social Justice* (Chicago: University of Chicago Press, 1976), p. 86. On freedom as elimination of the arbitrary through operation of the market, see James M. Buchanan, *Liberty, Market and State: Political Economy in the 1980s* (New York: New York University Press, 1986), p. 5. The quote is from p. 169.

15. See David Miller, "Constraints on Freedom," *Ethics* 94 (Oct. 1983):68.

16. F. A. Hayek, "Kinds of Order in Society," in Kenneth S. Templeton, Jr., ed. *The Politicization of Society* (Indianapolis: Liberty Press, 1979), p. 507; idem, *Law, Legislation and Liberty: A New Statement of the Liberal Principles of Justice and Political Economy,* vol. 3, *The Political Order of a Free People* (Chicago: University of Chicago Press, 1979), pp. 163–64.

17. Milton Friedman, *Capitalism and Freedom* (Chicago: University of Chicago Press, 1962), p. 8; Friedman and Friedman, *Free to Choose,* pp. 56–58.

18. Milton Friedman, *The Invisible Hand in Economics and Politics* (Singapore: Institute of Southeast Asian Studies, 1981), p. 8; Friedman and Friedman, *Free to Choose,* p. 3; Friedman, *Capitalism and Freedom,* p. 28.

19. George J. Stigler, *The Economist as Preacher and Other Essays* (Chicago: University of Chicago Press, 1982), pp. 22–24.

20. See Karl de Schweinitz, Jr., "The Question of Freedom in Economics and Economic Organization," *Ethics* 89 (July 1979):336–53. It is not possible to be outside the market. One must earn an income *and* the market is the model for analyzing all behavior and motivation.

21. *Individual Freedom: Selected Works of William H. Hutt,* ed. Svetozar Pejovich and David Klingaman (Westport, Conn.: Greenwood Press, 1975), p. 82; Ludwig von Mises, *Liberalism: A Socio-Economic Exposition,* trans. Ralph Raico, ed. Arthur Goddard (Kansas City: Sheed Andrews and McMeel, 1978), pp. 67, 20–23; Hayek; *Constitution of Liberty,* p. 139; Hayek, *Law, Legislation and Liberty,* 1:107; Murray N. Rothbard, "Freedom, Inequality, Primitivism and the Division of Labor," in Templeton, *Politicization of Society,* pp. 90–91.

22. Friedman and Friedman, *Free to Choose,* pp. xvi, 58; Friedman, *Capitalism and*

Freedom, pp. 39, 15, 16. See Friedman and Friedman, *Free to Choose*, p. 139; Friedman, "The Goldwater View of Economics"; Hayek, *Road to Serfdom*, p. 145.

23. Friedman, *Capitalism and Freedom*, p. 15.

24. Ibid., pp. 9–10, 15; Friedman and Friedman, *Free to Choose*, pp. xvi–xvii; Milton Friedman, *Essays in Positive Economics* (Chicago: University of Chicago Press, 1953), pp. 317–18; idem, "Threat to Freedom in the Welfare State," p. 12.

25. F. A. Hayek, *Studies in Philosophy, Politics and Economics* (Chicago: University of Chicago Press, 1967), p. 229; idem, *Freedom and the Economic System*, Public Policy Pamphlet no. 29 (Chicago: University of Chicago Press, 1939), p. 2; idem, *Road to Serfdom*, pp. 13, 100, 113.

26. Buchanan, *Liberty, Market and State*, p. 5 and passim.

27. Friedman, *Capitalism and Freedom*, pp. 21, 108–15; Hutt, *Individual Freedom*, pp. 7, 59; George Gilder, *Wealth and Poverty* (New York: Basic Books, 1981), pp. 66, 128–39.

28. James M. Buchanan, *Economics: Between Predictive Science and Moral Philosophy* (College Station: Texas A&M University Press, 1987), pp. 278–85. Cf. Buchanan, *Liberty, Market and State*, p. 153.

29. Friedman, *Capitalism and Freedom*, p. 15.

30. Hayek, *Road to Serfdom*, pp. 15, 13; Milton Friedman and Rose Friedman, *Tyranny of the Status Quo* (San Diego: Harcourt Brace Jovanovich, 1984), p. 131. See also Friedman and Friedman, *Free to Choose*, p. 57.

31. See Buchanan, *What Should Economists Do?* p. 168: The pure, albeit rare, form of political relation is "abject slavery," while the economic relation emphasizes "cooperative endeavor."

32. See Hayek, *Road to Serfdom*, p. 120.

33. See Buchanan, *Liberty, Market and State*, p. 170.

34. Milton Friedman, *There's No Such Thing as a Free Lunch* (LaSalle, Ill.: Open Court, 1975), pp. 187–96, 229–32; Friedman and Friedman, *Tyranny*, pp. 137–41.

35. Political values as independent variables are discounted. The conservatives employ a Stalinist model. Liberal intervention, democratic and market socialism, and all varieties of the welfare state are unstable and always risk deteriorating into authoritarianism. Safety lies in preventing any of these from developing. But the historical record is not that simple. Even in so-called communist countries, dissent may be possible, as long as there are opposing institutions; consider Poland, its Solidarity movement, and the role of the Catholic church there. In the absence of alternative institutions, there would be no dissent, even in the free market.

36. See Dan Usher, *The Economic Prerequisite to Democracy* (New York: Columbia University Press, 1981). Usher accepts the argument that a free market relieves the political system of a great deal of pressure and conflict and that economic freedom is necessary to political freedom. Yet he argues (p. 89) that there "is a crucial distinction between 'all' and 'some'".

37. de Schweinitz, "The Question of Freedom," p. 345.

38. Hayek, *Constitution of Liberty*, pp. 12–13, 20–21; idem, *Law, Legislation and Liberty*, 3:163.

39. Hayek, *Law, Legislation and Liberty*, 2:103, 128. Taxation is coercion. Hayek, *Law, Legislation and Liberty*, 3:42, 126. See also Buchanan, *What Should Economists Do?* p. 168–69. Friedman believes that any time government substitutes for the market, coercion becomes likely. "Morality and Controls I," *New York Times*, Oct. 28, 1971, p. 41. See also his *There's No Such Thing*, p. 2; and *Capitalism and Freedom*, p. 39.

40. Friedman, "Threat to Freedom in the Welfare State," p. 15. See also Hayek, *Constitution of Liberty*, p. 20.

41. Hayek, *Law, Legislation and Liberty,* 2:70, 99.

42. Buchanan, *Liberty, Market and State,* p. 5.

43. Hutt, *Individual Freedom,* p. 79.

44. Hayek, *Law, Legislation and Liberty,* 2:102; idem, *Constitution of Liberty,* pp. 137, 141, 135–37. See also Hayek, *Law, Legislation and Liberty,* 3:83–85.

45. von Mises, *Liberalism,* pp. 91–93. For von Mises, a manufacturing monopoly can exist only with government aid. Cf. Hayek, *Law, Legislation and Liberty,* 3:83.

46. Hayek, *Constitution of Liberty,* p. 136. See also Friedman, "Threat to Freedom in the Welfare State," p. 15; idem, *Capitalism and Freedom,* p. 14.

47. See Charles E. Lindblom, "The Market as Prison," *Journal of Politics* 44 (May 1982):324–36. There is a long history to the claim that power dissolves in the market, that pursuit of self-interest in the market is innocent, harmless, and substitutes for or curbs undesirable passions. See Albert O. Hirschman, *The Passions and the Interests: Political Arguments for Capitalism before Its Triumph* (Princeton, N.J.: Princeton University Press, 1977).

48. Hayek, *Law, Legislation and Liberty,* 3:77–81.

49. Hayek, *Road to Serfdom,* pp. 45–46.

50. Robert L. Heilbroner, *Behind the Veil of Economics: Essays in the Worldly Philosophy* (New York: W. W. Norton and Co., 1988), pp. 80–103; John Kenneth Galbraith, *The Anatomy of Power* (Boston: Houghton Mifflin Co., 1983).

51. Hayek, *Constitution of Liberty,* p. 120; see also pp. 136–37. On p. 119 he identifies the growing number of employed people with a threat to the "driving force" of a free society. See Hutt, *Individual Freedom,* pp. 92–93.

52. Friedman, *Capitalism and Freedom,* p. 14; Hayek, *Law, Legislation and Liberty,* 3:80. See also Friedman and Friedman, *Free to Choose,* pp. xvii–xviii: Nineteenth-century immigrants were free to work for themselves or for others "at terms mutually agreed."

53. Hutt, *Individual Freedom,* pp. 83–86, 91. Hayek, *Road to Serfdom,* p. 199, identifies growth of monopoly with "deliberate collaboration" of privileged groups: organized labor and capital. Capital drops out of subsequent discussions. In *Law, Legislation and Liberty,* 3:144, he refers to unions as a greater danger than business because they are able to use coercion.

54. See Friedman, *Capitalism and Freedom,* pp. 2, 15. On the last point, see also Hayek, *Law, Legislation and Liberty,* 3:82; Hayek cites Friedman.

55. See Lester C. Thurow, *The Zero-Sum Society: Distribution and the Possibilities for Economic Change* (New York: Basic Books, 1980), pp. 178–89; idem, *Generating Inequality: Mechanisms of Distribution in the U.S. Economy* (New York: Basic Books, 1975), pp. 155ff, 162–69, 203–5.

56. John Kenneth Galbraith, *Annals of an Abiding Liberal* (Boston: Houghton Mifflin Co., 1979), p. 355. In *American Capitalism: The Concept of Countervailing Power,* rev. ed. (Boston: Houghton Mifflin Co., 1956), p. 61, Galbraith sees power when business has the ability to influence or affect the lives and welfare of many people.

57. Galbraith, *Anatomy of Power,* p. 4 and passim.

58. Galbraith sees advertising as an important means of manipulation and control. He and Thurow criticize conventional economics for ignoring its role and impact, claiming that this neglects the social environment in the belief that wants are formed autonomously. See John Kenneth Galbraith, *The Affluent Society,* 4th ed. (Boston: Houghton Mifflin Co., 1984), pp. 126–27, 198–99; idem, *Economics and the Public Purpose* (Harmondsworth, Eng.: Penguin, 1973), pp. 150ff. On p. 245 Galbraith argues that resistance to advertising promotes freedom. Cf. Lester Thurow, *Dangerous Currents: The State of Economics* (New York: Random House, 1983), pp. 175, 219–20.

59. Galbraith, *Anatomy of Power*, pp. 87, 56–57; idem, *Economics and the Public Purpose*, p. 98.

60. Galbraith, *Anatomy of Power*, pp. 50, 138–39, 82–83; Lindblom, "The Market as Prison"; and idem, *Politics and Markets: The World's Political-Economic Systems* (New York: Basic Books, 1977), pp. 161–88.

61. Galbraith, *American Capitalism*, p. 156; idem, *Economics and the Public Purpose*, pp. 108–9ff.

62. Thurow, *Dangerous Currents*, pp. 220–22; Galbraith, *American Capitalism*, pp. 24–30; idem, *Anatomy of Power*, pp. 119–20, 140–41, xiii; idem, *Economics and the Public Purpose*, pp. 22–24; idem, *Annals of an Abiding Liberal*, p. 355.

63. Galbraith, *Affluent Society*, p. 65.

64. Galbraith, *Anatomy of Power*, pp. 109, 186–87.

65. Friedman and Friedman, *Tyranny*, p. 58, see also p. 59. Hayek's *Road to Serfdom* is the progenitor of contemporary arguments that government, welfare, and regulation are the primary dangers to freedom.

66. Friedman, quoted in the *New York Times*, Feb. 23, 1974, p. 44; idem, *Tyranny*, pp. 9, 38–41; William H. Hutt, *The Keynesian Episode: A Reassessment* (Indianapolis: Liberty Press, 1979), p. 54; Hutt, *Individual Freedom*, p. 81; George J. Stigler, *The Citizen and the State: Essays on Regulation* (Chicago: University of Chicago Press, 1975), pp. 16–19. Hayek adds the government monopoly on issuing money as a danger to individual freedom. See F. A. Hayek, *Denationalisation of Money: An Analysis of the Theory and Practice of Concurrent Currencies* (London: Institute of Economic Affairs, 1976), esp. pp. 96–97.

67. Friedman, "Threat to Freedom in the Welfare State," pp. 8–11; idem, *There's No Such Thing*, pp. 206–7; idem, *Capitalism and Freedom*, pp. 31–32, 57. Friedman and Friedman, *Free to Choose*, p. 60.

68. Friedman and Friedman, *Free to Choose*, p. 109; Hayek, *Road to Serfdom*, pp. iii, viii; Friedman and Friedman, *Free to Choose*, pp. 58–61. For an argument rejecting the substance of these assertions, especially the dependence claim, see Fred Block et al., *The Mean Season: The Attack on the Welfare State* (New York: Pantheon Books, 1987).

69. See Hayek, *Road to Serfdom*, pp. 93–94.

70. Hayek, *Constitution of Liberty*, pp. 12–13, 16–19; idem, *Road to Serfdom*, pp. 25–26; Friedman, *Capitalism and Freedom*, p. 14. See also Buchanan, *Liberty, Market and State*, p. 128.

71. See Elizabeth Anderson, "Values, Risks, and Market Norms," *Philosophy and Public Affairs* 17 (1988):54–65.

72. Hayek, *Road to Serfdom*, pp. 96–97. Discussing free speech, Friedman states that "[i]t is entirely appropriate that people should bear a cost . . . for speaking freely. However, the cost should be reasonable and not disproportionate." *Free to Choose*, p. 60. This insight is missing from the discussion of market costs in, for example, the loss of a job.

73. Amy Gutmann, *Liberal Equality* (Cambridge: Cambridge University Press, 1980), p. 10.

74. Friedman, *Capitalism and Freedom*, p. 12.

75. See Brian Barry, "Lady Chatterley's Lover and Doctor Fischer's Bomb Party: Liberalism, Pareto Optimality, and the Problem of Objectionable Preferences," in Jon Elster and Aanund Hylland, eds., *Foundations of Social Choice Theory* (Cambridge: Cambridge University Press, 1986), p. 26.

76. Hayek, "Kinds of Order in Society," p. 510.

77. F. A. Hayek, "The Use of Knowledge in Society," in Adrian Klaasen, ed., *The Invisible Hand* (Chicago: Gateway Editions, 1965), p. 130.

78. Though Buchanan is more cautious than the others (cf. *Liberty, Market and State*, p. 34), he has little room or hope for behavior that does not conform to these expectations.

79. Gilder, *Wealth and Poverty*. The quote is from George Gilder, *The Spirit of Enterprise* (New York: Simon and Schuster, 1984), p. 255. Hayek, *Law, Legislation and Liberty*, 2:30; Hayek, *Constitution of Liberty*, pp. 120–21; idem, *Road to Serfdom*, pp. 204–5; idem, *Law, Legislation and Liberty*, 1:104. On Friedman, see Sidney Blumenthal, *The Rise of the Counter-Establishment: From Conservative Ideology to Political Power* (New York: Times Books, 1986), p. 119. See also Ludwig von Mises, "The Economic Nature of Profit and Loss," in Klaasen, *Invisible Hand*, pp. 170, 177.

80. See Hayek on the errors of constructivism, throughout *Law, Legislation and Liberty*, especially vol. 3.

81. See Isaiah Berlin, *Four Essays on Liberty* (London: Oxford University Press, 1969), p. xlviii.

82. Ibid.; see also pp. 130–33.

83. See Becker, "Individual Rights," p. 202.

84. Berlin agrees that planning, the welfare state, etc., can be defended from a negative perspective. See *Four Essays*, p. xlvi. On p. lxi he states that "[i]f it is maintained that the identification of the value of liberty with the value of free choice amounts to a doctrine of self-realization . . . and that this is closer to positive than negative liberty, I shall offer no great objection." See also Sen's reference to "a positive concept of negative freedom." *On Ethics and Economics*, p. 56 n. 25.

85. See Hayek, *Constitution of Liberty*, pp. 15–17; idem, *Law, Legislation and Liberty*, 3:130–31.

86. Berlin, *Four Essays*, esp. pp. 141–44, 167–69.

87. When a person learns economics, he will "understand the principle of spontaneous order" and "understands" that there are no arbitrary decisions in the market. Buchanan, *Liberty, Market and State*, p. 5.

88. *The Collected Writings of John Maynard Keynes*, vol. 9, *Essays in Persuasion* (London: Macmillan, 1972), p. 224.

89. John Stuart Mill, *On Liberty*, in Marshall Cohen, ed., *The Philosophy of John Stuart Mill: Ethical, Political and Religious* (New York: Modern Library, 1961), pp. 197, 221, 255, 294, 191. The quotes are from chaps. 1, 2, 3, and 5.

90. Hayek, *Constitution of Liberty*, pp. 119–20.

91. John Kenneth Galbraith, "The Uses and Excuses for Affluence," *New York Times Magazine*, May 31, 1981, p. 50. Adam Smith believed that education could greatly improve the lot of the common people, who would be "mutilated and deformed" without it. They and society would benefit from the increased political stability and an implied improvement in the chances for freedom. Adam Smith, *An Inquiry into the Nature and Causes of the Wealth of Nations*, ed. Edwin Cannan (New York: Modern Library, 1965), pp. 736–37, 740.

92. Frank H. Knight, *Freedom and Reform: Essays in Economics and Social Philosophy* (New York: Harper and Bros., 1947), p. 382.

93. See Berlin, *Four Essays*, p. lvi.

94. David Dale Martin, "The Uses and Abuses of Economic Theory in the Social Control of Business," *Journal of Economic Issues* 8 (1974):274.

95. See Henry C. Wallich, "Economic Freedom versus Organization," in Klaasen, *Invisible Hand*, pp. 188–89, 198–99.

96. Hayek, *Law, Legislation and Liberty*, 1:61.

97. Robert E. Goodin, *Political Theory and Public Policy* (Chicago: University of Chicago Press, 1982), p. 213.

98. Smith, *Wealth of Nations*, p. 308.

Chapter Four. Equality

1. Douglas Rae, *Equalities* (Cambridge, Mass.: Harvard University Press, 1981).
2. Sidney Verba and Gary R. Orren, *Equality in America: The View from the Top* (Cambridge, Mass.: Harvard University Press, 1985), partially succeed in sorting out some of these meanings; see pp. viii, 4–6, 120, 250–51, and passim. Sanford A. Lakoff, *Equality in Political Philosophy* (Cambridge, Mass.: Harvard University Press, 1964), p. 238, notes that competing concepts of equality exhibit "fundamentally different . . . attitudes toward human nature and social order." See Rae, *Equalities,* passim; Michael Walzer, *Spheres of Justice: A Defense of Pluralism and Equality* (New York: Basic Books, 1983).
3. Attenuation is a common fate for universal statements. The first amendment to the United States Constitution begins "Congress shall make no law," but this has not been interpreted to mean that Congress shall make *no* laws on the subject, only that Congress shall not make very many laws.
4. John Locke defined "A State of Equality" in terms of freedom: no "Subordination or Subjection," each is *"equal and independent* . . . in his Life, Health, Liberty, or Possessions." *The Second Treatise of Government,* in *Two Treatises of Government,* ed. Peter Laslett (New York: Mentor Books, 1965), secs. 4 and 6. Cf. Adam Smith, *An Inquiry into the Nature and Causes of the Wealth of Nations,* ed. Edwin Cannan (New York: Modern Library, 1965), pp. 627–28; Murray N. Rothbard, "Freedom, Inequality, Primitivism and the Division of Labor," in Kenneth S. Templeton, Jr., ed., *The Politicization of Society* (Indianapolis: Liberty Press, 1979), p. 124; Amy Gutmann, *Liberal Equality* (Cambridge: Cambridge University Press, 1980), pp. 8ff; and Lakoff, *Equality,* pp. 7, 100, 128–29, 148, and passim.
5. Milton Friedman, *Capitalism and Freedom* (Chicago: University of Chicago Press, 1962), pp. 5, 139, 195; Milton Friedman and Rose Friedman, *Free to Choose: A Personal Statement* (New York: Avon Books, 1979), p. 119; F. A. Hayek, *The Constitution of Liberty* (Chicago: Gateway Editions, Henry Regnery, 1972), p. 85.
6. Friedman, *Capitalism and Freedom,* p. 195; Milton Friedman, *There's No Such Thing as a Free Lunch* (LaSalle, Ill.: Open Court, 1975), p. 38; F. A. Hayek, *The Essence of Hayek,* ed. Chiaki Nishiyama and Kurt R. Leube (Stanford, Calif.: Hoover Institution Press, 1984), p. 358; idem, *Constitution of Liberty,* pp. 85, 93; James M. Buchanan, *Liberty, Market and State: Political Economy in the 1980s* (New York: New York University Press, 1986), p. 125; Friedman and Friedman, *Free to Choose,* p. 139. See Hayek, *Constitution of Liberty,* p. 87: Freedom requires equality before the law and that "leads to material inequality."
7. Hayek, *Constitution of Liberty,* pp. 85–87; idem, *Essence,* p. 82; idem, *Law, Legislation and Liberty: A New Statement of the Liberal Principles of Justice and Political Economy,* vol. 2, *The Mirage of Social Justice* (Chicago: University of Chicago Press, 1976), p. 82; ibid., vol. 1, *Rules and Order* (Chicago: University of Chicago Press, 1973), p. 141; James M. Buchanan, *What Should Economists Do?* (Indianapolis: Liberty Press, 1979), pp. 246–49; Friedman and Friedman, *Free to Choose,* pp. xvi, 119–22.
8. Hayek, *Essence,* pp. 141, 358; Buchanan, *Liberty, Market and State,* p. 144; Buchanan, *What Should Economists Do?* p. 231; Hayek, *Constitution of Liberty,* p. 87; Samuel Brittan, *The Economic Consequences of Democracy* (London: Temple Smith, 1977), p. 277; Friedman and Friedman, *Free to Choose,* p. 126; George Gilder, *Wealth and Poverty* (New York: Basic Books, 1981), p. 95.
9. Lakoff, *Equality,* p. 8.
10. Friedman, *Free to Choose,* pp. 122–28, 166; Friedman, *Capitalism and Freedom,* pp. 88, 164; Milton Friedman and Rose Friedman, *Tyranny of the Status Quo* (San Diego: Harcourt Brace Jovanovich, 1984), pp. 159–61.

11. Hayek, *Constitution of Liberty*, pp. 91–92.

12. Hayek, *Essence*, pp. 339, 84, 152, 335–36, 92; idem, *Law, Legislation and Liberty: A New Statement of the Liberal Principles of Justice and Political Economy*, vol. 3, *The Political Order of a Free People* (Chicago: University of Chicago Press, 1979), pp. 142, 73; idem, *Law, Legislation and Liberty*, 2:9–11.

13. Buchanan, *What Should Economists Do?* p. 259; Buchanan, *Liberty, Market and State*, pp. 140, 132–33, 141.

14. Buchanan, *Liberty, Market and State*, pp. 132–40; see p. 150 for his acceptance of limited hiring quotas. Buchanan, *What Should Economists Do?* pp. 247–48. See also James M. Buchanan, *Economics: Between Predictive Science and Moral Philosophy*, comp. and with a preface by Robert D. Tollison and Viktor J. Vanberg (College Station: Texas A&M University Press, 1987), pp. 277–88.

15. Substantial inequality would remain under socialism. Under pure communism, results would be according to each person's needs, and needs would differ.

16. David Thomson, *Equality* (Cambridge: Cambridge University Press, 1949), p. 3.

17. Verba and Orren, *Equality in America*, passim.

18. Rae analyzes this as relative equalities; *Equalities*, pp. 104–29. See also p. 57.

19. Lawrence B. Joseph, "Some Ways of Thinking about Equality of Opportunity," *Western Political Quarterly* 33 (1980):393–400. See also Verba and Orren, *Equality in America*, p. 301.

20. Friedman and Friedman, *Free to Choose*, p. 139.

21. Ibid., p. 124.

22. In Conrad Waligorski and Thomas Hone, eds., *Anglo-American Liberalism: Readings in Normative Political Economy* (Chicago: Nelson Hall, 1981), p. 29.

23. Hayek, *Constitution of Liberty*, pp. 85–87; Friedman, *Capitalism and Freedom*, p. 195; Buchanan, *What Should Economists Do?* p. 233.

24. Friedman and Friedman, *Free to Choose*, pp. 135–36, 139, 126; Friedman, *Capitalism and Freedom*, pp. 17–18; Friedman, *There's No Such Thing*, p. 33; Hayek, *Constitution of Liberty*, pp. 124–28. This claim that economic inequality protects freedom, dissent, and other desired values is similar to traditional conservative claims that an aristocracy is necessary to protect the same values. Cf. Russell Kirk, *A Program for Conservatives* (Chicago: Henry Regnery Co., 1962), pp. 272, 287–89.

25. See Buchanan, *Liberty, Market and State*, p. 153.

26. Milton Friedman, *Essays in Positive Economics* (Chicago: University of Chicago Press, 1953), p. 134; Friedman and Friedman, *Free to Choose*, p. 125.

27. Buchanan, *Liberty, Market and State*, pp. 141–42; Friedman and Friedman, *Free to Choose*, pp. 137, 6; *Individual Freedom: Selected Works of William H. Hutt*, ed. Svetozar Pejovich and David Klingaman (Westport, Conn.: Greenwood Press, 1975), p. 82; Hayek, *Law, Legislation and Liberty*, 2:123. This is a constant theme in vol. 2; see pp. 72, 92, 119. Hayek, *Essence*, p. 82; idem, *The Confusion of Language in Political Thought: With Some Suggestions for Remedying It*, Occasional Paper no. 20 (London: Institute of Economic Affairs, 1968), p. 30; Friedman, *Essays in Positive Economics*, p. 134. Friedman and Hayek claim that freedom encourages equality; see Friedman, *Capitalism and Freedom*, pp. 139, 195; and Hayek, *Constitution of Liberty*, p. 85.

28. Gilder emphasizes this the most, Hayek the least, though it is never absent from anyone's underlying assumptions.

29. Gilder, *Wealth and Poverty*, pp. 96–97, 101, 245, 259. Friedman accepts an incentive argument; *Free to Choose*, pp. 14–15.

30. Friedman and Friedman, *Free to Choose*, pp. 14, 278; Milton Friedman, "Choice, Chance and the Personal Distribution of Income," *Journal of Political Economy* 61 (1953): 277–90; Hayek, *Law, Legislation and Liberty*, 2:128; Buchanan, *What Should Economists*

Do? pp. 247, 331–52; idem, *Liberty, Market and State,* pp. 128–29; Gilder, *Wealth and Poverty,* chap. 5 and passim.

31. Gilder, *Wealth and Poverty,* p. 259.

32. Ibid., pp. 245, 67, 96, 83; George Gilder, *The Spirit of Enterprise* (New York: Simon and Schuster, 1984), p. 257.

33. Hutt, *Individual Freedom,* p. 82.

34. Friedman and Friedman, *Free to Choose,* pp. 52, 137; Ludwig von Mises, *Liberalism: A Socio-Economic Exposition,* trans. Ralph Raico, ed. Arthur Goddard (Kansas City: Sheed Andrews and McMeel, 1978), pp. 31–32.

35. Hayek, *Essence,* p. 141; Hayek, *Constitution of Liberty,* pp. 42–47, 121.

36. Hayek, *Law, Legislation and Liberty,* 2:9–10; idem, *Constitution of Liberty,* pp. 90–91; idem, *Essence,* p. 337; Friedman and Friedman, *Free to Choose,* pp. 13–14, 123, 126–29; Friedman, *Capitalism and Freedom,* pp. 164–65.

37. Friedman and Friedman, *Free to Choose,* p. 14. Buchanan, *Liberty, Market and State,* pp. 128–30, identifies choice, luck, effort, and birth as factors in inequality; on genetic and cultural luck, see p. 141.

38. See Robert Nozick, *Anarchy, State, and Utopia* (New York: Basic Books, 1974), pp. 161–64, for an attempt to justify with a sports analogy inequality caused by choice and luck.

39. Hayek, *Essence,* p. 339.

40. Gilder, *Wealth and Poverty,* p. 30.

41. Friedman and Friedman, *Free to Choose,* pp. 133–36.

42. Hayek especially makes this argument, ignoring its implications. If deserving good (or ill) fortune – property, wealth, etc. – is not a reason for having it, there can be no moral justification of inequality. Its justification becomes purely utilitarian: inequality produces more good than harm. This encourages examination of the assumptions the conservatives take as axiomatic.

43. Hayek, *Essence,* pp. 340, 346; Hayek, *Law, Legislation and Liberty,* 2:72–74, 80–82, 91, 117, 122, 130–31, 180.

44. Buchanan, *What Should Economists Do?* pp. 94, 239; idem, *Liberty, Market and State,* p. 126; Friedman, "Choice, Chance, and the Personal Distribution of Income," passim.

45. Buchanan, *Liberty, Market and State,* pp. 152–53; F. A. Hayek, "The Miscarriage of the Democratic Ideal," *Encounter* 50 (1978):16; idem, *Law, Legislation and Liberty,* 2:131, 10–11, 3:103, 172. Presumably, this would lead them to oppose compensatory policies for the descendants of slaves.

46. What Rae refers to as subject, domain, and value of equality and equalities of opportunity. *Equalities,* chaps. 2–5.

47. *The Collected Writings of John Maynard Keynes,* vol. 7, *The General Theory of Employment Interest and Money* (London: Macmillan, 1977), pp. 33, 324, 373–74, 320, 378.

48. John Kenneth Galbraith, *The Affluent Society* (Toronto: Mentor Books, 1965), pp. 247, 71; Lester C. Thurow, *Generating Inequality: Mechanisms of Distribution in the U.S. Economy* (New York: Basic Books, 1975), p. 146. See also John Kenneth Galbraith, *American Capitalism: The Concept of Countervailing Power,* rev. ed. (Boston: Houghton Mifflin Co., 1956), pp. 82–83.

49. Thurow, *Generating Inequality,* p. 49; John Kenneth Galbraith, "Afterword," *The Affluent Society,* 4th ed. (Boston: Houghton Mifflin Co., 1984), p. 276.

50. Keynes, *Collected Writings,* 7:372; John Kenneth Galbraith, *Economics and the Public Purpose* (Harmondsworth, Eng.: Penguin, 1973), pp. 282–83, 287; Lester Thurow, *The Zero-Sum Society: Distribution and the Possibilities for Economic Change* (New

York: Basic Books, 1980), pp. 7, 155; idem, *Generating Inequality,* pp. viii, xii, 44–45, 149–51, 207.

51. Verba and Orren, *Equality in America,* p. 250.

52. Thurow, *Zero-Sum Society,* pp. 194–95, 123. See also Thurow, *Generating Inequality,* pp. 19–21; Lester C. Thurow, "The Illusion of Economic Necessity," in Robert A. Solo and Charles W. Anderson, eds., *Value Judgment and Income Distribution* (New York: Praeger, 1981), pp. 250, 252, 256, 258. Thurow finds no correlation between income equality or inequality and economic growth.

53. Hayek, *Law, Legislation and Liberty,* 2:32–33, 67, 70, 1:141.

54. Thurow, *Zero-Sum Society,* p. 20; F. A. Hayek, *Economic Freedom and Representative Government,* Occasional Paper no. 39 (London: Institute of Economic Affairs, 1973), p. 13; idem, *Essence,* pp. 69, 345.

55. Friedman, *Capitalism and Freedom,* p. 34, summarizes this common position.

56. Buchanan, *What Should Economists Do?* p. 181; idem, *Liberty, Market and State,* p. 243.

57. "Nor is inequality in political influence regarded as an incentive to good citizenship in the way that income inequality is defended as an incentive to hard work." Verba and Orren, *Equality in America,* p. 222.

58. Cf. Jonathan W. Still, "Political Equality and Election Systems," *Ethics* 91, (1981):375–94. Still emphasizes equality in voting, not equality of influence over who will run, agenda setting, or influence after elections.

59. Hayek, *Law, Legislation and Liberty,* 2:4, 131.

60. Thomson, *Equality,* p. 100; Verba and Orren, *Equality in America,* p. 90; Rae, *Equalities,* passim.

61. Referring to road taxes, Smith noted that purposes determine what is equal. *Wealth of Nations,* p. 686.

62. That equality "need not lead to uniformity" is illustrated by "the growth of religious equality." Thomson, *Equality,* p. 43. Compare this with medicine, which focuses on results. Equal treatment means treating people differently, according to their needs.

63. Michael B. Levy, "Liberal Equality and Inherited Wealth," *Political Theory* 11 (1983):549; Rae, *Equalities,* p. 70.

64. Plato also proposed complete equality of opportunity, but his Republic was steeply hierarchical. Frank H. Knight stated that "[e]qual right to use unequal power is not equality but the opposite." *Freedom and Reform: Essays in Economics and Social Philosophy* (New York: Harper and Bros., 1947), p. 72. Quoting Warren Burger, Robert Lekachman notes that "'not only overt discrimination but also practices that are fair in form, but discriminatory in operation'" undermine opportunity. "Economic Justice in Hard Times," in Arthur L. Caplan and Daniel Callahan, eds., *Ethics in Hard Times* (New York: Plenum Press, 1981), p. 92.

65. This is a major theme in E. D. Hirsch, *Cultural Literacy: What Every American Needs to Know* (Boston: Houghton Mifflin Co., 1987).

Chapter Five. Democracy

1. Aristotle, *Politics,* trans. T. A. Sinclair (Harmondsworth, Eng.: Penguin, 1962), bk. 3, chap. 10; bk. 6, chap. 3.

2. James M. Buchanan, *Economics: Between Predictive Science and Moral Philosophy* (College Station: Texas A&M University Press, 1987), pp. 303–14; idem, *Liberty, Market and State: Political Economy in the 1980s* (New York: New York University Press, 1986), pp. 23, 90, 179–80, 270–71, 307–8. Buchanan regularly refers to Wicksell's *Finanz-*

theoretische Untersuchungen, not his later work. See also James M. Buchanan, Charles K. Rowley, and Robert D. Tollison, eds., *Deficits* (Oxford: Basil Blackwell, 1986), pp. 186–88, 382–84.

3. Anthony Downs, *An Economic Theory of Democracy* (New York: Harper and Row, 1957). The quote is from p. 27. Downs's analysis of the costs of information and participation is also absent.

4. Kenneth J. Arrow, *Social Choice and Individual Values* (New York: John Wiley and Sons, 1963).

5. James M. Buchanan and Richard E. Wagner, *Democracy in Deficit: The Political Legacy of Lord Keynes* (New York: Academic Press, 1977), pp. 9ff, 24; Richard E. Wagner and Robert D. Tollison, *Balanced Budgets, Fiscal Responsibility and the Constitution* (San Francisco: Cato Institute, 1980), p. 1; James M. Buchanan and Richard E. Wagner, eds., *Fiscal Responsibility in Constitutional Democracy* (Leiden and Boston: Martinus Nijhoff, 1978), pp. 9–10.

6. The source of this constitutional rule and its possible inconsistency with the rule of law is never adequately discussed.

7. William Breit, "Starving the Leviathan: Balanced Budget Prescriptions before Keynes," in Buchanan and Wagner, *Fiscal Responsibility,* p. 10. For the "rule's" application to Britain, see John Burton, "Keynes's Legacy to Great Britain: Folly in a Great Kingdom," in James M. Buchanan, Richard E. Wagner, and John Burton, eds., *The Consequences of Mr. Keynes: An Analysis of the Misuse of Economic Theory for Political Profiteering, with Proposals for Constitutional Disciplines* (London: Institute of Economic Affairs, 1978), pp. 36–38. See also Buchanan and Wagner, *Democracy in Deficit,* pp. 21ff.

8. Buchanan and Wagner, *Fiscal Responsibility,* p. 23.

9. Keynes defended intervention on political and economic grounds. Economic instability undermined democracy and created an environment for extremism. Correcting economic instability supported capitalism and democracy. Buchanan and Wagner criticize Keynes for abandoning belief in "an equilibrating mechanism" that is "self-correcting," leaving no choice but intervention. See Buchanan and Wagner, *Fiscal Responsibility,* p. 86; idem, *Democracy in Deficit,* p. 25.

10. Buchanan and Wagner, *Democracy in Deficit,* p. 56.

11. The short quotes are selected almost at random from Buchanan and Wagner, *Democracy in Deficit,* but similar statements are found in each author. The quote about Keynes turning the politicians loose is from p. 4.

12. Buchanan, *Liberty, Market and State,* pp. 210, 215–18.

13. F. A. Hayek, *Denationalisation of Money: An Analysis of the Theory and Practice of Concurrent Currencies* (London: Institute of Economic Affairs, 1976), pp. 25, 89.

14. Keynes repeatedly denied Say's law and the existence of natural systems which ensure a high level of economic welfare. If there is no guarantee that things will work well, it followed that government should attempt to improve the situation. Doing nothing favored one possible outcome. On Say's law see George Gilder, *Wealth and Poverty* (New York: Basic Books, 1981), pp. 31–40; Buchanan and Wagner, *Fiscal Responsibility,* p. 86; and idem, *Democracy in Deficit,* pp. 24–25. See also Thomas Sowell, *Say's Law: An Historical Analysis* (Princeton, N.J.: Princeton University Press, 1972).

15. The quote is from Buchanan and Wagner, *Democracy in Deficit,* p. 88. See also Samuel Brittan, *The Economic Consequences of Democracy* (London: Temple Smith, 1977), p. xii. Each author shares these sentiments. See Milton Friedman, *There's No Such Thing as a Free Lunch* (LaSalle, Ill.: Open Court, 1975), p. 233: "[T]here is something innate in the political process that produces this result."

16. William A. Niskanen, "The Prospect for a Liberal Democracy," in Buchanan and Wagner, *Fiscal Responsibility,* p. 158.

17. Brittan, *Economic Consequences,* p. xi.

18. This is a common argument and justification for the market. See Brittan, *Economic Consequences,* pp. 247–59.

19. See Friedrich A. Hayek, *Economic Freedom and Representative Government,* Occasional Paper no. 39 (London: Institute of Economic Affairs, 1973), p. 9: "I have belatedly come to agree with Joseph Schumpeter . . . that there was an irreconcilable conflict between [existing] democracy and capitalism." Hayek, *Law, Legislation and Liberty: A New Statement of the Liberal Principles of Justice and Political Economy,* vol. 3, *The Political Order of a Free People* (Chicago: University of Chicago Press, 1979), p. xiii, argues that the behavior of existing democracies is inevitably tending to totalitarianism.

20. Brittan, *Economic Consequences,* p. 255; Buchanan, Wagner, and Burton, *Consequences,* p. 74; Buchanan and Wagner, *Fiscal Responsibility,* p. 134; Arthur Seldon, preface to Buchanan, Wagner, and Burton, *Consequences,* p. 9.

21. See Buchanan, *Liberty, Market and State,* pp. 210–21.

22. Brittan, *Economic Consequences,* pp. 254–56.

23. See Buchanan, *Liberty, Market and State,* pp. 108–9.

24. See W. Mark Crain and Robert B. Ekelund, Jr., "Deficits and Democracy," *Southern Economic Journal* 44 (1978):813–15. See also Jack Kemp, *An American Renaissance: A Strategy for the 1980s* (New York: Harper and Row, 1979).

25. Milton Friedman and Rose Friedman, *Tyranny of the Status Quo* (San Diego: Harcourt Brace Jovanovich, 1984), p. 45; Hayek, *Economic Freedom,* p. 9.

26. Edgar K. Browning, "Why the Social Insurance Budget is Too Large in a Democracy," *Economic Inquiry* 13 (1975):117.

27. Allan H. Meltzer and Scott F. Richard, "Why Government Grows (and Grows) in a Democracy," *Public Interest,* 52 (Summer 1978):117.

28. These theorists often raise the issue of class interest. It is not necessarily the poor who demand programs but middle class professionals who administer and benefit from them.

29. Hayek, *Law, Legislation and Liberty,* 3:1–3, 6–7; idem, *Economic Freedom,* pp. 9, 12–13; Buchanan, *Liberty, Market and State,* pp. 241, 59; Brittan, *Economic Consequences,* pp. 81, 288.

30. See Hayek, *Economic Freedom,* pp. 15–16; Hayek, *Law, Legislation and Liberty,* 3:9–16, 31–32, 51–53; idem, *The Confusion of Language in Political Thought: With Some Suggestions for Remedying It,* Occasional Paper no. 20 (London: Institute of Economic Affairs, 1968), pp. 31–35.

31. F. A. Hayek, "The Miscarriage of the Democratic Ideal," *Encounter* 50 (1978): 16; Friedman, *There's No Such Thing,* p. 210, among many such statements. See also Milton Friedman, *The Invisible Hand in Economics and Politics* (Singapore: Institute of Southeast Asian Studies, 1981).

32. Brittan, *Economic Consequences,* p. 261.

33. Wagner and Tollison, *Balanced Budgets,* pp. 46–47; Hayek, *Law, Legislation and Liberty,* 3:11–12, 15–16, 99, 129; idem, *Economic Freedom,* pp. 17–18; Brittan, *Economic Consequences,* pp. 63–64, 248. This is a common theme in Friedman. See Milton Friedman and Rose Friedman, *Free to Choose: A Personal Statement* (New York: Avon, 1979), pp. 191–92, 279ff. See also Kemp, *American Renaissance,* pp. 27–28; Gilder, *Wealth and Poverty,* pp. 238ff; and William Simon, *A Time for Truth* (New York: Reader's Digest Press, 1978), p. 221. Hayek, *Law, Legislation and Liberty,* 3:138–39, gives a thirteen-point indictment of democracy.

34. For example, see Friedman, *There's No Such Thing,* pp. 208–9; Gilder, *Wealth and Poverty,* p. 38; Brittan, *Economic Consequences,* pp. 237–44, 18–19.

35. Milton Friedman, *Capitalism and Freedom* (Chicago: University of Chicago

Press, 1962), pp. 8–14; idem, *There's No Such Thing,* pp. 32–33; Hayek, *Law, Legislation and Liberty,* 3:150; idem, *The Road to Serfdom,* with a new preface by the author (Chicago: University of Chicago Press, Phoenix Books, 1976), pp. 69–70.

36. This goes far beyond identifying voting in elections with the market as a social choice mechanism. Arrow, *Social Choice,* pp. 1, 2, 5, and passim.

37. Milton Friedman, "The Threat to Freedom in the Welfare State," *Business and Society Review* 21 (Spring 1977):15; Friedman and Friedman, *Free to Choose,* p. 57; Friedman, *Capitalism and Freedom,* p. 23.

38. George Gilder, *The Spirit of Enterprise* (New York: Simon and Schuster, 1984), p. 91; *Individual Freedom: Selected Works of William H. Hutt,* ed. Svetozar Pejovich and David Klingaman (Westport, Conn.: Greenwood Press, 1975), pp. 82, 79. See also Gilder, *Wealth and Poverty,* p. 38.

39. Hayek, "Miscarriage," p. 14. See also Hayek, *Law, Legislation and Liberty,* 3:xiii, 180 n. 14.

40. For example, see Hayek, *Economic Freedom,* p. 12; Wagner and Tollison, *Balanced Budgets,* pp. 208–9.

41. On the last point see especially Buchanan, *Liberty, Market and State,* pp. 215–17.

42. See Buchanan, *Liberty, Market and State,* p. 250.

43. This too is a constant theme. See Hayek, "Miscarriage," p. 14; idem, *Law, Legislation and Liberty,* 3:5, 98, 134; idem, *Road to Serfdom,* pp. 70–71; Buchanan, *Liberty, Market and State,* p. 65.

44. Buchanan, *Liberty, Market and State,* p. 253. See also Hayek, *Law, Legislation and Liberty,* 3:5, 38–39.

45. Gilder, *Wealth and Poverty,* p. 259, and Buchanan and Wagner, *Democracy in Deficit,* pp. 64–65, link Keynesianism and economic decline with sexual liberation, and erosion of both manners and the Puritan ethic. Buchanan sees "Keynes as a Moral Revolutionary." "The Moral Dimension of Debt Financing," *Economic Inquiry* 23 (1985):3, and *Liberty, Market and State,* pp. 191–92. Hayek sees constructivism coupled with growth of government as dangers, not only to "wealth, but of morals and peace." *Law, Legislation and Liberty,* 3:129. Hayek also links public support for modern art and space exploration to democratic breakdown(3:32). See also Buchanan, *Liberty, Market and State,* p. 217, where he calls for "moral and/or constitutional constraints" on democratic deficit spending. For one of the more blatant linkages between Keynes, sex, and the breakdown of traditional political economy, see Charles K. Rowley, "John Maynard Keynes and the Attack on Classical Political Economy," in Buchanan, Rowley, and Tollison, *Deficits,* pp. 114–42, esp. 120–22.

46. Niskanen, "Prospect," in Buchanan and Wagner, *Fiscal Responsibility,* p. 158; Hayek, "Miscarriage," p. 14; Buchanan and Wagner, *Democracy in Deficit,* p. x; Hayek, *Law, Legislation and Liberty,* 3:150–51, 16.

47. Hayek "Miscarriage," p. 14; idem, *Law, Legislation and Liberty,* 3:138. See also Buchanan, *Liberty, Market and State,* pp. 210, 219; fiscal restraints on democracies must be more limiting than for authoritarian government: "[O]ne of my purposes here is to indicate the need for such [borrowing] constraints on democratic process."

48. See Buchanan and Wagner, *Democracy in Deficit,* pp. 8, 121.

49. See Buchanan, *Liberty, Market and State,* pp. 60–63. On pp. 215–17 he claims that democratic legislatures will always fall into the temptation of deficit financing. Hayek agrees.

50. Gilder, *Wealth and Poverty,* pp. 230–31, does not.

51. Buchanan and Wagner, *Democracy in Deficit,* pp. 175, 11; cf. p. 159.

52. Wagner and Tollison, *Balanced Budgets,* pp. 25–32; Buchanan and Wagner, *Democracy in Deficit,* pp. 176–82; Buchanan and Wagner, *Fiscal Responsibility,* passim;

Brittan, *Economic Consequences,* passim. For an argument that this proposal would undermine constitutional processes, see Dan Usher, *The Economic Prerequisite to Democracy* (New York: Columbia University Press, 1981), pp. 119–22.

53. See Buchanan and Wagner, *Fiscal Responsibility,* pp. 134–35; Wagner and Tollison, pp. 44–49.

54. Friedman, *There's No Such Thing,* p. 90.

55. Friedman and Friedman, *Free to Choose,* pp. 287–97, 301–2, support at least six amendments to reduce the federal government's role.

56. Buchanan, Wagner, and Burton, *Consequences,* p. 80; Buchanan and Wagner, *Democracy in Deficit,* p. 180; Friedman and Friedman, *Free to Choose,* pp. 287–97; Wagner and Tollison, *Balanced Budgets,* pp. 40–42; Kemp, *American Renaissance,* p. 113.

57. See Milton Friedman, "Why Deficits Are Bad," *Newsweek,* Jan. 2, 1984, p. 56. The political, rather than purely economic, reasons for opposition are quite explicit in this essay. See also Buchanan, *Liberty, Market and State,* p. 194 n. 4.

58. Friedman, *There's No Such Thing,* pp. 86–91. See also "Why Deficits Rather than Higher Taxes," Friedman and Friedman, *Tyranny,* pp. 39–41. See also the discussion of the Reagan administration's deliberately running deficits to destroy resources and public support for intervention and welfare in Sidney Blumenthal, *The Rise of the Counter-Establishment: From Conservative Ideology to Political Power* (New York: Times Books, 1986), p. 236. Blumenthal quotes Hayek as saying that such deliberate deficits are "partly excusable."

59. Buchanan, Wagner, and Burton, *Consequences,* pp. 81ff.

60. Brittan, *Economic Consequences,* pp. 279–90.

61. Hayek, *Law, Legislation and Liberty,* 3:xiii.

62. F. A. Hayek, *Law, Legislation and Liberty: A New Statement of the Liberal Principles of Justice and Political Economy,* vol. 1, *Rules and Order* (Chicago: University of Chicago Press, 1973), p. 3; Hayek, *Law, Legislation and Liberty,* 3:22, 106–19. On p. 150 the purpose behind this procedure is revealed: It would "make all socialist measures for redistribution impossible." Hayek, *Confusion of Language,* pp. 34–35; idem, *Economic Freedom,* pp. 18–21.

63. Buchanan, *Liberty, Market and State,* chap. 6, esp. 56–57. This chapter subtly accuses those who disagree with Buchanan (p. 63) of calling Buchanan a fascist and of themselves being anticonstitutional.

64. Hayek, *Law, Legislation and Liberty,* 3:5; Brittan, *Economic Consequences,* pp. 266–67.

65. Wagner and Tollison, *Balanced Budgets,* p. 46; Brittan, *Economic Consequences,* pp. 267ff; F. A. Hayek, *Studies in Philosophy, Politics and Economics* (Chicago: University of Chicago Press, 1967), pp. 232–45, 172–73; idem, *Economic Freedom,* p. 13.

66. See Brittan, *Economic Consequences,* p. 277.

67. Joseph A. Schumpeter, *Capitalism, Socialism and Democracy* (New York: Harper and Row, 1976), believed that the requirements for democracy could be satisfied even if all adults were not allowed to vote. See pp. 243–45.

68. See James M. Buchanan, *What Should Economists Do?* (Indianapolis: Liberty Press, 1979), p. 236. If everyone were identical, the constitutional order and form of government would not matter.

69. Cf. Friedman and Friedman, *Free to Choose,* pp. 119–25, 139.

70. Given conservative human nature and the political market, not very much good and a great deal of harm can be expected from the people.

71. Hayek regrets that in *Constitution of Liberty* he defended democracy on the grounds of educating people. Hayek, *Law, Legislation and Liberty,* 3:180 n. 14. Each author ignores education for and through democracy.

72. See Hayek, *Law, Legislation and Liberty,* 3:96–97.

73. Ibid., 3:120.

74. Participatory democrats doubt that this would produce more seriousness in voters unaccustomed to making such decisions.

75. Friedman, *There's No Such Thing*, pp. 208–10, 258.

76. See Albert O. Hirschman, *Exit, Voice and Loyalty: Responses to Decline in Firms, Organizations, and States* (Cambridge, Mass.: Harvard University Press, 1970); idem, *Essays in Trespassing: Economics to Politics and Beyond* (Cambridge: Cambridge University Press, 1981); and idem, *Rival Views of Market Society and Other Recent Essays* (New York: Viking, 1986), esp. pp. 77–101.

77. Wagner and Tollison, *Balanced Budgets*, p. 33; Brittan, *Economic Consequences*, pp. 279, 181, xi; Hayek, *Law, Legislation and Liberty*, 3:8, 14, 22, 134–35; Friedman, *Capitalism and Freedom*, p. 24; Friedman and Friedman, *Free to Choose*, p. 57; Buchanan, *Liberty, Market and State*, pp. 243–44; idem, *What Should Economists Do?* p. 153.

78. Hayek, *Law, Legislation and Liberty*, 3:18. On p. 134 he claims that a majority in a legislative body where bargaining is the norm "can never represent the opinion of the majority of the people." See p. 6 for "alleged majority" as well as pp. 7–11, 99. Hayek, *Constitution of Liberty*, p. 120, says that "the employed majority" tends to impose its views on others, threatening freedom. Friedman argues that the present form of majority rule leads to decisions of which the majority disapproves. *Tyranny*, p. 52.

79. Usher does not agree with the attack on majorities. See *Prerequisite to Democracy*, pp. 10, 116–19.

80. See chap. 6.

81. See Buchanan, *Liberty, Market and State*, p. 21. Hayek occasionally refers to consent in *Law, Legislation and Liberty*, vol. 3 (for example, pp. 3–4, 17, 35), but it is significant and symptomatic that he does not discuss consent in his chapters on democracy (16), a model constitution (17), or containing power (18). Since these authors define politics as the realm of coercion, consent may be impossible in politics except for Buchanan at a mythical constitution-making stage.

82. Votes are spent, people choose from what is presented, self-interest predominates, common interest is shared interests, policies are responses to the largest number of votes/dollars—all in a political *market*. People have little voice in protesting undesirable situations.

83. Even evolved procedures may involve deliberate planning. The United States Constitution may evolve, but it was created and is a prime example of constructivism in politics.

Chapter Six. The Good Society:
Justice, Morality, and Community

1. National Conference of Catholic Bishops, *Economic Justice for All: Pastoral Letter on Catholic Social Teaching and the U.S. Economy* (Washington, D.C.: United States Catholic Conference, 1986).

2. See Richard J. Regan, *The Moral Dimensions of Politics* (New York: Oxford University Press, 1986), pp. 107–44. For an extended traditional argument, presented as a textbook, see Austin Fagothey, *Right and Reason: Ethics in Theory and Practice* (St. Louis, Mo.: C. V. Mosby Co., 1963).

3. See J. Philip Wogaman, *The Great Economic Debate: An Ethical Analysis* (Philadelphia: Westminster Press, 1977), esp. pp. 34–54, 77–124.

4. National Conference, *Economic Justice for All*, pp. 142, v, 3.

5. Ibid., pp. 28–44.

6. Ibid., pp. 130, 35–37, 155, 167, 12, and passim.

7. Stanley I. Benn, "Justice," *The Encyclopedia of Philosophy*, 8 vols. (New York: Macmillan, 1967), 4:300.

8. Regan, *Moral Dimensions*, p. 121.

9. Russell Kirk, *A Program for Conservatives* (Chicago: Henry Regnery Co., 1962), pp. 167–92, 140–50, 210.

10. Graham Walker, *The Ethics of F. A. Hayek* (Lanham, Md.: University Press of America, 1986), pp. vii, 56–58, 96–97, 101–22.

11. The bishops are accused of overemphasizing values and underestimating difficulties of modifying economic arrangements. A convenient compendium of criticisms is in Paul Heyne, *The U.S. Catholic Bishops and the Pursuit of Justice*, Cato Institute Policy Analysis no. 50 (Washington, D.C.: Cato Institute, 1985). He asserts that values and facts cannot easily be separated; economics is a positive science; social systems do not have goals; markets are autonomous; the poor partially cause and are responsible for their poverty; the impersonal market relieves people of personal responsibility for undesirable outcomes; the bishops ignore information exchange and coordination in markets; justice is procedural without substantive content; specific proposals have already failed; implementing proposals will create oppressive government; mankind is too ignorant to implement these proposals; the bishops ignore voluntary action; and the bishops do not understand the Bible.

12. See Thomas Robert Malthus, *An Essay on the Principle of Population*, 7th ed. (London: Reeves and Turner, 1872; Fairfield, N.J.: Augustus M. Kelley, 1986), pp. 276, 494, 422, 431–32.

13. Joan Robinson, *Economic Philosophy* (Harmondsworth, Eng.: Penguin, 1962), p. 19. See also Wogaman, *Great Economic Debate*, passim.

14. See Vincent Bladen, *From Adam Smith to Maynard Keynes: The Heritage of Political Economy* (Toronto: University of Toronto Press, 1974), pp. 358–60, 368, 370, 395–402.

15. Bladen, *From Smith to Keynes*, pp. 322–57; Robinson, *Economic Philosophy*, p. 65; John Kenneth Galbraith, *Economics in Perspective: A Critical History* (Boston: Houghton Mifflin Co., 1987), pp. 124–25.

16. Andrew Schotter, *Free Market Economics: A Critical Appraisal* (New York: St. Martin's Press, 1985), pp. 8–11, 22–26; Warren J. Samuels, *Pareto on Policy* (Amsterdam: Elsevier, 1974), pp. 200–206; Amartya Sen, *On Ethics and Economics* (Oxford: Basil Blackwell, 1987), pp. 31–40.

17. See Schotter, *Free Market Economics*, p. 94.

18. See Joseph J. Spengler, *Origins of Economic Thought and Justice* (Carbondale: Southern Illinois University Press, 1980); C. B. Macpherson, *The Rise and Fall of Economic Justice and Other Papers* (Oxford: Oxford University Press, 1985), esp. chap. 1. Robert E. Lane, "Market Justice, Political Justice," *American Political Science Review* 80 (1986):383–402; Robert Nozick, *Anarchy, State, and Utopia* (New York: Basic Books, 1974); John Rawls, *A Theory of Justice* (Cambridge, Mass.: Belknap Press of Harvard University Press, 1971).

19. F. A. Hayek, *Law, Legislation and Liberty: A New Statement of the Liberal Principles of Justice and Political Economy*, vol. 1, *Rules and Order* (Chicago: University of Chicago Press, 1973), pp. 138, 141; ibid., vol. 2, *The Mirage of Social Justice* (Chicago: University of Chicago Press, 1976), pp. 38–39, 63–65, 70–73, 31–33; cf. p. 19. F. A. Hayek, *The Essence of Hayek*, ed. Chiaki Nishiyama and Kurt R. Leube (Stanford, Calif.: Hoover Institution Press, 1984), pp. 70–73.

20. James M. Buchanan, *Liberty, Market and State: Political Economy in the 1980s* (New York: New York University Press, 1986), pp. 123–39, 114.

21. Buchanan is not consistent in his references to Rawls or in his construction of a contract model. See, however, Buchanan, *Liberty, Market and State*, pp. 123–39, 144, 168–70, 240–47; idem, *Economics: Between Predictive Science and Moral Philosophy*, comp. and with a preface by Robert D. Tollison and Viktor J. Vanberg (College Station: Texas A&M University Press, 1987), pp. 253–68, 311–13. This latter section cites the influence of Knut Wicksell on Buchanan's development. See also Geoffrey Brennan and James M. Buchanan, *The Reason of Rules: Constitutional Political Economy* (Cambridge: Cambridge University Press, 1985), esp. pp. 19–45; Rawls, *Theory of Justice*.

22. See Lane, "Market Justice," pp. 388–96.

23. Milton Friedman and Rose Friedman, *Free to Choose: A Personal Statement* (New York: Avon, 1979), pp. 13–14; Milton Friedman, *Capitalism and Freedom* (Chicago: University of Chicago Press, 1962), pp. 161–62.

24. Hayek, *Law, Legislation and Liberty*, 2:31–32, 64–65, 69–70; idem, *Economic Freedom and Representative Government*, Occasional Paper no. 39 (London: Institute of Economic Affairs, 1973), p. 13; idem, *Essence*, p. 80; idem, *Law, Legislation and Liberty: A New Statement of the Liberal Principles of Justice and Political Economy*, vol. 3, *The Political Order of a Free People* (Chicago: University of Chicago Press, 1979), p. 136. See also Hayek, *Law, Legislation and Liberty*, 1:141.

25. Buchanan, *Liberty, Market and State*, pp. 124, 141, 167. Cf. Buchanan, *Economics*, p. 267 n. 25.

26. *The Collected Writings of John Maynard Keynes*, vol. 9, *Essays in Persuasion* (London: Macmillan, 1972), pp. 311, 283, 224, 141–42; ibid., vol. 5, *A Treatise on Money*, vol. 1, *The Pure Theory of Money* (London: Macmillan, 1971), pp. 152–53; John Maynard Keynes, "Democracy and Efficiency," *New Statesman and Nation*, Jan. 28, 1939, p. 121. See also Keynes, *Collected Writings*, vol. 7, *The General Theory of Employment Interest and Money* (London: Macmillan, 1973), p. 33, on classical theory explaining and justifying "much social injustice." See also John Kenneth Galbraith, *Economics and the Public Purpose* (Harmondsworth, Eng.: Penguin, 1973), p. 43; Lester C. Thurow, *Dangerous Currents: The State of Economics* (New York: Random House, 1983), pp. 226–27; idem, "Toward a Definition of Economic Justice," *Public Interest* 31 (1973):56–80.

27. Given the conservatives' condemnation of transindividual conceptions of justice, this chapter employs social, distributive, and economic justice interchangeably.

28. Hayek, *Economic Freedom*, p. 13; idem, *Essence*, pp. 63, 67–69, 83, 85, 345; idem, *Studies in Philosophy, Politics and Economics* (Chicago: University of Chicago Press, 1967), pp. 244–45; idem, *Law, Legislation and Liberty*, 2:62–67, 96–97. The title of this volume is *The Mirage of Social Justice*. See also *The Collected Works of F. A. Hayek*, vol. 1, *The Fatal Conceit: The Errors of Socialism*, ed. by W. W. Bartley III (Chicago: University of Chicago Press, 1989), pp. 114–19; Samuel Brittan, *The Economic Consequences of Democracy* (London: Temple Smith, 1977), p. 267. In *Law, Legislation and Liberty*, 3:10, Hayek links development of social justice to growth of majoritarian democracy.

29. Hayek, *Law, Legislation and Liberty*, 2:65–68; idem, *Essence*, p. 69.

30. Buchanan, *Liberty, Market and State*, pp. 271–72, 130, 125; Buchanan, *Economics*, pp. 278–85.

31. Hayek, *Law, Legislation and Liberty*, 3:82; Friedman and Friedman, *Free to Choose*, p. 97; Friedman, *Capitalism and Freedom*, pp. 133–34, 120; "Milton Friedman Responds," *Business and Society Review* 1 (Spring 1972):5–16; Milton Friedman, *The Essence of Friedman*, ed. Kurt R. Leube (Stanford, Calif.: Hoover Institution Press, 1987), pp. 36–42.

32. Buchanan, *Economics*, pp. 78, 68. The quote is at page 68. Sen, *On Ethics and Economics*, appeals to economists to expand understanding of the role of ethics in eco-

nomics and decision making and to broaden economics to include moral decisions and bring more economic reasoning into moral and ethical analysis.

33. Buchanan, *Economics*, pp. 6, 17. This is very different from claiming that either his work or his recommendations are ethically neutral, though this distinction is lost in the argument.

34. Buchanan, *Liberty, Market and State*, pp. 108–20. See also James M. Buchanan, *What Should Economists Do?* (Indianapolis: Liberty Press, 1979), pp. 211–13. Buchanan admits that his work has normative implications; see "Contractarian Political Economy and Constitutional Interpretation," *American Economic Review* 78 (1988):135–39.

35. Buchanan, *What Should Economists Do?* pp. 201–17, 84.

36. Buchanan, "The Moral Dimension of Debt Financing," chap. 17 of *Liberty, Market and State*, pp. 189–94, originally published in *Economic Inquiry* 23 (1985):1–6.

37. Wogaman, *Great Economic Debate*, pp. 1–13, 34–54; Fagothey, *Right and Reason*, passim; A.D. Woozley, "Law and the Legislation of Morality," in Arthur L. Caplan and Daniel Callahan, eds., *Ethics in Hard Times* (New York: Plenum Press, 1981), pp. 143–74; Robert L. Heilbroner, *Behind the Veil of Economics: Essays in the Worldly Philosophy* (New York: W. W. Norton and Co., 1988), pp. 108–9; Walter A. Weisskopf, "Hidden Value Conflicts in Economic Thought," *Ethics* 61 (1951):195–204.

38. Weisskopf, "Hidden Value Conflicts," p. 198; Sen, *On Ethics and Economics*, p. 52.

39. Buchanan, *Liberty, Market and State*, pp. 189–94, 116–17, 165–77, 108–20. These limits are not simply narrow "economic self-interest" but include other, perceived self-interest. See p. 175. Buchanan equates norms of conduct with morality.

40. Milton Friedman, *Essays in Positive Economics* (Chicago: University of Chicago Press, 1953), p. 4.

41. Milton Friedman, "Morality and Controls I," *New York Times*, Oct. 28, 1971, p. 41; Friedman and Friedman, *Free to Choose*, p. x.

42. Hayek, *Essence*, p. 358; idem, *Law, Legislation and Liberty*, 3:120, 129, 170–71; idem, *The Road to Serfdom*, with a new preface by the author (Chicago: University of Chicago Press, Phoenix Books, 1976), pp. 211–15; idem, *The Constitution of Liberty* (Chicago: Gateway Editions, Henry Regnery, 1976), pp. 321–23; Hayek, *Studies*, pp. 230–31.

43. Hayek, *Law, Legislation and Liberty*, 2:77, 88–91, 144–47, 3:160–65; idem, "The Miscarriage of the Democratic Ideal," *Encounter* 50 (1978):16. See also Hayek, *Road to Serfdom*, pp. 138, 146; idem, *Collected Works*, 1:11–21, 48–75, and passim. In this volume, Hayek claims that socialism is an appeal to instinctual behavior that will overthrow civilization. Hayek uses "instinct" as if it were a demonstrated fact rather than a fanciful hypothesis.

44. Buchanan, *Liberty, Market and State*, pp. 190–92; See also pp. 108–20, reprinted also in Buchanan, *Economics*, pp. 289–301.

45. See Ruth Levitas, ed. *The Ideology of the New Right*, (Cambridge: Polity Press, 1986), pp. 30–31.

46. Donald W. Shriver, Jr., "Lifeboaters and Mainlanders: A Response," *Soundings* 59 (1976):240.

47. Hayek, *Law, Legislation and Liberty*, 2:26–27, 83, 97–100, 143, 149, 180 n. 28, 3:160–62; Buchanan, *Liberty, Market and State*, pp. 108–120, 109–91; Friedman, *Capitalism and Freedom*, pp. 23–24. Nozick, *Anarchy, State, and Utopia*, passim.

48. Hayek, *Law, Legislation and Liberty*, 2:27.

49. Hayek, *Constitution of Liberty*, pp. 62–63, 69; idem, *Road to Serfdom*, p. 211; idem, *Law, Legislation and Liberty*, 1:10, 17–19, 74–76, 3:xi, 159–66. See also Hayek, *Collected Works*, vol. 1; Walker, *Ethics of Hayek*, esp. pp. 10, 22.

50. Buchanan, *Liberty, Market and State*, pp. 189–94.

51. See Friedman and Friedman, *Free to Choose*, pp. 16–18.

52. Buchanan, *Liberty, Market and State*, pp. 189–94, 165–77, 240, 249–53, 269, 126. Making the individual the ultimate, and perhaps sole, source of value explains Buchanan's interest in unanimity in public choices. See Buchanan, *Economics*, p. 309, among many sources. This position is consistent with Pareto.

53. Buchanan, *Liberty, Market and State*, pp. 169, 262.

54. Hayek, *Road to Serfdom*, p. 211; idem, *Law, Legislation and Liberty*, 1:33. The quote is from Hayek, *Law, Legislation and Liberty*, 2:26.

55. Friedman, *Capitalism and Freedom*, pp. 25–26. His proposal to eliminate licensing requirements for many services and professions illustrates the belief that there are no "objective standards by which practitioners . . . can and should be judged." J. Harvey Lomax, "Economics or Political Philosophy: Which Should Prevail in Public Policy?" *Interpretation* 10 (1982):270.

56. Buchanan, "Contractarian Political Economy," p. 138.

57. Friedman and Friedman, *Free to Choose*, pp. 109–10; Milton Friedman, "Value Judgments in Economics," in Sidney Hook, ed., *Human Values and Economic Policy* (New York: New York University Press, 1967), pp. 85, 89.

58. George Gilder, *Wealth and Poverty* (New York: Basic Books, 1981), p. x. Gilder believes that religious belief is necessary to support capitalism.

59. This includes Hayek, Gilder, and Buchanan. Buchanan, *What Should Economists Do?* pp. 211–13.

60. See Amartya Sen, "The Moral Standing of the Market," *Social Philosophy and Policy* 2 (1985):2.

61. Wogaman, *Great Economic Debate*, p. 113.

62. National Conference, *Economic Justice for All*, p. xi, is a strong statement.

63. Buchanan, *Liberty, Market and State*, pp. 267–68.

64. Jose Ortega y Gasset, *The Revolt of the Masses* (London: Unwin Books, 1961); Walter Lippmann, *The Public Philosophy* (New York: Mentor Books, 1955).

65. How this capacity is related to primitive morality remains unexplored.

66. Hayek, *Law, Legislation and Liberty*, 1:95, 3:158, 140, 2:12; Hayek *Collected Works*, vol. 1, passim; Anna Elisabetta Galeotti, "Individualism, Social Rules, Tradition: The Case of Freidrich A. Hayek," *Political Theory* 15 (1987):163–81.

67. Friedman, *Capitalism and Freedom*, pp. 1–2, 22–25, 13; idem, *The Invisible Hand in Economics and Politics* (Singapore: Institute of Southeast Asian Studies, 1981), p. 7.

68. See Buchanan, *Economics*, pp. 271–72; idem, *Liberty, Market and State*, pp. 189–94; Hayek, *Law, Legislation and Liberty*, 2:88–91.

69. This section treats public interest as synonymous with common good.

70. Richard E. Wagner and Robert D. Tollison, *Balanced Budgets, Fiscal Responsibility and the Constitution* (San Francisco: Cato Institute, 1980), pp. 45–46; "Milton Friedman Responds," p. 14; Friedman and Friedman, *Free to Choose*, p. 281; Buchanan, *Economics*, p. 61; James M. Buchanan and Gordon Tullock, *The Calculus of Consent: Logical Foundations of Constitutional Democracy* (Ann Arbor: University of Michigan Press, 1965), p. 12; Hayek, *Road to Serfdom*, pp. 59–61.

71. Friedman, *Capitalism and Freedom*, pp. 1–2; Buchanan, *Liberty, Market and State*, p. 117. See also Friedman and Friedman, *Free to Choose*, p. 104.

72. Kenneth J. Arrow, *Social Choice and Individual Values* (New York: John Wiley and Sons, 1963). Cf. Buchanan, *Liberty, Market and State*, p. 265.

73. Buchanan, *Economics*, pp. 16, 309; idem, *Liberty, Market and State*, p. 138; Friedman, *Capitalism and Freedom*, pp. 22–23.

74. See discussion of "[t]he bias against collective needs," in Thomas Balogh, *The Irrelevance of Conventional Economics* (New York: Liveright, 1982), pp. 89–92.

75. See Lippmann, *Public Philosophy,* pp. 135–36.

76. Frank H. Knight, "Abstract Economics as Absolute Ethics," *Ethics* 76 (1966): 171.

77. Robert L. Heilbroner, "On the Limited 'Relevance' of Economics," in Ryan C. Amacher, Robert D. Tollison, and Thomas D. Willett, eds., *The Economic Approach to Public Policy: Selected Readings* (Ithaca, N.Y.: Cornell University Press, 1976), p. 64.

Chapter Seven. Conservative Economists' Theory of Government

1. F. A. Hayek, *Economic Freedom and Representative Government,* Occasional Paper no. 39 (London: Institute of Economic Affairs, 1973), p. 9; James M. Buchanan and Richard E. Wagner, *Democracy in Deficit: The Political Legacy of Lord Keynes* (New York: Academic Press, 1977), pp. 104, 118, 102–3; Samuel Brittan, *The Economic Consequences of Democracy* (London: Temple Smith, 1977) pp. 255–57; John Burton, "Keynes's Legacy to Great Britain: Folly in a Great Kingdom," in James M. Buchanan, Richard E. Wagner, and John Burton, eds., *The Consequences of Mr. Keynes: An Analysis of the Misuse of Economic Theory for Political Profiteering, with Proposals for Constitutional Disciplines* (London: Institute of Economic Affairs, 1978), p. 73; Jesse Burkhead and Charles Knerr, "Congressional Budget Reform: New Decision Structures," in James M. Buchanan and Richard E. Wagner, eds., *Fiscal Responsibility in Constitutional Democracy* (Leiden and Boston: Martinus Nijhoff, 1978), p. 134.

2. See James M. Buchanan, *Liberty, Market and State: Political Economy in the 1980s* (New York: New York University Press, 1986), p. 133 and passim; James M. Buchanan, *What Should Economists Do?* (Indianapolis: Liberty Press, 1979), p. 211. Government failure due to self-interest is a central theme in Buchanan's public-choice theory. See Buchanan, Wagner, and Burton, *Consequences,* pp. 85–86.

3. Adam Smith and other early political economists may have argued for limited government but not the inevitability of government failure. Cf. George J. Stigler, *The Citizen and the State: Essays on Regulation* (Chicago: University of Chicago Press, 1975), pp. 41–45. For a partial history of the government failure argument in the United States, see Sidney Fine, *Laissez-Faire and the General Welfare State: A Study of Conflict in American Thought 1865–1901* (Ann Arbor: University of Michigan Press, Ann Arbor Paperbacks, 1964), pp. 55–56 and passim.

4. F. A. Hayek, *Denationalisation of Money: An Analysis of the Theory and Practice of Concurrent Currencies* (London: Institute of Economic Affairs, 1976), p. 80; Milton Friedman and Rose Friedman, *Tyranny of the Status Quo* (San Diego: Harcourt Brace Jovanovich, 1984), pp. 19–20; George Gilder, *Wealth and Poverty* (New York: Basic Books, 1981), p. 225; Buchanan and Wagner, *Democracy in Deficit,* p. 69. See also Buchanan, *What Should Economists Do?* p. 211.

5. Buchanan, *Liberty, Market and State,* p. 217.

6. Milton Friedman and Rose Friedman, *Free to Choose: A Personal Statement* (New York: Avon, 1979), pp. 279–86, 107–9, 191, and passim; Buchanan and Wagner, *Democracy in Deficit,* p. 133 and all of chap. 9.

7. F. A. Hayek, *Law, Legislation and Liberty: A New Statement of the Liberal Principles of Justice and Political Economy,* vol. 1, *Rules and Order* (Chicago: University of Chicago Press, 1973), pp. 42, 144; ibid., vol. 2, *The Mirage of Social Justice* (Chicago: University of Chicago Press, 1976), pp. 128–29; Buchanan, *Liberty, Market and State,* pp. 132–33.

8. Friedman and Friedman, *Tyranny,* pp. 14, 52, 105–23, 146; Friedman and Fried-

man, *Free to Choose,* passim; Milton Friedman, *Essays in Positive Economics* (Chicago: University of Chicago Press, 1953), p. 117ff. The quote is from *Tyranny,* p. 148.

9. Friedman and Friedman, *Free To Choose,* pp. 62–81, 85; Buchanan, Wagner, and Burton, *Consequences,* pp. 85–86, referring to Friedman; Hayek, *Denationalisation,* pp. 13–14.

10. Gilder, *Wealth and Poverty,* pp. 39, 45, 110–11, 240, and passim; Ludwig von Mises, *Liberalism: A Socio-Economic Exposition,* trans. Ralph Raico, ed. Arthur Goddard (Kansas City: Sheed Andrews and McMeel, 1978), pp. 54, 75–85; Stockman and Simon are quoted in Sidney Blumenthal, *The Rise of the Counter-Establishment: From Conservative Ideology to Political Power* (New York: Times Books, 1986), pp. 216, 219–21, 254, 64–65.

11. Friedman and Friedman, *Tyranny,* p. 117; F. A. Hayek, *Law, Legislation and Liberty: A New Statement of the Liberal Principles of Justice and Political Economy,* vol. 3, *The Political Order of a Free People* (Chicago: University of Chicago Press, 1979), p. 150.

12. Buchanan, *What Should Economicsts Do?* pp. 168, 211; idem, *Liberty, Market and State,* p. 5; Friedman and Friedman, *Free to Choose,* pp. 56–61; Hayek, *Law, Legislation and Liberty,* 2:32, xiii.

13. Friedrich A. Hayek, *The Road to Serfdom,* with a new preface by the author (Chicago: University of Chicago Press, Phoenix Books, 1976), pp. 212–15; Buchanan, *Liberty, Market and State,* p. 116.

14. F. A. Hayek, *The Essence of Hayek,* ed. Chiaki Nishiyama and Kurt R. Leube (Stanford, Calif.: Hoover Institution Press, 1984), p. 83; Friedman and Friedman, *Tyranny,* pp. 73, 24–25, 8–9, 42, 117; Milton Friedman, *Capitalism and Freedom* (Chicago: University of Chicago Press, 1962), p. 34; idem, "The Threat to Freedom in the Welfare State," *Business and Society Review* 21 (Spring 1977):10; Buchanan, *Liberty, Market and State,* pp. 178–79.

15. Gilder, *Wealth and Poverty,* p. 68.

16. Milton Friedman, *There's No Such Thing as a Free Lunch* (LaSalle, Ill.: Open Court, 1975), p. 9; Gilder, *Wealth and Poverty,* pp. 12, 101.

17. Hayek, *Essence,* p. 87; Friedman, *Capitalism and Freedom,* p. 194; Friedman, *There's No Such Thing,* pp. 26, 206–7.

18. F. A. Hayek, *The Constitution of Liberty* (Chicago: Gateway Editions, Henry Regnery, 1976), pp. 100–102; idem, *Essence,* pp. 346–48; Buchanan, *Liberty, Market and State,* pp. 170, 263.

19. Friedman and Friedman, *Free to Choose,* pp. 110–15; Milton Friedman, *The Essence of Friedman,* ed. Kurt R. Leube (Stanford, Calif.: Hoover Institution Press, 1987), pp. 57–68, 137–38.

20. Buchanan, *What Should Economists Do?* pp. 271–73; Buchanan, *Liberty, Market and State,* p. 179.

21. Milton Friedman, *The Invisible Hand in Economics and Politics* (Singapore: Institute of Southeast Asian Studies, 1981); Hayek, *Road to Serfdom,* pp. xx–xxi, 5, 42; idem, *Law, Legislation and Liberty,* 3:150–51, 169–70; idem, *Freedom and the Economic System,* Public Policy Pamphlet no. 29 (Chicago: University of Chicago Press, 1939), pp. 33–34; idem, "The Use of Knowledge in Society," in Adrian Klaasen, ed. *The Invisible Hand* (Chicago: Gateway Editions, 1965), pp. 128–29; Hayek, *Law, Legislation and Liberty,* 2:86–87. See also F. A. Hayek, *Individualism and Economic Order* (Chicago: University of Chicago Press, 1948), pp. 119–208.

22. Gilder, *Wealth and Poverty,* pp. 3, 6, 26–27.

23. von Mises, *Liberalism,* pp. 85, 87–90.

24. Friedman, *Capitalism and Freedom,* p. 8; Friedman and Friedman, *Free to Choose,* pp. 46–47.

25. Friedman and Friedman, *Tyranny*, p. 138; idem, *Free to Choose*, p. ix. See also Buchanan, *Liberty, Market and State*, p. 267.

26. Malthus's reasons for the failure of the poor laws—they violate human nature and the natural system of social-economic relations; successful intervention in natural processes is impossible; the poor laws perpetuate poverty and cannot alleviate it; poverty is ultimately an individual concern, not caused by the existing political and social economy; the laws violate the freedom of taxpayers and the poor—are almost prototypical of contemporary claims that government cannot be effective, that it cannot successfully intervene in economic relations, and that it can only be destructive.

27. Adam Smith, *An Inquiry into the Nature and Causes of the Wealth of Nations*, ed. Edwin Cannan (New York: Modern Library, 1965). The quotes are from pp. 651, 740. The relevant sections are bk. 4, chap. 9, and bk. 5, chap. 1.

28. von Mises, *Liberalism*, p. 58; Hayek, *Law, Legislation and Liberty*, 1:45, 47.

29. von Mises, *Liberalism*, pp. 52–58, 38–39, 80–85, 75, 79.

30. Hayek, *Constitution of Liberty*, pp. 221–23; idem, *Law, Legislation and Liberty*, 1:48.

31. Hayek, *Law, Legislation and Liberty*, 3:139–140, 41–46, 60–63, 2:2–7; idem, *Constitution of Liberty*, pp. 221–24; idem, *Law, Legislation and Liberty*, 1:132–33, 48; idem, *Denationalisation*.

32. Friedman, *Capitalism and Freedom*, pp. 25–32; Friedman and Friedman, *Free to Choose*, pp. 21–25. See also Friedman, *There's No Such Thing*, p. 37.

33. Cf. Milton Friedman, *Adam Smith's Relevance for 1976*, Original Paper no. 5, (Los Angeles: International Institute for Economic Research, 1976).

34. This presumably serves self-interest more than in bureaucracies directly subject to publicity. About one-fifth of weapons research and procurement funds for 1989 are in the "black" part of the budget, classified even from most members of Congress. George C. Wilson, "The Only Thing Visible about Stealth Is Its Rising Cost," *Washington Post National Weekly Edition*, May 23–29, 1988, p. 31.

35. Consider Federal Bureau of Investigation requests, revealed in early 1988, that librarians provide lists of people with foreign-sounding names who use declassified technical data, on the grounds that they may be spies.

36. Hayek, *Law, Legislation and Liberty*, 3:54–56, 125, 132.

37. Friedman and Friedman, *Tyranny*, pp. 22–26, 69–80.

38. Albert O. Hirschman, *The Passions and the Interests: Political Arguments for Capitalism before Its Triumph* (Princeton, N.J.: Princeton University Press, 1977), is the best historical analysis of this claim.

39. Buchanan, *What Should Economists Do?* p. 161; Ryan C. Amacher, Robert D. Tollison, and Thomas D. Willett, "The Economic Approach to Social Policy Questions: Some Methodological Perspectives," in Ryan C. Amacher, Robert D. Tollison, and Thomas D. Willett, eds., *The Economic Approach to Public Policy: Selected Readings* (Ithaca, N.Y.: Cornell University Press, 1976), p. 25; Friedman, *There's No Such Thing*, p. 31.

40. See Charles E. Lindblom, *Politics and Markets: The World's Political-Economic Systems* (New York: Basic Books, 1977); Robert A. Dahl, *After the Revolution?: Authority in a Good Society* (New Haven, Conn.: Yale University Press, 1970); idem, *Democracy, Liberty, and Equality* (Oslo: Norwegian University Press, 1986); Benjamin Barber, *Strong Democracy: Participatory Politics for a New Age* (Berkeley and Los Angeles: University of California Press, 1984).

41. Dan Usher, *The Economic Prerequisite to Democracy* (New York: Columbia University Press, 1981). This is an issue in the debate over comparable worth.

42. See the discussion in David Dale Martin, "The Uses and Abuses of Economic Theory in the Social Control of Business," *Journal of Economic Issues* 8 (1974):280.

43. Hayek, *Law, Legislation and Liberty*, 3:151.

44. See Lindblom, *Politics and Markets*, esp. pp. 161–200.

45. Buchanan, *Liberty, Market and State*, pp. 253–54; Hayek, *Road to Serfdom*, pp. 106–13. The quote is from Hayek, *Constitution of Liberty*, pp. 282–83.

46. Friedman, *Capitalism and Freedom*, pp. 15–16, 23; Friedman and Friedman, *Free to Choose*, pp. 6, xvii.

47. Friedman, *Capitalism and Freedom*, pp. 23–24.

48. See "Gains from Privatization May Be Small without Measures to Boost Competition," *IMF Survey* 16 (Mar. 23, 1987):82–84; "Gains from Privatization Depend on Competition and Policy Measures," *IMF Survey* 17 (Feb. 8, 1988):39.

49. Hayek, *Law, Legislation and Liberty*, 3:46–49, 79, 186 n. 8; idem, *Denationalisation*.

50. Friedman and Friedman, *Free to Choose*, pp. 140–217; idem, *Tyranny*, pp. 101–4, 132, 142–64; Friedman, *Capitalism and Freedom*, pp. 35–36.

51. The assumption may be Hobbesian, but the conclusions are not. Hobbes relied on government power to produce order, not markets. Economic self-interest and desire for esteem were too frail to ensure order, given the savage passions of self-interest.

52. Hayek, *Law, Legislation and Liberty*, 1:1–3; Buchanan and Wagner, *Democracy in Deficit*; Buchanan, *Liberty, Market and State*, pp. 116–17; idem, "The Potential for Taxpayer Revolt in American Democracy," *Social Science Quarterly* 59 (1979):691–96; Friedman, *There's No Such Thing*, p. 6; Friedman and Friedman, *Tyranny*, pp. 41–47 and passim.

53. Milton Friedman, "Election Perspective," *Newsweek*, Nov. 10, 1980, p. 94; Friedman and Friedman, *Tyranny*, pp. 42, 3; Milton Friedman, "Why Deficits Are Bad," *Newsweek*, Jan. 2, 1984, p. 56; Friedman and Friedman, *Tyranny*, p. 9; James M. Buchanan, "Quest for a Tempered Utopia," *Wall Street Journal*, Nov. 14, 1986, p. 30.

54. Buchanan, *Liberty, Market and State*, pp. 22, 62; idem, *What Should Economists Do?* pp. 165–66, 180, 275.

55. Hayek, *Law, Legislation and Liberty*, 1:2, 64.

56. Hayek, *Law, Legislation and Liberty*, 3:128, 150; Friedman and Friedman, *Tyranny*, pp. 27, 168, 58–59.

57. This is valid if self-interested people assume they will be winners. A different assumption—that they desire to minimize losses or that they may be among the losers—can lead to a welfare or redistributive system.

58. Friedman, *There's No Such Thing*, p. 87; Hayek, *Law, Legislation and Liberty*, 3:126; Buchanan, *What Should Economists Do?* pp. 195–96; Friedman and Friedman, *Tyranny*, pp. 47, 51–55. See also Milton Friedman, "Reply," in Milton Friedman and Walter Heller, *Monetary vs. Fiscal Policy* (New York: W. W. Norton and Co., 1969), pp. 73–74.

59. Friedman, *There's No Such Thing*, p. 91.

60. Buchanan uses the term more than Friedman or Hayek, but it is consistent with Friedman's proposed constitutional amendments and Hayek's rule of law.

61. Buchanan and Wagner, *Democracy in Deficit*, pp. 13, 21–22, 77; James M. Buchanan, "The Moral Dimension of Debt Financing," *Economic Inquiry* 23 (1985):5; William Breit, "Starving the Leviathan: Balanced Budget Prescriptions before Keynes," in Buchanan and Wagner, *Fiscal Responsibility*, pp. 9–10; Buchanan, *What Should Economists Do?* pp. 180, 195. See also Buchanan, Wagner, and Burton, *Consequences*; Richard E. Wagner and Robert D. Tollison, *Balanced Budgets, Fiscal Responsibility and the Constitution* (San Francisco: Cato Institute, 1980).

62. Breit, "Starving Leviathan," in Buchanan and Wagner, *Fiscal Responsibility*, p. 10; Buchanan and Wagner, *Democracy in Deficit*, p. 9.

63. Buchanan and Wagner, *Democracy in Deficit*, pp. 147–59, 175–82; Buchanan,

Wagner and Burton, *Consequences,* pp. 81–86; Friedman and Friedman, *Tyranny,* pp. 51–65, 167; idem, *Free to Choose,* pp. 289–97, 301–2. See also Buchanan, *What Should Economists Do?* p. 195; idem, "Potential for Taxpayer Revolt."

64. See Friedman, *Capitalism and Freedom,* pp. 52–53; Friedman and Friedman, *Tyranny,* pp. 135–36.

65. Hayek, *Road to Serfdom,* pp. 73–76; idem, *Law, Legislation and Liberty,* 1:86, 108, 2:14.

66. Hayek, *Road to Serfdom,* p. 79; idem, *Law, Legislation and Liberty,* 3:102, 2:159, n. 4, 34–35.

67. Leonard Silk, *The Economists* (New York: Avon, 1976), p. 69.

68. Friedman, *Essays in Positive Economics,* pp. 181, 268. See also Friedman and Heller, *Monetary vs. Fiscal Policy;* Friedman and Friedman, *Tyranny,* p. 84; Friedman, *Capitalism and Freedom,* pp. 51–55; Friedman, *Essence,* pp. 285–445.

69. Hayek, *Denationalisation,* p. 90–93, 29, 80, and passim. See also Hayek, *Law, Legislation and Liberty,* 3:57–59; idem, "Toward a Free Market Monetary System," *Journal of Libertarian Studies* 3 (1979):1–8.

70. Buchanan, *What Should Economists Do?* pp. 275, 180; idem, *Liberty, Market and State,* p. 22, 153; Buchanan, *Economics* p. 269.

71. Friedman and Friedman, *Tyranny,* p. 42.

72. Hayek, *Law, Legislation and Liberty,* 1:2.

73. Friedman and Friedman, *Free to Choose,* pp. 25, 29; Peter Brimelow, "Why Liberalism Is Now Obsolete: An Interview with Nobel Laureate Milton Friedman," *Forbes,* Dec. 12, 1988, pp. 168–74.

74. *New York Times,* Dec. 2, 1977, p. 16; Milton Friedman, "A Biased Double Standard," *Newsweek,* Jan. 12, 1981, p. 68. On his influence see Jonathan Kandell, "Chile, Lab Test for a Theorist," *New York Times,* Mar. 21, 1976, sec. 4, p. 3.

75. Friedman, "Threat to Freedom," pp. 8–10.

76. "A Draconian Cure for Chile's Economic Ills?" *Business Week,* Jan. 12, 1976, pp. 70–72.

77. *New York Times,* May 22, 1977, sec. 4, p. 18.

78. Friedman, "A Biased Double Standard," p. 68; Milton Friedman, "Free Markets and Generals," *Newsweek,* Jan. 25, 1982, p. 59. See also Blumenthal, *Rise of Counter-Establishment,* pp. 111–14.

79. Buchanan, *Economics,* pp. 253, 258; idem, *Liberty, Market and State,* pp. 167, 274 n. 5.

80. This is a continuing theme in Lindblom, *Politics and Markets.* See also Charles E. Lindblom, "The Market as Prison," *Journal of Politics* 44 (1982):324–36.

81. See Hayek, *Law, Legislation and Liberty,* 1:10, 69–70, 100, 3:153–76; Buchanan, *Liberty, Market and State,* pp. 58, 190–91, and passim.

82. Law evolves for these authors, but government and politics are not the ultimate source of law.

83. Garrett Hardin, "The Tragedy of the Commons," *Science,* Dec. 18, 1968, pp. 1243–48. Given the conservative picture of human nature and private property, there is hardly any commons, but that is a definitional trick. If one assumes a wider commons, individual self-interest is insufficient in many areas. See also Robert E. Goodin, *Political Theory and Public Policy* (Chicago: University of Chicago Press, 1982), pp. 168–69, 176.

84. See Friedman and Friedman, *Tyranny,* p. 119, where they voice a common criticism of the U.S. government for financing anti-smoking campaigns and subsidizing tobacco farming. Instead of seeing this as evidence that government is not monolithic, Friedman uses it to condemn government for not being unified.

Chapter Eight. Conclusions

1. Friedman calls for "a detailed program of action." Milton Friedman and Rose Friedman, *Tyranny of the Status Quo* (San Diego: Harcourt Brace Jovanovich, 1984), p. 3.

2. See B. Burkitt and M. Spiers, "The Economic Theory of Politics: A Reappraisal," *International Journal of Social Economics* 10, no. 2 (1983):12–21; Robert L. Heilbroner, "On the Limited 'Relevance' of Economics," in Ryan C. Amacher, Robert D. Tollison, and Thomas D. Willett, eds., *The Economic Approach to Public Policy: Selected Readings* (Ithaca, N.Y.: Cornell University Press, 1976), pp. 54–66; idem, *Behind the Veil of Economics: Essays in the Worldly Philosophy* (New York: W. W. Norton and Co., 1988); Robert Kuttner, "The Poverty of Economics," *Atlantic Monthly*, Feb. 1985, pp. 74–84; Paul J. Quirk, "In Defense of the Politics of Ideas," *Journal of Politics* 50 (1988):31–41; Joseph J. Spengler, "The Problem of Order in Economic Affairs," *Southern Economic Journal* 15 (1948):1–29.

3. Burkitt and Spiers, "Economic Theory," p. 12.

4. *The Collected Writings of John Maynard Keynes*, vol. 9, *Essays in Persuasion* (London: Macmillan, 1972), p. 224.

5. James M. Buchanan, *What Should Economists Do?* (Indianapolis: Liberty Press, 1979), p. 84. See also Amacher, Tollison, and Willet, "The Economic Approach to Social Policy Questions: Some Methodological Perspectives," in their *Economic Approach*, p. 19.

6. Amartya Sen, "The Moral Standing of the Market," *Social Philosophy and Policy* 2 (1985):1–19. Results are important in general, systemic terms of promising that things will be better for more people in the long run.

7. A conservative such as Robert Nozick can, although he relies on suing in court rather than regulation. See *Anarchy, State, and Utopia* (New York: Basic Books, 1974), pp. 79–81. The conservatives also ignore the possibly centralizing tendencies of such technologies as nuclear power.

8. Frank Kahn, "Some Keynesian Reflections on Monetarism," in Fausto Vicarelli, ed., *Keynes's Relevance Today* (Philadelphia: University of Pennsylvania Press, 1985), p. 18.

9. For brief discussions on why economists often ignore the impact of economics on politics, see Dan Usher, *The Economic Prerequisite to Democracy* (New York: Columbia University Press, 1981), pp. 2–3; George Stigler, *The Economist as Preacher and Other Essays* (Chicago: University of Chicago Press, 1982), p. 16; J. Harvey Lomax, "Economics or Political Philosophy: Which Should Prevail in Public Policy?" *Interpretation* 10 (1982):251–71.

10. Amartya Sen, *On Ethics and Economics* (Oxford: Basil Blackwell, 1987), p. 81.

11. Eric Willenz, "Why Europe Needs the Welfare State," *Foreign Policy* 63 (1986): 88–107.

12. The United States and Germany faced similar economic circumstances in 1932, but Germany underwent a revolution. Strong belief by Americans in the legitimacy of their constitutional system and methods of problem solving allowed a system-strengthening shift in policies to implement reinterpretation of widely shared fundamental values. The Weimar Republic lacked such acceptance. Large numbers, perhaps a majority, considered it illegitimate, and it could not weather the economic crisis.

13. Russell Kirk criticizes von Mises for dispelling the myths by which people live. *A Program for Conservatives* (Chicago: Henry Regnery Co., 1962), pp. 146–49.

14. Albert O. Hirschman, *Rival Views of Market Society and Other Recent Essays* (New York: Viking, 1986), p. 53.

15. See Friedrich A. Hayek, *The Road to Serfdom*, with a new preface by the author (Chicago: University of Chicago Press, Phoenix Books, 1976), p. 209; James M. Buchanan, *Liberty, Market and State: Politcal Economy in the 1980s* (New York: New York University Press, 1986), p. 114. See also his discussion of secession.

16. Jon Elster, "The Market and the Forum: Three Varieties of Political Theory," in Jon Elster and Aanund Hylland, eds., *Foundations of Social Choice Theory* (Cambridge: Cambridge University Press, 1986), p. 111.

17. Burkitt and Spiers, "Economic Theory," p. 17. See also Samuel Brittan, *The Economic Consequences of Democracy* (London: Temple Smith, 1977), p. 242.

18. James M. Buchanan, "An Economist's Approach to 'Scientific Politics,'" in Malcolm B. Parsons, ed., *Perspectives in the Study of Politics* (Chicago: Rand McNally and Co., 1968), p. 80.

19. Neither Freud, experimental psychology, nor the sociology of behavior appears in conservative accounts of behavior. Noninstrumental behavior is also missing. See Hirschman, *Rival Views*, pp. 150–58.

20. See Michael Walzer, "Liberalism and the Art of Separation," *Political Theory* 12 (1984):325.

21. These comments were sparked by Larry M. Preston's essay, "Efficiency and Political Theory" (paper presented at meeting of American Political Science Association, September 1987).

22. James M. Buchanan, *Economics: Between Predictive Science and Moral Philosophy*, comp. and with a preface by Robert D. Tollison and Viktor J. Vanberg (College Station: Texas A&M University Press, 1987), p. 5. This insight is not developed.

23. Stephen Jay Gould, *Time's Arrow Time's Cycle: Myth and Metaphor in the Discovery of Geological Time* (Cambridge, Mass: Harvard University Press, 1987), p. 9.

24. The quote is from Hayek, *Road to Serfdom*, p. 42. See also Friedrich A. Hayek, *Law, Legislation and Liberty: A New Statement of the Liberal Principles of Justice and Political Economy*, vol. 2, *The Mirage of Social Justice* (Chicago: University of Chicago Press, 1976), esp. pp. 142–43; ibid., vol. 3, *The Political Order of a Free People* (Chicago: University of Chicago Press, 1979), esp. p. 151; Buchanan, *What Should Economists Do?* pp. 231–52; Milton Friedman and Rose Friedman, *Free to Choose: A Personal Statement* (New York: Avon, 1979); Thomas Sowell, *A Conflict of Visions: Ideological Origins of Political Struggles* (New York: Quill, 1987).

25. George Kateb, "Remarks on the Procedures of Constitutional Democracy," in J. Roland Pennock and John W. Chapman, eds., *Constitutionalism*, Nomos 20 (New York: New York University Press, 1979), p. 217.

26. See Buchanan's market-based theory of economic and political decision making. Hayek believes that *"the Great Society is still held together mainly by what vulgarly are called economic relations." Law, Legislation and Liberty*, 2:112. Leonard Silk, *The Economists* (New York: Avon, 1976), pp. 55–56, discusses Friedman.

27. For an intemperate discussion of the "invisible hand" in politcs, see Milton Friedman, *Adam Smith's Relevance for 1976*, Original Paper no. 5 (Los Angeles: International Institute for Economic Research, 1976).

28. See Geoffrey Brennan and Loren Lomasky, "The Impartial Spectator Goes to Washington: Toward a Smithian Theory of Electoral Behavior," *Economics and Philosophy* 1 (1985):192; Aanund Hylland, "The Purpose and Significance of Social Choice Theory: Some General Remarks and an Application to the 'Lady Chatterley Problem,'" in Elster and Hylland, *Foundations of Social Choice Theory*, pp. 45–74, esp. 46–47.

29. Quirk, "Defense," p. 39. For the conservatives, this is not a mitigating reason because, by definition, anything outside the market serves narrow, selfish special interests.

30. See Silk, *Economists*, p. 247; Walter A. Weisskopf, "Hidden Value Conflicts

in Economic Thought," *Ethics* 61 (1951):198; Donald N. McCloskey, *The Rhetoric of Economics* (Madison: University of Wisconsin Press, 1985), pp. 4–5 and passim.

31. See Homa Katouzian, *Ideology and Method in Economics* (New York: New York University Press, 1980), pp. 138–39, 146–47.

32. See Jan-Erik Lane: "A social decision involves two [interrelated] things, a consideration of what is feasible and a deliberation about what is desirable." Lane, ed., *State and Market: The Politics of the Public and Private* (London: Sage, 1985), p. viii; McCloskey, *Rhetoric*, pp. 140–41; Wesley C. Mitchell, "Facts and Values in Economics," *Journal of Philosophy* 41 (1944):216–17. Richard McKeon, "The Interpretation of Political Theory and Practice in Ancient Athens," *Journal of the History of Ideas* 62 (1981):3: "Facts are conditioned by men's philosophies in as definite a sense as philosophies are conditioned by relevant facts."

33. See Buchanan, "An Economist's Approach," p. 80.

34. There is always a reason why predictions fail: We did not wait long enough; all relevant variables were not examined; more data will prove the theory correct. If one believes strongly enough, results that do not fit expectations must be dismissed as inaccurate observations. Joan Robinson claims that given the impossibility "of controlled experiment, we have to rely on interpretation of the evidence, and interpretation involves judgment." *Economic Philosophy* (Harmondsworth, Eng.: Penguin, 1962), p. 26; see also pp. 28, 76. Cf. Lester Thurow, *Dangerous Currents: The State of Economics* (New York: Random House, 1983), pp. xvi, 3, 8, 16–20, 49, 126–27, 173–74, 216–17, and passim; McCloskey, *Rhetoric*, p. 14, 58–61; Charles K. Wilber, "Empirical Verification and Theory Selection: The Keynesian-Monetarist Debate," *Journal of Economic Issue* 13 (1979):977–81.

35. Buchanan seems more aware of these problems than do the others, though he too engages in this enterprise. See Buchanan, *What Should Economists Do?* p. 57.

36. They share remarkable similarities: deep roots in classical economics; a nineteenth-century picture of science as discovering preexisting laws of nature; mistrust of politics; a view of government as controlled by dominant interests; economics as the real basis of politics; downplaying of citizenship and participation; the belief that rules and institutions evolve rather than result from rational analysis and conscious decisions and that values do not have independent standing; and the assertion that people often fail to see their real interests.

37. George Gilder, *Wealth and Poverty* (New York: Basic Books, 1981); idem, *The Spirit of Enterprise* (New York: Simon and Schuster, 1984), pp. 70, 257; James M. Buchanan and Richard E. Wagner, *Democracy in Deficit: The Political Legacy of Lord Keynes* (New York: Academic Press, 1977), p. 9. Geoffrey Brennan and James M. Buchanan call for a "civic religion." *The Reason of Rules: Constitutional Political Economy* (Cambridge: Cambridge University Press, 1985), pp. 149–50. Cf. Thurow, *Dangerous Currents*, p. xviii: Conservative economics is "also a political philosophy, often becoming something approaching a religion." The religious nature of their enterprise remains, even though they reject many traditional moral injunctions and despite the scientific claims of Friedman's positivism and of Buchanan's and Hayek's partial positivism.

38. Gilder, *Wealth and Poverty*, p. 24.

39. *The Collected Writings of John Maynard Keynes*, vol. 7, *The General Theory of Employment Interest and Money* (London: Macmillan, 1973), p. 3; Keynes, *Collected Writings*, 9:284.

Selected Bibliography

Amacher, Ryan C. Robert D. Tollison, and Thomas D. Willett, eds. *The Economic Approach to Public Policy: Selected Readings*. Ithaca, N.Y.: Cornell University Press, 1976.

Anderson, Carol Leutner. "Economics and Metaphysics: Framework for the Future," *Review of Social Economy* 40 (1982): 199–226.

Anderson, Charles W. "The Place of Principles in Policy Analysis." *American Political Science Review* 73 (1979): 711–23.

Anderson, Elizabeth. "Values, Risks, and Market Norms." *Philosophy and Public Affairs* 17 (1988): 54-65.

Aristotle. *Politics*. Trans. by T. A. Sinclair. Harmondsworth, Eng.: Penguin, 1962.

Arrow, Kenneth J. *Social Choice and Individual Values*. New York: John Wiley and Sons, 1963.

Balogh, Thomas. *The Irrelevance of Conventional Economics*. New York: Liveright, 1982.

Barber, Benjamin. *Strong Democracy: Participatory Politics for a New Age*. Berkeley and Los Angeles: University of California Press, 1984.

Barry, Brian. "Lady Chatterley's Lover and Doctor Fischer's Bomb Party: Liberalism, Pareto Optimality, and the Problem of Objectionable Preferences." In *Foundations of Social Choice Theory,* ed. Jon Elster and Aanund Hylland, 11–44. Cambridge: Cambridge University Press, 1986.

Becker, Lawrence C. "Individual Rights." In *And Justice for All*, ed. Tom Regan and Donald Van De Veer, 197–216. Totowa, N.J.: Rowman and Littlefield, 1982.

Bennett, John G. "Ethics and Markets." *Philosophy and Public Affairs* 14 (1985): 195–204.

Berlin, Isaiah. *Four Essays on Liberty*. London: Oxford University Press, 1969.

Bladen, Vincent. *From Adam Smith to Maynard Keynes: The Heritage of Political Economy*. Toronto: University of Toronto Press, 1974.

Blaug, Mark. *Great Economists since Keynes: An Introduction to the Lives and Works of One Hundred Modern Economists*. Totowa, N.J.: Barnes and Noble Books, 1985.

———, ed. *Who's Who in Economics: A Biographical Dictionary of Major Economists, 1700–1986*, 2d ed. Cambridge, Mass.: MIT Press, 1986.

Block, Fred, Richard A. Cloward, Barbara Ehrenreich, and Frances Fox Piven. *The Mean Season: The Attack on the Welfare State*. New York: Pantheon Books, 1987.

Blumenthal, Sidney. *The Rise of the Counter-Establishment: From Conservative Ideology to Political Power*. New York: Times Books, 1986.

Boorstin, Daniel J. *The Discoverers: A History of Man's Search to Know His World and Himself*. New York: Vintage Books, 1985.

Breit, William, and Roger W. Spencer, eds. *Lives of the Laureates: Seven Nobel Economists*. Cambridge, Mass.: MIT Press, 1986.

Brennan, Geoffrey, and Loren Lomasky. "The Impartial Spectator Goes to Washington: Toward a Smithian Theory of Electoral Behavior." *Economics and Philosophy* 1 (1985): 189–211.

Brennan, Geoffrey, and James M. Buchanan. *The Reason of Rules: Constitutional Political Economy.* Cambridge: Cambridge University Press, 1985.

Brimelow, Peter. "Why Liberalism Is Now Obsolete: An Interview with Nobel Laureate Milton Friedman." *Forbes*, Dec. 12, 1988, 161–176.

Brittan, Samuel. *The Economic Consequences of Democracy.* London: Temple Smith, 1977.

———. "The Economic Contradictions of Democracy." *British Journal of Political Science* 5 (1975): 129–59.

Bronowski, J. *The Ascent of Man.* Boston: Little, Brown and Co., 1973.

———. *The Common Sense of Science.* Cambridge, Mass.: Harvard University Press, 1967.

Brown, Alan. *Modern Political Philosophy: Theories of the Just Society.* Harmondsworth, Eng.: Penguin, 1986.

Browning, Edgar K. "Why the Social Insurance Budget Is Too Large in a Democracy." *Economic Inquiry* 13 (1975): 373–88.

Buchanan, James M. "Contractarian Political Economy and Constitutional Interpretation." *American Economic Review* 78 (1988): 135–139.

———. "The Economic Theory of Politics Reborn." *Challenge* 31, no. 2 (Mar. 1988): 4–10.

———. *Economics: Between Predictive Science and Moral Philosophy.* Comp. and with a preface by Robert D. Tollison and Viktor J. Vanberg. College Station: Texas A&M University Press, 1987.

———. "An Economist's Approach to 'Scientific Politics.'" In *Perspectives in the Study of Politics*, ed. Malcolm B. Parsons, 77–88. Chicago: Rand McNally and Co., 1968.

———. *Explorations into Constitutional Economics.* Comp. and with a Preface by Robert D. Tollison and Viktor J. Vanberg. College Station: Texas A&M University Press, 1989.

———. *Liberty, Market and State: Political Economy in the 1980s.* New York: New York University Press, 1986.

———. *The Limits of Liberty: Between Anarchy and Leviathan.* Chicago: University of Chicago Press, 1975.

———. "The Moral Dimension of Debt Financing." *Economic Inquiry* 23 (1985): 1–6.

———. "Positive Economics, Welfare Economics and Political Economy." *Journal Of Law and Economics* 2 (1959): 124–138.

———. "The Potential for Taxpayer Revolt in American Democracy." *Social Science Quarterly* 59 (1979): 691–96.

———. *Public Finance in Democratic Process: Fiscal Institutions and Individual Choice.* Chapel Hill: University of North Carolina Press, 1967.

———. "Quest for a Tempered Utopia." *Wall Street Journal*, Nov. 14, 1986, p. 30.

———. *What Should Economists Do?* Indianapolis: Liberty Press, 1979.

Buchanan, James M., and Roger L. Faith. "Secession and the Limits of Taxation: Toward a Theory of Internal Exit." *American Economic Review* 77 (1987): 1023–31.

Buchanan, James M., and Marilyn Flowers. "An Analytical Setting for a 'Taxpayers' Revolution.'" *Western Economic Journal* 7 (1969): 349–59.

Buchanan, James M., Charles K. Rowley, Albert Breton et al. *The Economics of Politics.* London: Institute of Economic Affairs, 1978.

Buchanan, James M., and Warren J. Samuels. "On Some Fundamental Issues in Political Economy: An Exchange of Correspondence." *Journal of Economic Issues* 9 (1975): 15–38.

Buchanan, James M., and Gordon Tullock. *The Calculus of Consent: Logical Foundations of Constitutional Democracy.* Ann Arbor: University of Michigan Press, 1965.

Buchanan, James M., and Viktor J. Vanberg. "The Politicization of Market Failure." *Public Choice* 57 (1988): 101–13.

Buchanan, James M., and Richard E. Wagner. *Democracy in Deficit: The Political Legacy of Lord Keynes.* New York: Academic Press, 1977.

Buchanan, James M., Charles K. Rowley, and Robert D. Tollison, eds. *Deficits.* Oxford: Basil Blackwell, 1986.

Buchanan, James M., and Robert D. Tollison, eds. *Theory of Public Choice: Political Applications of Economics.* Ann Arbor: University of Michigan Press, 1972.

Buchanan, James M., and Richard E. Wagner, eds. *Fiscal Responsibility in Constitutional Democracy.* Leiden and Boston: Martinus Nijhoff, 1978.

Buchanan, James M., Richard E. Wagner, and John Burton, eds. *The Consequences of Mr. Keynes: An Analysis of the Misuse of Economic Theory for Political Profiteering, with Proposals for Constitutional Disciplines.* London: Institute of Economic Affairs, 1978.

Buckley, William F., Jr., ed. *American Conservative Thought in the Twentieth Century.* Indianapolis: Bobbs-Merrill, 1970.

Burke, James. *The Day the Universe Changed.* Boston: Little, Brown and Co., 1985.

Burkitt, B., and M. Spiers. "The Economic Theory of Politics: A Reappraisal." *International Journal of Social Economics* 10, no. 2 (1983): 12–21.

Caplan, Arthur L., and Daniel Callahan, eds. *Ethics in Hard Times.* New York: Plenum Press, 1981.

Crain, W. Mark, and Robert B. Ekelund, Jr. "Deficits and Democracy." *Southern Economic Journal* 44 (1978): 813–15.

Dahl, Robert A. *After the Revolution?: Authority in a Good Society.* New Haven, Conn.: Yale University Press, 1970.

———. *Democracy, Liberty, and Equality.* Oslo: Norwegian University Press, 1986.

David, Miriam. "Moral and Maternal: The Family in the Right." In *The Ideology of the New Right,* ed. Ruth Levitas, 136–68. Cambridge: Polity Press, 1986.

Downs, Anthony. *An Economic Theory of Democracy.* New York: Harper and Row, 1957.

Eatwell, John, Murray Milgate, and Peter Newman, eds. *The New Palgrave: A Dictionary of Economics.* 4 vols. London: Macmillan, 1987.

Elster, Jon. "The Market and the Forum: Three Varieties of Political Theory." In *Foundations of Social Choice Theory,* ed. Jon Elster and Aanund Hylland, 103–32. Cambridge: Cambridge University Press, 1986.

Fagothey, Austin. *Right and Reason: Ethics in Theory and Practice.* St. Louis, Mo.: C. V. Mosby Co., 1963.

Fine, Sidney. *Laissez-Faire and the General Welfare State: A Study of Conflict in American Thought 1865–1901.* Ann Arbor: University of Michigan Press, Ann Arbor Paperbacks, 1964.

Friedman, Milton. *Adam Smith's Relevance for 1976.* Original Paper no. 5. Los Angeles: International Institute for Economic Research, 1976.

———. "A Biased Double Standard." *Newsweek,* Jan. 12, 1981, p. 68.

———. *Capitalism and Freedom.* Chicago: University of Chicago Press, 1962.

———. "Choice, Chance and the Personal Distribution of Income." *Journal of Political Economy* 61 (1953): 277–90.

———. "Economists and Economic Policy." *Economic Inquiry* 24 (1986): 1–10.

———. "Election Perspective." *Newsweek,* Nov. 10, 1980, p. 94.

———. *Essays in Positive Economics.* Chicago: University of Chicago Press, 1953.

———. *The Essence of Friedman.* Ed. Kurt R. Leube. Stanford, Calif.: Hoover Institution Press, 1987.

———. "Free Markets and Generals." *Newsweek,* Jan. 25, 1982, p. 59.

———. "The Goldwater View of Economics." *New York Times*, Oct. 11, 1964, sec. 6, p. 35.

———. *The Invisible Hand in Economics and Politics*. Singapore: Institute of Southeast Asian Studies, 1981.

———. "The Keynes Centenary: A Monetarist Reflects." *Economist*, June 4, 1983, pp. 17–19.

———. *Market Mechanisms and Central Economic Planning*. Washington, D.C.: American Enterprise Institute, 1981.

———. "Monetary Policy." *Proceedings of the American Philosophical Society* 116 (January 1972): 183–96.

———. "Morality and Controls I." *New York Times*, Oct. 28, 1971, p. 41.

———. "Noble Lecture: Inflation and Unemployment." *Journal of Political Economy* 85 (1977): 451–72.

———. *Tax Limitation, Inflation and the Role of Government*. Dallas, Tex.: Fisher Institute, 1978.

———. *There's No Such Thing as a Free Lunch*. LaSalle, Ill.: Open Court, 1975.

———. "The Threat to Freedom in the Welfare State." *Business and Society Review* 21 (Spring 1977): 8–16.

———. "Value Judgments in Economics." In *Human Values and Economic Policy*, ed. Sidney Hook. New York: New York University Press, 1967.

———. "What All is Utility?" *Economic Journal* 65 (1955): 405–09.

———. "Which Budget Deficit?" *Newsweek*, Nov. 2, 1981, p. 88.

———. "Why Deficits Are Bad." *Newsweek*, Jan. 2, 1984, p. 56.

Friedman, Milton, and Rose Friedman. *Free to Choose: A Personal Statement*. (New York: Avon, 1979).

———. *Tyranny of the Status Quo*. San Diego: Harcourt Brace Jovanovich, 1984.

Friedman, Milton, and Walter Heller. *Monetary vs. Fiscal Policy*. New York: W. W. Norton and Co., 1969.

"Gains from Privatization May Be Small without Measures to Boost Competition." *IMF Survey* 16 (Mar. 23, 1987): 82–84.

"Gains from Privatization Depend on Competition and Policy Measures." *IMF Survey* 17 (Feb. 8, 1988): 39.

Galbraith, John Kenneth. *The Affluent Society*. 4th ed. Boston: Houghton Mifflin Co., 1984.

———. *The Affluent Society*. Toronto: Mentor Books, 1965.

———. *American Capitalism: The Concept of Countervailing Power*. rev. ed. Boston: Houghton Mifflin Co., 1956.

———. *The Anatomy of Power*. Boston: Houghton Mifflin Co., 1983.

———. *Annals of an Abiding Liberal*. Boston: Houghton Mifflin Co., 1979.

———. *Economics and the Public Purpose*. Harmondsworth, Eng.: Penguin, 1973.

———. *Economics in Perspective: A Critical History*. Boston: Houghton Mifflin Co., 1987.

———. "The Uses and Excuses for Affluence." *New York Times Magazine*, May 31, 1981, p. 50.

Galeotti, Anna Elisabetta. "Individualism, Social Rules, Tradition: The Case of Friedrich A. Hayek." *Political Theory* 15 (1987): 163–81.

Gilder, George. *The Spirit of Enterprise*. New York: Simon and Schuster, 1984.

———. *Wealth and Poverty*. New York: Basic Books, 1981.

Ginsberg, Morris. *On Justice in Society*. Harmondsworth, Eng.: Penguin, 1965.

Goodin, Robert E. *Political Theory and Public Policy*. Chicago: University of Chicago Press, 1982.

Gould, Stephen Jay. *Time's Arrow Time's Cycle: Myth and Metaphor in the Discovery of Geological Time*. Cambridge, Mass.: Harvard University Press, 1987.

Gray, John. *Liberalism*. Minneapolis: University of Minnesota Press, 1986.

Gutmann, Amy. *Liberal Equality*. Cambridge: Cambridge University Press, 1980.

Hardin, Garrett. "The Tragedy of the Commons." *Science*, Dec. 18, 1968, pp. 1243–48.

Hayek, Friedrich A. *The Collected Works of F. A. Hayek*. Vol 1., *The Fatal Conceit: The Errors of Socialism*. Ed. W. W. Bartley III. Chicago: University of Chicago Press, 1989.

———. *The Confusion of Language in Political Thought: With Some Suggestions for Remedying It*. Occasional Paper no. 20. London: Institute of Economic Affairs, 1968.

———. *The Constitution of Liberty*. Chicago: Gateway Editions, Henry Regnery, 1976.

———. *Denationalisation of Money: An Analysis of the Theory and Practice of Concurrent Currencies*. London: Institute of Economic Affairs, 1976.

———. *Economic Freedom and Representative Government*. Occasional Paper no. 39. London: Institute of Economic Affairs, 1973.

———. *The Essence of Hayek*. Ed. Chiaki Nishiyama and Kurt R. Leube. Stanford, Calif.: Hoover Institution Press, 1984.

———. *Freedom and the Economic System*. Public Policy Pamphlet no. 29. Chicago: University of Chicago Press, 1939.

———. *Individualism and Economic Order*. Chicago: University of Chicago Press, 1948.

———. "Individualism and Economic Order." In *The Conservative Tradition in European Thought*, ed. Robert Lindsay Schuettinger. New York: G. P. Putnam's Sons, 1970.

———. "Kinds of Order in Society." In *The Politicization of Society*, ed. Kenneth S. Templeton, Jr., 501–23. Indianapolis: Liberty Press, 1979.

———. *Law, Legislation and Liberty: A New Statement of the Liberal Principles of Justice and Political Economy*. Vol. 1, *Rules and Order*. Chicago: University of Chicago Press, 1973.

———. *Law, Legislation and Liberty: A New Statement of the Liberal Principles of Justice and Political Economy*. Vol. 2, *The Mirage of Social Justice*. Chicago: University of Chicago Press, 1976.

———. *Law, Legislation and Liberty: A New Statement of the Liberal Principles of Justice and Political Economy*. Vol. 3, *The Political Order of a Free People*. Chicago: University of Chicago Press, 1979.

———. "The Miscarriage of the Democratic Ideal." *Encounter* 50 (1978): 14–17.

———. "The Moral Element in Free Enterprise." In *The Invisible Hand*, ed. Adrian Klaasen, 69–77. Chicago: Gateway Editions, 1965.

———. *The Road to Serfdom*. With a new preface by the author. Chicago: University of Chicago Press, Phoenix Books, 1976.

———. *Studies in Philosophy, Politics and Economics*. Chicago: University of Chicago Press, 1967.

———. "Toward a Free Market Monetary System." *Journal of Libertarian Studies* 3 (1979): 1–8.

———. "The Use of Knowledge in Society." In *The Invisible Hand*, ed. Adrian Klaasen, 121–35. Chicago: Gateway Editions, 1965.

Heilbroner, Robert L. *Behind the Veil of Economics: Essays in the Worldly Philosophy*. New York: W. W. Norton and Co., 1988.

———. "On the Limited 'Relevance' of Economics." In *The Economic Approach to Public Policy: Selected Readings*, ed. Ryan C. Amacher, Robert D. Tollison and Thomas D. Willett, 54–66. Ithaca, N.Y.: Cornell University Press, 1976.

Heyne, Paul. *The U.S. Catholic Bishops and the Pursuit of Justice*. Policy Analysis no. 50. Washington, D.C.: Cato Institute, 1985.

Hirsch, E. D. *Cultural Literacy: What Every American Needs to Know*. Boston: Houghton Mifflin Co., 1987.

Hirschman, Albert. *Essays in Trespassing: Economics to Politics and Beyond*. Cambridge: Cambridge University Press, 1981.

———. *Exit, Voice and Loyalty: Responses to Decline in Firms, Organizations, and States*. Cambridge, Mass.: Harvard University Press, 1970.

———. *The Passions and the Interests: Political Arguments for Capitalism before Its Triumph*. Princeton, N.J.: Princeton University Press, 1977.

———. *Rival Views of Market Society and Other Recent Essays*. New York: Viking, 1986.

Hutt, William H. *Individual Freedom: Selected Works of William H. Hutt*. Ed. Svetozar Pejovich and David Klingaman. Westport, Conn.: Greenwood Press, 1975.

———. *The Keynesian Episode: A Reassessment*. Indianapolis: Liberty Press, 1979.

Hylland, Aanund. "The Purpose and Significance of Social Choice Theory: Some General Remarks and an Application to the 'Lady Chatterley Problem.'" In *Foundations of Social Choice Theory*, ed. Jon Elster and Aanund Hylland, 45–74. Cambridge: Cambridge University Press, 1986.

Joseph, Lawrence B. "Some Ways of Thinking about Equality of Opportunity." *Western Political Quarterly* 33 (1980): 393–400.

Kahn, Frank. "Some Keynesian Reflections on Monetarism." In *Keynes's Relevance Today*, ed. Fausto Vicarelli. Philadelphia: University of Pennsylvania Press, 1985.

Kammen, Michael. *Spheres of Liberty: Changing Perceptions of Liberty in American Culture*. Madison: University of Wisconsin Press, 1986.

Kateb, George. "Remarks on the Procedures of Constitutional Democracy." In *Constitutionalism*, ed. J. Roland Pennock and John W. Chapman, 215–37. Nomos 20. New York: New York University Press, 1979.

Katouzian, Homa. *Ideology and Method in Economics*. New York: New York University Press, 1980.

Kemp, Jack. *An American Renaissance: A Strategy for the 1980s*. New York: Harper and Row, 1979.

Ketcham, Ralph. *Individualism and Public Life: A Modern Dilemma*. Oxford: Basil Blackwell, 1987.

Keynes, John Maynard. *The Collected Writings of John Maynard Keynes*. Vol 5, *A Treatise on Money*. Vol. 1, *The Pure Theory of Money*. London: Macmillan, 1971.

———. *The Collected Writings of John Maynard Keynes*. Vol. 7, *The General Theory of Employment Interest and Money*. London: Macmillan, 1973.

———. *The Collected Writings of John Maynard Keynes*. Vol. 9, *Essays in Persuasion*. London: Macmillan, 1972.

———. *The Collected Writings of John Maynard Keynes*. Vol. 14, *The General Theory and After*. London: Macmillan, 1973.

———. "Democracy and Efficiency." *New Statesman and Nation*, Jan. 28, 1939.

Kirk, Russell. *A Program for Conservatives*. Chicago: Henry Regnery Co., 1962.

Klaasen, Adrian, ed. *The Invisible Hand*. Chicago: Gateway Editions, 1965.

Knight, Frank H. "Abstract Economics as Absolute Ethics." *Ethics* 76 (1966): 163–77.

———. *Freedom and Reform: Essays in Economics and Social Philosophy*. New York: Harper and Bros., 1947.

Kuhn, Thomas S. *The Structure of Scientific Revolutions*. Chicago: University of Chicago Press, 1970.

Lakoff, Sanford A. *Equality in Political Philosophy*. Cambridge, Mass.: Harvard University Press, 1964.

Lane, Jan-Erik, ed. *State and Market: The Politics of the Public and Private*. London: Sage, 1985.

Lane, Robert E. "Market Justice, Political Justice." *American Political Science Review* 80 (1986): 383–402.

Lekachman, Robert. "Economic Justice in Hard Times." In *Ethics in Hard Times,* ed. Arthur L. Caplan and Daniel Callahan, 91–115. New York: Plenum Press, 1981.

Levitas, Ruth, ed. *The Ideology of the New Right.* Cambridge: Polity Press, 1986.

Levy, Michael B. "Liberal Equality and Inherited Wealth." *Political Theory* 11 (1983): 545–64.

Lindblom, Charles E. "The Market as Prison." *Journal of Politics* 44 (1982): 324–36.

———. *Politics and Markets: The World's Political-Economic Systems.* New York: Basic Books, 1977.

Lippmann, Walter. *The Public Philosophy.* New York: Mentor Books, 1955.

Locke, John. *The Second Treatise of Government,* in *Two Treatises of Government,* ed. Peter Laslett. New York: Mentor Books, 1965.

Lomax, J. Harvey. "Economics or Political Philosophy: Which Should Prevail in Public Policy?" *Interpretation* 10 (1982): 251–71.

McCloskey, Donald N. *The Rhetoric of Economics.* Madison: University of Wisconsin Press, 1985.

McKeon, Richard. "The Interpretation of Political Theory and Practice in Ancient Athens." *Journal of the History of Ideas* 62 (1981): 3–12.

McMahon, Christopher. "Morality and the Invisible Hand." *Philosophy and Public Affairs* 10 (1981): 247–77.

Macpherson, C. B. *Democratic Theory: Essays in Retrieval.* Oxford: Clarendon Press, 1973.

———. "The Economic Penetration of Political Theory: Some Hypotheses." *Journal of the History of Ideas* 39 (1978): 101–118.

———. *The Rise and Fall of Economic Justice and Other Papers.* Oxford: Oxford University Press, 1985.

Malthus, Thomas Robert. *An Essay on the Principle of Population.* 7th ed. London: Reeves and Turner, 1872. Reprint. Fairfield, N.J.: Augustus M. Kelley, 1986.

Martin, David Dale. "The Uses and Abuses of Economic Theory in the Social Control of Business." *Journal of Economic Issues* 8 (1974): 271–85.

Meltzer, Allan H., and Scott F. Richard. "Why Government Grows (and Grows) in a Democracy." *Public Interest* 52 (Summer 1978): 111–18.

Mill, John Stuart. *On Liberty.* In *The Philosophy of John Stuart Mill: Ethical, Political and Religious,* ed. Marshall Cohen. New York: Modern Library, 1961.

Miller, David. "Constraints on Freedom." *Ethics* 94 (Oct. 1983): 66–86.

"Milton Friedman Responds." *Business and Society Review* 1 (Spring 1972): 5–16.

Mini, Piero V. *Philosophy and Economics: The Origins and Development of Economic Theory.* Gainesville: University Presses of Florida, 1974.

von Mises, Ludwig. "The Economic Nature of Profit and Loss." In *The Invisible Hand,* ed. Adrian Klaasen, 166–79. Chicago: Gateway Editions, 1965.

———. *Epistemological Problems of Economics.* Trans. George Reisman. New York: New York University Press: 1981.

———. *Liberalism: A Socio-Economic Exposition.* Trans. Ralph Raico, ed. Arthur Goddard. Kansas City: Sheed Andrews and McMeel, 1978.

Mitchell, Wesley C. "Facts and Values in Economics." *Journal of Philosophy* 41 (1944): 212–19.

Morris, Charles R. *A Time of Passion: America, 1960–1980.* New York: Penguin, 1986.

National Conference of Catholic Bishops. *Economic Justice for All: Pastoral Letter on Catholic Social Teaching and the U.S. Economy.* Washington, D.C.: United States Catholic Conference, 1986.

Nelson, Alan. "Economic Rationality and Morality." *Philosophy and Public Affairs* 17 (1988): 149–66.

Nisbet, Robert. *Conservatism: Dream and Reality.* Minneapolis: University of Minnesota Press, 1986.

Nozick, Robert. *Anarchy, State, and Utopia.* New York: Basic Books, 1974.

Oliver, Henry M., Jr. "Economic Value Theory as a Policy Guide." *Ethics* 68 (1958): 186–93.

Olson, Mancur, Jr. *The Logic of Collective Action: Public Goods and the Theory of Groups.* New York: Schocken Books, 1971.

Ortega y Gasset, Jose. *The Revolt of the Masses.* London: Unwin Books, 1961.

Pareto, Vilfredo. *Manual of Political Economy.* Trans. Ann S. Schwier, ed. Ann S. Schwier and Alfred N. Page. New York: Augustus M. Kelley, 1971.

Parsons, Malcolm B., ed. *Perspectives in the Study of Politics.* Chicago: Rand McNally and Co., 1968.

Pateman, Carole. *Participation and Democratic Theory.* Cambridge: Cambridge University Press, 1970.

Patinkin, Don. "Keynes and Economics Today." *American Economic Review, Papers and Proceedings* 74 (1984): 97–102.

Paul, Ellen Frankel. "Liberalism, Unintended Orders and Evolutionism." *Political Studies* 36 (1988): 251–72.

Pennock, J. Roland, and John W. Chapman. *Constitutionalism.* Nomos 20. New York: New York University Press, 1979.

Preston, Larry M. "Efficiency and Political Theory." Paper presented at meeting of American Political Science Association, September 1987.

Quirk, Paul J. "In Defense of the Politics of Ideas." *Journal of Politics* 50 (1988): 31–41.

Rae, Douglas. "The Egalitarian State: Notes on a System of Contradictory Ideals." *Daedalus* 108 (Fall 1979): 37–54.

———. *Equalities.* Cambridge, Mass.: Harvard University Press, 1981.

Rawls, John. *A Theory of Justice.* Cambridge, Mass.: Belknap Press of Harvard University Press, 1971.

Regan, Richard J. *The Moral Dimensions of Politics.* New York: Oxford University Press, 1986.

Regan, Tom, and Donald Van De Veer, eds. *And Justice for All.* Totowa, N.J.: Rowman and Littlefield, 1982.

Robinson, Joan. *Economic Philosophy.* Harmondsworth, Eng.: Penguin, 1962.

Rothbard, Murray N. "Freedom, Inequality, Primitivism and the Division of Labor." In *The Politicization of Society,* ed. Kenneth S. Templeton, Jr. Indianapolis: Liberty Press, 1979.

Rowley, Charles K. "John Maynard Keynes and the Attack on Classical Political Economy." In *Deficits,* ed. James M. Buchanan, Charles K. Rowley, and Robert D. Tollison, 114–42. Oxford: Basil Blackwell, 1986.

Saccaro-Battisti, Giuseppa. "Changing Metaphors of Political Structures." *Journal of the History of Ideas* 44 (1983): 31–54.

Samuels, Warren J. *Pareto on Policy.* Amsterdam: Elsevier, 1974.

Schotter, Andrew. *Free Market Economics: A Critical Appraisal.* New York: St. Martin's Press, 1985.

Schuettinger, Robert Lindsay, ed. *The Conservative Tradition in European Thought.* New York: G. P. Putnam's Sons, 1970.

Schumpeter, Joseph A. *Capitalism, Socialism and Democracy.* New York: Harper and Row, 1976.

Schwarz, John E. *America's Hidden Success: A Reassessment of Twenty Years of Public Policy.* New York: W. W. Norton and Co., 1983.

de Schweinitz, Karl, Jr. "The Question of Freedom in Economics and Economic Organization." *Ethics* 89 (July 1979): 336–53.

Sen, Amartya. *On Ethics and Economics.* Oxford: Basil Blackwell, 1987.

———. "The Moral Standing of the Market." *Social Philosophy and Policy* 2 (1985): 1–19.

———. "Rational Fools: A Critique of the Behavioral Foundations of Economic Theory." *Philosophy and Public Affairs* 6 (1977): 317–44.

Shriver, Donald W., Jr. "Lifeboaters and Mainlanders: A Response." *Soundings* 59 (1976): 234–43.

Sidorsky, David, ed. *The Liberal Tradition in European Thought.* New York: G. P. Putnam's Sons, 1970.

Silk, Leonard. *The Economists.* New York: Avon, 1976.

Simon, William. *A Time for Truth.* New York: Reader's Digest Press, 1978.

Smith, Adam. *An Inquiry into the Nature and Causes of the Wealth of Nations.* Ed. Edwin Cannan. New York: Modern Library, 1965.

Solo, Robert A. "Values and Judgments in the Discourse of the Sciences," In *Value Judgement and Income Distribution*, ed. Robert A. Solo and Charles W. Anderson, 9–40. New York: Praeger, 1981.

Solo, Robert A., and Charles W. Anderson, eds. *Value Judgement and Income Distribution.* New York: Praeger, 1981.

Sowell, Thomas. *A Conflict of Visions: Ideological Origins of Political Struggles.* New York: Quill, 1987.

———. *Say's Law: An Historical Analysis.* Princeton, N.J.: Princeton University Press, 1972.

Spengler, Joseph J. *Origins of Economic Thought and Justice.* Carbondale: Southern Illinois University Press, 1980.

———. "The Problem of Order in Economic Affairs." *Southern Economic Journal* 15 (1948): 1–29.

Spitz, David. *The Real World of Liberalism.* Chicago: University of Chicago Press, 1982.

Staniland, Martin. *What Is Political Economy: A Study of Social Theory and Underdevelopment.* New Haven, Conn.: Yale University Press, 1985.

Stigler, George J. *The Citizen and the State: Essays on Regulation.* Chicago: University of Chicago Press, 1975.

———. *The Economist as Preacher and Other Essays.* Chicago: University of Chicago Press, 1982.

———. *Memoirs of an Unregulated Economist.* New York: Basic Books, 1988.

———. "Nobel Lecture: The Process and Progress of Economics." *Journal of Political Economy* 91 (1983): 529–45.

———. "The Politics of Political Economists." *Quarterly Journal of Economics* 73 (1959): 522–32.

Still, Jonathan W. "Political Equality and Election Systems." *Ethics* 91 (1981): 375–94.

Stockman, David. *The Triumph of Politics: The Inside Story of the Reagan Revolution.* New York: Avon, 1987.

Sumner, William Graham. *Social Darwinism: Selected Essays of William Graham Sumner.* Englewood Cliffs, N.J.: Prentice-Hall, 1963.

———. *What Social Classes Owe to Each Other.* Caldwell, Idaho: Caxton Printers, 1974.

Templeton, Kenneth S., Jr., ed. *The Politicization of Society.* Indianapolis: Liberty Press, 1979.

Thompson, Dennis. "Philosophy and Policy." *Philosophy and Public Affairs* 14 (1985): 205–18.

Thomson, David. *Equality.* Cambridge: Cambridge University Press, 1949.

Thurow, Lester C. *Dangerous Currents: The State of Economics.* New York: Random House, 1983.

———. *Generating Inequality: Mechanisms of Distribution in the U.S. Economy.* New York: Basic Books, 1975.

———. "The Illusion of Economic Necessity." In *Value Judgment and Income Distribution,* ed. Robert A. Solo and Charles W. Anderson, 250–75. New York: Praeger, 1981.

———. "Toward a Definition of Economic Justice." *Public Interest* 31 (1973): 56–80.

———. "Why Do Economists Disagree?" *Dissent* 29 (Spring 1982): 176–82.

———. *The Zero-Sum Society: Distribution and the Possibilities for Economic Change.* New York: Basic Books, 1980.

Uhr, Carl G. *Economic Doctrines of Knut Wicksell.* Berkeley and Los Angeles: University of California Press, 1960.

Usher, Dan. *The Economic Prerequisite to Democracy.* New York: Columbia University Press, 1981.

Verba, Sidney, and Gary R. Orren. *Equality in America: The View from the Top.* Cambridge, Mass.: Harvard University Press, 1985.

Wagner, Richard E., and Robert D. Tollison. *Balanced Budgets, Fiscal Responsibility and the Constitution.* San Francisco: Cato Institute, 1980.

Waligorski, Conrad, and Thomas Hone, eds. *Anglo-American Liberalism: Readings in Normative Political Economy.* Chicago: Nelson Hall, 1981.

Walker, Graham. *The Ethics of F. A. Hayek.* Lanham, Md.: University Press of America, 1986.

Wallich, Henry C. "Economic Freedom versus Organization." In *The Invisible Hand,* ed. Adrian Klaasen, 187–99. Chicago: Gateway Editions, 1965.

Walzer, Michael. "Liberalism and the Art of Separation." *Political Theory* 12 (1984): 315–30.

———. *Spheres of Justice: A Defense of Pluralism and Equality.* New York: Basic Books, 1983.

Wanniski, Jude. "The Burden of Friedman's Monetarism." *New York Times,* July 26, 1981, sec. 3, p. 2.

Weisskopf, Walter A. "Hidden Value Conflicts in Economic Thought." *Ethics* 61 (1951): 195–204.

———. "The Method Is the Ideology: From a Newtonian to a Heisenbergian Paradigm in Economics." *Journal of Economic Issues* 13 (1979): 869–83.

Wilber, Charles K. "Empirical Verification and Theory Selection: The Keynesian-Monetarist Debate." *Journal of Economic Issues* 13 (1979): 973–82.

Willenz, Eric. "Why Europe Needs the Welfare State." *Foreign Policy* 63 (1986): 88–107.

Wogaman, J. Philip. *The Great Economic Debate: An Ethical Analysis.* Philadelphia: Westminster Press, 1977.

Woozley, A. D. "Law and the Legislation of Morality." In *Ethics in Hard Times,* ed. Arthur L. Caplan and Daniel Callahan, 143–74. New York: Plenum Press, 1981.

Index

Air pollution, 163–64
Aristotle, 4, 117, 152, 168; on democracy, 101, 102, 108; on equality, 76, 85; on justice, 49, 126, 131
Arrow, Kenneth, 11, 102, 103, 149

Baker v. *Carr,* 86
Balanced budget, 10–11, 104–6, 113–14, 170–72, 174. *See also* Budget deficits
Balanced budget amendment, 113, 171, 174
Begin, Menachem, 11
Brittan, Samuel, 42, 80
Buchanan, James M., ix, 9–10, 12–13, 44; on balanced budgets, 104, 113–14; on common good, 148–49; on discrimination, 58–59; on economics as key to political analysis, 39, 218n56, 219n72, 83; on equality, 79–80, 82–83, 87; on equal opportunity, 80, 82–83; on evolution, 143–45; on failure of government, 239n2; on failure of Reagan administration, 170–71; on freedom, 54, 57–58, 221n11; on immorality of debt financing, 140; on individual valuation, 144; on justice, 133–34; on Keynes, 140; on majority rule, 108, 121; on market limits on government, 167; on market order, 36–37; on Marxism, 158; on methodological individualism, 26–28; on morality, 137–44; objectivity claim of, 20; on Rawls, 133, 236n21; on social justice, 136; on spontaneous order, 34–35; on tax system, 172; on Wicksell, 20, 102–3
Budget deficits, 104–6, 107, 113, 114, 172, 199, 233n57, 58. *See also* Balanced budget; Government, limiting available resources of; Government, proposed solutions to problems of
Burger, Warren, on equality, 229n64
Burke, Edmund, 6–7, 27, 68, 85, 147, 151, 201, 212n11

Coercion, 61
Chile, 11, 177–79
Common good, 148–50
Common interest, 147–50, 154
Community, 126, 147–48
Consent, 36–37, 55, 122–23, 234n81
Conservatism, meaning of, 5–9, 211n8
Conservative argument. *See* Justification of conservative argument; Neglected issues in conservative argument; Starting assumptions of conservative argument
Conservative economics as political theory, ix–xi, 3–4, 10, 11–12, 13–17, 185–88, 199–204, 208–10, 213n30
Conservative economists, 12–14, 44
Conservative political economy, 187–200, 204–8
Constitutional amendments to reform government, 113–14, 173–74. *See also* Balanced budget amendment

Defense, 116, 164–65
Democracy, 7, 101–25; and balanced budget, 106; common elements in democratic theories, 116–23; and consent, 122–23; and conservative argument, 116–25; conservative economists' critique of, 40–42, 101–12, 231n19; conservative economists' picture of, 8–9, 110–12, 219n80; and economic constitution, 103–4; and equality, 95, 117–18; extent of, 116–17; and freedom, 118; and human nature, 111; and majority rule, 41–42, 108, 120–22; and market, 110–11; and morality, 112; participation in, 118–20; as a political market, 109–11; proposed solutions to problems of, 112–15 (*see also* Government); and self-interest, 103, 106–9, 120
Discrimination, 58, 67, 84–85, 94, 98–99, 132, 182
Downs, Anthony, 103

257